ARCA

ARCANA
MUSICIANS ON MUSIC

EDITED BY
JOHN ZORN

GRANARY BOOKS / HIPS ROAD 2000

Book design by Philip Gallo,
Heung-Heung Chin consultant.

Library of Congress Cataloguing-in-Publication Data

Arcana : Musicians on music / edited by John Zorn
p. cm
Discography: p.
Includes bibliographical references.
ISBN 1-887123-27-X (pbk. : alk. paper)
1. Musicians as authors. 2. Music—20th century—
history and criticism. I. Zorn, John, 1953-
ML90.A73 2000
780'.9'04—dc21   99-047434

First published in 2000
Third printing 2005
Printed on acid-free paper
Printed and bound in the United States of America

Granary Books, Inc.
168 Mercer Street   #2
New York, NY 10012

http://www.granarybooks.com

Distributed to the trade by D.A.P / Distributed Art Publishers
155 Avenue of the Americas, Second Floor
New York, NY 10013

Orders: (800) 338-BOOK   Tel: (212) 627-1999
Fax: (212) 627-9484

CONTENTS

i

PREFACE

JOHN ZORN

Rock. Jazz. Punk. Dada. Beat. These words and their longer cousins, the ism-family (surrealism, postmodernism, abstract expressionism, minimalism), are used to commodify and commercialize an artist's complex personal vision. This terminology is not about understanding. It never has been. It's about money. Once a group of artists, writers, or musicians has been packaged together under such a banner, it is not only easier for work to be marketed—it also becomes easier for the audience to 'buy it' and for the critic to respond with prepackaged opinions. The audience is deprived of its right to the pleasure of creating its own interpretation, and the critic no longer has to think about what is really happening or go any deeper than the monochromatic surface of the label itself, thus avoiding any encounter with the real aesthetic criteria that make any individual artist's work possible.

It is understood that a critic's job is not an easy one, but it is a source of great surprise and disappointment to me that after more than twenty years of music-making on the New York scene, except for the occasional review in trade magazines/periodicals (which because of the context in which they appear and the speed with which they are written don't really count anyway), not one single writer has ever come forward to champion or even to intelligently analyze exactly what it is that we have been doing. Indeed, they hardly seem able even to describe it.

This is almost entirely unprecedented for an artistic movement of such scope and involving as many important figures as it does. Perhaps it is due to the fact that the music explicitly and violently resists the classifications that these so-called thinkers have so desperately tried to impose on it: from the ludicrous *comprovisation* to the ambiguous *postmodernism* to the meaningless *totalism*. More likely it is because of the musicians' understandable and very deliberate antagonism to such catchwords—their rejection of attempts to simplify the work, package it for the market place, and conceal the subtle (and sometimes not so subtle) distinctions between the works of the many individual artists concerned.

I am not so naive as to believe it could be because our work is in any way more difficult, more original, or indeed any less commercially viable than other experimental work throughout the ages. After all, history has shown us how artists whose work has eluded traditional genres and transcended boundaries have been ignored in their own lifetime, suffering the pain of alienation and rejection, sometimes even paying the ultimate price of being 'suicided by society.'

The *Arcana* project began six years ago. The authors here represent a small cross section of a much larger body of musicians. Many more people were invited to contribute, but for one reason or another not all were able to participate. For the most part musicians do not like to write about their work. And perhaps the artists themselves are not always the best people to do so, since they have chosen a largely non-verbal medium in which to work.

As a result, the writing here is often on the raw side, but by virtue of that very fact it provides a helpful insight into the artists' inner mind. Musical thought has vast scope, enormous depth, and approaches to it are various and dynamic, and my hope was to elicit material that would be much more direct than an interview after it's been sanitized or manipulated by someone with an agenda or an article after it's been cut, recontextualized, or sensationalized by a hungry editor trying sell an issue of a magazine or newspaper.

Very special thanks to Lyn Hejinian and Travis Ortiz, who took over this project when it threatened to become a reality and got out of hand. They did all the dirty work, and without them this book would still be just an idea surrounded by mountains of paper.

I wish more people were represented here, but this book is at least a first step, filling a very real gap. This book exists to correct an unfortunate injustice, the incredible lack of insightful critical writing about a significant generation of the best and most important work of the past two decades. In this sense putting it together was not a 'labor of love' but an act of necessity.

—John Zorn, *Taipei, January 1997*

ARCANA

PLUNDERSTANDING ECOPHONOMICS

Strategies for the Transformation of Existing Music
An Inteview by Norm Igma with John Oswald

JOHN OSWALD

You are often asked *how you get away with doing these plunderphonic projects.* The assumption is that any sort of creative activity that blatantly refers to some other existing creative activity has potentially dire legal consequences.

Does it?

The initial activity of creating the music is something i presume i'm allowed to commit in the privacy of my own studio, and nobody else will care. It gets more complicated when a large number of people want to hear the fruits of this creative activity. So i've experimented with different strategies for dissemination, some of which are a little unorthodox.

First there was *Mystery Tapes,* where nothing at all was revealed to indicate what the sounds were. Everything was anonymous, and ideally also unfamiliar; or at least each thing was of a mysterious state of existence. I can't say much else about *Mystery Tapes* without spoiling the premise.

A performance corollary to *Mystery Tapes* is *Pitch,* where sounds are presented in absolute darkness. Both in *Pitch* presentations and in *Mystery Tapes* any fixation on things like the wardrobe, gender, race, hairdo, and even species of musicians is totally avoided.

Plunderphonics is, in a way, the opposite of *Mystery Tapes. Plunderphonics* is the radical transformation of very familiar music. In keeping with this obvious familiarity it doesn't make much difference whether i credit the sources or not; but when i started to conspicuously cite my sources there was a tendency elsewhere in the music business not to reference obvious quotations. I remember looking at the credits and thankyous to a Public Enemy release. There were over three hundred names; everyone was mentioned except James Brown, whose sampled essence was the pervasive element in their music.

So they didn't credit him because they hadn't licensed the samples?
This was before sample licensing had become a common procedure. The unfortunate aspect of sample licensing is that if you absolutely can't afford the fee (which is negotiable and can vary extremely) or if they just say "no," absolutely, your thing won't happen. Even though you may have already created the music. The plunderphonic pieces i had created at this time were initially private experiments. They were done well before i thought of releasing them. If i had retroactively asked permission from let's say Dolly Parton to transform her voice and she had said absolutely not, then i would have felt obliged not to play that piece for anyone, which i feel would have been unfortunate for everyone, including Dolly Parton. It's imaginable that Dolly Parton would be more sensitive about her aural-sex transformation[1] than most. But part of the validity of life in the public arena is the freedom to parody. Witness the common image of everyone laughing except for the person who is the subject of the joke. Humor is a healthy sort of cruelty. It's like a vaccination. And parody is not necessarily funny. Plunderphonics is not necessarily funny. Plunderphonics is parody that is not necessarily funny. Or not necessarily not funny either.

1. John Oswald, "Pretender," *Plunderphonic* (1988-89), crushed.

Did you send Dolly Parton a copy of the finished product?
Yes i did, via her management—Velvet Apple in Hollywood. No reply. But it matters more how people generally react to Dolly Parton's sex change than what Dolly Parton thinks about what is after all her foisted-upon-the-public image. So i avoided asking permission. I absolutely avoided selling the thing; and i probably set up a situation of unfair competition by doing that, because i was giving away for free a record which was a lot more interesting and various and loaded than the records of all the people i had electroquoted, which were being sold. The free thing was obviously a better value.

Following the plunderphonic CD there were a couple of instances of a musical source or the business partners of a source initiating plunderphonic projects. Elektra paid me to transform anyone i chose from their roster, past or present, and an invitation from The Grateful Dead to transform The Grateful Dead paid for itself.

And in between these two examples you created Plexure *for Avant.*[2]
Plexure is another angle on plunderphonics altogether. In this case i'm once again an outsider: no one is inviting me or permitting me to do this. In *Plexure* i'm not picking on a singular per-

2. John Oswald, *Plexure*, CD (Avant 016) 1992.

former. I'm scanning a whole genre. And i'm not providing references to all sources, for two main reasons: one: pop is so rarely original that a reference is usually a subreference to some antecedent which is in turn...somewhat infinitely.

But there are a finite number of quotations in the piece. You've said there are about a thousand.

There are approximately a thousand songs being referred to. There are several thousand morphs; each with reference to a composite of pop hooks. These are based on correspondent similarities among various pieces. The reference game is potentially an infinite genealogy. Plexure-bits are references. Each source fragment has been blended with other similar fragments. The spectre of appropriation amongst the quoted material is rampant in these aggregates. Perhaps this is a practical fail-safe mechanism. Any perceived infringement is embedded in the proof of its dire lack of originality.

So, anyway, what you hear are not strict electroquotations. In fact there are some hand-drawn waveforms in there, which are like tracings of a sound.

How do you do that?

A sonic snapshot of a sound can be reproduced as a printout of an intensity-by-time graph. These are like two single-line worms across the page (the left and right components of a stereo image). These drawings can be placed on a tablet-like surface. A waveform can be traced accurately, or transformed in some aspect by a pen which has a function similar to the more conventional computer mouse. The waveform can be made sharper or smoother—harmonics, for instance, can be given a different emphasis. This type of coloring is not integral to the compositional intent of *Plexure,* but it was an early way of attempting sonic-image transformation. It's a method which is only practical for very brief durations of sound. Initially i drew a hyperrealistic image of a sung word, sort of a Chuck Close-like sonogram, just for the satisfaction of having done it. This was before i got Larry Polansky's Spectral Mutation function[3] which enables something analogous to the sort of visual morphing you see in motion pictures in which there is a transformation which convolutes between a recognizable initial image and a recognizable final image.

3. Part of the computer program *Sound Hack.*

So there are at least a thousand songs being directly referred to. Although in preparing a database for *Plexure* i directly cloned about twelve hours of fragments of commercial pop CDs, each a few seconds long, these exact facsimiles have gone through the sender bender blender by the time they get to the end listener.

So instead of Bruce Springsteen you get Bing Stingspreen...

Yes, a fictional, Frankenstein-like assemblage of raw parts. These credits concocted of plunderphonies are, by-the-way, a further red herring; so you won't find anyone related to, for instance, Mariane Faith No Morrisey on the track of *Plexure* which is thusly credited.

With this constant morphing going on you hear pop music in a constant upheaval of novelty, which is contrary to the way pop music is usually presented. Most pop music is about seventy to ninety percent redundancy. All the information in your typical pop song can be packed into less than half a minute. Although the average pop song has increased in length from two to four minutes over the last couple of decades, that doesn't mean you get twice as much information. There are just more repeats of the same information. *Plexure* has low fat content—very little redundancy and lots of hooks, each one an attractive musical entity.

This brings up the question of value of information in music. The cost of a CD, unlike many computer programs, is not dependent on production costs. A CD which had an initial recording budget of $50. will cost a consumer in a store approximately the same amount as a Michael Jackson CD with a $5,000,000. production budget. Also a CD with a few variations of a few loops played over and over, will cost approximately the same as a recording of a hundred people in a symphony orchestra playing thousands of notes, which in some cases is then pieced together with a thousand edits. The price is flat, independent of the production costs. The price only varies dramatically according to format (single, EP, or album, or reissue) which in all cases can be provided on exactly the same five-inch disc. The manufacturing costs are the same.

Any attempt at standardizing a sample clearance rate would, i suppose, necessarily consider how long the sample is and how often it is repeated. It should also (but probably won't) consider the depth of the mix. Something plexure-like could be a sample concentrate—it would be much denser and info-rich than another piece where someone talks over one repeating loop. So far, concentrated music has not been demonstrably marketable as an acceptably pricey item, like concentrated detergent. I'm surprised when people complain that the *Plexure* disc is only twenty minutes long, given how much happens in that twenty minutes. It's music concentrate (twelve songs, twenty-four sub-tracks, a thousand references, thousands of hooks) in which the prominence of any particular reference is diluted.

How do you define a hook?

Any point in music in which you feel like you've arrived at a place of relief or well-being or familiarity or all of these. A place like home. I'm not an avid radio, jukebox, disco or MTV listener but there are often bits of these songs which will immediately, psychoacoustically meld with my nervous system. The reason may be melodic, timbral, rhythmic, textual, dramatic, or even just temporal, but the hooks are where the hits hit. My referent at *Billboard* magazine has a tendency to utter the cliché, "there's a reason you can hear why each of these songs became hits." I think it's true. Each really successful song, above and beyond marketing insinuation, has sonic viral elements, or hooks, which get inside you and stay there and become part of you. The virus is emotionally-laden information. When you hear one of these elements again you get emotionally engaged and your body sings along so even if some sociologically-oriented part of your mind is saying "i hate this song," your body will ecstatically sing along with Debby Boone in "You Light Up My Life."

The word plexure is a relatively archaic term for weaving.

From the Latin *plexura*: a plaiting or weaving together. "An intruding rose has stolen a nest among the plexures of the vine."[4] And it also is a homonymic graft of 'pleasure' and 'texture' as in "plexually seizing." The word has more recently been used in a renegade tangent by a new age philosopher named Zindell to mean "the ability to see knowledge as through different lenses"[5]; but i just recently heard about this nonsense. It has nothing to do with my use nor the traditional meaning of the term.

4. John P. Kennedy, *Swallow barn, or a sojourn in the old dominion* (1832).
5. David Zindell, *The Broken God*.

It could be construed as referring to how different listeners will hear Plexure *differently.*

I think it's more interesting to consider similarities in the habits of listeners based on a common background of exposure to the sources and some basis of bias to these pop sounds. The major distinction among listeners is degree of recognition. Some people have listened to more pop music than others and some of them have a greater degree of reconnaissance-confirmation than others. Jim O'Rourke for instance says he can identify 340 sources (although i have yet to see his proof of this). I can't identify this many from unaided listening, and neither can Phil Strong who categorized all the song fragments for the tempo map. Everyone who has listened to the first version seems to recognize and identify at least one source. I've consequently made the most often recognized references more obscure in subsequent versions. This positive I.D. function is somewhat independent of recognition overload, which seems to happen to almost everybody. This is a state of recognition without the ability to identify or put a name on something, which is immediately superseded by further recognitions which in a sense mask the previous memory tendril by writing over one's short-term mnemonics. This is the nagging riddle flavor which constitutes the nature of the piece.

Anyway, getting back to plunderphonic viability strategies, the facetious one for *Plexure* is that it's got everyone in pop music on it so no one act should consider themselves the focus of appropriation. No one is being particularly quoted because everyone is being referentially treated. *Plexure* is a crowd shot, or let's say a panoramic view. You can't see the trees at this resolution for looking at the forest. The boundary of this forest is the first decade of the CD era, 1982-92, from a Euro-American dominant perspective, which is the way it is in pop music, 'pop' being defined as music that is popular. Beethoven is pop music and cool-period Miles Davis is pop music, and both of these are pop music on CD in the eighties, and both Elvis and The Doors were million-sellers in '92; but i've limited the scan to music generated during that decade, so the piece will eventually have a period flavor, although when i was first working on it, some of the sources were absolutely current, and nothing sounded really old, even though some songs were released prior to '82; i included them if they didn't remind me of the seventies—if they were in a sense still percolating through the fads of current musical culture in '82.

So what is the definition of 80s pop?

Oh, i have no idea. There were a variety of tangents and a few marriages of hitherto disparate streams, like funk and metal, but categorizing any period would be too much of a generalization; and categorizing any particular example is something i've found difficult to do. Phil and i thought about trying to tag each song to keep track of what we had, but i for one couldn't do it. In a record store the categories are all based on race, gender, and geopolitical distinctions, none of which describe the music. A black man in Jamaica might produce a reggae tune, but so might a white woman in Finland. For a while almost everyone did at least one quasi-reggae tune, but other non-rhythmic influences would make all this reggae less than homogeneous.

What i find i do in trying to organize relationships is to make a hypertextual web. One selected song might be related to another in its anomalous use of flute as a soloing instrument which has a melodic shape similar to another song in which the singer affects the mannerisms of the singer of another popular song which is in a particular tempo pocket.

Tempo in the end became the pervasive organizing element. Very little of the music from this period was tempo nebulous, or in free time. So we could measure tempo as an absolute rational value which we could apply to all the pieces. At worst there would be a choice of a tempo harmonic—a doubling or halving of the sense of the beat, depending on what rhythmic element was pushing forward in the mix to establish the pulse; and there was the odd piece that wasn't in 4/4 which wouldn't fit comfortably in our rhythm continuum, but given the overall parameters of selection, tempo was a useful organizing device which eventually became the prime structural factor.

Why have you continued to work on Plexure?

Nineteen ninety-two has come and gone. When i first worked on *Plexure* it felt like i was doing something contemporary. Most of the plunder-phonic work has an historical perspective. Now, even though it's only three or four years later, *Plexure* has an historical perspective too. Also, the selection process back in '92 was a bit too arbitrary: i found all the material on CDs from a friendly alternative radio station and a friendly used record store. I knew there were some very apparent hits that i didn't have examples of, but given the wealth of material i had that didn't feel like a problem. My historical perspective is that now it does feel like a problem, and so i've done a much more thorough search for a couple of hundred pieces which i missed the first time around which according to my statistics of sales, international charting, and my personal hook meter, are essential. The great thing about the most magnetic songs is that i need much less of their essence to make their presence be suspected in the mix, than i would require of less popular items. And of course this additional material is what is being used to mask/morph those quotes which have been persistently too obvious. *Plexure* in a way is like a garden which i'm now weeding. In the past i always considered that through my recordings i was attempting to create masterpieces—in other words pieces which would not need to change; their existence would set an historical precedence, and any further modification would undermine their effectiveness. Listeners might change but there is no need for the composition to change. *Plexure* has such a complex relationship with listeners, including myself, that i haven't yet been able to pin down its masterpiece potential. I may be misguided in thinking that adding to its comprehensiveness is going to help, but, whatever the outcome, i enjoy weeding the garden.

So the weeds are the recognizable electroquotes?

Exactly, especially if its viability as a marketable item is to be considered in the equation. That's the nice practical consequence to the prime concern of maintaining the threshold of recognition.

Are there any other plunderphonic presentation strategies that you'd like to mention?

Over the last few years, partly with the encouragement of written-music performers such as the Kronos Quartet, and the existence of the big instrument—the symphonic orchestra, i've been playing around with the re-writing of classical music. A lot of the applicable documents are in the public domain and as a result of this practicality there has been a quite a bit of plunder-phonicizing by people other than myself. But relatively recent hi-fi recordings of performances of the classical repertoire are copyright-protected just like a pop recording. It's nice that someone gets credited for any distinction they might make. But a lot of these recordings don't seem very distinct to me. The rule to recording the classics is to commit an accurate interpretation of the score. As a result, most of these interpretations which faithfully follow the recipe are quite similar. In preparing materials for some plunderphonic transformations of recorded material i've been working in the opposite way to what i did in the GRAYFOLDED project.[6] For that i gathered over a hundred versions from The Grateful Dead's vaults of the band playing "Dark Star" in concert over a twenty-five year period. These versions had some pervasive similarities—the moments which were expected in order to define this music as "Dark Star" and not as something else. But the major mass of the piece was improvisation, which encourages the opportunity for distinctions—for exceptions to the rules of "Dark Star." And these distinctions from particular performances are the substance of GRAYFOLDED. It is a particularly unusual "Dark Star."

6. John Oswald and The Grateful Dead, *GRAYFOLDED*, 2CD (Swell/Artifact S/A (19691/1996) 1996.

With the classics of the classical genre i've been making conglomerates that focus on the rules rather than the exceptions. I combine the sum of normality in several performances to make a generic version which wouldn't be associated with any particular performer. This could result in a nebulous or multi-faceted version of the piece, depending on instrumentation in combination with my choice of editing techniques. Acoustic aspects such as the perspective, seating pattern, and reverberance are variable. This is something which never happens in a traditional classical recording. It's more pop-like or cinematic. It can also have some of the effects of an O.M.N.I.V.E.R.S.E.[7]

recording—it can be spatially volatile.

A lawyer who runs a recording mechanical rights organization took great exception to my concept of generic version. He said that even though specifics of what is purloined might not be detectable, i am still categorically a thief because i'm conscious of my thievery.

7. O.M.N.I.V.E.R.S.E. *Orbital Microphonic Navigational Imaging Via Ecotonic Radial Stereo Eccentricity:* Following the cinematic convention of camera motion as in tracking, tilting, zooming etc.—a moving microphone. Featured on Gordon Monahan, *THIS PIANO THING*, CD (Swerve 001) and Christopher Butterfield, *Pillar of Snails*, CD (unnumbered). The latter also has an ensemble piece in which a musical-chairs perspective has been edited together where phrase by phrase the positions of the players are completely rearranged or progressively tracked in relation to a fixed microphone.

Note: Further definitions of the terms used in Chapter 1 can be found at: http://www.6q.com

To my reply that it would perhaps be best that we stop calling no-loss situations (the appropriation and manipulation of intellectual endeavors) thievery, he asked if i would be upset if someone broke into my house in an undetectable fashion and perused, or manipulated or took something, and that i wasn't able to detect that this had taken place, but that i would be aware of these things happening. My reaction is that such fastidious thievery would be commendable; it sounds more like housekeeping. His scenario in part calls for a reaction to an invasion of privacy. I don't think any of plunderphonics constitutes such an invasion of privacy. It all deals with public acts and official releases. I'm not at all interested in studio outtakes, sonic laundry, or personal phone messages.

Two variations of the generic versions: one is a compilation of aspects of various arrangements of Debussy's *Clair de Lune,* from the original piano score through various easy-listening orchestral confections; which is a nice bridge from classical to pop. The other is twenty-four simultaneous versions of Richard Strauss's Introduction (Einleitung) to *Also sprach Zarathustra,* which are all lined up to the first horn entry; so they begin in synch and then the musical picture gets progressively more thick and diffuse as each version runs its course at a slightly different tempo. It's a particularly wonderful transition because by the middle of the piece it sounds more like something by Ligeti; so the piece is like the soundtrack to the movie *2001* in a nutshell, with a continuum between the romantic tradition and the 20th century third-quarter avant garde.

But i challenge any orchestra that may object to their non-complicit inclusion to identify themselves in this mix. I bought all the versions of the piece on CD that i could find, but there were, or there are now more than two dozen versions (classical music is also like detergent in that there are so many competing packages of the same product—for instance there are over sixty currently-available versions of Stravinsky's *Le Sacre du Printemps*). It's indetectable who is in this meta-Zarathustra and who isn't. In the end my derivative version is probably the most distinct and non-derivative version of all.

THE COUNTERPOINT OF SPECIES

SCOTT JOHNSON

Naming and defining the generations born since World War II has become a
popular pastime in recent years, but one shared feature on their cultural landscapes remains constant for all. Every group has come of age in a society which
acknowledges the Western art music tradition with an increasingly faint and uncertain voice, and which has little use for the composers who are the living offshoots of that tradition. While our indigenous popular musics thrive, the vast
majority of educated Americans cannot name a living composer, and most of
those who can are likely to know only one or two individuals who emblematic-
ally stand for a concept of serious music, in the way that one famous singer can
stand for all opera. Composers and their millions of non-listeners alike seem to
agree that there is little in common between an elaborately notated piece of
music in the European tradition, and a popular piece in which the decisions of
band-members, arrangers, or producers flesh out the details left open by the
songwriter's art. This enormous gulf in practice is reinforced by the disparity
between the instruments and musical materials used by classical and vernacular styles. The existence of such sharp contrasts has become self-perpetuating;
providing endless fuel for the critical distinctions with which art music professionals fence off their territory. Our culture teaches us a gut certainty about
which sounds belong with which technique, and there are no widespread contemporary equivalents of Schubert parlor songs or Bach church music to integrate popular sources into composed music, or composers into daily life.

But during the 1990s, the corrosive side effects of the isolation and
near-sacralization of art music became apparent even to those who had not
seen the trouble coming. For others, who had maintained a long-standing skep-
ticism about contemporary culture's airtight distinctions between serious and
popular music, the new realignments and reversals of opinion have been both
gratifying and full of surprises. It's no longer unusual to hear academic thinkers
or the directors of major classical music institutions soberly acknowledging

that the transplanted European tradition of serious music has run into serious problems adapting to the American climate. This same realization fueled many a late-night rant among my friends two decades ago, and such reactions retain their shape today as young musicians continue their weekend pilgrimages between obscure concerts of the post-classical avant-garde, and the marginally less obscure clubs of the popular avant-garde, where sonic extravaganzas involving the creative abuse of electronics, electric guitars, or saxophones are an anti-institution of long standing. Agreement between power brokers and art punks is not the usual state of affairs, and the emergence of similar conclusions in such disparate constituencies suggests that a very real crisis is being seen from multiple vantage points. How to best describe it? Is this a mere shift in fashion, or are there slower motions and larger principles involved?

At the heart of this *fin de siècle* crisis lies the very set of ideas which provided a solution to the last one. In their search for a way around a moribund romanticism, musical modernists drew upon many of the same ideas and events which animated other early 20th century progressives. The explanatory power of Darwinism and the unprecedented achievements of science and technology combined to create an atmosphere charged with an animating belief in an inevitable march of progress. With both Marxism and Freudianism contributing variations on an underlying theme of the malleability of human nature, the big question was "Why not?" and the possibility of leaping forward though expert redesigning of human experience must have been deeply compelling. But here at the end of that century, music is not the only field where exaggerated versions of utopian desires have created unforeseen and unwanted side effects. The visionary modernist impulse is now paying the price for its single-minded, reductionist misunderstanding of the nature of cultural evolution.

But regardless of the damage done to the health of post-classical music by an oversimplified belief in linear progress, the basic perception that there are similarities between cultural change and biological evolution is no mistake. The same basic mechanisms and accidents of evolution which have granted us our survival and the ability to communicate with each other are also at work within seemingly unnecessary "luxuries" like music. They aren't at work because they were designed with music in mind. They are just unavoidably present in all that we do, because that is how people are put together. Once we've learned to be suspicious of the old triumphal stories of progress, contemporary evolutionary thought offers a set of ideas which work equally well on matters great and small, physical and intellectual. The very distance of this non-musical vantage point shifts our perspective away from the customary ways of talking about music, suggesting alternative routes around familiar ideological entrenchments. But perhaps it's best to first connect these realms at the lowest level available.

It is nearly impossible to listen to or study music for any length of time without noticing both the chains of imitation which link pieces and styles of music together, and the leaps of invention which set them apart. In making these simple observations, we have already identified two of the three classic preconditions for evolution: inheritance and variation. Now off we go to a concert; choose any kind of music, in which we can hear any particular interplay of inheritance and invention. Each decision that you or I make between applauding, not applauding, or leaving the room transforms us briefly into minor ecological forces, making a judgment about relative fitness. At this point all of the Darwinian requirements have been fully met: 1) inheritance, in the style of music; 2) variation, from the personal expression of the musicians or composers; and 3) differential success among the variants, from the assessment that we voted with our palms. Regardless of whether we have ever put much thought into examining our intuitions about evolution, any evening's concert or any trip to the record store both fit snugly within its definition. And note that the match is not a matter of metaphor: here at this most basic behavioral level, it is a functioning, measurable process; as real as any chemical reaction.

So it is little wonder that people habitually sprinkle their conversations about music with references to genealogies of influence and the evolution of genres. Our instincts are correct, and it's not just a matter of poetic analogy. Culture, and all of its constituent branches, is a concrete expression of our nature. Although cultural details are far more free of narrow genetic control than individual physical traits are, our capacity for inventing and teaching behaviors and traditions is still as much a product of our species's evolution as the opposable thumbs on our hands, the upright posture which frees us to use them, or the brains that decide what to use them for. I should say at the outset that I think that "fitness" is a slippery concept in music, not particularly meaningful in the absence of a particular use or cultural niche. An obscure composer is as "fit" within a hushed roomful of devotees as a popular icon is in the roar of a stadium concert; but that roomful should be cautious about claiming to represent their civilization, rather than merely themselves. Fitness is a practical matter, and need will generate whatever ideological arguments prove necessary for survival. And so I'll try and leave fitness to sort itself out, because for the pleasures of contemplation and imagination, questions of inheritance and variation are far more interesting and fruitful. They throw light inward to the workings of musical minds, and outward towards the differences between human beings and the rest of the natural world.

A failure to fully recognize one of these differences has played a part in the misconceptions which have led serious music to its current insignificance in the culture at large. Artistic traditions seem to evolve like natural species in some respects, transmitting new adaptations along with a basic body of information; but nature enforces an uncompromising linear purism upon its creatures, because they cannot mix things up by interbreeding with distantly related species. But in the world of ideas, hybridism and cultural cross-pollination play a huge role. Nowhere was this more true than in the omnivorous European classical tradition, cobbled together as it is from the contributions of numerous distinct nations and languages. Hybridism has received a very bad press during the second half of the 20th century, but the patchwork logic of human culture is echoed by the very physical structure of our brains, in which jury-rigged modules are added to each other simply because they work, not because they are elegant or logical. Functions are often redundant, and sometimes work at cross purposes, but if this haphazard complexity lacks the crystalline beauty of good design, it still provides for surprise and unforeseen interactions.

But serious music's gradual retreat from its position of importance within 19th century culture has been marked by bouts of purist fervor from classicists and avant gardists alike. Both reflect a very real need to reduce an increasingly complex world to the more manageable proportions of a story, whether one of a golden age lost, or of progress towards some "higher" state. In the case of historical preservationists, a concern with lineage and purity makes practical sense, but as High Modernism embraced the idea of art music as specialized pure research, exporting new "conclusions" and importing nothing from the surrounding musical environment, it gradually dried up the wells which had periodically refreshed the European tradition. The inertia of this attitude is considerable, and even now the sometimes gleefully messy melting pot of the avant garde community is not immune to occasional fussy fits of house-cleaning, as the heirs of a previous generation's rebellious attempt to fortify the ground gained by their heroes.

Evolution always involves a relationship with the environment, not just with one's own ancestors and descendants. High Modernism may have gotten itself into trouble by thinking that progress and specialization are synonymous, but both modernism and classicism have shared another misreading of Darwinian principles; one which has also been used to provide a background justification for the separation of post-classical music from its surrounding culture. Fragments and descendants of once-popular forms which were long ago incorporated into the classical music tradition are now accepted as if their transmutation had erased their popular history. But they were not originally created to serve their "fine art" function, and newer influences still undergoing the same process are greeted with distaste, condescension, or embarrassment.

The most polite thing one could say about this way of thinking is that it is a Platonic or essentialist fallacy, which ascribes intrinsic qualities where there are only temporary and contingent ones. The fallacy rests on the notion that any genre of music currently occupying a certain cultural niche is somehow inherently well suited to it in part and whole, although its ancestors may have drifted in from elsewhere with plenty of unrelated baggage, and its descendants may head off in yet another direction. But a less polite and more direct observation is that such respect for safely pre-legitimized popular influences bears a distinct resemblance to a chimpanzee's increased grooming of a newly ascendant leader, who only a few days ago may have had to just deal with his fleas on his own. This status-oriented blindness to the power of context and social suggestion has been greatly exacerbated by the modern tendency to defend the purity of genres and to demean hybrids. Much of the damage to the classical tradition has resulted from a habit of investing the differences between serious and popular music with all of the gravity and exaggeration of the medieval distinction between sacred and profane. Talk of high and low culture has become a self-fulfilling prophecy, and in obeying it the classical tradition has turned its back on the very capacity for importation and hybridization which fueled its rise. All that art music seems to have gained in return for its insistence on these terms is a moderate amount of verbal convenience when discussing itself.

The concept of replication with variation receives an advertisement every time we note the resemblances between parent and child; and as for survival of the fittest, the next two guys that refer to it are welcome to step outside and give each other a fat lip. These concepts themselves are endlessly varied and replicated, and they refuse to be restricted to the job of explaining the genetic world. Since evolution-based explanations of musical events are a reflexive and often unconscious habit, this essay will compare such interpretations of culture to the biological forces which provide us with our mental templates of evolutionary change. We will need to make a few stops in the natural world to assemble

, but then it will be back to the world of music, to try to find
ntuitive understanding of evolution work, and which don't,
tools so useful that their inaccuracies are forgiven (at least
thumb). I'll begin with the simplest of evolutionary ideas,
ally tied to the most complex of living musical styles.

And A Staircase

itance not only provides us with a story, but the story suggests
Whether we are looking at creatures or culturally transmitted
f making things, our selective attention is especially drawn
are actually elaborations; when a species, a type of human
n-made object grows more complex, or just plain big. We are
eager to inner Guinness Book with amazing tales of intricacy or vast-
ness, and on our expeditions we frequently consult a conceptual compass
which predisposes us to associate "complex" with "higher." It saw constant
use during our growth from infant to adult, and it gradually establishes connections with our sense of social hierarchy. Is this desire-driven linkage of
complexity and advancement a learned tendency, a latent capacity waiting to
be activated, or a hardwired imperative? May the best sociobiologist or cultural
relativist win, but either way, it is a inclination which has a lifelong influence
on our cultural perceptions and attitudes, as well as our personal ambitions.
Unsurprisingly, our heads are filled with vaguely or explicitly triumphal stories
about the achievement of sophistication over time.

Although we generally shift over to the image of a branching tree if we
want to imagine the whole of evolution, a series of crawls and leaps along an
ever-ascending line is our usual way of picturing the history and development of a
single species, or a cultural tradition seen in isolation. This linear close-up is useful because it both focuses our attention on specifics, and it engages us emotionally with its air of storytelling. Often it's quite accurate as well: we all can conjure
up the familiar image of a series of ancestral primate skeletons, captured in their
spine-straightening march from the ape on the
left, through a few early hominids, and finally to
the modern human on the right. As Stephen Jay
Gould points out,[8] these simplified ladders of
ascent are often paths drawn retroactively
through the dense historical bushes of branching evolutionary experiments, following lineages which generally culminate in the current winner, or perhaps a

8. On this point, see Stephen Jay Gould's essays "Bushes and Ladders in Human Evolution," from *Ever Since Darwin* (New York: Norton, 1977); or "Life's Little Joke" from *Bully for Brontosaurus* (New York: Norton, 1991).

particularly spectacular loser. This template for explaining things is not the sole property of biology. We might picture technological evolution in mental snapshots of ever taller buildings leading to a skyscraper, or perhaps in the soaring ratio of information capacity to physical size implied in a line drawn from clay tablets to paper to computers. Even in a specialty like music, clearly evolutionary readings of history as an accumulation of complexity have existed since long before Darwin began to put our intuitions about genealogy and change in order.

If this sort of directional accumulation of design and complexity didn't actually happen in the real world, we wouldn't be here to make drawings or mental images of it; perhaps we'd be contentedly waving our flagella at passing algae. But although these pictures of linear progress may be true as far as they go, we still need to remember that they only go to the edge of the picture frame. They accurately describe certain bones and buildings and blank pages, but seldom include the environmental forces which made it advantageous or even possible to become what they have become. Left unexplained is the availability of fruit for the monkeys and steel for the skyscrapers, or the reasons why access to vertical real estate was worth the effort in either case.

The model of ascending lineages leaves an implication that all things evolve from simple to complex, when in fact they only evolve from what worked last year to what works this year. If a complex solution fits the environment without creating extra problems, it survives, and the same goes for simple solutions. In this realm of environment and ecology, we might imagine a web of lateral interactions radiating out from each individual or type in our line-up of evolutionary mug shots. A biologist or a structural engineer is unlikely to forget that a sequence of forms presents only half of the story, but it may be useful for the rest of us to make some distinction between linear inheritance and lateral ecology; particularly those of us who grew up in the midst of modernism's fastidious history of concern with the genealogy of pure shape and technique.

We all notice that which gives comfort to our desires, and post-classical 20th century music saw itself perched at the top of a logical progression, the outcome not of serendipitous and particular circumstances, but of an essentially directional European history in which voices multiply from plainsong to dense counterpoint, and acceptable pitch relationships make a slow crawl up the harmonic series from octaves and fifths towards increasingly dissonant intervals. It is no wonder that the second half of the century produced a modernist musical culture characterized by a growing indiscernibility to the ear of complex structures, and that it in turn bred a Cageian counter-culture; one which accepted much of the modernist premise, but employed intentionally non-intuitive, randomly derived structures as a means of inducing composers and listeners to confront their own expectations about music.

But rather than being an expression of some sort of inevitable, "natural" progression towards complexity, High Modernism is perhaps better understood as a specific adaptation of music to its new home in the post-World War II university. This environment has its own imperatives, and they are indispensable to the activities which usually go on there. Good science and scholarship require ideas designed to be defensible when challenged by colleagues, and a consistent and teachable methodology which generates reproducible results. This works very well as a way of testing and conserving practical knowledge, but it may not be an optimal or sufficient list of characteristics for a thriving art form. If there was a "natural" force operating within the complexity of late 20th century atonal modernism, it had less to do with linear evolution and more to do with the limits of the brain's processing abilities in the face of a dense flood of incoming sound information, whose organizing principles were often more attuned to study than listening. But High Modernist styles have survived despite an overwhelming hostility from listeners, and despite their failure to produce the long hoped for and often propounded "Sacre du Printemps" reversal of fortune: the initial rejection and eventual embrace experienced by aggressive avant-gardes earlier in the century. However, those earlier styles had retained the habit of making folk derivations, and thus maintained a conduit to and from the outside world. Late modernism did not, and today even its best work remains relatively impenetrable to the rest of the culture. But its once-secure home base in academia doesn't completely explain its long survival, because that security itself needs to be explained. Another reason suggests itself, a non-musical reason tied less to the evolution of form and more to the ecology of ideas.

A powerful paradigm animated High Modernism in its adventurous beginnings, an image which tapped directly into the 20th century's dreams of progress and the top-down redesign of human endeavors. From Webern on, the composer gradually took on the coloring of the research scientist: ahead of his time, and understood by few. In an elegant example of the human mind's ability to create conceptual hybrids from seemingly incompatible materials, this persona, elite yet understandable to popular culture, was lifted directly out of the history of science and merged with aspects of the very artistic paradigm which modernism had worked so hard to replace: the Romantic genius, the artist as conspicuous experiencer of emotions. Removing some of the emotionality and overripe stylistic conventions, but retaining the part about genius, the new century's avant-gardes preserved their increasingly tenuous link to their culture by merging Einstein and his violin. In music's own odd version of the "physics envy" so familiar to practitioners of the softer sciences, the most rigorous music generated both dislike and a respect which was denied to work that was more immediately comprehensible but less theoretically defensible.

This hybridized modern paradigm of the researcher as romantic genius makes a very snug fit with the vision of evolution as a ladder-like sequence of exemplary forms, because a string of such individuals of genius allows us to construct a morphing lineage similar to our familiar row of evolving skeletons. The merger of this modern artistic mythos and the image of mutating sequences creates a useful mental tool for making sense of a messy and sprawling human endeavor like music. But tools shape the hands that use them, and the appealing clarity of the insular modernist narrative has encouraged an atrophy of awareness regarding the environment, and an intellectual dismissal of the lateral cultural forces which push and prod musical lineages into the shapes which they temporarily assume. Our ideals of individual invention are easily offended when those forces intrude, and a quick listen to this month's imitation of last month's pop hit will explain why, but this esthetic gag reflex has become far too automatic among art music specialists. Much mud has been hurled over such matters, and fear of the accusation of seducing audiences has sometimes resulted in music intended to seduce the potential accusers with a stringent unseductiveness. But in practice no philosophical dike can completely prevent social forces from sneaking in around the edges, particularly with practitioners of such a social art as music.

Virgil Thompson suggested that much can be learned about music by finding out who paid for it. In its pursuit of purity, free from the economic and audience pressures which constitute much of music's ecological context, modernist music found a philosophical fit to its central paradigm within the university. This isn't terribly surprising, since the university was itself a major source of that paradigm. But art music found no escape in principle from audience pressures, only a narrowing of territory. The outcome brings to mind a species in a stable environment, growing ever more perfectly adapted to a given task, responding to the same question with better and better answers. In contrast, a successful species in a volatile or uncertain environment is like a flexible set of tools, capable of solving a number of related problems. This is what the

European tradition was for most of its history, and the irony of its descendants' radical effort to avoid the diluting hybridism of the marketplace is that the paradigm of the artist as research scientist is itself a conceptual hybrid, as is modernism's romance with mathematical imagery and ideas. As is the essay that you are reading, for that matter.

Splitting The Adam

The world of Western art music spent much of the 20th century engrossed in an argument between modernists dedicated to the image of musical evolution as an ever-ascending lineage, and classicists who devoted themselves to selecting and preserving the best of a finished heritage. Both branches believed that they were engaging in the same sort of behavior as those who had actually created the European tradition, but they were right in only a limited sense. Each represented a experiment in specialization and the compartmentalization of effort; in effect, the differentiation of new musical subspecies from the common stock of the old. But by mid-century, neither side wanted much to do with their surrounding environment of folk and popular musics, and in this respect both were making a momentous departure from their parent tradition.

While High Modernism embraced a utopian vision of progress detached from environmental interaction with outsiders, thus emphasizing only half of the evolutionary equation, performer-oriented classicism sought, within the boundaries of its own domain, to suspend the laws of ongoing evolution and the passage of time itself. Although both the laboratory and the museum were essential aspects of the old European tradition at its healthiest, in isolation neither one has proven to be as robust as their common ancestor. Work of excellence done in these still overlapping fields has not prevented them from presiding over a slow retreat from the days when their mutual predecessors could place an instrument in most homes, or turn out thousands for Beethoven's funeral.

But all ideological urgencies eventually wane, and the debate between the 19th and 20th centuries grows less compelling. Weary from its long dichotomous battle, the troubled world of "serious" music has begun to turn its attention towards an approach which was out of favor for decades: the idea that our living popular music is a candidate for a symbiotic relationship, rather than a rival to be defeated. Twentieth century tonal composition has maintained a version of this throughout its life as tolerated guest in the house of classicism, but the new revival of interest arises from a very different source. In its current incarnation this idea is a major constituent of the heterogeneous subculture sometimes known as the "downtown" new music scene, named after the formerly inexpensive neighborhoods in New York City where many of its practitioners once resided, including your essayist. Many people from around the world are familiar with this musical outlook, but not the local designation "downtown." Perhaps we should follow critic Gregory Sandow's suggestion and borrow a term from the world of rock: "alternative" classical music. I should say at this point that most of my own work as a composer has occurred within this niche in the musical world, and the desire to understand the relationship between popular and serious musics is a desire to sort out my immediate surroundings.

This "downtown" coalition of the miscellaneous is even further removed from the regulating influence of the classical canon than "uptown" mainstream 20th century modernism has been. Since alternative art music traces its descent from a series of relatively unaffiliated individualists, with heavy doses of cross-cultural hybridization, attempts to manufacture a genealogy to rival that of High Modernism always seem a bit strained until they get to the appearance of minimalism. This stylistic group has been the success story of the alternative new music world, replicating and mutating in a fairly stable way since the late 1960s. From the look of things at the moment, the downtown melting pot may even have sprouted a new post-minimalist mainstream, and many participants continue to experiment with the explicit reintroduction of the living vernacular into the "classical" world. But far from being a radical idea born downtown in the 1970s, disseminated a decade later, and made nearly respectable a decade after that, this sort of symbiosis between popular and serious music has in fact been an utterly normal state of affairs throughout most of the history of the Western tradition.

Long after the classical tradition coalesced out of its simple sources and accomplished its seminal achievement of hybridizing sacred and profane musical forms, it continued to maintain boundaries porous enough to import and transform folk or vernacular musical materials. The mechanism was fairly automatic and self-regulating because the composers doing the importing and transforming were working with popular materials they had personally internalized, simply by being members of their own culture or travelers among its subcultures and neighbors. At its best this had little to do with ideological stance: the focusing emotions of a group belief might motivate a person to actively edit out the signs of his or her cultural vernacular, but leaving them in happens all by itself.

Nevertheless, the taboos against such references accumulated during the 20th century, and contemporary high culture still presents us with the rather odd spectacle of extinct folk dances appearing as respectable musical topics for serious composition, while living forms excite controversy. This controversy depends on an inherited set of mental habits poorly adapted to our world, and as this becomes more unavoidably apparent the process of unlearning them gathers momentum. Our current folk forms cluster around rock music, and like people of other times and places, we look for a glimpse of our own face mirrored in the very art music that we hope will draw us outside of ourselves and our daily concerns. This sounds paradoxical in a sentence, but not in the listening experience. The resolution of the commonplace and the unique within a piece of music is such a basic pleasure that extensive training is required to teach people not to want it, and the relative scarcity of that pleasure among the specialized descendants of classical music has left them clinging precariously to shrinking patches of survivable environment, at a time when the increased ease of communication and travel should be constantly opening up new avenues of dispersal.

All that is real in an artistic dichotomy like "serious/popular music" is generated by shifting human behaviors and ideas circulating within a cultural ecosystem, not by polarized, formal, and immutable categories. The language of evolution offers a useful set of tools for explaining the virtual lineages and environments of such concepts. One could begin at either end of current evolutionary debates and still come out ahead: we might follow Daniel Dennett and ask an adaptationist question: "What problem did this dichotomy solve, and how did it benefit those who first used it?" or think of Stephen Jay Gould and ask: "Given that it's there and too embedded to be discarded, what is this dichotomy good (or bad) for now?" I am convinced that a musical world accustomed to talking within its own circle would profit from either answer.

Ideas And Organisms: What Translates, And What Doesn't

Music has both an inside and an outside. Its internal concepts and terminology are necessary for understanding and describing the music itself, but they are not sufficient for explaining the transactions it makes with the surrounding world—transactions involving education, economics, class, stylistic tribalism, audience demographics, and serendipitous inspiration from unexpected sources, whether romantic landscapes or modern math. Conversely, ideas imported from the philosophy of science are not going to be of much use in understanding any individual piece of music, much less enjoying it emotionally. But physical evolution has some illuminating and relevant tales to tell as we again redefine the modern musical world. It has something to say about extremes of purity, in the form of dangerously specific adaptations that put all of a creature's eggs in one basket. It has something to say about the fragmentation of habitat, and how shrinking gene pools and loss of species diversity can set isolated systems up for a crash under the pressure of healthy new invaders. And it underscores the unprecedented ability of the human mind to create hybrids and assimilate portions of seemingly distant and distinct virtual lineages; to trade bits of foreign thematic material and enter into a counterpoint of species.

As we have seen, the basic principles of evolutionary change travel well. From a young animal's hunting lessons all the way to rocket science, culture is a continuation by other means of life's basic business: transmitting its hard-won information into the future. Whether in an evolving species in the natural world or a cultural project like music, new uses are found for existing structures, previous transformations are transformed again, and things gradually lose their resemblance to their ancestors. The function of ecological forces also transfers comfortably, merely requiring us to acknowledge that our opinions, passions, or indifference exert selective pressures among ideas and behaviors just as surely as bugs or a particularly dry summer do among plants. But there are differences between the mechanisms and materials of nature and culture which are concrete and unavoidable, and we need to take note of the details and recognize the limits of analogy. Unlike genetic information, ideas can spread throughout a population within a generation. They are extremely mobile, divisible into parts, and utterly promiscuous. And they are capable of transmission and hybridization over the gulfs between widely divergent species of cultural endeavor: the intellect's lamb and lion indeed lay down together, and not for a nap either.

A discredited 19th century evolutionary heresy called Lamarckism speculated that a creature's life experience and learning could be somehow biologically passed along to its heirs, when in fact the "germ line" of reproductive cells spends an entire life cordoned off from the "somatic line," which consists of all of the other cells of the body. If Jean-Baptiste Lamarck had been right, it would have provided a huge enhancement of evolution's speed and efficiency. Each species would possess the ability to learn quickly from its mistakes, and then pass the news along on an individual basis. That, of course, is exactly what has been accomplished in the cultural realm of ideas, behaviors, and artifacts.

Compared to the slow and wasteful mechanisms of biology, the exchange of learnable behaviors and ideas provides huge advantages in speed and efficiency, both within and between separate cultural lineages. Inheritance becomes a network, as groups or even single individuals experiment with partial and selective hybridization; in essence, freely picking and choosing their own conceptual parents. Variation becomes directional through individual invention, which is simply a new way of putting proposals on life's table: a way of crafting targeted alternatives, rather than waiting for one of nature's accidental mutations. Selection's edge is blunted by choice and learning, as people switch strategies and drape layers of options over the hard-wired behaviors inherited from simpler animals. Conscious invention and continual revision can avoid much of the massive waste of time and effort involved in the biosphere's endless process of sorting through randomly generated variations, blindly searching for that one in a million which will somehow happen to work better.

Thus our ability to choose freely does not contradict or refute an evolutionary outlook on life; it is in fact the very essence of our particular evolutionary path, and the key to our success as a species. The human brain can break down and reassemble its knowledge of the past, and from these raw materials we can picture the possible future effects of our choices in the mind's eye before making a physical commitment, allowing what neurobiologist Antonio Damasio calls "memories of a possible future."[9] Once they have been mentally previewed, new combinations of invention and influence can be taken for trial runs as fast as they can come off the behavioral assembly lines. Experiments seldom have to wait generations to find out if selective pressures will make a judgment on their viability; unless, like most of the details of our lives, they are simply ignored because their positive or negative effects are so minuscule or counterbalanced that they fall beneath the radar of adaptation. In any given year, a human community can gossip, trade, and legislate its way through enough successful, failed, or indifferent experiments to keep whole species of bees busy for centuries.

Slow rates of change, linear inheritance, and formal purity within art forms is exactly what we would expect if they evolved in the way that the natural world does. Biological lineages can't undergo too much mutation in too short a time and still remain viable, and they are unforgivingly specific about the details. Without the right number of genes making the right chemicals in the right proportions, a would-be mutant cannot even win the right to fail. In the biosphere, breeding and blending over any evolutionary distance seems to be

9. Antonio Damasio, *Descartes Error* (New York: Grosset/Putnam, 1994), ch. 10, p. 239. *Descartes Error* is not specifically about evolution, but about its outcome. Damasio's examination of how the mind/brain/body allows us to imagine the future describes the operating system which gives cultural evolution its unique qualities. Also, his overall point about the crucial role which emotions play in reasoning should be both gratifying and intuitively familiar to most artists.

31

out of the question for complex organisms, with the mixing of DNA confined to closely related subspecies and to the pared-down parasitism of viruses. Past a certain point, divergence within individual lineages creates species which are forever separate. They can still interact on an ecological level: they can compete, they can cooperate, or they can move to opposite ends of the forest, but they can never again interbreed.

So there is no clear genetic parallel to the free and fast exchange of distant information that creates a Zeitgeist of shared ideas across a society's specialized branches. Although many genes serve nearly identical functions in species as distant as mammals and insects, they come by their similarity only by inheritance, not by communication. For example, eyes have been passed on along chains of descent, and they have been independently evolved in separate lineages (convergent evolution), but no blind species has ever obtained eyes by genetically "noticing" that everybody else seems to have them, and then copying their DNA (although selection by external forces could offer a species a more roundabout way of "noticing" everyone else's optical advantage through the death of its most photo-insensitive individuals, eventually growing its own eyes if it could survive long enough to do so). To create a true ecological version of a cultural Zeitgeist, free-floating genes would have to somehow splice themselves from species to species. But apparently that's not how it works above a single-celled level (although it's likely that cell organelles are the descendants of engulfed symbiotes). Stravinsky said that a great artist steals rather than borrows, but a great species doesn't have either option: it must experiment and develop from scratch, staying among its own kind.

This is not what we generally see when we look at cultural evolution: traditions with anything approaching this sort of stability and formal repetition usually require isolation or sacralisation to survive. They are very difficult to maintain in the presence of a large and varied culture, because some percentage of their members will adopt whatever borrowed practices appeal to them, and incorporate them into their own work. Hybrids abound, and altered artistic traditions can rarely be put back together outside of museum-like settings, dedicated to the appreciation of genres which are no longer producing new works.

Culture's talent for making hybrids suggests a variation on the single most common and useful image of evolution: that of a tree, with its trunk dividing into multiple branches as new forms of life arise. Since biological subspecies can't separate very far from each other without losing their ability to interbreed, the overall shape of the tree comes from pronounced, large scale divergences into whole new branches. The only convergences are within species, between organisms so close to each other that they appear to exist as a solid branch. Now if we climb up the animal branch to the vertebrates, take a left at the fish and go all the way through mammals and primates, we will find a place where the tree is looking very different. From the human twig, a complex culture has sprouted. The familiar genetic branches have started to grow vine-like extensions, which not only diverge under the pressures of variation and selection like everything else on the tree, but also curve back and wrap around each other, forming bundled branches of converged ideas and practices. These cultural constructs are themselves subjected to evolutionary forces, and we don't have to travel very far to find two examples of such vine-like composite limbs, assembled in mid-air. The "modern synthesis" in evolutionary thought is a 20th century hybrid of Darwinian principles and a post-Mendelian genetic biology which did not exist in his time, and I am borrowing some thoughts from it to throw a different light upon the current state of Western art music, a braided cable which came into its own centuries ago after it began to hybridize elements from separate sacred and profane branches within the music of earlier periods.

Artists and scientists alike fondly collect tales of inspiration from unlikely associations, proving again and again that fragments can be broken off from bodies of thought and still prove fruitful. This ability to merge separate lineages, in whole or in part, is called anastomosis, after the merging of blood vessels. The word itself makes the point that living cultural traditions, like their biological counterparts, exist as conduits for information, not simply as sequential collections of forms. Richard Dawkins's controversial concept of memes[10] proposes a mechanism for this transfer of ideational material. A meme is a memorable idea which easily copies itself into different minds, and provides a template for their activities. Here are some memes: the idea of an insurance company, or of an umbrella, or a bass drum, or of tending to play that bass drum on beat one. Such eminently imitate-able chunks of thought and behavior spread like viruses, and if one accepts the basic outlines of this scenario, then there are repercussions for group cultural endeavors which already have a difficult set of skills and concepts to teach to their members.

10. Richard Dawkins, *The Selfish Gene* (Oxford: Oxford University Press, 1976, new edition 1989), ch. 11. This book is a central text in contemporary evolutionary theory, which sometimes suffers from the long and unhappy history of attempts to derive right-wing political implications from knowledge about our place in the natural world. But the idea of memes is not necessarily responsible for the behavior of all of its relatives. For a brief and lucid summary of the concept, see also Daniel Dennett, "Memes and the Exploitation of Imagination," *Journal of Aesthetics and Art Criticism*, vol. 48 (1990).

The opening of new channels between cultural conduits tends to subvert the purity of genres by injecting competing memes, which suggest different ways of doing things, or different things to focus one's attention upon. What does this mean for individuals, whose curiosity drives the entire process? More stuff to learn; maybe even too much. The sheer difficulty of learning new and strange materials will offer a cultural tradition some protection from distracting influences, but if genres really wish to preserve their purity, they will also respond with social pressures upon their members, inducing them to reject such wayward impulses out of loyalty, shame, or disdain for the source of contamination. Thus is born both the concentration of the master and the obstinacy of the reactionary. A familial chain of masters and students, trained to operate according to biology's model of linear inheritance, discourages attention to the potentially distracting memetic messages arriving laterally from adjacent cultural conduits. Filtering incoming data to avoid overload and confusion is not a trivial function, and the advantages to members are obvious, but the group loyalty which enforces these attitudes is adapted from the same basic program as the local pride driving other human groupings: family and tribe, team and nation. This double-edged sword makes musical traditions prone to the rigidity and defensiveness which are so often the downfall of other cultural groupings, at the same time that it offers a means for conserving skills, and a buffer against the wasting of energy and attention.

Stir Thoroughly, And Not All At Once

The very ease and speed with which human culture invents, imitates, and reinvents the results not only makes us the biosphere's speediest test-driver of adaptive strategies this side of the virus, but also the chief manufacturer of non-adaptive byproducts: seemingly unpurposeful daydreams, digressions, pleasures, and play. If you consider the drifting details within a spreading rumor, the real wonder is that we have managed to come up with a few ways of making any accurate copies at all. In the genetic world, most mutations are deleterious; and although our brains provide us with a better-than-random success rate by allowing us to picture possible outcomes, our rapidity of cultural drift and experimentation requires a correspondingly good set of brakes.

Our desire for surprise and novelty is balanced against our limited time and energy, and the need to filter the world and focus our attention. Social loyalties which stigmatize influences from less respected sources are one of these filters. Another is that old enemy of avant-gardism, the suspicion that something which is not understood is either a hoax or laughably inept. These conservative and skeptical tendencies within the attitudes of individuals and cultures are analogous to the body's immune system, whose roving T-cells seek and destroy invaders from without and dangerous mutants from within. They provide social stability, as well as a cast of villains for our modern culture's creation stories; like the French academic painters of the late 19th century, whose ponderous pursuit of perfection set itself up for an upset by brash and lively interlopers like the Impressionists and Fauves. Defenders of tradition who wish to maintain continuity and avoid such catastrophic collapse are wise to approach challenges on their merits, and resist the tendency to think of their current array of genre definitions as essential and eternal, when in fact they are only convenient ways of dividing the world into teachable and discussible sized chunks.

But genre definitions are more than mere artificial constructs, because they create feedback loops with the real world. The niches they outline within the culture attract people who are eager to participate, and who voluntarily sort themselves into the available categories; but who also insist on continually customizing genre boundaries and job descriptions to fit their personalities and the changing circumstances. These divisions are neither completely foolish and arbitrary, nor particularly optimal or exact. They are simply what's available, and their proper use requires flexibility and occasional vandalism.

The Western classical tradition was so successful at binding together a fairly large group of cultures within a fairly consistent set of practices that it is easy to forget that it began its recorded life as a patchwork of regional styles and segregated genres, with strong feelings about the religious qualities of the human voice, and powerful taboos about when and where and within what style or technique it was appropriate to blend them with instruments. If we think of our own preconceptions about the proper place for saxophones or electric guitars, it is not all that difficult to imagine what such social conventions might have felt like, but we have nothing quite like the philosophical weight once accorded to such questions of passing taste. A thundering Romantic finale combining chorus, percussion, and pitched instruments would have seemed an abomination to many of the originators of the tradition.

So the assembly of a common practice was accomplished through gradual and successive transgressions against common sense; against gut instincts which said this technique or sonority does not belong with that one. Much of this could be accomplished by Trojan Horse incursions; "barbarous"

Turkish percussion, imported into Viennese classical pieces for sound color
and cultural references, gradually lost its exotic connotation and gained a new
European one. But it retained the sound color, which became a permanent part
of the orchestra. The ultimate success of these constant borrowings and appro-
priations depended on a balance between a willingness to accept outside influences as well as to redefine native ones, and the presence of a solid-enough core
of common practice to lend structure and to suggest uses for imported material.
But that core itself was constantly being changed; so much so that eventually
Europe's modern descendants bore less resemblance to their earliest notated
sources than those sources did to the foreign influences of their own time, with
whom they at least shared an environment, if not always a direct lineage.

Although its center may shift over time, the core of a common practice can
look very stable at a given moment, particularly after a good invention or synthesis has opened up a new plateau of as yet unexhausted possibilities, and
everyone seems to be converging on the same sort of work site. But the stability
is always temporary. The only unchanging quality inherent in a set of core
practices is its ability to unify and mediate between its constituent parts, each
of which were once either absent or very different from their current state.
Referring to genetic change, Daniel Dennett says that "nothing intrinsically
counts as a canonical version of anything,"[11] because of the difficulty in picking
significant mutations out of the imperceptible gradations in an evolutionary
chain. The difference between a mother and child is too tiny and microscopically diffuse in its details to afford us a clean
point where we can announce a species break,
and in any case it is only retrospectively that we
can decide which change was a significant one.
Identifying significant change is considerably
easier and more meaningful in a cultural tradition, because human invention is able to get away
with wider and more immediately recognizable leaps and variations than
nature's hit or miss, thanks to our ability to sort through the probable success
of possibilities before committing to them.

Not only are we occasionally capable of quickly picking out a significant cultural mutation, or a cluster of them which work well together, but once
found, we are eager to canonize them, build genres around them, and produce

11. Daniel Dennett, *Darwin's Dangerous Idea*
(New York: Touchstone, 1995), pp. 203-204. This
book is a sweeping attempt to make a whole of
biological Darwinism and its ethical, cultural,
and philosophical implications. The determined
attack on Gould as a threat to Darwinism may
seem puzzling to outsiders.

variations as soon as possible. The modern world, with its access to a long history, has drawn certain conclusions from observing this process. It is always on the lookout for promising new progenitors to bet on. In this sense the entire growth of avant-garde traditions in the Western arts looks very much like an attempt at the gradual institutionalization of foresight, or at least of a selection process for isolating it.

Maintaining a tradition during a string of transactions with local mutations and foreign imports requires a continuity of practice and outlook, but that inherited core is itself inherently composite; the product of a history of just the sort of transactions which it is now supposed to provide an anchor for. The only consistent purity of means or goal to be found between the various generations in a tradition resides in individuals, and their personal determination to pursue the emotional expression and experiences which the various genres of music were designed to deliver. This includes, of course, the emotional pleasures of simply manipulating musical materials in the most abstract way; not all music needs to refer outward. But much music prefers to.

Composers like Ravel, Milhaud, or Stravinsky who participated in the spread of jazz-influenced pieces during the 1920s and 30s didn't get their jazz at all right, but then again they weren't really trying in any serious sense, because that would have required improvisation. They were only making a picture of their surroundings, and its inclusion changed the nature of the post-classical music which followed. Since that time the 20th century was filled with messages sent between the European classical tradition and jazz, as populist as Ellington or Bernstein, or as arcane as Gunther Schuller or Anthony Braxton. But jazz and classical practice have rarely fused in equal parts, and the primary background of each of these composers is usually one or the other. Another approach currently thriving in a related territory is that of "downtown" and European improvisers. Their group and individual improvisations relate to jazz, but only occasionally follow its forms, while frequently referring both to 20th century avant-gardism and popular music. Regardless of whether this trend has speciated into a genre unto itself or not, it represents another extension of a long dialogue.

Given that both jazz and the post-classical traditions are themselves composed of many interleavings of invention and borrowing, why has the territory between them, which has been explored so many times from so many angles, been so difficult to establish permanent settlements in? The clearest and most commonly mentioned reasons involve the different sets of skills involved in composing and improvising, and the lack of a common practice; both of which are generally true, although solvable by talented individuals. These traditions are highly invested in complex characteristics which may not translate easily even when they are related: a classical virtuoso able to thread a way through harmonic change along the most perilous of composer-made paths will most likely lose his or her footing when first called upon to improvise a steady line through a jazz deployment of those same harmonies. Both sets of skills can be learned, but as long as they exist in separate toolboxes in the outside world that will never be a dependably common choice. But someone from either of these specialties could probably work up a respectable accompaniment for a popular song, so long as they understood stylistic nuances, thus blending their discipline with a simpler one. And either one could play music in their own field which required only a moderate influence from the other, not full command of an entirely new genre.

So if we step back and think in general about the convergences of lineages, we can imagine a sort of sliding scale of the practicality of influences, based on the relative complexity of the two genres involved, and the relative ambitions of a given merger. A 50/50 cross-pollination from two complex fields, such as the jazz and classical traditions we've been talking about, is the most ambitious and the most risky of all, as would be a hypothetical convergence of Japanese Gagaku and Indian classical music. But compositions incorporating a more modest influence, we'll say 20/80, are so common on the modern world that High Modernism's distaste for even that level of eclecticism stands in sharp contrast to its environment.

Genres of popular music, on the other hand, are quite capable of near-50/50 hybrids between equals, simply because there are so many variations of nearly the same level of complexity which use nearly the same harmonic, rhythmic, and structural materials. A small stylistic tic, inaudible to outsiders, can provide the rock cognoscenti with a clue to a new band's esthetic lineage and lateral borrowings. Furthermore, since the advent of recording nearly all such lineages are virtual, with no personal contact whatsoever between "master and student." This provides the greatest difference between rock and traditional folk musics: rock styles may begin as local phenomena, but they are quickly scouted out, evaporated up into the corporate clouds, and rained down across the country or the world. The transformation of rock and related forms into a corporate folk music for the corporate folks that we have become contains more than a little irony, given the rebellious impulses at the heart of nearly every interesting sub-genre.

But rock doesn't put up quite the same resistance to assimilation into modern post-classical composition that jazz does, because it has not had the time to evolve as far away from its folk sources, or to come up with a self-enclosed, fine art tradition of improvisation with the level of complexity and specificity found in jazz. And so, thanks to the very simplicity which excites so much high-brow scorn, rock might offer to the serious music world a relationship which could conceivably become similar to the long-lost relationship that the European tradition once had with its local folk musics. But unlike the mid-century style exemplified by Copland, which set American-sounding themes within European techniques and orchestrations, new serious music incorporating rock arrives with a whole new set of electric instruments, technologies, and timbres in tow; and its prolonged success would mean enormous changes in the sound and production of serious music.

Some composers interested in this field have called attention to the contrasts between their sources, while others have moved more incrementally, but over time these differences may not matter very much. To make a simple picture: if a generation of pieces influenced by a previous 20/80 merger engage in another 20/80 merger, their descendants' share of the "pure" heritage is down to 36/64. The next 20/80 change leaves 48.8/51.2, and thus successive approximation has landed us in 50/50 territory by another route. Obviously these arbitrary numbers are inadequate to describe the inexact nature of different people's mental "copies" of shared ideas, the inventive personalization built into human activities like art, and the unpredictable eddies of nuance where personality touches culturally shared style, but they do draw an outline of the sort of process which alters a living genre. Just as 20th century percussion pieces can in some way trace their genesis back to the Trojan Horse importation and later de-ethnicization of Turkish military percussion, then so might a future form spring from the borrowings, novelties, or heresies of our day, in a way which is not immediately apparent.

This is not to say that most hybrid mutations won't perish without establishing a lineage; they probably will. The more distant the leap they attempt, the greater their mortality rate is likely to be, pulled down by the lack of an internal commonality of practice, or by the attacks of their culture's purist "T-cells." But lateral dispersal is inevitable in a complex culture, and inheritance by direct lineage alone is increasingly unlikely.[12] Even an abandoned approach can leave its own home genre changed by the effort, and possibly point out an escape route from an overly stylized dead end. Only time will tell if any of our current experiments in gap-bridging will result in a permanent span, but if they do, the last gesture will be more like dropping a keystone into a nearly completed arch than building a bridge from the ground up.

12. As I was editing this essay, an article by Richard Taruskin appeared in the *New York Times* (24 September 1997) in which he referred to classical music's concern with artistic pedigree and inherited texts as "vertical," versus the "horizontal" influence of recordings, which reflect a cross-section of what is available in our living culture, regardless of source. As far as I can tell, his "vertical" is essentially identical to my "linear," and his "horizontal" to my "lateral." I hope that this concept enters into common use, under whatever name survives the selection process.

The internal influences of popular culture have probably had a greater effect than external imports on the inventions of most composers, if for no other reason than their sheer unavoidability by anyone who leaves the house or scans the media once in a while. But although Western classical music may not have met up with any single external tradition which pushed its center of gravity far enough to alter central tenets in areas like notation, harmony, or basic performance practice, the cumulative consequences of world influences have increased as travel and communication have became easier and more routine. In particular, cross-cultural translation was the rule among the early Minimalists, with significant influences appearing from India, Japan, Bali and Africa, and elsewhere. LaMonte Young and Terry Riley seriously studied Indian music, and Steve Reich found a model for his brand of shifting polyrhythm in African drumming, while Philip Glass tells how a friend's verbal description of counting systems in Indian classical music provided him with an inspiration that was as much invention as influence. In these latter cases, hybridization allowed an end run around High Modernism's prohibition against a stable pulse with a recognizable tie to dance forms. This has opened the gates on our musical culture's renewed ability to find interesting materials in its own popular backyard.

This end run around the insoluble and ingrown battle between modernism and classicism has led to numerous attempts to further hybridize minimalism with popular influences, or academic modernism, or romantic orchestral traditions, or any combination of the above, as required by any individual composer's desire to make a whole out of their imagination and their favorite tools and inherited musics. While the juries may be out for some time on all of these hybrid forms, it's clear that the logjam which had piled up around the clogged juncture between the 19th and 20th centuries is finally clearing as the 21st approaches.

Growing A Purpose

A little corner of human culture like music may exhibit all of the fingerprints of the big evolutionary forces, from mutation and differential selection to speciation, but at first glance there appears to be a missing link in its connection to its relatives. The arts certainly bear structural resemblances to other cultural endeavors. All have gradually assembled core histories and branching subdivisions, and all make similar use of local inventions and conceptual recipes appropriated from related cultural projects. But an undertaking like agriculture answers an obvious and immutable need to eat, while the desire to look at pictures remains mysterious and conditional. Some might be tempted to use this as a waiver, exempting the arts from discussions about the practical uses and origins of things; and might even feel that the utilitarian overtones of such talk deprives art of its sense of wonder. But it is not that difficult to speculate about what the fine arts might be "for," in an evolutionary sense, so long as one accepts that a uniquely human symbolic enterprise will behave in a more circuitous and indirect way than the simple adaptational cause and effect we might expect from life's most basic needs. And as for the fear of emotional deflation, I for one experience a sometimes surreal wonder in imagining the paths by which an animal might come to enjoy daubing mud or blowing into a hollow reed, always finding a place for such artifacts and activities alongside the necessities of life as it goes about the prosaic, sordid, and glorious business of generating its swarming cultures.

The accidents of history that make us sing and make images and symbols happened a very long time ago, so long ago that they could conceivably have as much to do with the way our brains are wired as with any specific cultural traditions. I suspect that our artistic proclivities are one of Gould and Lewontin's "spandrels"[13]: a side-effect of the abilities for symbol-making and symbol-understanding which allow us to do more practical things, like remembering how much stuff we have, or expressing contempt for Frog People while among our fellow Fish People. Such side effects are accidentally acquired and opportunistically developed evolutionary "habits" which survive because

13. Stephen Jay Gould and Richard Lewontin, "The Spandrels of San Marco and the Panglossian Paradigm: A Critique of the Adaptationist Programme," *Proceedings of the Royal Society of London*, vol. B205, no. 1161 (1979).

they turn out to be good for something else, or simply because they don't get in the way. For instance, vocalizing on the part of infants and mothers is a cross-cultural constant which serves a specific purpose: this apparently hard-wired behavior teaches the vowel sounds of a particular language to the child.

All that the birth of song requires is that people keep doing it beyond child-hood because it's pleasurable, and both copy others and think up rewarding new things to do with the habit.

Something useful can be repeated for strictly hedonistic reasons, and that act of hedonism can both retain emotional meaning from its source, and be reinvested with new meanings derived from its new use. Song branches into songs of social camaraderie, religious songs, love songs. Accidents and oppor-tunities for play can grow from targeted adaptations, and adaptations can build upon accidents. In a cultural medium, where branches of thought and practice are by nature constantly hybridizing, such multiple origins and causes are the rule. In light of this, it is difficult to imagine any satisfactory conclusion to an argument between a strict adaptationist search for causality, in which making and experiencing the arts would have directly benefited their first practitioners, versus a Gouldian awareness of the incorporation of side-effects into a system. Culture's blending of causes and effects would have quickly muddied up any readable tracks. Music is a particularly tough case, because prior to notation and recording, it left no fossils to study.

It's conceivable, but not necessary, that someone with the skills of hand, eye, and mental planning necessary to carve an ornamented version of a tool may also be more likely to come up with a new and better tool, incor-porating a subtle improvement in engineering. Basket-weaving and ax-making are matters of importance because something concrete is at stake, but like vocalizing, they also offer opportunities for what can only be called play. For children, play not only involves the sharpening of motor skills, it also involves practice at making mental models of the world and learning how to behave within them: they play house, or play war, and debate the rules amongst them-selves. We are not the only species which uses childhood as a period of concen-trated experimentation; we just keep it up for an extraordinarily long time, and never completely stop.

But experimentation is often fruitless, and adults have serious busi-ness to take care of. Whether the enjoyment of play is an end in itself, or nature's reward for exercising the imagination, a question still arises: how to get access to that sense of wonder when a child's eagerness is no longer present, when one's standards demand something more carefully constructed, and when there is no time to do it yourself? Hire a professional! Artists are sub-contractors of the imagination, hired to produce access to a purposeful and adult version of the emotional pleasures of discovery, wonder, fear, and "make-believe" of all descriptions, and the artistic sub-genres they work in are products of the same branchings and convergences which produce specialized job descriptions in other fields. Today Western artists tend to work with very personalized meanings and associations, but other times and places have seen more attention paid to the making of communal symbols, tools for rituals of membership which strengthened the devotion of members and thus contributed to their collective success as a group. It does have a certain ironic appeal to imagine that all of our cherished individuality and artistic freedom descended from a job as manufacturers of social glue.

In the end, it is neither necessary nor possible to resolve such dual purposes in the uses of music or any other art, even if they present us with such apparent contradictions. If a genre of art is as much a convergence of bundled influences and uses as a linear inheritance, than it should not surprise us if some of those constituent elements conflict with each other. After all, science has demonstrated that the very cells in our body frequently compete among themselves, to our ultimate benefit. Optimal design is not a guaranteed part of life's package; only adequacy, as defined by having survived the last major threat. If these artistic projects didn't work well for whatever it is that they are doing, some society would have figured out how to stop wasting the effort by now, and thus gained a competitive edge on everybody else.

It didn't happen that way; in fact, the expenditure of the "wasted" energy of art is one of humanity's favorite symbols of cultural power and success. An uneasy recognition of this lies beneath many a declaration of artistic purity on the part of people who honestly wish to hold to their ideals. Like the extravagant nests of certain birds, art can serve as a social sentence which says "I/We can afford this"; and that motivation accounts for much of the consumption of the arts, and for the existing relics of civilizations past. However, it doesn't account completely: a serious composer could find easier ways of making a living, and a marginally committed audience member or patron could find more brightly glittering toys to impress people with. But artist and patron might not be able to find an activity which so successfully combines their practical or social needs with the same emotional pleasures or sense of meaning. There is no purity of motive to be found here; rather, there is an historically successful habit of interweaving several disparate impulses.

This use of an art form to bundle several purposes together is not just a cultural strategy; in nature, multiple uses also tend to accumulate around a single action or structure. You could think of this as the Swiss Army Knife principle, and for the composer mentioned above, it's very efficient: in return for making interesting noise, he or she gets self expression, intellectual challenge, emotional gratification, social attention from fellow primates, and lunch. The wings of birds and insects provide us with an example of the same principle of multiple use at work in nature. In addition to providing flight, wings regulate body heat, and can also offer a billboard for colorful sexual advertisements to members of one's own species, or camouflage for the eyes of predator or prey.

Multiple uses multiply even further when spread out across time as well as space. Wings present a classic evolutionary puzzle: what force could have kept them evolving gradually towards the size necessary for flight, when half a wing isn't enough to get a bug or a bird off the ground?[14] This is the problem of the uselessness of intermediate stages, and Darwin himself pointed out the path to a solution, which has been supported by recent research into insects. During their early stages, the little quarter-wings and eighth-wings hadn't really been wings at all. They were devel-

14. Stephen Jay Gould, "Not Necessarily A Wing," from *Bully for Brontosaurus.*

oped to control body heat, and when these thermo-regulator flaps got big enough, the creature began to take advantage of their aerodynamic properties. Eventually this new, accidentally acquired and opportunistically developed function of flight gained primary importance (although wings do still work as thermal regulators). Thus our Swiss Army Knife principle takes on the added dimension of time: not every blade is out at once. In fact, it constantly grows new blades, and we don't even know what potentialities are folded into the handle until a new task appears to try it out on.

This little story tells us as much about our own perception as it does about bug wings. Our conception of exactly what kind of thing any multiple-use structure "really is" depends more on the order in which we discover its different functions than on any intrinsic essence. The first problem that we see it solve becomes, for us, its purpose: wings are for flying. But they weren't always for flying. Despite millennia of fascination with airborne creatures, the human tendency to look for purity of purpose made it difficult to conceptualize this indirect path of adaptation-with-change-of-function, or exaptation,[15] and thus to finally find out how and why wings came into being.

15. Stephen Jay Gould and Elizabeth Vrba, "Exaptation: A Missing Term in the Science of Form," *Paleobiology,* vol. 8 (1981).

Uses And Niches

Musical examples of the process of exaptation are very easy to find. Musicians are constantly importing and exporting ideas, both between individuals and between their stylistic tribes, using what they find, and changing what they use. Given time and intermediate stages, a musical technique can eventually show up anywhere doing anything. And, as with biological evolution, apparent purity of purpose for a feature can evaporate if one keeps an eye on the ball long enough.

Cloistered monks didn't intone medieval religious chants so that their melodies could later mutate into a cantus firmus within a florid pile of counterpoint, performed by professional musicians for powerful clients. Nor did African-American work songs employ call-and-response so that jazz masters could wow club audiences a century later by "trading fours" at dizzying tempos. The transmission and variation of ideas is clear in both of these cases, and it's equally clear that the end results of these evolutionary processes were not pre-ordained or written into their beginnings: they are simply what happened to happen as generations of creative people took whatever materials they had inherited or discovered, and adapted them for their own purposes. Although both of these examples moved in the direction of greater complexity, that motion did not render their original sources "obsolete." Nor did it render them ideal or exemplary in any way, making it somehow unnecessary for future musical cultures to make further exaptations from sacred uses to profane uses, or from folk to professional, or from anywhere else to elsewhere. The uses of music are not like a technological problem which can be once and for all solved by the invention of the wheel; rather, they demand the renewal of continuous rediscovery and reinvention.

Ideas from the chants and worksongs jumped genres at some point, whether in leaps, with individuals intentionally applying the techniques of one field to another purpose, or in gradual tides, as large numbers of musicians incrementally veered in a new direction. In both cases there was a general trend towards increasing difficulty over time, because the music became a profession, and because individuals wanted to provide themselves with a sense of personal accomplishment and invoke the admiration of others. But there were no inherent and immutable "essences" of sacred/profane, serious/pop, or high/low to be defended or transgressed upon. Rather, there were collections of tools which had worked before, and therefore were the first things likely to be picked up, tried out, and jury-rigged to fit when changing circumstances presented new challenges. And there were job sites, niches where there was something particular to be accomplished. Such niches can be occupied by any musical materials, regardless of their history or genealogy, that either satisfy the local requirements of the niche, or succeed in convincing the local users they will be better off if they redesign their habits to fit the new candidate.

Most of the available niches within a culture's ecosystem are sites where music is used to induce specific emotional states for specific occasions, and most often it gets straight to the point. Music is great for inducing mating, or generating reverence, whether religious or nationalistic. It can be used to strengthen bonds of class, age, consumer brand loyalty, or whatever else people can dream up in the way of groups to belong to. In such circumstances the connection of music to the Darwinian basics of a culture's needs is not terribly mysterious. Art music with no apparent purpose beyond itself offers a reflective access to some of these functional pleasures and to new inventions of its own as well, while escaping some of the ritualization and relentlessness which can accumulate around more utilitarian music.

But if serious, Sit-down-and-shut-up music began and continues as a sort of rebellion against the tyranny of the obvious, it is not therefore an escape from utility itself, and certainly not from ritualization. It is simply another type of use, conversant with the others. It is defined not by abstract principles, but by a behavior; a way of focused listening which generates a demand for more music that will satisfy our desire for more of these listening experiences. It is a system comprised of a niche and the stuff that fills it, partly invented and partly adapted from the culturally available materials. But that niche only partially defines the nature of the occupants who branch out within its space. Sit-down-and-shut-up music or Get-up-and-dance music each contain a set of broad instructions about what use you are supposed to make of what you hear, but Saturday night's set of dance tunes might evolve or be appropriated into a polite Sunday suite, and the suite with its minuet into a symphony with its scherzo. Simple music initially intended to serve as a soundtrack for mating can and has evolved offshoots which provide more satisfactory abstract listening, but less satisfactory social dancing.

And so as it goes about its not-quite-independent business, serious music's processes of abstraction from the simple sources which gave it birth not only can be repeated, but must be repeated, if the equation linking it to its culture is to be a living transaction, rather than an enshrined memory. Through the likes of Bach, Chopin, and Bartok, the older European tradition continually demonstrated that shifts in use are part of the evolutionary process; and we would breathe life into our own times by keeping that in mind. In the end, or rather in the beginning, the only unchanging, essential characteristics of music are those which are written into the physics of sound, and those which are wired into our nervous system or our primal experiences: sudden loud sounds startle us, sounds that remind us of adults cooing over an infant have the opposite effect. Beyond that sort of nearly involuntary analogy, the use to which people are putting a given music will gradually decide its nature.

Military bugle calls once effectively allowed synchronized advances and retreats on confused battlefields: here is a function so simple that it's really only a signal, and some might not want to call it musical at all. But after the fight, the same person picks up the same instrument and plays taps over the graves of his comrades. He plays slowly and well, people are moved: have we entered the realm of art yet? The space between reveille and taps is a tough place to go hunting for a line where mechanical uses can be cleanly walled off from the universe of the fine arts. Did we enter it when our bugler played trumpet on an anthem at a commemorative civic ceremony, or only when a symphony dedicated to the fallen is premiered the following year? In which situations is it sensible and fruitful to ask exactly when and where we enter the territory of esthetics? We all can recognize that there are differences in musical use here, but what we make of them often says as much about our affiliations and goals as it does about the differences themselves.

If the histories of each of those uses could be mapped, and the points where they diverged in the distant past could be found, then in biological terms this would become a question of speciation. Exactly when is the beginning of a species; with what individual or generation can we say that it came into existence? The answer is that you cannot. In a direct line of inheritance, individual Z may be of a new species when compared with individual A, but individual J might be considered to be of the same species as either A or Z. At no point in the alphabet was any one type of individual unable to interbreed with those types immediately before or after, or there would not be a line of inheritance at all.

Nevertheless, gradualism is broken into by circumstances, and every transfer of information provides an opening. Ernst Mayr observes that "Evolution is not a smooth, continuous process but consists, in sexually reproducing organisms, of the formation of a brand new gene pool in every generation."[16] Each moment in time has

16. Ernst Mayr, "An Analysis of the Concept of Natural Selection," from *Towards A New Philosophy of Biology* (Cambridge, Mass.: Harvard University Press, 1988), p. 99.

particular, lateral qualities not completely shared with its ancestors or descendants, and the potential volatility of a pool of cultural practices is even greater than that of a gene pool, since the merging of linear and lateral inheritances within culture gives every thought a multitude of parents. With so many characteristics to shuffle, and an active, choice-making human mind doing the shuffling, there are strong incentives for people to make distinctions which will help them by partially pre-programming their decisions.

Looking laterally across the range of jobs that are simultaneously available to our brass player there is a gradation, but it is marked by a few fairly pronounced distinctions, the results of previous audiences' requests, and previous musicians' agreements to clump together as genre specialists. Each incremental move, from the battlefield equivalent of an animal cry to the fine arts, shares characteristics with the next. But as we shall see, our very perception of genre differences tends to cause them to become more exaggerated, as we assign them jobs within the culture. People are drawn to identifiable quantities because it saves them sorting time. Twentieth century art has repeatedly proven that the very act of giving a name to a genre can contribute to a process which, if successful, attracts attention and causes it to become further differentiated from its sources and surroundings. Similarly, on the broadest possible level, separating music into the serious and the popular is a tool which our musical culture has used to help individuals focus on their divergent interests, and avoid wasting time on unpromising avenues when they have a general idea of what they are looking for. The subgroups and communities which result are simply social structures whose function is to act as cognitive filters for their members: what you don't like, or have been instructed not to like, you don't have to learn about. This is the reason why the blunt instrument of the serious/popular distinction survives, despite its pronounced resemblance to an attempted division of all plants into trees and grasses.

The Fools On The Hill Go Down In The Valley

As we have seen, there is no individual who provides a dividing line between successive species in the same lineage, but once two branches have incrementally divided far enough, they begin to embark on separate evolutionary paths. When this is noticeable enough we retroactively decide on where in the transition to draw the line between types. It's a bit easier with culture. Since a human invention can launch a new train of thought in a single leap, we occasionally have a clean place to draw a line and say "this was the first one." This remains a relatively infrequent occurrence, considering the number of artists' lives which have been filled with desire and labor towards this end. Nevertheless, even where gradualism persists, it is usually only a matter of time before genre boundaries appear. They appear because we induce them: distinctions have a practical value to us. We want to know when a new style begins, where its boundaries are, and who is in or outside of them. We draw demarcations because they are convenient and they help us to talk and focus our valuable time and attention; and once they are established they become self-fulfilling prophecies, because conventional delineations of style affect the distribution of rewards.

A successful and definable style will attract audience attention, and the associated rewards will attract even more people towards doing even more of such work, thus fleshing out the center of the bell-curve for whatever characteristics define that style, and emptying out the fringes. These less populous regions become the space between genres. We could picture them as dry, rocky topographical high ground, and imagine mainstream, center-of-the-bell-curve genres as fertile valleys rich in resources, population, and developed techniques for efficiently gathering the fruits of a rewarding environment. For an example of such a valley and an optimum valley dweller, think of the early 20th century orchestra, with the bugs worked out and some sonorities still underused, and Ravel there to orchestrate on it. Lucky orchestra, lucky Ravel.

Now back to our rocky ridge. It doesn't seem to offer a lot of ways to make a living, but a few people give it a shot anyway. Perhaps they grew up there, the child of an experimenter as Charles Ives was; or maybe they are slightly odd and cranky and prefer their solitude. Or perhaps the population explosion in the valley is pushing people up the slopes, and they believe that they can settle this sparsely populated ridge of possibility and prosper by finding a resource missed by others: a winery, a mine, a line of traps in the right place. If it works, others will follow. This is the structural essence of the "reproductive strategy" of a successful avant-garde, whether or not it was consciously conceived of or pursued as such by those first few up the ridge.

But remember that our high ground was only the space between genres, a lightly used group of possibilities outside of the valleys of successfully established practices. The very presence of more people changes its nature, and we can reflect that by giving our terrain the qualities of a seesaw. In our imaginary rubber landscape, the growing weight of our growing number of successful mountain people pushes the ridge downward, until it becomes a valley itself. Perhaps it draws so many converts from the former mainstream that it displaces

17. For several days, I thought this visual analogy was of my own imagining, but then I noticed that on page 192 of Dennett's *Darwin's Dangerous Idea,* which I had read several months earlier, there is a similar visual image in a quote from Manfred Eigen's *Steps Toward Life* (Oxford: Oxford University Press, 1992). It is populated by genetic mutations, with different meanings attached to the hills and valleys in the terrain, and no miners clomping around its abstract topography in their dirty boots. Well, at least I get a good example of the exaptation of an idea as a consolation prize.

the old valley upward, or perhaps the old valley survives, leaving us with two parallel troughs. Now our model[17] reflects the fact that a physical organism or cultural construct can redesign its own environment, and we can not only see the difference between avant-garde and mainstream behaviors as survival strategies, but another phenomenon as well: the often noted way that one gradually transforms itself into the other, given conspicuous success.

This image can also help us to see the pitfalls of searching for too coherent a lineage among the composers who have often been referred to as "American Mavericks." A school like the Serialists all settled on adjacent ridges, found a common way of mining, and were able to get enough people piled up in the same place to generate their own new valley in a fairly efficient way. What our now-honored mavericks have in common is only that they were "Ridge Guys" of one description or the other. Some miners, some vintners, some trappers, most living on different hills altogether; or like John Cage and Lou Harrison, plying different trades in close proximity. These two offer a cautionary argument against attempts to redefine the line of mavericks from Ives to contemporary experimentalists and minimalists as a "school" in quite the sense that serialism and East Coast rationalism in general were a school. In earlier years Cage and Harrison worked together as friends, participating in concerts and events in a milieu which in many ways set the tone for both West Coast experimentalism and New York's downtown environment. But like other important figures in this field, such as Cowell, Partch, or Nancarrow, their mature work offers very different experiences to the ear, across a wider and less unified range than the "uptown" Serialists. Although all parts of town see Ives as their ancestor, the later composers in the more miscellaneous lineage have provided much of the inspiration and impetus for downtown new music. This lively anti-tradition of mavericks has made and continues to make the world a far more interesting place, but it did not settle into a relatively stable or clearly defined genre until it gave rise to minimalism. Only with the appearance and success of a number of postminimal styles has a quorum of people congregated closely enough around a single shared inheritance to create a sizable new valley, and thus the potential for a new mainstream; to the extent that such a thing can still exist in a society with the diversity and complexity of our own.

The Urge To Procreate

Regardless of the eventual fate of any particular style, all which have participated to any great extent in the avant gardism of 20th century post-classical music have had more than a few bites out of the apple of historical self-awareness. The world of the modern avant-garde is one which is quite knowledgeable about the details of its own history of innovation, and is as eager to reproduce the conditions which led to its successes as any other group of people would be. Thus it should be no surprise that the values embodied in the maverick composers above should command a great deal of allegiance, nor that the founding research-oriented modernists should have the same effect. Here uptown and downtown agree: both of their central narratives tell of individuals who were willing to risk the scorn of others to stick to a difficult vision, who eventually succeeded in spreading their influence by wide dispersal or along a lineage, but who would have kept at their work regardless of wide attention or success. In a century whose primary features were specialization aimed at tightly targeted audiences, divergence of cultural functions, and the subdivision of a rich and successful musical inheritance, it is no wonder that the confluent processes of synthesis, hybridization, and populism should get something of a bad name. The bad name was only made worse as popular music came to be defined by corporate grazing among the sincere efforts of new bands, and film gradually learned to design broadly targeted products by committee, treating the artists executing them as being increasingly interchangeable.

I am not at all sure how our emphasis on individualism and specialization in the fine arts would have felt to composers of earlier times, or whether their more stable common practice generated different attitudes about innovation and invention; but these are our values, and the benefits to be derived from fulfilling them are now intuitively obvious to any aspiring student of contemporary music. As was true in the past, inheritances from older composers remain the most conflict-free and readily acknowledged of borrowings, because both generations benefit. But modern composers have strong social pressures upon them to be very cautious about lateral influences from their immediate peers. They do not want to be seen as engaging in imitative behavior which might disqualify them as potential progenitors; either in a line of their own, or more often as major contributors in the dispersed reproductive style of artistic schools. Shared characteristics can exacerbate rivalries, but a way around this problem can be found by creating coalitions, ranging from loose camaraderie to close associations of the Picasso/Braque sort. As usual, a common enemy helps things along.

On a more impersonal scale, the lateral spread of a new taste can also be problematic, because if its dissemination doesn't call to mind popular culture's fashions and fads on its own, you can be sure that its critics soon will. The price that we pay for the subversive pleasures of our admiration of mavericks is that it promotes an outlook in which any comparison to passing fashion seems to detract from the seriousness of an artistic endeavor. But these winds of common concern which sweep back and forth across the musical infosphere are audible in the best of work as well as the worst, and are not necessarily in conflict with originality, since shared ideas have often provided the raw material for an original treatment. Nevertheless, eclecticism beyond a circle of friends sometimes raises eyebrows, and referring to such lateral influences when talking to a composer about his or her work is potentially impolite, or worse. Making faddishly derivative work constitutes conduct unbecoming a prospective progenitor, and offense can easily be taken if such any such implication is perceived.

This sketch of the relative respectability and social comfort level of influences begins to paint a familiar picture, one with a strong preference for direct generational inheritance or a sort of tribal proximity. Tracing its outlines reveals the silhouette of biology's branching, linear tree of inheritance being superimposed on human invention, and there are places where this linear model pinches and fits poorly. These are the same places where composers' emotional discomfort over acknowledging influences from beyond a chosen circle appear: at the sites where vines of lateral cultural influence arrive from distant branches, or sprout off and reach towards them, or twine together in mid-air in hopes of making a branch where there was none before. The discomfort arises when the regulatory influence of group identity conflicts with an individual's outward-looking curiosity, and these conflicts are areas of endless social renegotiation. Up to a certain point, the interests of a group are furthered by a narrowed focus on inherited, indentifiable badges of membership; and individuals who participate are rewarded. But individuals do not want to be deprived of their conduits for acquiring lateral information, and often feel resistant to any group-friendly linear model of inheritance which fails to make full use of our capacity for intellectual hybridism.

Nevertheless, we hold on to the not-quite-sufficient tool of a linear inheritance wherever possible, for the same reason that we use prescriptive/descriptive genre boundaries which don't quite fit the facts on the ground: because they are both so useful. The points where biological branchings are closest to the truth, such as the relationship between teacher and student, are points of immediate contact between real people who know each other; where the transfer of detailed information itself is easier than across subcultures, and where there are opportunities to personally smooth over any rough spots and rivalries. But the linear model itself is still useful even when it doesn't fit. It filters data down to the point where it can be more easily grasped, isolating individual leaps of human inventiveness from the background of environmental forces operating both within and around that individual.

There is a distinctly game-like quality to all of this, with winners to be picked and rewards to be distributed. Focusing on the meandering tracks of lateral influence or ideas "in the air" interrupts the business of making competitive interpretations, identifying progenitors, and rating their subsequent lineages for their relative "fitness." When cultural evolution is recast as this sort of boiled down Darwinian drama of inheritance, variation, and selection, then lateral influences and hybridism constitute a muddying of the contestant's trail, a form of cheating in what was supposed to be a clean fight. Keeping the fight within the rules and the ring is the job of the purist. But even if you buy the idea that selection is always more interesting than variation, one problem remains: too much success at keeping the fight in the ring tends to shrink the ring itself, until there is no room left for anything but the musical equivalent of Bruce Lee's one inch punch.

Despite the reality of selection and competition, there is a damaging fallacy at work in all of this. Cultural selection does not operate solely on individuals; it also operates on group interests. Concerts of one composer's work remain the exception, and genre members depend on each other in many ways. Music is not in its entirety a zero sum enterprise, in which the ascendance of one practitioner damages the rest. On the contrary, a successful composer will send listeners hunting for another similar experience, thus benefiting the field or genre as a whole. This may not be immediately apparent at our moment in history because, as an unintended side-effect of the modernist adventure, the culture's interest in contemporary music is so slender that it will support only a handful of recognizable names at any given moment. This creates a winner-take-all situation where they must "stand for" contemporary composition in the same way that Pavarotti now stands for opera, and of course there is considerably less "all" for the winner to take at our end of the musical field. Nevertheless, if we composers indulge the misplaced exaggerations of natural rivalry which this system evokes in us, we simply become engines of its perpetuation. Serious music is a minority interest, and like most minorities, it fares best with a realization of shared interests.

Ideas are more often laterally dispersed than bequeathed in a line, and few cultural endeavors will ever have anything like the clarity and hard edges of natural lineages. Schoenberg got as close as possible, establishing a particularly definable branch because of his invention of a specific and unmistakable technique, but Stravinsky behaved more like most great composers have, sending vine-like tendrils of influence off into many corners of musical space, and entering into transactions with whatever sources fed into his personal vision. Stravinsky's influence still appears in unexpected quarters with unexpected results, because his genius for organizing a broad range of materials allowed him to carry his house on his back as he traveled through diverse territories. When in the end these territories included Schoenberg's own, it was more the logical extension of an omnivorous nature than the acceptance of an inherited, enclosed, and circumscribed role for art music.

Adam, Eve, Cain, Abel, The In-Laws, And The Kids

As we have seen, for most of its history Western art music was remarkably adept at absorbing, abstracting, and exploiting both outside influences and mutations in its local folk musics. As a multiple-use, multi-national tradition, it was able to survive profound change for centuries and still maintain the musical equivalent of a Pax Romana, but the 20th century experiment with fission into several specialized branches was probably inevitable as this very success began to generate too much information to fit comfortably between one set of ears. But this has caused as many problems as it has solved, and only time will tell if they can re-converge into something resembling dialects of a workable common language, or if they will be able to speak across divisions within a heterogeneous culture and eventually repopulate the fragmented or abandoned habitat of their ancestor.

Much of the old tradition's ability to speak to non-specialists by producing direct emotional experiences has now been bottled and shipped to Hollywood, much of its historical capacity for complexity has been condensed and stored in academia, and much of its propensity for synthesis and absorption has collected within the downtown wing of new music, after varying degrees of hybridization with modernism's experimentalist spirit. Here, some of what remains of the European tradition's ability to forge popular styles into unexpected forms mingles with experimentalists from the self-supporting world of jazz, and with the homegrown avant-gardes that periodically branch out from rock and roll, which in its more commercial forms is our culture's real folk music. Finally, there is classical music proper: the actual works written while the tradition was engaged in its vigorous balancing act between intellectual, emotional, and practical impulses. This music survives as our culture's most common form of art music, but it is not of our culture. It's beautiful, it's borrowed, it's a bit musty, and it's gradually withdrawing into the museum of humanity's past achievements, while its offspring and their new in-laws squabble over the inheritance.

Each of these factions has inherited a portion of the functions once served by the classical tradition, from the creative to the economic, but none has inherited the whole. No currently living segment of the field of composed music is fully analogous to the European art music of recent centuries, and a new cultural organism capable of filling that niche cannot be put together using only the leftover pieces of the old, because one very big piece is missing: the extinct popular musics which constantly fed "serious" music with raw material for its abstractions and transformations. This vital element needs to be found among the living. The engine that drove 19th century European music to its continuing worldwide acceptance (limiting our discussion here to canon, not cannon) wasn't solely its pure, abstract triumphs of functional harmony or elaborate structure. The classical repertoire also grew strong on the isometric tensions between its intellectuality and its continual absorption of folk musics, with their conventionalized portrayals of common emotions.

Ironically, only the world of jazz and improvisation comes close to approximating the structure of the bygone European musical ecosystem, in the sense that jazz still encompasses a complete range of simple and complex musical uses under one roof. Even the most technically advanced improviser retains an ability and a feel for playing the blues, which is both an historical source for jazz and a living folk music that now survives primarily as a branch of rock. This has made it a forerunner in a second and even wider way: the electrification of the blues during the 1950s is now being mirrored in scores of folk musics around the world. Local popular forms worldwide have been displaced or forever changed by the phenomenal success of American pop music, with its blend of

African rhythmic sensibility, European harmony, and electronic technology. But far from spelling doom for serious music, as worried devotees of the Western tradition often fear, this trend offers potentially fertile conditions for the incubation, on a global scale, of new art musics which have the hope of becoming as successfully adapted to our world as the classical tradition was to its own.

What would contemporary "serious" music sound like if it incorporated the commonplace musical materials of our culture as readily and extensively as Bach or Mozart did with their own? Early returns are already in, but if this becomes a conventionally acceptable question, most answers probably won't cruise anywhere near the speed of Ligeti. But however odd it might seem, the existence of a certain percentage of unsuccessful but earnestly well-intentioned attempts (as opposed to cynically market-driven ones, of which there is generally no shortage) would be a clear sign of a healthy and thriving musical culture. A figure like Brahms might be seen as a very large animal perched at the tip of a complex musical food chain; a creature who could not have thrived without the environment created by millions of clumsier claws scuttling across the parlor pianos which were a fixture of 19th century middle class homes. An omnivore like Schubert could work both ends of the system, penning popular parlor pieces and lofty symphonies alike. Theirs was a period when serious and popular, professional and amateur music-making were related dialects; is it completely coincidental that this very music continues to dominate our concert halls? As we move farther and farther away from that vanished world, our intuitive connections with the sounds and forms of 19th century classical music fade, but the work has outlived its culture because it grew up in, and created around itself, a robust musical ecosystem. It developed conventions for connecting a full range of human emotions to a huge store of musical techniques. The tradition was both adaptive and complex; a unified field theory which provided one of humanity's high water marks before it began to choke on the repetitions and reactions engendered by its own success.

In contrast, the passing century's more insular art music traditions accepted the loss of the parlor pianos and tended away from such generalistic endeavors, and towards a more partitioned view of the relationship between compositional problem-solving and emotional intent, often informed by a keen sense of dualism between high and low culture. Philosophically defensible or not, these distinctions have had the practical effect of creating an atrophy of dialogue between cause and effect, between the architectural and communicative aspects of music. Our categories shunt young composers towards the academy or the marketplace, experimentation or communication, structure or emotion. In effect, the 20th century seems to be preparing to send its composers walking into the 21st with their choice of either a strong left leg or a strong right one.

These attitudes have had profound repercussions on art music's place in the outside world. Artistic specialization, along with its cousin in marketing, tightly focused demographic targeting, has reached such extremes that serious composers live in a sort of internal exile, playing virtually no part in their parent culture. When the most gifted converse only among themselves, their complaints about a debased public sphere become a self-fulfilling prophecy. At some point it ceases to matter whether they withdrew first, or were driven away by Philistines; the end result is identical.

This all began as a plausible adaptation to a huge and complicated modern culture. When ancient difficulties of travel and communication allowed hundreds of little monocultures to survive in relative isolation, a person could investigate every lead in their limited environment and never be overwhelmed by information or contradictory instructions. As societies grow more complex, specialization erects barriers in the social environment that can help artists preserve command of their materials. But this gradual drift into a strategy of specialization has left the living inheritors of the once-dominant classical tradition in the evolutionary predicament of Australia's koala, which is so well suited to its eucalyptus trees that it's lost the ability to thrive on any other diet. If the forests disappear, so does the koala. If large enough patches manage to survive as carefully protected preserves, walled off from the invasive and evolving surroundings, so will the koala. The animal will not, however, go looking for adventure abroad, unless it's really determined to do something drastic about that weight problem.

Although our poor koalas will never make it out of the woods and onto the savannas by breeding with kangaroos, that is exactly the sort of leap that the human brain is best at. The Darwinian gene can't mix apples and oranges, but in the virtual reality of ideas, languages, and art, the Lamarckian mind can transmit to the future any non-linear concoction that it's capable of dreaming up, provided that the dream includes some sort of a plan for meshing the working parts, and some inspiration and inventiveness to lubricate their motions. Long ago, such combinations of experimentation and hybrid inheritance animated the assembly of the classical tradition, from a collection of converging influences into an omnivorous system which rarely forgot to refresh its core with input from its surroundings. A new attempt to re-establish this sort of a relationship with the world began three decades ago when minimalism began its end run around modernism, avoiding prohibitions against undisguised references to popular or folk forms by referring to musics from beyond the West's boarded-over frame of reference. This has opened the door for subsequent generations to re-examine the musical worlds around them, looking outside of the genealogical chain of post-classical music, and to blend those lateral influences with their linear inheritance. In a very important sense, the use of elements from popular music is more in keeping with the classical tradition than their exclusion by mid-century, post-classical modernism. Now these vernacular influences and instruments are gradually ceasing to be a novelty among serious composers, and are well on their way to becoming a basic option in the vocabulary of a new generation.

The Western tradition had become a kite flying at the end of a very long string, stretching backward across time, and one had to look back farther than most could remember to find the last places where it had habitually and "respectably" touched the ground of a living folk tradition. But now some lines of lateral communication with other areas of the culture have been re-established. Perhaps we'll see an end to the days when most people, educated or not, simply do without any music from their own time that's any longer or more involved than a song; giving very little thought to the historical and geographical oddity of automatically associating serious music with a European past. New solutions to this problem become more numerous every year: plenty of honest music, written from the inside out, as marked by our culture as its creators are.

The new century promises an art music which no longer needs to self-consciously purge itself of references to its environment, and which claims the right to use our native dialects as it records our moment in history.

Many thanks for the observations of those who read early portions or the penultimate draft of this paper: John Halle, Ed Harsh, Lyn Hejinian, Marlisa Monroe, Greg Sandow, and Randy Woolf.

TREATMENT FOR A FILM IN FIFTEEN SCENES

JOHN ZORN

1. BARE ROOM, WOMAN TIED UP ON BED
2. SHOES BEING COVERED BY DIRT
3. SPIDER CLOSE UP
4. OLD NEWSREEL CLIP
5. FOG OR SMOKE PATTERNS
6. BUTCHER IN SLAUGHTER HOUSE
7. CEMETERY GATES CLOSING
8. BOTTLE OF LIQUOR SPILLING OUT
9. TWO LANE BLACK TOP EXPANSE
10. GLOVES BEING PUT ON
11. MURDER VICTIM
12. TELEPHONE

13. WATER CURRENTS
14. HANDS LEAFING THROUGH BOOK
15. PRESSURE GAUGE RISING
16. TWO SHIPS PASS AT NIGHT
17. ELECTRIC OVERHEAD FAN STOPS
18. HOCKEY PLAYER'S ELBOW
19. MIXING OIL IN A HUGE VAT
20. MONKEY IN A ZOO
21. ROCKING CHAIR
22. DANCING PEOPLE
23. WRITING ON A BLACKBOARD
24. HAND WITH MANY RINGS
25. MONEY EXCHANGED BETWEEN TWO MEN
26. MIRROR REFLECTING ROPES

27. WATER BOILING
28. MAGIC ACT

29. LETTER DROPPED INTO MAIL SLOT
30. BED
31. BUBBLES IN THE AIR
32. DOOR OPENS
33. CHOPPING ICE
34. FRUIT IN A BASKET
35. TELEPHONE
36. SHIRTS HANGING IN A CLOSET
37. AERIAL SHOT
38. SCISSORS
39. CROWDED SUBWAY
40. PULLING TAPE OFF A MICROPHONE
41. INK SPILL
42. PULLING BOW BACK
43. EGG IN FRYING PAN
44. LAMP
45. HANGMAN'S NOOSE
46. SLEDGE HAMMER
47. WHEAT FIELD

48. FISH SCALES ON FULTON STREET
49. FACE, EYES DOWN
50. SHOWER
51. PAIR OF GLASSES
52. PAN UP FIRE ESCAPE
53. GLASS BREAKING
54. DRIVING IN A CAR
55. SNARE DRUM BEING BEATEN
56. FIREPLACE
57. EATING AN APPLE

58. TRAIN
59. HAIRCUT

60.   MUSHROOMS

61.   CHURCH SCENE

62.   FUR COATS WITH PRICES IN STORE WINDOW

63.   SAWING WOOD

64.   DISTORTION MIRROR/FUN HOUSE

65.   PINEAPPLE

66.   SHAVING FACE

67.   CAT'S CRADLE

68.   CAR PULLS UP TO EMPTY LOT

69.   EMPTY FACTORY LATE AT NIGHT

70.   RAZOR REFLECTS LIGHT

71.   DESSERT, WHIPPED TOPPING WITH CHERRY

72.   CLOSE UP OF CAMEL EYE

73.   MAP SECTION

74.   TWO TRACINGS PUT TOGETHER IN LIGHT

75.   SHEARS CUTTING LONG GRASS

76.   RIPPING DRESS IN HALF

77.   DENTIST DRILLING TOOTH

78.   KEY UNLOCKS CHEST

79.   LOTS OF BASEBALL BATS

80.   LIGHT BULB BEING PAINTED BLACK

81.   STIRRING A MARTINI WITH
      OLIVE/TOOTHPICK

82.   BLOTTER ON SIGNATURE

83.   THREE FRIENDS ARM IN ARM

84.   SAND POURED ON PAPER

85.   FIRE HYDRANT

86.   COUCH

87.   LOOKING DOWN FROM LIBRARY STAIRCASE

88.   MAN WITH GUN

89.   HUNDREDS OF FILING DRAWERS

90.   RECORD TURNS ON TURNTABLE

91.   TRAFFIC JAM

92.   BRIDGE SCENE

93. TOAST POPS UP
94. MAN IN GOGGLES
95. MICROSCOPE SLIDES
96. SHOT IN MAGNIFYING GLASS
97. RADIO
98. TWO ICE CUBES
99. ELEVATOR DOORS—PAN TO FLOOR LIGHT
    UNDER DOOR—GOES OUT, DOOR OPENS
100. HAIR
101. BALL BOUNCING
102. JIGSAW PUZZLE
103. WASHED ASHORE ON BEACH
104. CLOSE UP OF BAR GLASS
105. TARGET
106. COVER OF 50'S MYSTERY MAGAZINE
107. HOT / COLD TAP
108. BIG BELL
109. STEAM FROM A MANHOLE COVER
110. MAN IN A STOCKING MASK
111. CONSTRUCTION SITE—HUGE SHEETS OF METAL
112. CANDLE
113. COW
114. FEEDING FURNACE
115. HAND REACHES FOR BEAKER
116. CRUMPLED PIECES OF PAPER BLOW AWAY
117. CHANGING MARQUEE OF A MOVIE
118. BEES SWARMING
119. RINGING A HAND BELL
120. STORM CLOUDS GATHERING
121. A CHAIR
122. PENDULUM CLOCK
123. FULL ASHTRAY

124. CHESS MOVE
125. CITY MORGUE
126. PENGUINS

127. LONG STAIRS
128. TYPEWRITING
129. REFRIGERATORS
130. DEAD BODY
131. TAXI CAB
132. SHADOW
133. BIRD CAGE
134. CUTTING A CABBAGE IN HALF
135. PUPPET ON STRINGS
136. TREES AT NIGHT, BLOWING IN THE WIND
137. CARTESIAN DIVER
138. TWO HANDS SHAKING
139. FIRE HOSE
140. SHOVEL DIGGING
141. BALL ROLLING ON METAL TRACKS
142. ANCIENT LANGUAGE / HIEROGLYPHS

143. SWIMMING POOL
144. KNIFE CUTS THROUGH ROPE
145. GLASS OF MILK
146. FLAG OF BAHRAIN
147. BARE BACK WITH TATTOO
148. LEAFING THROUGH BOOK: PHOTO OF
     DEMILLE SETS
149. RACING CAR AROUND BEND
150. THE SUN
151. HALL OF JUSTICE
152. TAPING BOTTOM OF BRIEFCASE
153. CRAGGY MOUNTAIN TOP
154. UPSIDE DOWN NEON SIGN
155. BRACELETS ON WRISTS
156. HINDENBERG DISASTER
157. MAN OPENS DOOR—SHADOWS
158. FIVE SMALL STONES
159. HIGH FENCE
160. ARTIFICIAL LIMB

161. CURTAINS SLIGHTLY MOVING
162. CHIMNEYS
163. CHALK "SCULLY" DRAWN ON SIDEWALK
164. BARKING DOGS
165. METRONOME
166. HOT CUP OF COFFEE
167. WOMAN TAKES HER STOCKING OFF

168. CHOCOLATE GRINDER
169. KITES IN THE WIND
170. GRAVE STONE
171. PLUMBING PIPES
172. MAN WEARING A MASK
173. THE MOON
174. ROW BOAT ROWING
175. GARBAGE CANS
176. TWO MEN WALKING UP A SPIRAL STAIRCASE
177. STATUE OF VENUS OR APOLLO
178. ONE WAY SIGN
179. LIGHTNING
180. IDENTITY CARD
181. ELEVATOR
182. PEELING AN ORANGE
183. A CHILD ASLEEP
184. WEIGHT

185. BLANK WALL WITH ONE WINDOW
186. TYING A TIE
187. SIGHTS OF A RIFLE
188. PAPER BAG
189. ASIAN EYE
190. LIGHT ON PHONE BLINKS
191. WINDOW SHADE UP
192. FINGERS OPENING A SMALL CASE WITH
       INSTRUMENTS
193. WIND THROUGH THE CURTAINS

194.   OLD STYLE STREET LAMP
195.   KNIFE SLITTING OPEN ENVELOPE AND
       OPENING LETTER
196.   CANDY CANE
197.   VOODOO VÉVÉ ON DIRT

198.   KEYS OF A PIANO
199.   TRIMMING HEDGES WITH LARGE SHEARS
200.   BONES IN SAND
201.   BLACK NIGHT GOWN
202.   DEALING PLAYING CATCH
203.   FINDING MICROFILM IN BELT BUTTON
204.   DROPPING A STONE INTO WATER
205.   ROSE IN A LAPEL
206.   MOTOR OF A CAR
207.   UMBRELLA SCENE
208.   LIGHT BULB IN LEAVES OF MAPLE BUSH
209.   ICEBERG

210.   DINNER TABLE, SET
211.   HYPODERMIC SYRINGE
212.   BEAK OF A BIRD
213.   BOOKS WALL-TO-WALL
214.   LADDER
215.   OCEAN SHOT
216.   ORCHARD STREET MERCHANT STALLS
217.   KEY OPENS DOOR
218.   TELEGRAPH WIRES
219.   SIGN AT CORNER OF WILLIAM AND
       S. WILLIAM STREETS
220.   READING A NEWSPAPER
221.   WALL WITH NUMBERS ON IT
222.   LAUNDRY IN A MACHINE
223.   ENVELOPE WITH POSTMARK CHANGES HANDS
224.   SKULL, SKELETON
225.   GIANT CURTAINS

226. FIXING THE PLUMBING
227. THE PLANETARIUM

228. HAND WITH ROSARY BEADS
229. FISH IN A MARKET
230. BAG OR PACKAGE THROWN OUT OF A WINDOW
231. FLASHING LIGHT
232. MAN LOOKING THROUGH BINOCULARS
233. SWITCHBLADE OPENS
234. ROWS OF NUMBERS
235. KNIVES DANCING FROM UNDER CLOTH
236. TAPE RECORDER, FAST FORWARDING
237. BABY'S RATTLE
238. DRIED MUD FLATS
239. ELECTRIC SAW
240. A HOUSE
241. MAN SWIMMING

242. WIRES ON THE FLOOR
243. MAN TAKES HIS GLOVES OFF
244. DELIVERING BOXES OFF TRUCK
245. MIXING DOUGH OR BATTER
246. SMOKY JAZZ CLUB
247. POOL OF BLOOD ON THE FLOOR
248. THE TRACKS OF A CAR IN FLASHLIGHT
249. HANDS TAKING PULSE
250. FIRE BUCKET
251. SHADOW OF RUNNING MAN
252. TAKING TICKETS AT A THEATER
253. SWEEPING BROOM
254. CYCLONE FENCE

(Note: All foley and sound effects should be out of sync, never corresponding to its related image.)

AN ADVENTURE

FRANCES-MARIE UITTI

The idea of transforming the cello from a monodic instrument into a multi-dimensional performance and compositional tool, came to me while finishing my studies in Rome. I was just beginning to emerge from the sound world associated with music from the Classic and Romantic eras, a rich offering of seductive beauty. Aesthetically I needed a wider palette of color than was acceptable to the traditional canon, to reach beyond the limits of the 'beautiful' sound and give space to the rough, the wild, the unheard. I soon collaborated with composers active at the time—Giacinto Scelsi, Sylvano Bussotti, John Cage, Elliott Carter, and others—and immersed myself in their music. I was struck by the diversity of linguistic styles, each composer inhabiting a world of his own creation with its own particular language.

Improvising groups were being formed, and I participated in several very experimental ones. This had a liberating effect in the beginning, but as time passed I found myself wishing to explore free improvisation in solitude, as a means of generating ideas which could later be re-formed into my own pieces.

I felt that the intrinsic warmth of the instrument, with its rich overtones, six-octave range, and plaintive colors could stand on its own in a solo concert. No piano, no 'others'; a radical concept at the time. The monodic nature of the cello was expressive in a lyrical way, but limited grammatically. This presented problems. How could one suggest harmony when the bow could only sustain two note chords, or at best, swipe quickly at three or four? By arpeggiation? The Bachian model served well in its time, but to force new musical ideas into it seemed to me a deformation that was clumsy, and therefore futile.

I designed and commissioned the construction of a curved bow from an adventurous luthier and experimented with it for the next several months. At last a solution! It could intersect all four strings simultaneously, therefore creating the chordal instrument longed for. In this way one could sustain any adjacent combination of strings desired.

This later turned out to be precisely the problem; adjacent strings on the low-registered cello with its abundance of overtones produced a thick dark sound, gorgeous to the uninitiated ear, but very soon tiresome in its limitations. Like living on a diet exclusively of plum pudding, the timbric richness and unrelenting homogeneity of texture, and no less the dynamic and articulatory unity across the strings, became indigestible. Back to the drawing board.

But what to do? To retune the instrument higher would alleviate some of the heaviness, but it would put the table under too much tension, risking a crack in the wood. How to separate the strings at will. A bow in each hand? Silly. One could only play open strings. Months went by in frustration while I tried out many similar ideas, all to no avail.

The solution came in a dream. It was clear that by holding two bows in the right hand, one over the strings and the other one under, one could play any adjacent strings desired, but more importantly, any non-adjacent ones, and in any combination. This gave the possibility to switch from densely textured passages to single tones, or to two distant strings, cracking open the limitations of the instrument and throwing it into an entirely new realm.

Not only were the chordal possibilities transformed, but I found that the two bows could be manipulated separately to create simultaneous legato and staccato work. Contrasting accents between the bows could highlight two or more individual voices, or create contrapuntal rhythms. Phrasing could be emphasized by differing accents as well.

Sul ponticello and *sul tasto* contrasts between bows became possible as well as all intermediate colorings in order to vary the timbric contrast and textures. By employing these, one could lighten the fabric of sound, or intensify chosen voicings. The tone could also be split by using extreme pressure combined with slow speeds to create undertones one octave lower of hyper-expressive rough-hewn hoarseness.

By playing *ponticello* with varied pressure, speed and placement on the strings between the bows produced more than ten simultaneous multiphonic tones. These could be effectively contrasted with fundamental stopped notes to give an orchestral fullness.

The upper bow produces brighter colors than the under bow due to the direction of pressure (in this case, into the resonating box). This contrast can be used to produce 'shadow tones,' giving depth as well as a sense of the third dimension to sound.

Not only these capacities, provided by using two bows, have altered the chordal soundscape, but through them, the left hand ranged of expressivity has doubled. Wishing to expand further the left hand, bound physically by its reach of one position, I began experimenting with *scordatura*, or retuning the cello. Due to the position-oriented structure of harmonies, these tunings greatly influenced the modality and harmonically implied associations. With these techniques, one could broaden the frequency range enormously in chordal playing.

I began restringing the instrument to further the musical and sonoral expansion. These explorations not only expanded acoustical perceptions but transformed the instrument as well. At times it was indistinguishable from a synthesizer, at others it sounded like a hurdy gurdy, or even a string quartet. The cello lost its identity. Gradually this prided instrument, ever associated with its almost annoyingly gorgeous voice, revealed new dimensions not previously acceptable for musical expression.

It was at this time that I began presenting the work in public, over the radio and for various European television stations. A vinyl disc was produced entitled *The Second Bow* on the Milanese label Cramps/Interpresa. Luigi Nono took interest and used my restringing ideas in *Diario Polacco II*. A solo version was developed from this work as well after the premiere in the Venice Biennale. Giacinto Scelsi also wrote a wonderful work, *Sauh,* using the restringings. Later, Richard Barrett used them in his two-bow works *Dark Ages* and *Praha,* as did Clarence Barlow in *The Weather.* A miraculous piece arrived in the mail after a meeting in Vienna from György Kurtág, *Message to Frances-Marie* for two-bowed cello with optional violins and celestia. Jay Alan Yim has just finished a large work, *Orenda,* employing two bows and restringing as well. Louis Andriessen heard my work in the Holland Festival and then wrote *La Voce* for me, using my voice as a surrogate second bow.

As for my own work, what was most intriguing was the prospect of developing a three-dimensional perspective through the manipulation of multiphonics. shadow tones, and quasi-unison microtones: these restringings gave me the expanded parameters needed.

As the months passed into years, a slow change was taking place in my perceptual musical thinking. New formal ideas grew from the embryonic research, works that were somehow more spherical from the gained perception of depth. The tyranny of horizontal and vertical hierarchies began to disappear, and an architectural way of structuring music began to interest me. Density, weight, mass, and shape intrigued me as pure musical subject matter, as did the relationship of micro to macro structures.

These possibilities have opened my mind to a new way of perceiving sound, and hence a new way of conceiving music. The mind inventing the

techniques and the techniques re-inventing the mind. Working with stimulating limitations is for me essential to the development of new ideas as closed
structures free the mind for creative problem solving in a way that wouldn't
happen in another context. Boundaries are broken and new visions replace
them. Over the last twenty years I feel that my musical journeys have taken me
into unexplored realms due to the stimulus provided by this research.

Left hand possibilities (translated only in one position)

* same configurated pattern extended by ½ step.

2 NOTE CHORDS

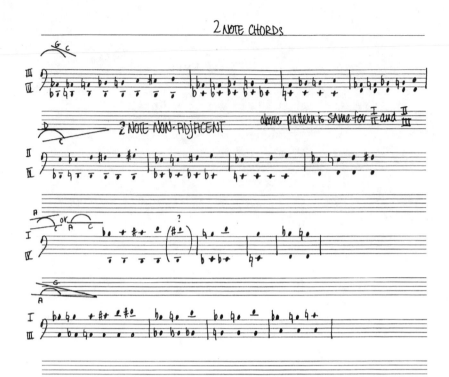

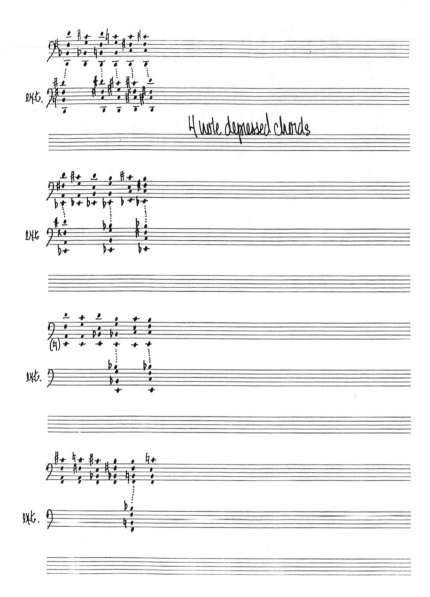

4 note depressed chords

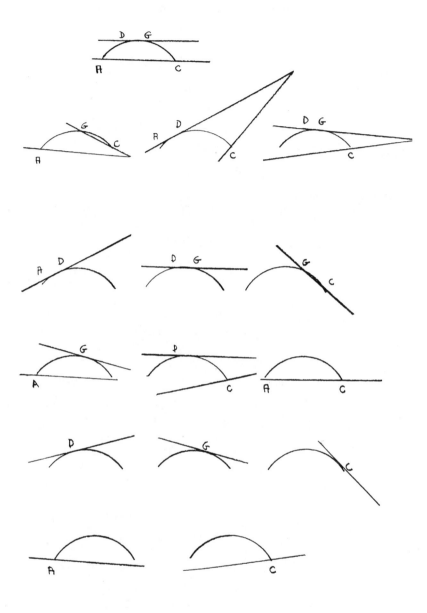

Excerpts from Two Works for Two-bowed Cello

Works for two-bowed cello:

Luigi Nono	*Diario Polacco II*
Giacinto Scelsi	*Sauh; Il Funerale di Carlo Magno*
György Kurtág	*Message to Frances-Marie; Homage to John Cage*
Richard Barrett	*Dark Ages; Praha*
Clarence Barlow	*The Weather*
Jonathan Harvey	*Untitled*
Jay Alan Yim	*Orenda*
James Clark	*Independence*
Elliott Sharp	*In Progress*
Horatio Radulescu	*lux animae*
Guus Jansen	*Untitled*
Frances-Marie Uitti	*75 Ricercari (on 75 tunings); Kepler's Last Dream; OaXANo; The End; Babaal; Purple Film Music; J de K; Rolf's Chorale; Message to György Kurtág; RR Lyrae; fffff fffff² fffff*

TEACHING IMPROVISED MUSIC:
AN ETHNOGRAPHIC MEMOIR

GEORGE E. LEWIS

Introduction

For the last several years, in my current position as a professor of music at the University of California, San Diego, a research-oriented university, I have found myself deeply involved in issues relating to the pedagogy of improvisation. These issues affect not only my interactions with my students, but increasingly, my approach to composition, improvisative performance, and critical theory. My observations in this essay with regard to these pedagogical issues do not seek to emulate scholarly discourse. Rather, I present here an experiential, first-person narrative, drawing upon my own twenty-six years of involvement with the peculiarly deterritorialized expressive medium of musical improvisation.

In the spring of 1992, I decided to declare, in the music department's official documentation and publicity materials, that my primary activity was "improvisor," just as others listed their practices as flutist, composer, music historian or contrabassist. This was done with the realization that, despite my extensive activity as a computer musician, my ongoing incursions into the world of notated forms (with and without interfaces with improvisation), and my performances as a trombonist, my primary research activity as an academician—my "field"—was the study of improvisation.

In fact, since 1970, the field of "improvised music" has arisen and come to some prominence. Improvised music may be usefully characterized as a sociomusical location inhabited by an considerable number of present-day musicians, from diverse cultural backgrounds and musical practices, who have chosen to make improvisation a central part of their musical discourse. Individual improvisors are now able to reference an intercultural establishment of techniques, styles, aesthetic attitudes, historical antecedents and networks of cultural and social practice. Media reports, scholarly essays and popular articles about such musicians have tended to coalesce around the term "improvised music" as a catch-all label for this field.

To encourage the articulation of a pedagogical and research environment for the study of musical improvisation within the academic context, students working on improvised music needed an institutionally supported and
sanctioned course of study—the kind of explicit institutional recognition
which students working in such canonically established fields as composition
or performance usually take for granted. Thus, the identification of improvised music as a field allowed a graduate student to come to UCSD with
improvisation as an explicitly defined primary area of research. Moreover, the
combination of my efforts with those of my students has created a site for a
wide-ranging exploration of critical, theoretical and practical issues surrounding musical expression. Classes, workshops, discussions, performances, critical
research and essays all serve as indispensable components of our integrated
approach to the study of improvisative modes of articulating musical meaning.

Part One: Clichés and creativity

I have learned that a good way to start a heated debate among experienced
improvisors is to pose the question of whether improvisation "can be taught"
—a question which, as often as not, refers to the kind of pedagogy associated
with schools. Both formal and informal discussions of these issues among
musicians recognize the crucial impact of pedagogical initiatives upon the
transmission of culture. As the study of improvisative modes of musicality,
regardless of tradition, has begun to assume a greater role in the music departments of a number of major institutions of higher learning, it is to be expected
that the nature, necessity and eventual function of such pedagogy would be
scrutinized—and eventually contested—from a variety of standpoints, both
inside and outside the academy.

Particularly among jazz musicians, the admonition that improvisation
"needs to go into the schools" is often heard. Once in the schools, however, an
aware improvisor cannot fail to notice the lack of experience with alternative
models of musical thinking that many students bring to the university. In my
experience, students who have been extensively trained in the European-based
musical practices and histories that continue to dominate academia are particularly susceptible to a range of prejudices regarding other musical forms, which
often accompany the folkways of European musical pedagogy and its American extensions.

In an atmosphere where non-European musical cultures are often not accounted for, or even actively disparaged, the resultant lacunae in the musical education which these students are receiving often becomes manifest in a certain tacit or even explicit disapprobation of improvisation. Thus, as a professor working in improvised music, I am rather frequently obliged to disabuse relatively naive "classical" music students of the notion that jazz improvisation is something they could pick up without any special effort, training, historical background or prerequisites other than those that they have picked up as a result of their backgrounds in Eurological music.

While the study of any improvisative musical tradition would seem valuable as a site for presenting alternative cultural models to young musicians, many improvisors, particularly jazz musicians, often express ambivalence about whether schools are the right environment for such study. In particular, many improvisors are loath to subject their art to a (justly) feared and hated process called "academicization." Quite often, those who advance the notion that the academic study of improvisation is either superfluous or even dangerous cite the example of "jazz," the African-American musical constellation most commonly associated with the exploration of improvisation in both Europe and America (the geographical "West").

As even a cursory acquaintance with the musical history of the United States reveals, the history of sanctions and segregation imposed upon African-Americans by the dominant white American culture made it difficult for jazz to find a place in the academic environment until fairly recently. Even as jazz began to find a place in these institutions, the diversification of music faculties to include African-American musicians proceeded at what a too-charitable observer might describe as a rather leisurely pace. In this post-civil rights context, such musical pioneers as Jackie McLean, Archie Shepp, and Max Roach were obliged to vigorously contest attempts by some colleagues and administrators within the system to marginalize and tokenize their nascent jazz programs.

Providing a sharp contrast to the exclusion and disapprobation of jazz in academic circles is the phenomenon of the "university composer," a creation which reached its maturity in the 1950s, as what is now termed "academic music"—a form whose primary historical and intellectual antecedents are ostensibly Eurological in content and origin (see Lewis 1996)—began to garner crucial support from both private and public (taxpayer-supported) institutions, private foundations and patronage, and later, the National Endowment for the Arts. It is evident that such support enabled this music to become a fixture on the pedagogical and research landscapes. At the present time, these kinds of institutions continue to provide a crucial link in the support net for newer versions of what has come to be called "new music" (see Pasler 1987, Fromm 1988).

Noting the discrepancies in sources, quality and quantity of financial and infrastructure support between Eurogenic new music and other American art music forms, both improvisors and jazz critics often cite as nothing short of miraculous the fact that, despite a near-total lack of access, before the 1970s, to the support of the networks of power and privilege that "academic music" took for granted, "jazz" has nonetheless produced some of the world's most important music. Indeed, the latest "free-market" version interpretation of this phenomenon—echoing the American debate over, say, welfare—often concludes that this withdrawal of support actually strengthened the music, and that a sudden infusion of support might well damage it—perhaps by causing some of its practitioners to indulge in undue "pretensions" as to their role in the cultural firmament.

Actively working musicians, while often expressing a somewhat less sanguine view of the virtues of neoliberal jazz economics, nonetheless question the necessity for, or even the desirability of, any "academicization" of the music, particularly where this term evokes the sacralizing, culturally hierarchical attitudes which many jazz musicians associate with the study of the theory, composition and performance of pan-European high-culture ("classical") music. On the other hand, particularly in the United States and in Europe, one can currently pursue studies in jazz, even at the doctoral level, at a fair number of reputable academic institutions.

Some musicians would undoubtedly regard as antithetical to the fostering of creativity the possibility of a "university improvisor" network that would simply reproduce, without interrogation, the class-based power and support structures, as well as the intellectual and aesthetic attitudes, characteristic of the university composer complex within the academic sector of American Eurological music. On the other hand, commentators such as Christopher Small (1987) have decried the erasure of improvisative modes of musical discourse in Eurogenic music pedagogy as directly antithetical to the kind of trenchant vibrancy and creative spontaneity that any great music offers to the human spirit. Indeed, Small—no fan of Eurological "contemporary music"—identifies the absence of pedagogy about improvisation as a primary factor in what he views as the gradual decline of this "Western" musical form.

These criticisms concerning the current state of pedagogy regarding improvised music can be seen as directly addressing questions of academicization and its effect upon creativity. I still remember one older Chicago musician (older than me, anyway) warning me against the overuse of the now widely available compilations of precomposed "jazz" patterns, or "licks"—a practice which he deemed to be a direct product of the academicization process. In particular, one oft-heard complaint about such "riff books" (in my colleague's disparaging terminology) was that they amounted to approved lists of melodies that musicians often feel obliged to reproduce, often verbatim, as part of an ersatz "improvisation." Indeed, many of these riff books do bear formidably erudite titles ("Structures for Jazz"), which announce a somewhat suspect strategy of classicization and canonization.

The saxophonist Eddie Harris, in his pedagogical text, *Clichés* (Harris 1975), explicitly identified, satirized and "signified on" these "riff books" in his own inimitable fashion. *Clichés* is simply a compilation of characteristic bebop, blues and swing licks—passages often derived or directly copied from the work of musicians such as Charlie Parker. Harris's reputation as an innovative, articulate artist whose musical mastery is unquestioned lends particular authority to his rather wry critiques and acerbic commentary upon the process of canonization through clichés.

These "clichés" which, as Harris notes, were regarded during the 1950s as canonic, have lately become embraced as part of the (re)presentation of this historical era in the form of a present-day "jazz revival." The recrudescence of earlier forms of jazz improvisation has received wide support from corporate print, electronic and recording media conglomerates, as well as from changes in the curatorial hierarchy at well-heeled high-culture presenting organizations, such as Lincoln Center and Carnegie Hall. In a number of cases, musicians have sought (somewhat ahistorically) to anoint these familiar forms as constitutive for the past, present and future of jazz music.

While it is often the case that at "jam sessions," and even in concert performance, faithful reproduction of key "licks" is taken as evidence of competency in the idiom—and as such, can be important to the budding jazz musician's career prospects—a widely-held view among musicians of Harris's generation casts doubt upon the desirability of such a methodology. Rather, Harris, like many other improvising musicians, maintains that intimate, near automatic familiarity with these "clichés" is to be regarded, not as an end in itself, but as the legacy of common practice, to be used as a springboard to the creation of a more personal approach.

A complex interaction between notions of literature, orature, tradition, canonization, personality and innovation is seen by jazz improvisors as being directly linked to the nature of musical learning. This interaction, moreover, conditions the articulation of musical meaning, as an integral part of the transmission and dissemination of culture. Thus, expressed as an uneasy relationship between "clichés" and "creativity," what is at stake in this debate is nothing less than the concept of originality itself. Thus, "improvisations" which appear to consist mainly of unquestioning, rote regurgitation of prepared patterns are viewed by many improvisors as failing to display the kind of independent creative investigation and spontaneous invention that can lead to the discovery of what jazz musicians often call "one's own sound," or the original creation of one's own musical material and lexicon (see Berliner 1994, Taylor [1977] 1993).

Viewed historically, perhaps the primary reason why "jazz," in its many forms, has continued to provide trenchant models of alternative musical thinking, is that musicians of every era in the music managed, on their own, to create community-based alternatives to segregated or otherwise exclusionary institutions. In particular, black musicians, recognizing that the hostile attitudes expressed toward African-American culture in such institutions had often proved inimical to the progress of the black student (see Davis 1989), took direct agency for providing alternatives—clearly affirming the view that the promulgation of pedagogy concerning improvisation is a key factor in the maintenance and extension of tradition. In this regard, Eddie Harris's pedagogical text may be seen as the product of a long tradition, in which musicians have moved to identify and create an alternative pedagogy through direct intervention in the pedagogical process—either without the support of traditional institutions, or in direct challenge to their perceived hegemony.

In recent years, musician-created institutions (see Backus 1976), such as the Black Artists Group (St. Louis), the Underground Musicians' Association (Los Angeles), the Creative Arts Collective (Detroit), Asian Improv aRts (San Francisco), the Creative Music Studio (Woodstock, New York), and quite notably, the Association for the Advancement of Creative Musicians (Chicago), have created formal scholastic structures providing a combination of experimentalism, performance-oriented practical experience and theoretical grounding. As a product of several such alternative institutions, I would like to examine the nature of this pedagogy from a personal standpoint, narrating the effect of this teaching upon me and observing its effect upon other musicians. Later, I intend to compare and contrast this experience with my current university-based activity, while posing the question of how these distinctly different pedagogical directions might fruitfully be combined.

Part Two: Apprenticeships

With varying degrees of success, I have tried to remember the oft-cited maxim that in order to be a good teacher it is necessary to be a good student. Thus, my work in the development of pedagogical concepts for improvised music has made it necessary for me to engage my own history as a student, examining the kinds of pedagogy that conditioned my development as a creative artist. In this regard, I count myself fortunate that so many of the improvisors I have known—whether affiliated with schools or not—have been so intensely involved with the investigation of the nature of musical creativity.

My first encounters with improvisation as an activity that I could actually do was in the context of trombonist Dean Hey's high school jazz improvisation classes at the University of Chicago Laboratory School. These classes also constituted some of the early improvisative experiences of my fellow trombonist, Ray Anderson, as well as New York trumpeter Randy Sandke. Mr. Hey, a trombonist with extensive experience in new Eurological ("contemporary") music and post-Fluxus performance art, was a stimulating, challenging teacher who infused the study of jazz improvisation with insights from these forms. Performances of our "jazz band" featured the juxtaposition of Kaprow-style "happenings" with challenging scores by composer-arrangers such as William Russo and Johnny Richards.

Moreover, Mr. Hey was directly responsible for exposing us to several events whose impact upon me, though delayed, was crucial to my future development. Making students aware of the new Afrological music that was developing in Chicago from the AACM, Mr. Hey helped to sponsor concert appearances at the Lab School by my future teachers—Muhal Richard Abrams, Fred Anderson, and the early Art Ensemble of Chicago.

The next step in my student odyssey, matriculation at Yale University in 1969, demonstrates that events rarely unfold in linear fashion. What might have seemed like a complete detour from improvised music, as I sought to leave the "hobby" of music behind in favor of "practical" preparation for a "real job" in law (!), was fortuitously transformed into one of my most salient early experiences with Afrological improvisative music.

As it happens, the "New Haven scene" of the early 1970s was a fluid mix of town and gown, centering on both Yale and Wesleyan University, as well as the surrounding communities. Among the students who benefited from the unexpectedly rich musical environment, both inside and outside the traditional structures of academic musical pedagogy, were pianist Anthony Davis, saxophonist Jane Ira Bloom, composer Alvin Singleton, flutist Robert Dick, percussionist Gerry Hemingway, contrabassist Wes Brown and vibraphonist Jay Hoggard. To intensify the jambalaya-like mix still further, more experienced artists, such as composer-trumpeter Leo Smith, and saxophonists Oliver Lake, Marion Brown and Bennie Maupin, all lived in the area, adopting many of us as students and musical partners.

A highlight of this period of swirling creativity was the tireless and prescient activity of Professor Willie Ruff, hornist and contrabassist in Yale University's music department. Professor Ruff's creation, in the early 1970s, of the Duke Ellington Fellowship program—his "Conservatory without Walls" —was an unprecedented attempt to marshal the resources and support of one of the nation's richest and most prestigious universities in the service of a highly innovative integration of academically oriented, literature-based approaches with the orature-based approach which, though foreign to academic manners, was Professor Ruff's own birthright as a jazz musician. The program included visits by Ellington himself, as well as Mingus, Gillespie, Roach, Papa Jo, Tony Williams, William Warfield, Slam Stewart, and Prof. Ruff's musical soulmate, pianist Dwike Mitchell. These and other Duke Ellington Fellows, in residence in one or another of Yale's residential colleges, made themselves available with regularity for meals and even for performances with undergraduate students (see Ruff 1991).

In 1971, I encountered what I believe to be the most important musical association of my life. My chance encounter with the pianist and composer Muhal Richard Abrams and other members of the Association for the Advancement of Creative Musicians led to what is by now a nearly thirty-year collegial and personal relationship with many of the organization's composers, improvisors, and artists. While it is possible to describe practically any musical activity as a "learning experience," I cannot pretend to have understood very much of what was going on during my initial encounters with the AACM. Being suddenly thrust into performance with artists such as trombonist Lester

Lashley, percussionists Steve McCall and Ajaramu, saxophonists Roscoe Mitchell and Joseph Jarman, contrabassist Malachi Favors, and guitarist Pete Cosey was at once revelatory and confusing.

Indeed, the membership of the AACM had anticipated that some potential colleagues, particularly young people, might find themselves lacking in prior context for understanding this emerging new music. For those people, they developed the AACM School of Music, a community-based alternative to traditional teaching environments, where Abrams, Mitchell, Leo Smith, and saxophonists Wallace McMillan and Anthony Braxton, among others, taught harmony, theory, and other compositionally-oriented skills. The work of the AACM School, an idea born in the crucible of the Black Arts Movement, exemplifies the nature of the process through which alternative institutions developed by African-American musical artists, working in the black community, tackled crucial issues related to creativity and innovation through the development of pedagogical methods which combined orature and literature.

Influenced in part by the work of Joseph Schillinger, Muhal Richard Abrams's composition and theory class was given every Saturday morning, beginning at nine o'clock and lasting until noon. The class utilized a "little red schoolhouse" model; a sincere desire to learn music counted over prior musical education, and more experienced students were required to help beginners. Improvisation and composition were discussed as two necessary and interacting parts of the total music-making experience, rather than essentialized as utterly different, diametrically opposed creative processes, or hierarchized with one discipline framed as being more important than the other.

Nonetheless, the clear implication of the pedagogical approach in the class was that students would use their newly-acquired knowledge of methods and materials to make compositions. Composing a short piece from the materials given in lesson one was each new student's first homework assignment, thus transforming each student from the very beginning into a composer. Improvisation was rarely discussed directly, though I do recall one interesting lesson given by Muhal on the symmetrically-based harmonic structure of Coltrane's "Giant Steps." Students were warned, however—recalling the debate between "clichés" and "creativity"—that they were to take this information as a means to the end of personal idea development, rather than simply regurgitating it on command in "improvisative" performance.

The Saturday theory class was not exclusively devoted to the study of African-American musical forms. On a given Saturday students were quite as likely to hear Igor Stravinsky, or perhaps Morton Subotnick (reflecting Abrams's ongoing engagement with electronic music) as Charlie Parker or Ornette Coleman. Moreover, the class sessions presented music along with its social, cultural, historical and political contexts. This included thoroughgoing discussions of the work of major authors in what is now called "Afrocentric" history, such as Yosef Ben-Jochannan, Jacob Carruthers, John G. Jackson, and Chancellor Williams.

Students and AACM members were encouraged to present music at the weekly membership-sponsored AACM concerts. Musicians were free to play any music desired, with the sole iron-clad rule being that all music presented had to be the original products of the musicians giving the event. Class leaders such as Abrams, Mitchell, Braxton and Smith served as role models for the students, presenting their latest compositions in class, and in these community-based performances.

Highly complex, virtuosic works that demanded considerable rehearsal and personal practice were often presented at the AACM concerts. But preparing the notated material for performance was just a small part of the process. Invariably, a pre-concert meeting would find the composers of the evening's music imparting to the other improvisors a general outline of how the pieces would fit into the framework of the concert itself. These instructions frequently consisted of sketches that outlined interactional forms; for instance, there might be an opening duo improvisation, followed perhaps by a "shower of bells" and little instruments, then the first of the notated pieces, an open group improvisation, and so on.

Organizing the entire concert in advance in broad outline, but leaving the details to the improvisors to structure and glue together as they wished, demanded that improvisors assume both personal and collective responsibility for the real-time articulation of form within form. This responsibility, based upon a welcoming to the performance of the musicians' own creative resources, included an awareness that any nominal pre-concert plan could be discarded or subverted at any moment; one would suddenly be called upon to create in a situation for which there could be no preparation other than one's own knowledge, no solutions other than those presented by one's own intelligence and intuition. This necessitated the development of a high degree of trust in both the musicians and in the moment, reflecting the desire to discover how the musicians would respond to the kinds of novel creative opportunities that only open improvisation could provide.

AACM saxophonist Fred Anderson's mid-1970s ensembles usually began a piece by negotiating a fearsomely difficult notated theme, such as Anderson's "Within" (Anderson 1994). Shortly thereafter, the leader would produce an improvised solo of ferocious intensity and brilliance of invention. In particular, Anderson's playing possesses a powerfully evocative timbral quality which completely enthralled the other group members, including saxophonist Douglas Ewart, percussionist Hamid Drake, contrabassist and trombonist Lester Lashley, and myself. Anderson was supremely supportive of his younger colleagues, often allowing extremely long solos to take place as a means of exploring form, method and technique. Moreover, since these concerts were often tape-recorded, rehearsals often included extensive discussion and critique of previous performances, as well as study of the work of other improvisors from various genres and historical periods.

Like the pedagogically active pianist, composer and performance artist Misha Mengelberg, with whom I first performed in the mid-1980s, Anderson would often invite less experienced musicians (such as myself) into the group, in the hope that they would one day assume responsibility for the exploration, discovery and nurturance of their own potential. In furtherance of this philosophy, Anderson eventually realized his long-standing dream of creating his own "club," which now functions as another kind of alternative pedagogical institution, directly nurturing the new improvised music by providing a place for musicians to play.

With the revival of 1950s forms of jazz now in full "swing," much has lately been made of the importance of the return of the jam session as a social institution articulating an alternative pedagogy. In this regard we are often referred to the legendary Minton's in Harlem, where the bebop pioneers were presumed to have cut their improvisative teeth. Contemporary accounts of these sessions, however, (see Gillespie [1979] 1985) refer not to learning, but to research, exploration and innovation as prime values.

Unfortunately, the same cannot be said for many contemporary jam sessions, which, though still important as forums for the maintenance of tradition, often degenerate into sites for the exchange of canonized "clichés." A symbol of this reification of traditional forms, used by both students and professional musicians, is the bootleg "Real Book," a compilation of (often inaccurate) lead sheets for various jazz compositions by composers whose copyrights have been ignored. While the title itself signifies upon the origin of this collection of "tunes" as part of the genre of "fake books" (where "faking" is a derogatory synonym for improvisation), in the world of jazz pedagogy, the "Real Book" serves both a canonizing function and a learning function in terms of performance.

Weekly "jam sessions" are held at Anderson's now highly successful "Velvet Lounge," but the vastly expanded range of aesthetic options open to visiting musicians at a club run by one of the pioneers of AACM's "Great Black Music" implicitly challenges the restrictions upon musical invention imposed by the culture of mainstream jazz. In sharp contrast to the conventional jam session, improvisors at the Velvet Lounge sessions—where the "Real Book" is rarely to be seen—combine traditional forms with frank exploration. Fred Anderson's perspicacity in renewing the jam session form along post-bebop lines encourages musicians to explore approaches to time, timbre, form and method which are all but excluded in sessions dominated by "Real Book" mentality. Thus, these sessions seek to recuperate the deeply probing, experimental spirit of Minton's, as a means of ensuring the continuous renewal of Afrological improvisative musics.

Another Chicago-style musical institution of higher learning with strong links to the exploratory is the more traditionally oriented jam session sponsored at the "New Apartment Lounge" by saxophonist Von Freeman. As with Anderson, nurturance is the order of the evening at these sessions. Though musicians of Freeman and Anderson's generation had grown up under the old "cutting" regimes, the two saxophonists clearly held no particular nostalgia for those tropes. Instead, Freeman and Anderson recognized that while the "cutting session" had been of prime importance for an earlier era, the attempt to build confidence mainly through competition was not necessarily a fruitful approach for this one. Recognizing the pressures facing African-American musical creativity at that moment, cooperative learning was, for many musicians, deemed more emblematic of the music to come, especially with respect to how this music has been understood to reflect its social environment.

The Freeman sessions of the mid-1970s, often incorporating the often laconic, acerbically witty brand of lounge pedagogy dispensed by pianist John Young, contrabassist David Shipp and drummer Bucky Taylor, provided the young Chicago musician with a needed forum in which to learn the art of improvisation. These older, more experienced artists took the lead in creating a learning environment where the emphasis was on creativity rather than (re)presentation. As with the AACM's activity, Freeman's sessions took place in the heart of Chicago's black South Side, attracting a diverse community of interested listeners and musicians who, along with Freeman, Young, Shipp and Taylor, did not hesitate to provide the budding improvisor with forthright and well-articulated critiques. Along with the analyses of one's work that were freely given by musicians such as Abrams, Anderson, Mitchell, trumpeter and AACM co-founder Phil Cohran, Eddie Harris, bandleader Morris Ellis, and many other Chicago community musical institutions, the atmosphere was such that it was possible for a young musician to obtain a particularly well-rounded exposure to a wide range of black musical directions, in the Chicago version, circa 1971-1976, of the "Conservatory Without Walls."

Another important pedagogical moment was my short (two-month) tenure in the USA and Japan with Count Basie and his Orchestra in 1976. It was very clear that the membership of this august organization—particularly trombonists Bill Hughes, Al Grey, and Mel Wanzo, saxophonists Charlie Fowlkes, Eric Dixon, Jimmy Forrest, Danny Turner, and Bobby Plater, trumpeters Sonny Cohn and Pete Minger, and guitarist Freddie Green—took a very proactive, explicit stance in making their musical knowledge and experience available to me. Of singular importance were the insights that I acquired into how the "Basie sound" resulted from the individual and collective interpretive and improvisative efforts of each musician. Two solos per night enabled me to put what I was discovering to immediate practical use, with absolutely no restrictions on what I could play, including the kinds of extended techniques and timbral resources that musicians of the time associated with "free" jazz. This was the literal embodiment of Philly Joe Jones's comment to the drummer Arthur Taylor concerning so-called "freedom" music: "Everybody's been playing free. Every time you play a solo you're free to play what you want to play. That's freedom right there" (Taylor [1977] 1993, 48).

In fact, the issue of free music, including discussions of such improvisors as saxophonists George Adams and Anthony Braxton, frequently came up in discussions on the band bus. My recollection is that the members of the orchestra were quite familiar with the work of these and other so-called "avant-garde" improvisors, not only from articles in magazines, but from first-hand attendance at concerts and close listening to recordings. Moreover, in sharp contrast to early statements by some of the 1980s jazz revivalists, neither Mr. Basie nor the band members I have cited dismissed the work of these musicians out of hand. Rather, important issues concerning materials, form, content and reception dynamics, rather than tart-tongued, corporate-backed denigration, held center stage in our frank and open discussions. Thus, it was possible to gain from the more experienced musicians a variety of informed perspectives on the "new music."

Despite the wide stylistic and aesthetic disparities among the musicians with whom I spent my early apprenticeships, I believe that certain common tropes were key. These included an explicit pedagogical nurturance; a valorization of the psychological connection between musician and the audience-as-community; a hybrid pedagogical experience and musical practice with particular emphasis upon diversity of intellectual and cultural outlook; catholicity of musical reference; a contextualization of music as incorporating personal narrative; and a framing of music, not as autonomous "pure expression," but as directly related to social and historical experience.

The issue of freedom, so central to the experience of African-Americans, underlies all these tropes. Ultimately, Ruff's "Conservatory Without Walls" is a hopeful metaphor that expresses the need to transgress and ultimately to do away with those borders that promote exclusion, nonpermeability and nonexchange. Both inside and outside traditional academia, African-American musicians sought to extend the academic concept to incorporate what was happening outside its walls, daring the institutions to respond in new ways to the challenges posed by free expression.

Part Three: Early teaching experiences

Eventually, opportunities arose to present my developing ideas about music to students of my own, while remaining very much a student myself, as I am today. During the summer of 1980, I was given the opportunity to head the summer workshop at the Creative Music Studio, founded by the musician, pedagogue and philosopher Karlhans Berger near the well-known village of Woodstock in upstate New York (see Sweet 1996).

The Creative Music Studio was, along with the AACM, one of the most innovative and ambitious attempts ever mounted by artists themselves to found an institution devoted to the study of improvisative musics, world musics, new musics, and the interfaces between them. Like the earlier "New Haven scene," the "Woodstock scene" included a diverse array of musicians, including the pianist Marilyn Crispell, composer-performers Pauline Oliveros and John Cage, cellist Tom Cora, percussionist Jack deJohnette, and musician and social activist Ed Sanders, as well as such eminent nonmusical artists as poet Allen Ginsberg and scientist R. Buckminster Fuller.

As director of the summer workshop, I had the opportunity to place students in contact with a variety of musical concepts, from an exciting array of guest artist-instructors. The summer program's actual pedagogy was very evidently dependent upon the personal styles of these invited composer-teachers. Each of the artists—Frederic Rzewski, Roscoe Mitchell, Anthony Davis and electronic composer Maryanne Amacher—worked with the students for one week, presenting workshops and preparing compositions for performance by the excellent student ensemble. At the same time, the ongoing innovative rhythm studies of Karl Berger and Ingrid Berger, which amounted to a kind of core curriculum for CMS, provided continuity over the course of the entire summer.

Following my AACM training, as well as the insights I had gained from associations with such musicians as pianist and composer Frederic Rzewski, and electronic musicians Richard Teitelbaum and David Behrman, the pedagogical methods I began to develop in these, my earliest teaching experiences, reflected the influence of the apprenticeship experiences I have described earlier. I taught as I had been taught, to some extent. The overall planning of the summer workshop reflected the very high priority which, then as now, I placed upon the presentation of diversity—not only with regard to musical discourses, materials, and forms, but in terms of cultural background, ethnicity, race, and gender. On this view it was undeniable that these supposedly "extra-musical" concerns would in fact have a great impact upon the musical discourses on view in the workshop; my experience in music indicates that many artists are loath to leave their culture behind to court a deracinated Muse.

Since that time, I have participated in these kinds of multi-week workshop experiences in a variety of venues, including eight seasons of summer intensives at Simon Fraser University ("Music of Two Worlds" and "Computed Art"), and a semester at the Royal Conservatory in the Hague. Creating such workshops, however, is very different from accepting responsibility for creating the kind of ongoing core curriculum that the Bergers created at CMS. Such core courses provide not only a sense of continuity, but an awareness of community, comprising notions of field, discipline, history, historiography and hermeneutics. My two years as a Visiting Artist at the School of the Art Institute of Chicago, where I taught academically-oriented courses both in computer-based sound installations and in 20th century music, provided valuable insights into the function of such courses in a more traditional academic environment that was nonetheless devoted to nontraditional expressive materials and forms.

My activity since 1991, as a professor of music at the University of California, San Diego, has confronted me with the further challenge of helping to creating such a core program, even to the extent of helping to foster the development of a newly emergent academic field, that of "improvised music." UCSD's Music Department, as I found it in 1991, could not be characterized as exemplifying traditional music pedagogy alone. In fact, the department is often described by its faculty as having a "mission" concerning something called "contemporary music." This mission is best described as having emerged from the legacy of its early leaders, the composers Will Ogdon and Robert Erickson (see Shere 1995), and later, the decisive leadership role later taken by such current senior faculty members as Pulitzer laureate composer Roger Reynolds.

In the case of UCSD, the explicit emphasis placed on "contemporary music" may be taken to refer to a set of musics with a relatively unswerving Eurological profile. Within the bounds of pan-European forms, however, musicality at UCSD was quite varied, including both improvisative and compositional discourses as well as other hybrid approaches to real-time music making. Unusual choices of faculty, including the formidable presences of psychoacoustician Gerald Balzano, computer music researchers F. Richard Moore and Miller Puckette, and composer Brian Ferneyhough, are indicative of the department's ambitious, even somewhat dangerous attempt to forge a certain commonality, within the competition-oriented world of academia, between extremely divergent intellectual, aesthetic and cultural viewpoints. This diversity of practice, in my view, accounts for much of the intellectual strength and musical power of the department.

Several artist-professors who had been involved in real-time music-making at UCSD prior to my arrival, including composer-performer Pauline Oliveros, and the improvisation and intermedia group KIVA, led by professors John Silber (trombone), Keith Humble (piano) and Jean-Charles François (percussion), had created a strong and effective base upon which to build a new vision of improvisative musicality in the academic environment. At the time I arrived, with all these figures having moved on, senior professor Jimmy Cheatham was doing large-form jazz ensemble, while pianist Cecil Lytle was active in a demanding triple role as interpreter of classical repertoire, gifted improvisor, and Provost of UCSD's Thurgood Marshall College.

My first few years at UCSD posed a particular challenge for me in that I had, for the most part, never before been part of any sort of academic music school or department, either as a student or teacher. Beginning by teaching courses in jazz performance, 20th century music literature, and interactive computer music, I once again taught as I had been taught, bringing my alternative pedagogical heritage—the AACM, New Haven, Basie and CMS—into the arena of high academia. Gradually, with the support of composer and then-department chair Rand Steiger, I moved to redefine my pedagogical role.

Shortly after my arrival, a number of new students had come to UCSD with the desire to explore improvisative modes of musicality in depth, in a fashion that had perhaps not been fully explored at UCSD since the departures of Oliveros, Silber, Humble and François. To address the needs of these students, it was decided to start a new graduate performance course devoted exclusively to improvisation. This course, dubbed "Music 201B" (Music 201A being devoted to notated music) has become a primary catalyst and engine for improvised music performance at UCSD.

201B provides a pedagogical site, not only for the development of improvisors, but for the articulation of a multi-voiced creativity. Students are challenged to combine critical methods, intercultural practice, and interdisciplinary experimentalism in an environment that, instead of subsuming the practice of improvisation as a sub-category of the Eurological notion of "performer," explicitly centers improvisation, improvisors and improvisative practice. In 201B, the traditional divisions separating the disciplines of composition and performance—which have now become tenuous in any event—become even more permeable, permitting the promulgation of multiply-mediated creative work that cannot be described with simple labels.

One complaint among students new to 201B is that the course often functions as more of a sit-down seminar than a traditional performance course. That is, why do we have to do all this talking? Why can't we just play music? The answer to this question has to do with both the expanding context in which performance itself is currently being considered, and the particular position of improvised music in the academic context.

It was clear from the outset that 201B would necessarily differ radically from courses devoted either to jazz or to notated Eurological music. Framing improvised music as part of an overall departmental pedagogical initiative that centers non-improvised, highly Eurological work requires an understanding of background and situatedness of both students and faculty in the course. Such recognition involves negotiation and interchange through a complex network of (after Messaien) "modes, valeurs et intensités." This has included a recognition of my own mix of Afrological and Eurological backgrounds, my activity as improvisor, computer musician and composer and installation artist, and the varied discourses and backgrounds of the students, most of whom locate the performance of Eurological "contemporary music" as a central part of their musical practice.

My experience as a teacher indicates that students do not leave their backgrounds at home when they enter the classroom. Part of my pedagogical function involves attention to the fact that it is easily possible for the average UCSD music student to go through his or her entire undergraduate or graduate music career without encountering an African-American in class, either as a professor, or even more problematically, as a student. This reproduces my own experience as a student at Yale in the early 1970s, where I had exactly one African-American professor in four years of study.

In fact, a fair number of the students with whom I work have never worked with a black teacher at any academic level, from kindergarten on. Any and all assumptions or prejudices that such students have been developing and nurturing, often since childhood and usually with the help of their parents, their community, and the news and entertainment media, become disclosed in the dialogic process—sometimes with results that can be painful for both student and professor.

This intercultural moment, however difficult, must be squarely faced. As 201B participants address the recognition and negotiation of identity, location and difference as part of our contextualization of improvisative utterance, we find it necessary to take particular note of the ways in which race, ethnicity, gender, class and power issues condition the production and reception of any music. At the same time, we strive to avoid the kinds of vulgar essentializing and stereotyping of the cultural backgrounds of either students or faculty that encourage needless worry about how "black," "white," "Asian" or "Latino" their music is supposed to be. Participants in the class have to come to grips with the fact that improvisative musical activity today necessarily reflects its provenance—the global, transcultural environment.

Through discussions, critical writing, and the study of recordings, our class gives particular attention to critique and documentation of process. Students are encouraged to develop an understanding of why and how they do what they do, including attention to issues of form, method, materials, lexicon, aesthetics, and historical position. Issues fundamental to improvised music, such as the nature and function of "practicing" as part of the development of style and personality, the relationship between individuality and collectivity, the function and nature of authorship, as well as a variety of historiographical issues, are all part of the exploration of the ontology of the improvisative work that students eventually come to grips with as part of the course.

One of the foremost of the so-called "new musicologists," my UCSD colleague Jann Pasler, has devised the "Critical Studies/Experimental Practices" program (CSEP), designed to meet the needs of music students who wish to explore the kinds of intercultural, interdisciplinary issues that students in her classes and mine were investigating. Our CSEP faculty currently consists of myself, composer and improvisor Anthony Davis, and ethnomusicologist Margaret Dilling, and European music historian Jane Stevens, as well as Professors Pasler and Balzano.

From Professor Pasler I learned that as students interrogate themselves, taking a critical stance toward the sources of their work as musicians, they should be encouraged to become aware of the possibility that theoretical discourses current in other arts, humanities and science disciplines could have important implications for their work. As a part of CSEP, I began to realize that the fields of critical theory and cultural studies, including the emerging areas of feminist musicology, ethnic studies, "queer theory" and other postcolonial and post-modern discourses, were becoming central to an understanding, not only of what the students were doing, but of my own activity as composer, improvisor, and my emerging role as scholar.

A deeper recognition of these discourses, long active in the visual arts and humanities but relatively new to academic music, allowed me to begin to establish communication with cultural workers operating in fields outside of music and the arts—including, but hardly limited to, anthropology, sociology and psychology, cognitive science and literary theory. Discovering and affirming the intrinsically multi-voiced nature of improvisative musicality—thus explicitly acknowledging the general validity and utility of interdisciplinary practice—promotes dialogue and collaboration with workers in other fields, while concomitantly bringing ideas developed from improvised music into an expanded intellectual and social context.

A further development of this process involves the creation of support structures for musicians and scholars working directly with the new improvised music who are moving to produce new scholarship, first-person narratives and other documentation. A number of musicians and scholars have identified important new ways in which musical meaning is articulated through improvised music, thus providing a rich area of study for people interested in studying improvisation. Among the musicologists and cultural studies researchers working on issues related to improvised music are George Lipsitz, Krin Gabbard, Ronald Radano, Paul Berliner, Gerhard Putschögl, Gary Tomlinson, Peter Niklas Wilson, Michael Heffley, Jörg Solothurnmann, Christopher Small, Chad Mandeles, Bert Noglik, Ingrid Monson, Robert Walser, Wolfgang Charles Keil, Wolfram Knauer, Steven Feld, Ulrich Kurth, Scott DeVeaux, and Ekkehard Jost. The increasing number of improvisors, acting in accord with a philosophy of self-determination, who have written on musical issues includes Steve Coleman, Jerome Harris, Anthony Brown, La Donna Smith, Frederic Rzewski, Jon Jang, Vinko Globokar, Charles Moore, Francis Wong, Georgina Born, Dwight Andrews, John Corbett, Fred Wei-Han Ho, Yusef Lateef, Malcolm Goldstein, Derek Bailey, Anthony Braxton, Eddie Prevost, Roger Dean, Didier Levaillant, Miya Masaoka, Steve Lacy and Vernon Reid.

Thus, in order to provide my students with models and a place to be, it became clear that I had to start producing such scholarship myself. With the encouragement of Professor Pasler, cultural theorist George Lipsitz of UCSD, musicologists Philip Brett at the University of California at Riverside and Ronald Radano of the University of Wisconsin, and Dr. Samuel Floyd at the Chicago-based Center for Black Music Research, I have begun this process, in which this essay plays an important role.

My own writing often becomes drawn toward an examination of the culture-based assumptions behind the musical education that students are receiving. In this context, the presence or absence of curricular intertextuality becomes an important concern. For example, in most university music departments, the valorizing of pan-European music of all historical periods is reinforced in myriad ways in the aggregate of courses taken by a typical music student. Framed as an integral part of both European and American history and culture, this music is lauded, lionized and applauded on an hourly basis. Reproduced in other sectors of the university arts and humanities curriculum, this constant interdisciplinary, intertextual cheerleading becomes transformed into a exonominated authority through which pan-European-based cultural products achieve both apparently unlimited credence and presumed universality.

At the same time, cultural products lacking this ethnic base, or partaking of different historical traditions, are often treated, particularly in the crucial allocation of courses, personnel resources and financial support, as marginal or peripheral (see Levine 1996). This marginalization is none too subtly embedded in the common characterization of classes in ethnomusicology or other non-European musical forms as "enrichment" courses—a curiously contradictory characterization, which seems to implicitly admit that, like Wonder Bread, the Eurocentric music education being received is somehow impoverished in terms of overall content.

Particularly in music, an absence of interaction between discourses representing different formal approaches and social histories can promote a particularly deleterious form of monocultural ignorance, with the concomitant lowering of intellectual standards which invariably accompanies the promulgation of unchallenged dogmas. To combat this tendency, it is necessary for individual faculty and students to be in constant dialogue and contact, forming a community which is aware of and respectful toward a diversity of sociomusical histories. This provides an environment in which faculty and students feel encouraged to participate in interdisciplinary, multicultural pedagogy, moving toward an embodiment of dialogue and diversity as a part of their musical practice.

Exemplifying the view that exposing students and other members of an intellectual community to diversity of discourse is crucial to the quality of pedagogy in a given field, UCSD composition students may choose among six different models of compositional aesthetics, in the persons of a group of composers who form part of a "composition faculty." Working toward a similar diversity, students at UCSD whose primary research interests lie in the area of improvised music are able to choose between my own approach, as I have outlined it here, and the very different approaches of two highly experienced pedagogues, Anthony Davis and the contrabassist Bertram Turetzky.

Already, a number of institutions have incorporated experimental forms of improvised music into their programs. Faculty members such as computer musician David Rosenboom, Wadada Leo Smith, contrabassist Charlie Haden and harpist Susan Allen at the California Institute of the Arts, flutist and composer James Newton at the University of California at Irvine, computer musician Chris Brown and saxophonist Glenn Spearman at Mills College, and Anthony Braxton at Wesleyan University, have sought to create environments where experimental music becomes a site for investigating and eventually refashioning concepts of music and musicality. In such an environment, improvisative discourses disclose the extent to which musicians have a vital stake in the ongoing dialogue concerning the future of our planet. Music becomes a necessity for existence, rather than merely a pleasant way to pass lived time.

Part Four: Music 133—a case study

In the winter of the 1995-96 academic year, I taught an undergraduate performance project, Music 133, where the majority of UCSD's music majors were required to come to terms with the reality of real-time music-making—in the lecture hall, in weekly class sections, in readings, in their personal practice sessions, on recordings, and in a culminatory class concert.

As with other kinds of subjects that young college students are obliged to study, it is not necessarily the case that undergraduate students come to UCSD with a strong interest or even familiarity with any kind of improvised music tradition. A few students had extensive backgrounds in jazz or rock, and at least one student was familiar with the work of the AACM via summer jam sessions in Chicago with master saxophonist Fred Anderson. While such prior experience did not necessarily place these students in a superior position with regard to the course, all of the students taking the course were obliged to come to grips with the fact that, for at least one brief, ten-week academic quarter, a different set of criteria for musical excellence in performance was being institutionally promulgated. For most, the awareness was implicitly established that educational institutions do establish cultural priorities; whether or not one notices may depend upon whether or not one's particular ox is being gored.

Because almost all of the senior undergraduate students were required to take Music 133, I was able to glean from personal observation some notion of the race, gender and ethnicity mix of our music students. As is the case in many of the classes in our department, ethnic diversity—a subject of intense debate in the California educational system at the moment—was fairly minimal. The ethnic composition of the class was overwhelmingly Anglo; there were a few Asians, but hardly any Latinos or African-Americans. This mix, of course, bears little resemblance to the ethnic makeup of the state of California. Gender was a bit more balanced, with the male-female ratio approaching (my thumbnail estimate) sixty to forty percent.

Of course, this unreflective ethnic mix is part of the reason why most UCSD students do not encounter, or are able to avoid encountering, musical cultures similar to mine. Thus, most of these students were in for a period of intense adjustment. My observation is that the students who had the most difficulty in adjusting to the novelty of their status as tyros were those who in other, more Eurologically oriented classes, had achieved some status as especially talented or advanced students. Nonetheless, some of these students, used to achieving excellence through hard work, applied themselves diligently to

99

the new challenge. For others, the sudden reversal of priorities and modes of evaluation could have seemed unfair.

The class met for two sessions per week—one general lecture and one playing/discussion section, for which the student population was divided among three teaching assistants. Each of these teaching assistants—Patrick O'Keefe, clarinet; Ulfar Haraldsson, contrabass; and Glen Whitehead, trumpet—was an experienced improvisor who had participated in my graduate-level classes before and were familiar with the mix of practical, theoretical and experimental pedagogies. Moreover, each of them had extensive experience with the complexities of postwar Eurological notated music.

The teaching assistants, who attended all lectures, were assigned the centrally important tasks of illuminating and contextualizing the reading and listening assignments in their class section, treating the musicians in their section as their "band" to lead, developing compositions or improvisative environments for this band, presenting real-time musical examples on their chosen instrument, and encouraging students to create their own environments for real-time music-making. O'Keefe and Whitehead, who with fellow students Scott Walton (contrabass) and Jason Stanyek (electric guitar) had already founded a highly cohesive, musically vigorous working ensemble, were simultaneously enrolled in my graduate seminar on "Improvised Music since 1950," for which they elected to write essays about their experiences in teaching improvised music. Included in their essays were discussions of how they conceived the class environments, how the students responded and how they developed their own approaches to pedagogy.

The course requirements for Music 133, though not particularly onerous, were substantial. Weekly exercises and listening assignments were given, and reviewed both in the lecture and in discussion sections. Grading was tough, and assignments, incorporating both written and oral modes of learning, were frequent and demanding. Assignments designed to get the students to create music were given right at the outset, as I had been taught in the AACM School. These beginning exercises emphasized listening, sensitivity to environment, form and structure, location and tradition, and awareness of internal dialogue. The exercises were meant to be related to the reading assignments; the readings for the course privileged first-person narratives by improvisors, including articles by some of the scholars and musicians I have mentioned earlier.

In order to establish a notion of field (if not canon) regarding improvised music, students were exposed to a multi-national view of the field, reflecting the transcultural nature of the music. The students listened to examples of European improvised music, such as the work of contrabassist Joelle Léandre and Barry Guy, guitarist and theorist Derek Bailey, pianists Misha Mengelberg, Alexander von Schlippenbach and Irene Schweizer, trombonists Paul Rutherford, Radu Malfatti and Günter Christmann, vocalists Maggie Nicols and Phil Minton, and saxophonists Peter Brötzmann and Evan Parker. They were exposed to AACM composer-improvisors, such as Muhal Richard Abrams, Fred Anderson, the Art Ensemble of Chicago, Anthony Braxton, Wadada Leo Smith, violinist Leroy Jenkins, pianist and composer Amina Claudine Myers and saxophonist Henry Threadgill.

Students became aware of the so-called "downtown" New York improvisors, such as violinist Malcolm Goldstein, flutist Robert Dick, saxophonist John Zorn, guitarists Fred Frith, Eugene Chadbourne and Elliott Sharp, vocalists Shelley Hirsch and David Moss, and electronic improvisor Bob Ostertag, as well as the Western improvisors, including pianists Jon Jang, Glenn Horiuchi and Vijay Iyer, guitarist Henry Kaiser, saxophonists Russel Baba, Vinny Golia, Gerald Oshita, and Francis Wong, contrabassist Mark Izu, vocalist Tina Marsh, percussionists Adam Rudolph and Anthony Brown, storyteller Brenda Wong Aoki, kotoist Miya Masaoka, and the ROVA Saxophone Quartet. Finally, the new school of Chicago improvisors, including clarinetist Ken Vandermark, contrabassist Kent Kessler, saxophonist (and former Creative Music Studio participant) Mars Williams, and guitarist Jim O'Rourke were studied as part of the course.

Other requirements included a two-part midterm examination centered around class readings and listening assignments. As part of the midterm each student handed in a solo improvisation on tape, along with documentation as to how it was made and as to the kinds of issues that came up during the creation of the piece. Those students whose midterm projects had been particularly interesting were given extra credit assignments in the form of solo and duo spots on the class concert. Some of these people had never improvised before and were frankly astonished at their selection for a special spot.

Some 133 students—especially those used to heavy competition among each other for the attention and approbation of professors, as well as for the approval of the society that privileges pan-European music so highly, displayed distinct reluctance to participate in the preparation and performance of an original improvised work to be presented in front of their peers. Indeed, this kind of intense peer group pressure tended to make the establishment of a supportive learning environment problematic. For some, this somewhat negative attitude carried over into their response to the other assignments in general, and to the midterm exam in particular. Only a few students, however, felt sufficiently emboldened to decide that they needed to test the waters by not doing any reading or listening and then showing up for the midterm. These students, of course, flunked. Flunking *improvisation* class—supposedly an easy A if ever there was one—had obviously been deemed an impossibility by these fairly smug individuals, who placed themselves in particular difficulty because, unlike their normal electives, they were unable to drop the class.

For the final performance project, each undergraduate student was required to participate in two ensembles at a final class concert, featuring group improvisations led by teaching assistants and by other class participants. In lieu of a traditional term paper, students were required to maintain a "process journal" to be turned in at the end of the quarter, presenting their reflections on the exercises and their responses.

This leads us to the question of how the assignments were evaluated, a subset of the general issue as to how any creative work is judged. This question comes up in other academic pursuits—the construction of a literature term paper, for example. Of course, students challenged me to come up with fixed criteria for judgment. My position was that such criteria were unrealistic in this creative context, just as they are in other pedagogical contexts where musicality is being evaluated. It was necessary to keep in mind that in this course, which was devoted to a form of music-making which was utterly new to most of the students, students were placed on the edge of creativity in a radical way. This allowed the process journals to be graded, not on the basis of polished excellence (very suspicious in a journal that is supposed to be formulated over time), but for depth of expressive content. My evaluation procedure with regard to the improvisation exercises attempted to frame "quality," not only with regard to the more intangible factor of whether or not I found the audible results to be interesting, but as to the thoroughness of engagement with the assignment itself.

With respect to the fact that students were learning from more experienced people, this class was no different from other music classes. What was new to the students was that there was indeed such a thing as a field of improvised music, where judgment tempered by experience could be a factor in evaluation, just as in other forms of music. I felt it necessary to disclose my own implication in what I was teaching—my twenty-five years as an improvisor, my experience, my training, my background—a summary of which I distributed to the students, for their information. I made it clear that these factors gave me a certain confidence in evaluating assignments in terms of quality; at the same time, I wanted to encourage students to develop their own evaluative criteria.

The process journals allowed me an important window into the experiences of the students. In the best of these journals, I saw at first hand the dynamics of the development of aesthetic and methodological criteria, as students reflected upon their psychological states, their soundscape and their own place in it, as well as the place of music in society. Topics included issues of technique, form, timbre, tonality, time, and sound, as well as critical questions about the class process, my teaching and that of the assistants, and the notion of improvisation itself.

One student became interested in the concept of originality, remarking upon the difference between a recorded and a live performance. Listening to her recorded performance, she realized that she might have "missed" certain experiential possibilities, while at the same time expressing reluctance to repeat things she had already done: "I was afraid to go back and attempt to do similar things to what I heard on the recording." Other topics included practicing and rehearsals ("How do you practice improvisation"); personality development ("I feel as if improvisation is not only an expression of who you are, but a continuing discovery of yourself"); inner experience and emotional states ("I was continually searching for emotion in my music. Making it really "me."); and value ("Is there a right or a wrong way to play when involved in free improvisation?").

From the comments I read in several of the journals, intense debates were taking place in the playing and discussion sections about the music being made, especially concerning the nature of instrumental performance and sound. At times, confrontations erupted between students, as in the case of one student whose major instrument was the Australian didgeridoo, who complained that "I don't think anyone knows how to listen to the didgeridoo. They don't see any music, just weird noise...How can you do anything new on a didg—it's just a weird sound already. Well, what can you do on a piano except notes?" The student's account continued with a discussion of contention over issues of vocabulary and interactivity: "There's a lot of potential in [the piano], but [some people] seem to get literally offended when you suggest anything different...People are playing the same thing all the time and never listening." This student, who was already active doing didgeridoo concerts as a professional, complained that it was "hard to come back to class and be back in the role of the guy making weird noises. It's also hard because my duo performed and was very well received...people couldn't get the idea out of their heads that they had to make "real music."

Some students expressed impatience with the attitudes of others among their contemporaries over what they saw as narrowly constructed attitudes about what "real music" was—even to the point of active struggle or harsh critique. In particular, students who felt the need to actively engage the material in the course framed the resistance they encountered from some other students as part of an active attempt on the part of these students to sabotage the course. In this regard one might observe that this process of engagement with difference, in the form of musical viewpoints strikingly dissimilar to one's own, was either highly unusual, or at least more anxiety-producing than some students had wished for.

At least one student wrote—unbidden, after the class was over and the grades were in—an extra paper evaluating her fellow students. Titled "Frustration," this essay was a detailed account of what she perceived to be a lack of engagement, or even disdain, that some students were manifesting toward the course. She revealed that "it was very obvious that the atmosphere of the students in the class was one of apathy and disinterest...the fact that this class was one on improvisation was another factor that made the students even more antsy to find some way around learning a little of what was going on...I got very tired, very quickly, at the extremely narrow-minded and closed mentality of the so-called music majors."

Another student, a contrabassist, related a similar frustration at rehearsing with his class section: "I just couldn't handle playing music with people who very obviously thought the music was stupid and unpleasant. They were like black holes that sucked up any energy or joy that I brought to the class." According to this student, some of his fellows used a variety of apocryphal excuses to avoid engagement, such as "my teacher says it will hurt my voice." This student went on to describe attempted acts of sabotage of the music, leading him to withdraw the piece he had created for the concert. Somewhat later, however, this student did manage to find a kindred spirit. Describing his work with a fellow contrabassist, he declared: "All doubts about the music vanish and I am enjoying playing and interacting and being challenged and thinking and this is what it's all about...If only the section had been like that..."

The pressure of the final public concert obliged some students to face, perhaps for the first time, the uncomfortable responsibilities that go with the public presentation of personally created experimental music. Some students felt completely out of their depth, and angry about having that fact exposed to their peers—even though, for the most part, their peers were in exactly the same situation. One student described her mental and physical state just before the concert: "I feel ill-prepared, ill-equipped, ill! " Another student wrote, in a stream-of-consciousness style: "I'm scared, even when I (nervous) know the written music—either in front of my face, sight-reading, or committed to rote—still it's been written somewhere! Improv is scary!...I feel kind of stupid, don't know what to do...I haven't been exposed to this kind of thing before. Just go with your instincts!! It'll be fine."

The process journals, due at the end of the course, provided an excellent opportunity for the graduate student assistants to experience, from their own students, the kind of contentiousness, and even active hostility toward personal creativity or new musical forms that they could expect to find in some circles beyond the protected world of academic music. In evaluating student responses to the course, both positive and negative, I arrived at a number of possible explanatory scenarios:

1) I was a poor teacher who was unable to inspire the students with my vision of the power of improvised music. For the sake of completeness and frankness, I am obliged to consider this possibility.

2) Students had little preparation for the experience of improvisation. This is partly due to the nature of Eurological music pedagogy, which perhaps more than other arts and humanities disciplines, tends toward the promotion of class-based antagonism toward popular culture. At the same time, the emphasis upon rote learning, unproblematized technocratic repetition, and obedience to, rather than dialogue with traditional authority, privileges aspects of musicality that improvisative performance necessarily interrogates.

3) It may well be the case that requiring students to learn improvised music runs counter to what Jerry Garcia (see Marre 1991) once called the "anti-authoritarian" tendency in improvisation. One student's journal described how other students were careful to try to tell me things they thought I wanted to hear; the frustrating problem for such students was that rather than imposing

ideas, I tended to leave the very notion of development of criteria as to what "works" to the students themselves. Given this policy of never telling people what to do or not do, finding out what I wanted to hear was difficult.

4) Written documentation about improvised music tends to be poorly distributed and thus somewhat obscure, making it difficult for music students to experience serious contemporary writing on the subject. Where present, documentation can be spotty, of dubious quality, at times subtly or frankly racist, or otherwise lacking in authorial credibility.

In a society (such as that of the geographical West) which privileges literature over orature, written texts have far more authority than their recorded (aural-oral) counterparts. Particularly within the Western academic environment, where what is not written has a tenuous ontology, the relative paucity of quality written materials on improvised music has had quite deleterious consequences. Thus, recent initiatives by improvisors to produce and disseminate not only recorded performances, but textual documentation of their own practice—thereby directly intervening in the documentary process—is an important and necessary step in redressing an apparent imbalance between literature and orature in the society at large.

5) Even for those improvisors who are producing recordings, the domination of the American cultural landscape by powerful corporate forces that act as media gatekeepers (see Hirsch [1972] 1991, Hirsch [1973] 1985 and Bagdikian 1992) serves to severely impede access to alternative musics through the promotion of a self-serving ideology that privileges commercially-based notions of value. This dominance is reflected in the extreme difficulty that listeners experience in obtaining recordings of new and unusual music in most American record stores.

It has become painfully evident that both students and the general public have been extremely poorly served by the current version of the so-called "free-market" distribution of cultural resources. The use by creative artists of new electronic and computer technologies for disseminating new work promises a certain release from this domination, but only to the extent that such cyberspatial networks as the World Wide Web do not themselves succumb to the dominion of the gatekeeping system itself.

Conclusion

Written documentation plays an important role as part of a composite social environment that conditions the understanding of sonic utterance. In particular, the activities of musicians who move to produce reflective and thoughtful documentation of their activities will hasten the coming of a multi-methodological, intercultural musical environment in which the philosophical poverty of ethnocentric declarations of musical value will be more clearly disclosed.

With this in mind, questions naturally arise as to the kinds of strategies that can be articulated to encourage the development of such an environment. The organization of concerts, recordings, workshops and other opportunities for direct musical experience, while a fundamental part of the process of helping people to understand new music, must not be pursued to the exclusion of other important activities that directly affect the understanding of music. Such a short-sighted agenda, often justified with recourse to notions about how "hearing music is more important than reading about it," expresses, I believe, a certain fear that is based in part on a recognition of the seemingly superior position of literature over orature in this culture. Nonetheless, what I am arguing for is that in a rich cultural environment, a zero-sum framing of the relative positions of orature and literature is both unnecessary and detrimental to the advancement of the music.

One important strategy calls for an internal reconstitution of university faculties of music to embrace new possibilities. One way to achieve this is to initiate cross-disciplinary outreach to researchers working in other disciplines who nonetheless have music as a primary focus. This broadening of both the intellectual and social bases for new music, challenging the common division of "arts" and "humanities," recognizes that a fruitful meeting of the two areas places expanded notions of musical creativity before new, and I believe, highly receptive audiences, that are prepared to work toward the development of still newer discourses about music.

Exchanges between improvisors working both inside and outside the academic system will become more frequent, foreshortening the distance between "inside" and "outside." This is particularly important when one considers that many of the improvisors currently holding academic positions base their claim to legitimacy as much upon a long period of work and experience outside of the academic system as upon their achievements within academia itself. In many cases, this period of time spent in the world of professional music performance has greatly exceeded the amount of time that would have been required to obtain a doctoral degree. Such musicians are unlikely to forget the long absences from family and friends, the dreary train, bus, and car trips, the dislocation of time and space, the microscopically small hotel beds, and the sometimes indifferent, thoughtless or even unscrupulous promoters.

When experienced improvisors enter the academic environment, they bring with them the very valuable understanding of the conditions under which improvisors work. This increases their value to students who need to be aware of life outside the academy. Moreover, experienced improvisors are aware of how the pressure to produce new work often overwhelms the documentary process for existing work—a phenomenon which can cause the important process of reflective exploration concerning method and process to appear as a kind of luxurious indulgence. Thus, in addition to short-term concerts, lectures and workshops, I would propose the creation of long-term residencies in which the documentary work of improvisors would be supported, perhaps with the help of student and faculty researchers. This process, through the medium of "artists' colonies," is routinely available to artists classified as "composers"; improvisors, suitably disguised with scores, are at times admitted. A new model of direct support for improvised music would allow the disguise to be jettisoned, directly addressing and supporting the nurturance of improvisative musical creativity.

Finally, an appropriation of the concept of the academic "conference" would facilitate the exchange of information, methodologies, and musical ideas among improvisors. Unlike the standard academic conference, which is effectively limited to those within the academic system who can obtain financial support from their institutions, this kind of conference would need to directly support appearances by artists outside the academic system. Such a conference presents a formidable fund-raising challenge, but a potentially democratizing reality.

The new possibilities that are being uncovered by the broad transformations taking place in musical artworlds are breathtaking in their potential.

Thanks are due to Bonnie Wright of Spruce Street Forum, Lyn Hejinian, and Travis Ortiz for helpful suggestions and clarifications.

The transformation of the pedagogical process to engage these possibilities will play a crucial role in advancing a 21st century musicality that invites all of us to take part.

Works Cited:

Anderson, Fred, and Steve McCall. *Vintage Duets* CD (Okkadisk OD12001, 1994).

Bagdikian, Ben H. *The media monopoly* (Boston: Beacon Press, 1992).

Berliner, Paul F. *Thinking in jazz* (Chicago: University of Chicago Press, 1994).

Davis, Miles, and Quincy Troupe. *Miles: The Autobiography* (New York: Simon and Schuster, 1989).

Backus, Rob. *Fire music: a political history of jazz* (Chicago: Vanguard Books, 1976).

Fromm, Paul. *A Life for New Music: selected papers of Paul Fromm.* David Gable and Christoph Wolff, eds. (Cambridge, Mass.: Dept. of Music, Harvard University, distributed by Harvard University Press, 1988).

Gillespie, Dizzy, and Al Fraser. *To Be, or Not—to Bop: Memoirs* (New York: Da Capo Press, [1979], 1985).

Harris, Eddie. *Clichés* (Chicago and Los Angeles: Wardo Enterprises, 1975).

Hirsch, Paul M. "Processing fads and fashions: an organization-set analysis of cultural industry systems." In Mukerji, Chandra, and Michael Schudson, eds. *Rethinking Popular Culture: Contemporary Perspectives in Cultural Studies* (Berkeley: Universityof California Press, [1972], 1991).

Hirsch, Paul M. *The Structure of the Popular Music Industry: the filtering process by which records are preselected for public consumption* (Ann Arbor, Mich.: Institute for Social Research, University of Michigan, [1973], 1985).

Lewis, George. "Improvised Music Since 1950: Afrological and Eurological Perspectives." In *Black Music Research Journal*, vol. 16, no.1, Spring 1996.

Levine, Lawrence. *The Opening of the American Mind: Canons, Culture, and History* (Boston: Beacon Press, 1996).

Marre, Jeremy. "Improvisation: Its nature and practice in music." Video documentary (1991).

Pasler, Jann. "Musique et insitution aux États-Unis." *Inharmoniques*, no. 2 ("Musiques, identités"), May 1987. Distributed by IRCAM.

Ruff, Willie. *A Call to Assembly: the Autobiography of a Musical Storyteller* (New York: Viking, 1991).

Shere, Charles. *Thinking Sound Music: the Life and Work of Robert Erickson* (Berkeley: Fallen Leaf Press, 1995).

Small, Christopher. "On Improvisation." *Music of the Common Tongue* (London: Calder, 1987).

Sweet, Robert. *Music Mind, Music Universe* (1996).

Taylor, Arthur. *Notes and Tones: Musician-to-Musician Interviews* (New York: Da Capo, [1977], 1993).

SOUL MECHANICAL

Raw Tech in Real Time

IKUE MORI

I have been working with the drum machine as an instrument, trying to find a way to play more organically and colorfully within the possibilities of its particular system. Using the drum machine one can make loops, play a sequence, select from hundreds of sound sources (voices), program each pad to a key, control pitch, trigger other sound sources…multiplying and manipulating the sounds by adding effects, by combining them, and by causing them to interact in real time.

One can use the drum machine's features as a means for constructing a music as raw as possible.

Loops

Working with patterns (variations) and loops (repeats) is the main function of a drum machine, and patterns are the source of my composition. A hundred patterns from each of three drum machines can be organized into groups to obtain sound material or rhythms. Sound patterns include explosions and textures, and rhythm patterns include melody and phrase. The event loop determines when to change.

So, for example, one might choose four rhythm patterns and three textural patterns, and event patterns could be added spontaneously:

rhythm loop	12b	→	B35	→	B49	→	B30	→	12b	→	B35
texture loop		A88	→	A78	→	A40	→	A88	→	A78	→
event loop	B48	→	19b	→	39b		01a	→	B36	→	19a

The rhythm pattern changes when an event starts and texture changes when the event is over.

The order of patterns should be fixed but the duration of each patten is controlled by the event.

Rhythm and texture patterns are generated through the looping (repeating).

An event is not continuous only; the order of patterns is looped (repeated).

The events in the above example are:

B48: power tom, aggressive tom, conga, wrench, trash can, scratch tuned very low, falling
B36: pipes tuned high, alarm whistle
01a: cold block tuned in 6 notes sequenced, siren
19b: impact, LoBigHL, Backwrdz, XLoCanon, Pop Shot, mechanical blast

Thistle dexterous in the morning after rain: texture

Texture patterns are made using similar kinds of sound groups, programmed by assigning each voice a different sound quality, for example, that of wood, a low drum, or metal, etc. One can record the pattern with no beat, let it loop, creating streams of sounds which become colorful through the addition of reverb and are vitalized with effects.

– a texture:	A40 (rain, stream), faint mix of hand clapping, maracas, claves, triangle
– layers of texture:	B46, A95, 40 simulate various rain sound
– texture:	B50 (brewing), A78 (bells)

Recipe: *cooking*

"Cooking" has been one of my methods for working with patterns: Chop, mix, and simmer.

Let the stop/continue option divide the phrase and distribute it across all three drum machines; make new combinations of the chopped phrase creating other odd rhythms. Simmer the patterns by layering them with delay and reverb, and vary their intensity; simmering becomes boiling.

PIDGIN MUSICS

CHRIS BROWN

Pidgin is the practical way that people speaking different languages communicate with each other: dispensing with grammar, words

In the following article, sections in
italic are taken from interviews conducted in June 1995 in Havana, Cuba;
sections in bold italic are taken from
an interview made in December 1992
in Quezon City, Philippines.

taken from all the languages present are used in whatever way it takes to get across the meaning. Patterns that
work survive, and bastard languages form. The world
today is a hot-house for musical pidgins, as musicians
with different training and influence figure out how to play with each other.

*Composer Juan Piñera describes himself as a "basurero," a garbage man, because
he lives in Cuba and garbage is what he has to work with. But he embraces this
quality not only out of necessity, but because "there's something beautiful about
ugliness."*

The second half of the 20th century is almost over, and musical issues
that concerned composers at the mid-century (like tonality vs. atonality, complexity vs. simplicity, order [tone] vs. disorder [noise], etc.) seem increasingly
distant and irrelevant. Our music now uses any and all resources available to
respond to these social issues: 1) the electronic recording media and the new
audiences they create; 2) the global collision of musical cultures, their new
awareness of each other, and their pidgin-hybrids.

Without embracing either its risks or its challenges, the American
classical musical establishment has recently co-opted the experimentalist musical tradition. As an ethos of novelty and rebellion becomes the norm, it makes
sense that interesting work is more likely to be found where the media glare is
not, where community can develop because the commercial blare is relatively
weak, in the cracks of the global culture where people still invent art to enter-
tain and enliven themselves. I recently met and interviewed two great composers, Juan Blanco and Jose Maceda, whose music, though informed by their

experience with Western compositional practices, primarily addresses the concerns of their own societies.

Blanco is the founder of the Cuban electro-acoustic music, which he developed in contact with composers and studios world-wide, while still managing to integrate it into the modernist, socialist fabric of Cuban society. This meant an emphasis on music designed not only for the concert hall, but also for theater and film, gymnastics events, multi-media expositions, and multi-track, ambient sound installations for interior public spaces, including hospitals. The musical material draws its inspiration from abstract sources, including the techniques of film-animation, two and three dimensional geometric algorithms, and forms derived from geology, chemistry, acoustics, and electronics. As with other Cuban musics, there is an emphasis on a free mixture of styles: for example in his 1983 work *Circus-Toccata*, an ostinato synthesizer sequence with a carnival, melodic flavor complements high-energy improvisations by Afro-Cuban percussionists Tata Guines (congas) and Guillermo Barreto (timbales) in a continuous fifteen minute piece.

Blanco trained a younger generation in musical invention, only to have the rug pulled out from under him with the collapse of the Soviet-supported socialism. His students, Juan Piñera among them, have been left in the difficult but creative position of having to invent for themselves a new context for their music.

Piñera's Quando el aura...*uses an East German rhythm machine/effects processor, with the rich resonances of inductive coil filters. But lacking any context for electronic music, he has turned to opera, and has had a number of recent successes. His first opera was* A Cup of Coffee, *an opera buffa, for full orchestra, chorus, and soloists, the libretto written to be understood on many levels, one of which was clearly political, but in a characteristically Havana, joking, satirical way. It was written to intentionally flatter the voices of the opera singers, giving them ample opportunity for display, gracious arias, etc. making some fun of themselves in a clowning way while still allowing them to do what they do best. Many musical styles are mixed together in the music, for example, and the final scene is a reworking of Beethoven's "Ode to Joy" theme set to Cuban dance rhythms His new opera deconstructs the figure of the Cuban nationalist hero Jose Marti. Marti is sung by three different characters, one representing the actual, historical Marti, the second representing the idealized, heroic Marti, and the third representing the degenerate Marti.*

Jose Maceda of the Philippines trained in Paris in the thirties for a career as a concert pianist, got interested instead in composition and met Varèse while studying in New York in the fifties, and produced his first compositions while studying ethnomusicology at UCLA in the sixties. He then returned to the University of the Philippines and is considered the founder of Philippine ethnomusicology, playing a major role in recording, analyzing, and preserving pre-Hispanic musical cultures. His early pieces in the sixties were written for massive ensembles (hundreds to thousands) of performers playing bamboo percussion and wind instruments. These pieces were realizable for him not only because bamboo instruments are easily made in the Philippines, but because the participatory function of music is still primary there.

How can you approach music as a study of culture, instead of only as acoustics/ science, etc.? The tools for this are not just electronic, they are all the instruments of the world. What made me go into ethnomusicology was the perception that there was something that went beyond dominant/tonic relations and their modernist extensions. There are certain generalities that we now know about Asian music that form a background that may help us as contemporary musicians to decide on where to go. Over 1000 cultures each one repeating or redoing his own culture in order to make another culture — there are so many components now, very different from the European culture which had no precept of anything else.

The scores for these early pieces use simple musical materials which through multiplication create complex sonic textures with obvious relationships to those of Western avant-garde and electronic music. Maceda insists that the idea of being a composer is in itself a Western idea, for which there is no comparable tradition in Asia.

When you compose new music you are looking for new expressions in thought: that is a European concept. "Composers" are a particularly Western concept. A Javanese guru has a different kind of role. When I make my music I am not trying to add to, for example, Kalinga music, I am trying to add something to Western composition. It's like science, it's like an expression in thought, music is something like that, you are searching for things, and that is Western. It's not the nose flute, it's what the nose flute represents: you can go about it placidly, without too much technique. How do you transfer those techniques, non-dexterity, gentleness into music composition? What is there in the culture of gongs and bamboo that can be brought to the post-Varèse traditions of composition?

You just don't start from scratch—like I will just shake these gongs, break them, there's a background to what you do. Are you attacking the tradition by using an instrument in a new context? My use of jaw-harps parallels the use of string instruments taken from the Middle East by Italians: they brought their ideas to an instrument without the idea of extending the Middle Eastern culture.

Waves and language, how the twanging of the instrument can give you the perception of electronic means, but made with natural means in performance, it creates something that is different. It is a study of forty waves that become a diffused sound, the waves vary with the movement of the piece, as against the human voice.

In 1974 he realized *Ugnayan* ("working together") for transistor radios which used radio stations as musical instruments and radio listeners as performers: over twenty radio stations in Manila simultaneously broadcast the different instrumental parts for the piece, and performers throughout the city tuned in the signals on small hand-held receivers, playing them together while moving around, creating musical atmospheres of sound.

Writing for many people is not orchestral, orchestra is volume and loudness. My idea is the opposite—dispersion and thinness. Why so many people? My concept of melody is no longer a melodic line, I became interested in sounds that are combinations, several sounds going on. A melody is a culture, the moment you play a melody you identify a culture, and I don't want to be a culture. I would like to propose that you can have interesting sounds without single tones being identified as such and having a meaning as such. When you have forty tones, it's another meaning, it is the concept of blurring a melody.

With growing interest in his music in Japan, Maceda has recently been writing music for Western orchestral instruments in which he intentionally obscures their exact pitches, focusing instead on their tone-color and pitch-range.

Exact pitch in orchestral instruments hinders expression of color qualities in inexact pitch. What is the meaning of pitch that is not quite pitch? When you have many things going on at the same time, then there is the possibility of using pitches without having to deal with clear pitches. The less pure the pitches are, the more conducive they are to color blends. Pitch and color are forced to merge into combinations outside the logic of temperament. The instruments used are only a means toward the fulfillment of another music with more flexible pitch-colors. The problem is how to limit this, what is the number that it takes to get the blurring effect, what is the right number of voices to get this effect?

The musical present *is* multiplicity. Maceda's blurring effect with pitches now applies to the mixing of musical traditions. Post-modern, as a descriptor, is a cop-out; multi-cultural is what we are. Traditional musics carry the wealth of millennia of accumulated musical intelligence, and a return to one's cultural roots is a way to mine this inheritance. Without a serious understanding of their depth, the use of other cultures' instruments and music is a rip-off. Instead of new musics, we get fashionable but shallow collages of images, and a reduction instead of proliferation of musical diversity. But the yeast of all cultural activity is the need to solve contemporary problems; music becomes relevant, and widely practiced, when it provides solutions to our life, delightfully. Devotion to the musical solutions of the past is no answer for the modern composer of any era. So there must be a focus on both the quality and variety of our musical pidgins, on growing strong hybrids that can synergistically activate the musical intelligence of their ancestors.

Jose Maceda at home in Quezon City, Philippines.

Electronic recording has changed everything in the twentieth century, and especially music. Musical cultures are face-to-face with each other primarily because of recordings, and audience participation via the replication of musical performances has become the dominant social form of musical activity. Since the seventies, even classical composers publish their music first as recordings; but the elevation of aural traditions to the pantheon of musical history began far earlier, as popular music (followed by film, then video) became the leading vehicle for the development of the technology that delivers culture to its consumer-society. Now with the explosion of digital media, the recorded music medium starts to move away from its function as a reinforcer of cultural hegemonies, and becomes a network within which multiple layers of interactions take place. With the Internet, individuals have become network broadcasters. The avant-garde is dead in this new electronic culture because there is no single line or center, only networks of inter-connected centers, each with many different frontiers. Within this culture there can be no High Art, and no need for critics to define it, because there is no single system of value. Information (and music) is all free-flow, it's just the packages that hold and the tools that mold it that are sold. It's only packaging that distinguishes one product from another; so if art is a form of activity that provides relief from the survivalist logics of commerce, shouldn't artists concern themselves with something besides packaging?

Instead of electronic products, we should be developing instruments that help us to play, and encourage our development of pidgins. The culture we're moving towards is both local and global. It encourages us all to be artists, so the best art is my art and that of my friends, and it is local; but my locality is a global network, because my friends are spread throughout the world, from different cultures, and I have immediate communication channels with them. This exists now for words and still images, but musical situations that take advantage of it are yet to be invented. And electronic instruments alone may not be enough; since the electronic genie is always changing shape, we never have enough time to develop a physical language to use with them. And since electronic technology evolves with miniaturization, musical instruments developed exclusively with it tend to be based on amplifying tiny amounts of physical motion. With acoustic instruments the body learns to integrate a large number of subtle controls into larger gestures; we like to play them partly because of the physical challenge that they bring, and because they provide a discipline for integrating mind and body. The ethereal medium alone becomes entirely a head-trip, yet another expression of that culturally explosive Western idea of locating our whole self in the head, in reason without emotion, in becoming an immortal being, a Composer (a bust), whose life is forever frozen as data on a metal disc.

The following speculative suggestions are glimmerings received from the baby-steps of my fifteen years of experience with computer-mediated musics. We can't abandon our head-life, but we do need to keep working at integrating it with our body-life. Our electronic instruments can be free from our bodies, we don't need to strap them on, or to bind ourselves to them— they are software. Rather than trying to make them better controllers over the musical universe, we should release them to become participants in our musical practices, to become free-floating abstractions that respond to the physical music that we already make, thus transcending the artificiality of their own limited intelligences. Interactive programs display the workings of our own minds as we play them, because they are mirrors that change with time, revealing the consequences of our actions in time without repeating, framing us by the growth and decay of their structure. Interactive networks are transparent to their users, freely recombining the musical languages that are input to them, enabling musical interactions over distances in time, space, and culture. They are both worth aspiring to.

How high can a man be born? What can he listen to? That's the same problem. What's the relation to mankind, what is a human being, what does a human being think? You cannot ignore science and electricity, concepts like that, Western music. At the same time, you cannot ignore Asian music, you cannot, it would be too one-sided. Yes, you need to know another culture, that people eat rice and that we eat bread, you cannot conceive of that.

AURAL ARCHITECTURE:
THE CONFLUENCE OF FREEDOM

MYRA MELFORD

A man sets himself the task of drawing the world. As the years pass, he fills the empty space with images of provinces and kingdoms, mountains, bays, ships, islands, fish, houses, instruments, stars, horses and people. Just before he dies, he discovers that the patient labyrinth of lines traces the image of his own face.[19]

"Where is the plan you are following, the blueprint?"

"We will show it to you as soon as the working day is over; we cannot interrupt our work now," *they answer.*

Work stops at sunset. Darkness falls over the building site. The sky is filled with stars.

"There is the blueprint," they say.[20]

19. Jorge Luis Borges, *El Hacedor (Dreamtigers)* (Austin: University of Texas Press, 1964), from the epilogue.

20. Italo Calvino, *Invisible Cities,* trans. William Weaver (New York: Harcourt Brace Jovanich, 1974).

21. G. Gilbert, "Patterns of Faith," *Darshan* 97 (New York, April 1995).

...vivid forms have been created in man's search to experience the divine. These spaces are the embodiment of deeper reality, maps that point the way and offer pathways back to the Self within...These spaces are enlivened by the power of the One who resides there, whom we meet on our own inner ground.[21]

The house in which I lived from the ages of three to eighteen, designed and built by Frank Lloyd Wright, had a major impact on my development and direction as a composer and improvising pianist.

Another such building is the mosque, La Mezquita, in Cordoba, Spain, which I visited in 1994. I happened to walk into this building one morning before it was officially open to the public. As soon as I entered I felt like a different person. All the distracting thoughts and chatter in my mind were suddenly stilled. The space was beautiful, quiet, and dark except for occasional shafts of dusty sunlight; and it was completely empty except for a forest of stone columns and arches which my guide book aptly described as a meditation in stone. This experience kindled an aspiration for me as a musician: to create an aural space, if you will, that is not only structurally and esthetically satisfying, but that also allows for the individual listener or player within it to have her own experience—an experience that perhaps leaves one feeling alone, but that brings one back to one's Self, that affirms one's deepest feelings or longings.

Architectural concepts, in particular those of Frank Lloyd Wright, have both inspired and informed my approach to creating music. And music, it seems, was an important inspiration for Mr. Wright. In the first volume of his *Collected Writings,* Wright discusses the development of his vision for modern architecture, and he describes his affinity with music: "...as a small boy...I used to lie and listen to my father playing Beethoven...To my young mind it all spoke a language that stirred me strangely, and I've since learned it was *the language, beyond all words, of the human heart*...to me architecture is just as much an affair of the human heart...I know there are possibilities in the way of putting things together that are to my eyes or sense of fitness what music is to my ear or sense of sound."[22] These words suggest the importance of an intuitive as well as an intellectual process, which is very much the way I work. What's crucial is the connection between the language of the human heart and the act or purpose of creation.

22. Frank Lloyd Wright, *Collected Writings: Volume 1 1884-1930* (New York: Rizzoli, 1992), pp. 31, 311 [emphasis mine].

The house in which I grew up is the earliest extra-musical influence on my direction and development as an artist. It was designed by Frank Lloyd Wright and was located at 1023 Meadow Road in Glencoe, Illinois, a suburb about twenty-five miles north of Chicago on Lake Michigan. Built in 1915 in the 'Prairie Style,' it is one of five houses that Wright intended for middle-income housing, situated near the larger Booth House which was built for his lawyer. This subdivision was called Ravine Bluffs and had elegant poured concrete markers at either end of the roadways leading into the neighborhood and a beautiful bridge spanning the ravine on one end, all designed by Wright. As a little girl I loved this house but didn't realize until I'd lived in many other places how special it was. It was truly a beautiful esthetic experience. The exterior of the house was white stucco with dark brown wood trim defining the major horizontal lines and flat roof. In winter it blended beautifully with the snow and bare trees around it. There were many windows bringing in a lot of sunlight, and there were lovely details in the light fixtures and woodwork. One in particular was an interior window, trisected with wooden slats, between the staircase and the living room, allowing air, light, and sound to filter through. There was a beautiful big gray brick hearth and fireplace in the middle of the first floor, around which the dining area flowed into the living room. Everything exemplified Wright's idea that the wall as wall was vanishing—that interior space should be fluid, not boxy, and in turn should flow out and blend into the surrounding landscape. Wright aspired to "the natural building, naturally built, native to the region...a building as beautiful on its site as the region itself."[23] The Booth House was an even more dramatic example of this, with its many rooms and levels seeming to grow out of its hilltop perch and its cantilevers jutting out over the ravine.

23. Ibid., p. 311.

In high school, I began studying Wright's architecture and philosophy. I visited many of his buildings in the Chicago area and in Spring Green, Wisconsin, where he had built Taliesen East, his home and school. I haven't yet had the opportunity to visit his house, Fallingwater, in Bear Run, Pennsylvania, but I came across a description which would apply to many of his designs: "For Wright's rooms were rarely enclosed by four walls; rather areas were defined by a change in ceiling height or the position of built-in furniture, so that functions as well as spaces interpenetrated and overlapped, especially at corners. What constituted the indoors and outdoors was deliberately left vague; even the continuous metal windows...touched the walls without a frame to emphasize the same materials used either side of them. The same stone floors seep out under the doors."[24]

After moving to New York City, when I began to practice composition and improvisation seriously, I realized there were certain of Wright's ideas I could apply to creating music:

> In music the Romanza is only a free form or freedom to make one's own form. A musician's sense of proportion is all that governs him in it. The mysterious remains just enough a haunting quality in a whole—so organic as to lose all tangible evidence of how it was made—and the organic whole lives in the harmonies of feeling expressed in sound. Translate 'sounds and the ears' to 'forms and the eye,' and a Romanza, even, seems reasonable enough, too, in architecture.... To be potentially poetic in architecture, then, means—to create a building free in form (we are using the word Romanza), that takes what is harmonious in the nature of existing conditions inside the thing and outside it and with sentiment (beware of sentimentality)—bringing it all out into some visible form that *expresses those inner harmonies perfectly, outwardly,* whatever the shape it may take.[25]

24. Charles Knevitt, *Shelter* (San Francisco: Pomegranate Artbooks, 1996), p. 128.
25. Wright, *Collected Writings*, p. 314.

This idea of working within a free form, guided by one's sense of proportion, not being able to tell how the form was created, as well as allowing for a free flow between inside and outside, made sense to me metaphorically as I started to develop my musical and compositional vocabulary. I was exploring sound and texture within mostly free and structured improvisations, experimenting with different frameworks, playing with the balance of composed and improvised material within a piece and also trying to create an invisible seam between what was notated and improvised. I was also developing my keyboard and inside-the-piano vocabulary—playing directly on the strings and soundboard. At the same time I was beginning to write within more traditional sounding song forms using the language of jazz, classical, folk, blues, and gospel music, and I was looking for a way to synthesize or make sense of these seemingly contradictory tendencies—improvising both within and without form; playing inside the harmony or rhythmic feel as well as with a greater sense of tonal and rhythmic freedom. Through my understanding of Wright's approach to architectural design and subsequent composition lessons with Henry Threadgill, I began to find a way to integrate these ideas into a coherent whole through combining composition and improvisation in an organic way. Both Wright and Threadgill likened the creation of their work to that of a living organism.

One of the key ideas of Wright's philosophy pertained to what he called 'organic architecture': the building growing out of the site, out of materials that fit with the site, out of the function it needs to serve, without imposing a design, rather, letting the design create itself. He explained it this way: "An architect must 'grow' his buildings from his motif, so that his building is just as natural an expression of thought and feeling directing power toward ultimate purpose as any tree or any engine for that matter...Things of themselves begin to proceed from generals to particulars—they begin to build of themselves, to develop, emerge, and take inevitable form, forcing nothing, imposing not at all...There is destiny inherent in every chosen motif and it finds destiny anew in your hands guided by imagination to your heart's desire."[26] During my composition lessons, Threadgill talked about organic composition—starting with a small cell or musical phrase and allowing a whole composition to grow naturally, through an infinite number of permutations, out of that initial material including the form or structure of the piece. This lesson from Henry continues to be the basis for my approach to composing and improvising—allowing/following this organic growth.

Some of the techniques I use for developing the initial musical cell are familiar to many composers. They include the analysis of the phrase in terms of

26. Ibid., pp. 259, 261.

its intervals and the transposition of the phrase into all those keys (i.e., a 4th above, a minor 3rd below, etc.); finding the inversion, retrograde inversion, and complement; reordering the notes within the phrase; and deriving the harmony from stacking or verticalizing the horizontal phrase (putting it on another axis) and then developing permutations of that through a concept that Edgar Varèse called crystallization: "...internal structure expanded and split into different shapes or groups of sound constantly changing shape, direction and speed, the form of the work is the consequence of this interaction—limitless as the external form of crystals—the dimension of the infinite."[27] This process of crystallization has much larger implications in terms of overall compositional structure, which accorded with both Threadgill's concept of organic composition and Wright's organic architecture. Varèse was working with a very visual and sculptural approach to music—creating and manipulating timbral blocks of sound within space.

27. Jonathon W. Bernard, *The Music of Edgar Varèse* (New Haven: Yale University Press, 1987), p. 43.

The Varèse techniques I use include rotation, projection, expansion, and contraction. Here's a simple example of using rotation to derive variations in harmony: say you have a chord like e-a-c, a perfect 4th with a minor 3rd above it. You rotate the middle note (a) from a 4th above to a 4th below the lowest note creating this chord: b-e-c; or from a minor 3rd below to a minor 3rd above the c: e-c-eb (e-flat). So this traditional sounding 2nd-inversion minor triad evolves into something more unusual [Fig. 1].

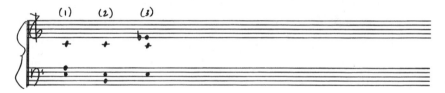

Figure 1.

One way I'll use expansion is to widen the intervals of a phrase by a minor 2nd (or larger) and then play two or more of these lines simultaneously to derive the harmony [Fig. 2].

I once read that Picasso would intentionally take an initially pretty idea and work it over and over again to find something more substantial, and that Stravinsky had a penchant for a certain awkwardness in a work of art. The techniques to which Henry Threadgill introduced me gave me the tools to take what might be a pretty or conventional idea and develop it into something more compelling. The ear plays a crucial role in all of this. It's the ear that

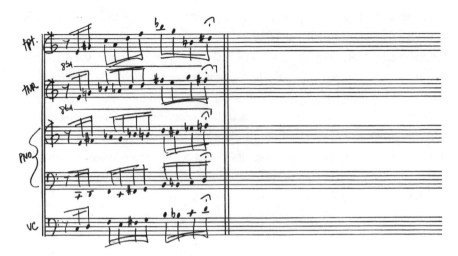

Figure 2. *Changes I*, last measure.

decides finally which of the many permutations get used and how; determining order, rhythmic feel, and tempo. My own hand size and physical tendencies influence my choices as well. Sometimes I'll deliberately choose something that's awkward to play in order to break away from habit and arrive at a new sound or feeling.

The first piece that I worked on with Threadgill was in fact the piece I titled "Frank Lloyd Wright Goes West to Rest." The title comes from the headline of an editorial in the *New York Times* about how Wright's second wife was having his remains disinterred from his burial site in Wisconsin and sent to be buried next to her in Scottsdale, Arizona, where Wright had lived the latter part of his life and where he built Taliesen West. At the time, I had been thinking about writing some kind of homage and quasi-portrait of Wright ('quasi,' because I was basing the piece more on subjective feelings of having grown up in and around his architecture and persona; it's really a very personal impression).

The musical cell I chose to start with is this one [Fig. 3]:

Figure 3.

Then I began making worksheets using the processes I've described, and came up with the first incarnation of this piece which was originally given a reading by the Brooklyn Philharmonic Chamber Ensemble. I learned a tremendous amount from that experience, having never written for chamber ensemble before, nor ever having asked classically trained musicians to improvise. This piece has had many lives since then—I later reduced it to a solo piano piece from the original orchestral score and since then have arranged it both for trio and quintet.

That initial phrase and the ensuing permutations became this opening theme [Fig. 4]:

Figure 4.

This theme is then developed through improvisation, sometimes structured and sometimes not, depending on the situation. One thing I enjoy is to change the game plan for the improvisation sections from one performance to the next. For instance, I might begin my improvisation by playing through the material backwards in another tempo, or turning the score literally upside down. I also use the same techniques for developing the vocabulary or language for the improvisation as I use for writing the material. In these times, when composers' music is so personal, standard jazz, blues, and even so-called 'free' improvisational vocabulary isn't necessarily or always appropriate. Whether I'm improvising on my own music or someone else's, I find that I need to mine the piece for ideas, rather than trying to apply some vocabulary that worked in other music. In a group situation, I might set up revolving duos and trios interspersed with overlapping quartets and quintets, or assign textural qualities to the smaller groups, using different devices like this in an attempt to keep the music fresh. This idea of rearranging the music on the spot was something I experienced working with both Threadgill and Butch Morris.

Many of the techniques used in developing the pitch material can be applied with regard to rhythm; for example, expanding and contracting the units—a group of four sixteenth notes becomes a group of four quarters and evolves into a walking bass line for Part II of the piece with an even more temporally spread out melody floating on top of it.

A more encompassing compositional process, that of integrating musical as well as extra-musical material, is exemplified in my piece called "Even the Sounds Shine." Before writing this piece I collected the following ideas which I intuitively felt belonged together: numerous melodic phrases I had transcribed from a bird I heard in Wiesen, Austria, that sounded like a cross between Ornette Coleman and Leroy Jenkins [Fig. 5];

Figure 5.

an impression of that bird singing accompanied by hundreds of other birds and animals chattering one dawn that was one of the most beautiful sonic textures I'd ever heard; and the following poem by Fernando Pessoa:

In broad daylight even the sounds shine
On the repose of the wide field they linger.
It rustles, the breeze silent.
I have wanted, like sounds, to live by things
And not be theirs, a winged consequence
Carrying the real far.[28]

This poem inspired both the title and an image or feeling I wanted to convey—the idea that sound can shine ('seeing' with the ears) and that this sound has the potential to carry us beyond ourselves, to an understanding or awareness of something greater. Sound itself, a moving, transformative expression of energy, doesn't rest in its place of origin, but continually carries the message of its existence into the surrounding space. Within this poem are both the Zen idea of experiencing the senses in relation to sense objects typically associated with another sense, thereby short-circuiting the intellect and producing an experience of nonduality; and the potential for sound to transport one to an altered state of union with the Self.

28. Fernando Pessoa, *Selected Poems*, trans. Jonathon Griffin (London: Penguin, 1974).

I started with these birdcalls, and I came up with all kinds of permutations, and then played with them until I heard a theme emerge. The entire theme consists of the birdcall material. I then constructed the rest of the piece out of this same material used in different ways, as a series of landing points between improvisations and/or backgrounds for improvisation. Where I didn't use actual musical notation, I gave verbal instructions about the texture I was after.

The piece starts with the ensemble playing very loud and dense for a few seconds and then immediately getting quiet setting up a very soft texture with little bits of melody jumping out until the piano gives a cue and the theme is played [Fig. 6-8].

Figure 6.

Figure 7.

Figure 8.

The piece then moves into a slower tempo to set up an open bass and trumpet duet improvisation that leads into a trumpet solo over this material [Fig. 9].

Figure 9.

At the end of the trumpet solo, the piano sets up a background for the saxophone to solo over which sounds like this [Fig. 10]:

Figure 10.

This develops into either a piano and saxophone duet or trio with drums. As the improvisation develops, the trumpet and bass come back in with another written background and this moves into a high-energy, densely textured piano trio with bass and drums, based on the diminished triad material, which is also one of the birdcalls [Fig. 11].

Figure 11.

Figure 12.

This is followed by a call-and-response section between the horns, over the original quiet texture that builds to a repetitive phrase played by the group [Fig. 12].

Then I give the original cue, and we play the opening theme one more time to end.

Recently I've been considering the ideas of Heraclitus as I compose for my new quintet project, "The Same River, Twice": "All things flow; opposition brings together, and from discord comes perfect harmony; the hidden harmony is better than the obvious one; it is in change that things find rest; and you can't step twice into the same rivers, for other waters are ever flowing onto you." His ideas perfectly express my evolving aspirations as a composer and improvisor: to synthesize and find beauty in atonal and polytonal vocabularies, in dense, highly energetic passages as well as in more serene and consonant sections; and to create music that is constantly evolving within each piece, as well as from performance to performance. My techniques include the use of cross-fades and overlapping sections of improvisation and written material, one plane of music dissolving to reveal another, as well as the juxtaposition of contrasting materials. I'm interested in finding new ways of using improvised sections to develop the music—exploring how a player might improvise his or her part in a particular section without it being a featured 'solo' per se, or how a group might improvise a section with the emphasis on ensemble texture and interplay, again, rather than featured solos. For me, the use of improvisation is the key to making 'expansive' music— music that's fresh, vital, and spontaneous with a sense of inevitability to it, like the flow of a river or the flow of space in a Frank Lloyd Wright building. "The contrast of light and shade, different materials, solids and voids, and varying bright colours and textures, create a rich tapestry where inside, outside, and their interface merge imperceptibly." [29]

29. Knevitt, *Shelter*, p. 136.

In recent years, my practice of the martial arts (*aikido* and *nei kung*) and meditation has provided inspiration for pursuing my musical goals. It has increased my overall energy level and my understanding of the subtle presence of *chi* (life-force or universal energy), and how to begin to use it to create/perform music by focusing on the movements of chi within the player, amongst the players, and between players and audience. The process of learning to still and focus the mind in the present moment has strengthened my ability to concentrate. I'm able to react with greater flexibility and to trust my spontaneous musical choices, both as a composer and improviser. But more than this, the insights and the physical experiences I've had while meditating have become the goal that I want to reach through playing music and to communicate experientially with the audience. There's a tangible link for me between being in a meditative state of focus—experiencing vast, infinite internal space; the dissolution of boundary between self and other (the sense of being a separate body/person); a sense of timelessness; and a deep sense of well-being and joy— and the aural space I want to build through music.

Through my studies of Eastern philosophy I've come across two ideas which seem to shed some light on my own creative process and aspirations and point me in a direction for further investigation. One is the Sanskrit word *spanda* which is the root for our word 'expand,' and which contains within it the unstruck sound *om*, from which the universe arises. The other is *Saraswati*, originally the river goddess and later the goddess of knowledge, language, the arts, and music, which is directly linked to *spanda* through the potent quality of sound contained within her. "Saraswati is the embodiment of the purity of supreme Conscious- ness from which all creation flows."[30]

30. E. Grimbergen, "'Sweet Flows the Voice': Deities of Inspiration," *Darshan* 97: 8.

I'm reminded of a childhood ritual I had when I would go swimming in the Wisconsin River where it flowed through Spring Green, not far from Taliesin and right next to a restaurant that Wright had designed. Whenever I entered the water for the first time, I'd face upstream, hold up my arms, and ask the spirit of the river to heal me. In some way I was talking to Saraswati then, as I am now, working with "The Same River, Twice" and related ideas and projects.

I've read that all music is an attempt to recreate this internal, divine music, the primordial *om*, that is itself the same energy that creates all forms — buildings, cities, compositions—and which is also the source of supreme bliss. Emotion is projected through sound, and when that sound vibrates at the right frequency to harmonize or create a resonance with the physical world, a space of union and healing is created. The key is in "identifying and expressing the appropriate combination of vibrations for the effect you desire...the right use of intention, awareness, and sound."[31] This gives rise to the experience of time- lessness—when there's no distraction or awareness of duality, no separation from immediate experience. Again, the concept of flow—that meditative state of focus in which there's no awareness of past or future. There's only a sense of merging and the knowledge that everything that exists in the universe comes from the same source of universal consciousness which dwells within all people in the space of the heart. Everything we create, whether material, conceptual, aural, or imaginary, is only a projection or reflection of ourselves, the universal speaking through the personal. "A man sets himself the task of drawing the world."[32]

31. T. Kenyon and V. Essene, *The Hathor Material* (Santa Clara: S.E.E. Pub. Co., 1996), p. 162.

32. Borges, *El Hacedor,* from the epilogue.

33. Kabir, *Songs of Kabir,* trans. Rabindranath Tagore (York Beach: Samuel Weiser, Inc., 1974).

Unity is the goal. A transient experience that longs for eternity. In that moment when the musician, the listener (which includes the performer as well as the audience), and the music are One, this aural space of union is created and one experiences the Self of all. It's for this experience referred to as 'the confluence of freedom' that I look forward to continuing my exploration of the relationship between internal, external, and aural space—meditation and architecture; and the healing and transformative power of music and sound.

The flute of the Infinite is played
without ceasing, and its sound is love:
When love renounces all limits, it reaches truth.
How widely the fragrance spreads! It has no end,
nothing stands in its way.
The form of this melody is bright like a million suns:
incomparably sounds the vina, the vina of the notes of truth.[33]

THAT SILENCE THING

ANTHONY COLEMAN

Article.

In the air—months behind. Deadlines become pointless. Abstract.
The idea that saying something is more than opinion. More than taste.

Grasping at it. No faith.

Believing in the idea of language without really knowing what that
means.

Writing about music.

Thinking?

What about it?
A) It's a job like any other.
B) It's not my job (I have too much respect for it to do it).
C) (But, seriously), what kind of thought goes into (my?) music?

The thing about 'silence.'
And me—the attraction to it.

"Poetry after Auschwitz."[34]

To talk about nothing.

The thing about silence.

Mistrust of verbal language.

34. Adorno's comment, "After Auschwitz,
to write poetry is an act of barbarism," is to
be found in his 1949 essay, "Cultural Criticism and Society," in Theodor W. Adorno,
Prisms (Cambridge, Mass.: MIT Press, 1981).

I'm just at the beginning of this. All this time I feel as if I've been
living/working an extended prelude. A vague desire for a confrontation with
some idea about language—semantics, rhetoric, manner, cliché, etc....

What idea?

Atomization, for example.

That Webern thing: "To express a novel in a single gesture."[35]

Mistrust of (verbal) language.

35. See Arnold Schoenberg's introduction to Anton Webern's *Six Bagatelles for String Quartet,* opus 9, reprinted in Walter Kolneder, *Anton Webern: An Introduction to His Works* (Berkeley: University of California Press, 1968).

36. George Steiner, *Language and Silence* (New York: Atheneum, 1967).

"The idea that music *is* deeper, more comprehensive than language, that it rises with immediacy from the sources of our being, has not lost its relevance and fascination."[36]

But which music? How can music be looked at as one generalized *thing?*

Musical language (I really can only speak for myself here) is *also* a battlefield, filled with so many embarrassing stumbling blocks, pitfalls, holding actions.

Also prone to lies, half truths, overstatements.

The dream of a common language.

"…there ought to be acknowledgment of the elementary fact that musical languages have to be transmitted, and a utopian vision of a common language that will allow music and musicians to speak…. Without this covertly implied and perhaps unrealizable ideal, music cannot move, loses one of its dialectical reasons for existing and drifts from one mannerism to the next. It's useful to search for things we know we can't find…"[37]

37. Luciano Berio, *Luciano Berio—Two Interviews,* trans. & ed. David Osmond-Smith (New York: Boyars, 1985).

The dream of a common language.

The search for something beyond taste (Cage).

Beating life into an exhausted language (sounds like Beckett).

Or…the drift from one mannerism to another.

At a certain point one of them chooses *you.*

Then you have to find a rationale—*a raison d'être.*

I found a kind of stumbling pitch idiocy—a teaching process whereby the piece teaches its component parts to itself. Little scraps treated. Horizontalized—verticalized. You can't move on until the piece is memorized. Written *x* number of times on the blackboard.

(thematizing stuck-ness—the banging of the head against the wall [traces of Cage and Beckett])

(a sometimes absurd emphasis on and stress of the individual pitch [traces of Webern and Feldman])

It's about patience, limits, pattern recognition, formal dialectic—play between repetition and change, similarity and difference—it's about memory and its inexorability. You'd *like* to forget.

Or remember.

It's about stuckness. Paralysis.

The spaces between the things said.

Ellipses.

Being a musician—being a composer —this arises out of all kinds of loves, desires, and drives. But one thing that should never be gainsaid—it also arises out of a basic mistrust of the descriptive and/or emotive power of verbal language.

One reason I am a musician comes out of a negative: my distrust of spoken/written language's ability to express whatever it is I want to 'say.'

Words—*mere* words. One person's opinion.

Heidegger comes to mind—the site of authentic language—the point where language breaks down. Babies and lovers.[38]

The idea of essence.

(A simple musical example—Monk. Pianistic language *depouillé* [stripped, skinned, divested or denuded of....])[39]

38. The reference to Heidegger and the site of authentic language comes from my class notes to Prof. Karsten Harries's seminar, "Language, Poetry, and Silence," given at Yale University, 1977-78.

39. For an example of recent interpretation of Monk's language, hear Jacky Terrasson's recording of "I Should Care" on *Reach* (Blue Note, 1996).

Pianistic language?

Musical language stripped.

And then ... the current uses to which Monk's music is put—for example, when *Young Lions of Jazz* pay homage. And then reinstate all the pianistic detritus that Monk expunged—constant arpeggios, rows of 16th notes smooth voice leading—a seamless carpet of harmony.

> Monk didn't exist only to create
> but also to destroy. Or at least erase.

It seems to me that to miss this point is to miss everything.

Lip service. Co-option.

(Can the sound of music be divorced from its project? *Should* it be?)

"Language remains unlost, in spite of everything."[40]

Historicity.

It's almost 50 years since Adorno's rejection of "poetry after Auschwitz."[41] And? It's a hoary classic. The whole vocabulary for challenging the idea that language *can* express—the whole project of "challenging signification"—has passed into history. A movement—a moment.

40. Paul Celan, "Bremen Speech, 1958," reprinted in Sander L. Gilman, *Jewish Self-Hatred: Anti-Semitism and the Hidden Language of the Jews* (Baltimore: Johns Hopkins University Press, 1986).

41. The concept of language's *challenge to signification* comes from Adorno; it is articulated in several places in his works; see, for example, his essay "Commitment," in *Aesthetics and Politics* (London: NLB, 1977).

And now?

"It seemed to me at the time an absolutely natural and crucial thing to say; and it hoped for disproof."[42]

And now?

42. George Steiner in an interview entitled "The Art of Criticism II," *Paris Review* 137, Winter 1995.

All those quotes: ideas about the end of art; the impossibility of expression; the breakdown of language....

(Is that a legacy or an inheritance? What is its claim? On me, on anything? I listen to a few of my pieces: *by the book; a hurtful angle; The Bosnians; Sarajevo...* I think they have something to do with all of this.)

—what a conceit. Language went on. And so what now? A dated avant-garde. What a screwed-up oxymoron.

AN APPROACH
TO GUITAR FINGERING

BILL FRISELL

Most of the method books I've seen for guitar deal mostly with fingerings based on staying in a particular 'position,' or, less frequently, moving up and down individual strings. Here are some exercises showing fingerings for step-wise passages that will allow notes to sustain simultaneously wherever possible. This is something that's done easily on the piano—by holding down the sustain pedal or simply holding down the fingers. Getting smaller intervals (major and minor 2nds) to sound together on the guitar doesn't come so easily. The examples that follow make ample use of open strings and harmonics—you won't find many symmetrical patterns here.

I find this way of thinking interesting because it opens possibilities for dissonant or closely voiced chords not so commonly used on the guitar. It also will give a very different articulation for melodic passages. Hopefully, what's here will lead you on to other possibilities. There are many.

Note:

Numbers above the notes refer to left hand fingers (1-4)

O = open string

Circled numbers below the note refer to the string

An X designates a harmonic; I've used only those found on the 12th, 7th, and 5th frets [Example 1]

All notes within a bracket should sustain together [Example 2]

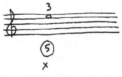

Example 1. (3rd finger, 5th string, harmonic on the 7th fret)

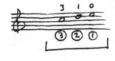

Example 2.

As a general rule, you should hold your fingers down until it's absolutely necessary to move, so that as much of what you're playing as possible will ring simultaneously.

Scales

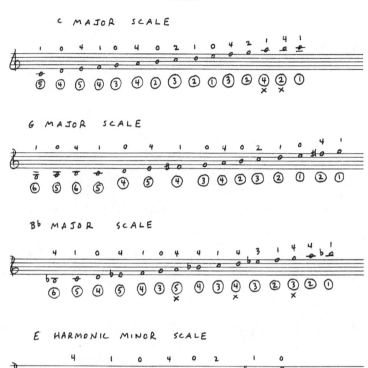

Chromatic Scale

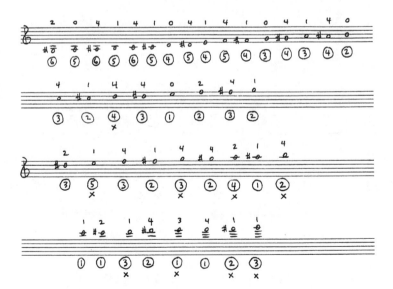

Exercises

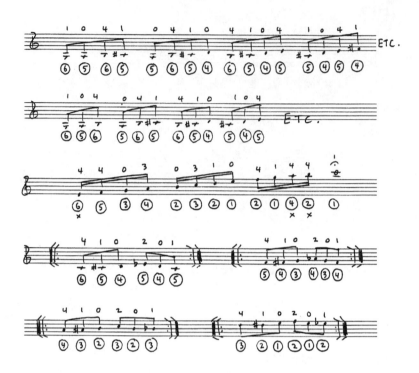

Etude #1

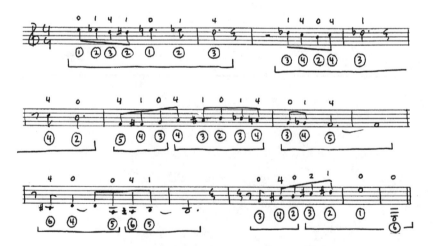

Etude #2

Etude #3

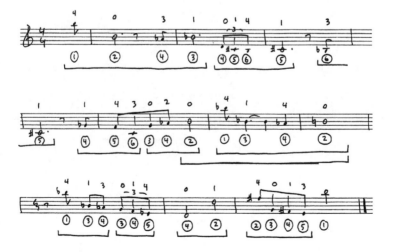

Etude #4

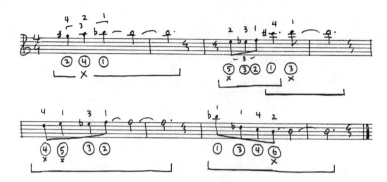

Etude #5

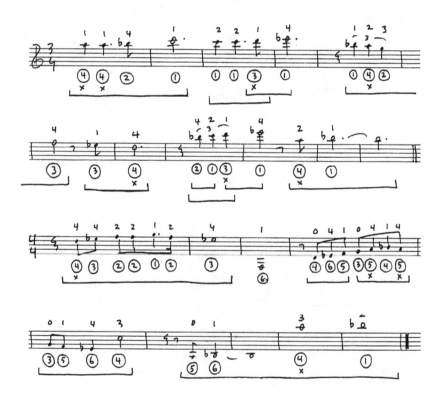

ONE/TWO

DAVID SHEA

The combination of one element with a second, or its other, does not create a synthesis or a unified whole, but rather a layering or network of connections creating a temporal space event of change. The whole, or the one and one that are two, is always larger than the combination of the individual things being combined. One thing and its opposite are not two but a network of connections that thought and language separate, and create difference between, in order to distinguish one from another.

Fragmentation and holism have their origins in thought. Distinctions of natural and technological, individual and unified, are born of the mind. These changes and connections of material orders exist in both limited time and space. For connection to exist there must be separation. Thought systems use these differences for pragmatic solutions to material needs and desires. That which lies outside limitation cannot be seen through thought alone nor can thought be perceived by using only its own limited mechanisms. A change in individual thought can change only a limited range of material form or energy. Those related to time, space, and concept.

Combination of one intention or desire with a second does not create a single synthesized intention, but rather a network of desire, connections that have no center or single point of origin. This combination is neither subjective nor objective unless the network is then formed as a thought-object and given a material role. The roles become useful and practical through the creation of an economy of these objects.

If you don't know where to put it down, don't pick it up.

—Tompkins Square Park chess player

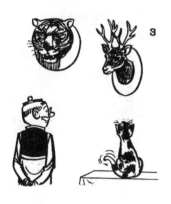

Limited by space a frog in a well cannot understand what is an ocean; limited by time, an insect in summer cannot understand what is ice.

—Chuang Tzu

The conditioning of each individual through genetic, cultural, religious, psychological, and linguistic information, forms a separate and totally unique thing. These things can be known because of their differences and their connections to things outside themselves. Each fragment has its own network with its own intentions, times, spaces, and histories. Conditioned experience creates this uniqueness, and therefore non-conditioned or non-mind experience can be said to be devoid of unique things or differences. If the state of non-mind and mind are considered to be two separate states, then the combination of the one with the other creates a third state that is neither a new synthetic whole nor a direct result of intentional thought.

How can a thinking creator realize these combinations in the form of practical works? First, a separate or individual thing must be understood to be a network in and of itself. A single culture or language, a single piece of music or economic principle, is composed of smaller parts that are collections of networks and are connected to external and recursive references. All writing, history, music, and thought are connected to all other materials through their difference. Each arrangement is recognized by its difference from another and each new combination creates a network of new combinations. The work of composing is not one of invention but of arrangement. All materials being both unique and fundamentally connected, the strategy and art of connecting forms creative work.

These changes and combination works are being made at an increasing speed by many people in many areas, through the use of things external to their own conditioning and minds, by utilizing particular technological machines. Computers are easily performing simple functions at a speed much faster than the human mind. The creation of works that combine machine and mind is occurring in a new territory that is only recently possible. These machines, though produced by thought, are independent of it. They make possible a type of thought process that is external to the mind. Technology is a territory of pure reference. It provides total connection to thought without a direct will or mind of its own. This combination of technology with intuitive and rational thought is only one example of recent change. Many other examples can be seen in works which combine old world and new world cultures, mysticism and scientific thought, Eastern and Western traditions and methodologies, that have been, historically, in opposition. The multiple purposes of the arranged elements create a layered work that is the product of a single creator and a network separate from its origin of intention. The individual work is connected to things outside itself always pointing to external references. An obvious example would be a work that was made only from references. However, when performed or communicated the piece comes in contact with a conditioned perceiver. It then becomes a theater of memory and direct experience.

The principles I have written here are deliberately general because I believe that the generative forces behind combination works apply to any area or discipline. I am a composer of music but my works are attempts at musical solutions to general issues. Specific parallels in new combinations of western medical science and traditional eastern healing, Hong Kong cinema, traditional and modern political economies, and many other areas point to issues that I consider central to my work now. These combinations produce works that are radically individual, nationalist, and separatist with the understanding that each individual is in fact not individual at all; that each separate element is defined and connected to that which is outside itself; that all argument is based on fundamental agreement, all separation based on fundamental connection. The work of arranging consists then of composing a form in which these layered differences can become practical pieces.

Architectural composition primarily calls for a happy combining of similarity and difference. —Feng Shui lecture

When fighting with enemies if you get to feeling snarled up and are making no progress, you toss your mood away and think in your heart that you are starting everything anew. As you get the rhythm you discern how to win. This is "becoming new." Anytime you feel tension and friction building up between yourself and others, if you change your mind at that very moment, you can prevail by taking advantage of radical difference. This is "becoming new."

—Miyamoto Musashi, *The Book of Five Rings*

I now would like to turn to the ways in which I have approached these questions in my work, and in particular the pieces that combine sampled material with live playing and the use of multi-method collage structure. Each work, in the past few years, has been focused on combining recorded sources, records, cds, etc., played on electronic instruments with traditional electric and acoustic instruments. The first pieces of collage were made with sources found on tapes of prerecorded music with text, video, and various objects. Usually they were performed by simply placing the materials in the same place at the same time. None of the materials were directly created by myself and the actions were usually performed by others. the purpose was, at some level, to remove myself from the process and allow the materials to change in some way, free of my control and conditioned intentions. Lacking in these works was my own personality and a connection to spontaneous action and physicality. I found this in free improvisation of solo vocal work. The voice was a physical, personal instrument and the music was rarely planned before a concert exploring both my own conditioned habits and intuitive changes.

When an adversary wields his sword in a large rhythm, you should use yours with a small rhythm. If an adversary uses a small rhythm, you should use a large rhythm. Here too the idea is to use your sword in such a way that the rhythm is incongruous with that of your opponent.

—Miyamoto Musashi, *The Book of Five Rings*

Knowing that the being of any form is created on the basis of non-being, an architect acquires a maximum freedom of expression. —Feng Shui lecture

ll _ h_ o_ _ _ ↔ _ _≺ _ _o_ ↦ _h_ _

All right you guys pair up in twos and threes. —Yogi Berra

The development of my compositional methods never has been based on musical questions alone. the choices have been shaped by practical situations. Questions like: how do I eat? what is possible in my living situation? what are the economics of the materials used? how can I remain healthy making this work? and many other pragmatic, religious, political, historical, and personal questions, have been just as important as questions of compositional method, tonality, serialism, chance, improvisation, collage, classicism, silence, or noise. Particular choices of musical style or method in each individual work have changed according to the conditions. Musical virtuosity is often important in some works while in others it's a handicap. A single piece may employ one method or the methods may change as fast as possible.

One area of music in which I've seen composers dealing with these issues is that of the film score. In the history of film scoring, musical solutions to problems have often been created through practical limitations. Composers encountered dramatic situations with limited resources and time, in contexts that they often did not have a hand in creating or controlling. The works were made with musical questions, economic considerations, and the issues of the particular film in mind. Only later was the core separated from part of its source and allowed to become an independent work. the intention of the final work was multiple and individual. Any style or method might be used to score scenes, and choices changed with respect to the conditions of the musical whole and the action or psychology of the images. I am, in particular, referring to soundtracks of the American and European cinema circa 1930-80, since that is what I've been familiar with.

Another time period that was influential were the years when hip-hop (rap) music and house music changed the role of the club DJ from a record selector to an active mixing musician with a personal style and musical techniques. Here the composer of the final product was multiple in a unique sense. Pre-recorded music of many styles and time periods were (re)composed by a mixer performer where the original source material could be primary or abstract sound source material in a continuous mix. The turntable was used by composer-mixers who were not, usually, motivated by theoretical explorations but

The cinema is both a window and a mirror. The window looks out on the real world both directly (documentation) and vicariously (adaptation). The mirror reflects what the director feels about the experience.

This statement is false.
This statement is true.

—Classical paradox

When five people would stand over the chess board in this park, one of them would see the next move, one wouldn't see a damn thing, one would see a mate in five, and one would be smiling about something he thought he saw but was wrong about. Everybody had a different experience with this game even though they were looking at the same thing. This I like very much.

—Washington Square Park chess player

Often when two things
seem
opposed, like east
and west, it is found that
what is lacking
in one system is
perfectly supplied by the other.

—Lao Tzu

through the practicality of street knowledge, the logic of club culture, and the limitations of the dance floor. The actions of playing or mixing music created or recorded at another time or era is actively paralleled by people who make works, in many areas, combining their traditional cultures with technological pop culture. The social context shifted for me when the experimental vocal music combined with the old school hip-hop and funk music I had grown up with. Because of my living situation at the time, I connected with many MCs (rappers) in my neighborhood and used my vocal sounds to play beats for their raps. I began working as a 'human beat box' in hip-hop groups and I soon realized that the direction the DJs were taking the music was nearly identical, in theory, with what many experimentalists had been doing for the last fifty years, and were also similar to the cassette collages of my own work. Many DJs at that time used scratching and noise techniques, a wide range of sources, and would play with tempo shifts, in subtle and sophisticated ways within the restraint of the beats. The idea seemed to be that the records were the musical material but the mixer was the composer. I then began using turntables both as a DJ in dance clubs and for experimental solo works and improvisations. The connection for me was clear. The techniques and instruments would remain the same, allowing the social and musical contexts to be the defining factor. What one situation lacked, the other provided. The club musics were about repetition, subtle variation, and a direct connection to audience response. The improvised playing was about non-repetition, constant invention, radical changes, and independence from judgment. The differences were extreme in the social situations, audiences, money and physical spaces, yet the combination of the two created a balance for me.

In order to work on this balance more directly in the compositions, I began making works with turntables and samplers. I wanted to work directly and accurately with phrases and sounds found on records. Pieces that layered sources with the changes focused on the combinations of the materials themselves and less on the manipulation of those sources. The sampling keyboard was the perfect instrument for these works. The pieces combined sound effects, sampled records, concrete sources, etc., and were often made for theater or dance. Since material and process were primary, the sources were taken from a large number of styles, time periods, and cultures. Information was fluid and the structures equally changeable. The sampler is able to record a large amount of material which can be played back on keyboards. The keyboard provides the triggers for the recorded sounds in the sampler's computer memory. This combined the electronic mixing-playing with varying levels of keyboard technique. The samples were fixed fragments that would be played back, as they were recorded, to create collages of layered individual materials. The use of the sampling keyboard led to works that combined the technique of triggering samples with traditional keyboard technique and later with ensembles of live players.

The combination of the one with the other, the sampling and electronic mixing/playing with combinations of live players, has been the focus of my work of the last few years. Some large scale pieces have been sound cinema collage pieces and some explorations of the playing techniques of samplers. Each work is structured as a field of connections, combinations, and references.

I believe that a radical, violent, yet organic process of change forms this period in history where neither the old world nor new world cultures can survive without the other. The principles that generate pieces of music are the same as those that are not music. Culture is, at any point in time, fundamentally connected on every level. If music can express and explore psychological, spiritual, and emotional connections that can complement spoken and written language, then music can be an essential part of understanding

The way to weaken is to strengthen.

If an adversary is positioned such that the tip of his sword is facing you, strike as he raises it. When you intend to strike an opponent, let him hit at you. As long as your adversary lashes out at you, you have as good as struck him.

—Miyamoto Musashi, *The Book of Five Rings*

these changes and point to practical ways of creating balance. I have avoided writing specifically about musical issues in isolation in this work. This is never how I have thought of or made music, so it made no sense to write about it that way. Perhaps future writings will be concentrate more on aspects of musical structure, issues raised by sampling as a technique, and on other things such as memory theater performance. However, if so, I hope those writings will be read, and my musical works will be heard, in the light of the whole I have presented here.

This is called going into the mind to see the mind.

—The Diamond Sutra

NOTES FROM
A TRANS-CULTURAL DIARY

MIYA MASAOKA

The KOTO-monster (Japanese Frankenstein, mutant godzilla, deformed hybrid) has its foot in three millennia. The ancient hollow-bodied wooden instrument of Japan is wired to a Sensorlab, a microcomputer that reads switches, pots, pressure pads and other sensors, and translates that information into midi data, while the accompanying SPIDER control language lets the user program multiple, dynamically re-configurable instruments based on a single hardware core. Koto-monster combines live sampling, ultra sound rings, and various digital signal processing. These components are patched, sewn, soldered, and glued together to create a new sonic creature (or monster) that can generate sounds that wed the human brain, acoustic technology, analog and, of these the most primitive, digital technology.

Why should we, as post-contemporary composers, be concerned with such worldly and out-of-our-discipline notions? How is social context relevant to music-making, and has technology shifted the balance of power? How should we as artists view the commodification of our work and hence of ourselves, and what can we do to subvert the flow of the status quo? How do our musical raw materials, of sound and its metaphorical and phenomenal opposite, silence, position themselves in this meta-narrative?

I am a kotoist and a composer, simultaneously navigating the varied worlds of Gagaku (Japanese court music), jazz, improvisation, new music and electronic music. Informed and inspired by a wide spectrum of musics and traditions, I've performed with Pharoah Sanders, whose music and philosophy is driven by a deep spirituality; the Berkeley Symphony; the Cecil Taylor Orchestra; L. Subramaniam; ROVA Saxophone Quartet; Steve Coleman; virtuoso Indian violinist Rohan de Saram of the Arditti String Quartet, who taught me bowing techniques for the koto; saxophonist Francis Wong and bassist Mark Izu, leaders in Asian-American jazz; George Lewis, innovative composer and trombonist; Fred Frith; Henry Kaiser; and my esteemed Gagaku teacher, Suenobu Togi.

When I was a child, my cousin, Midori, who was five years older than me, played the koto, and at Christmas time I received beautiful pictures of her in her kimono, dressed perhaps for a recital. As a youngster, I would hear Japanese music at church bazaars and at Buddhist funerals, and at home from my grandpa's singing old Japanese folksongs when he lived with us. In my twenties, I began studying traditional koto with Shimaoka Sensei, and eventually I learned other styles of koto-playing. The koto has an understated but crucial role in the Gagaku orchestra, and I became fascinated with this ancient music. Notated Gagaku scores date back to the seventh and eighth-century Tang Dynasty in China, a vital period when musicians from Persia, India, Japan, Korea, Vietnam, and China performed and improvised together. My Gagaku teacher, Suenobu Togi, traces his lineage through more than one thousand years of Imperial Court musicians. It was a member of the Togi family that first broke the tradition of teaching Gagaku only to men and began accepting women, as well as non-court lineage people, as students.

- 1928: My grandfather is standing on the pier at Fukuoka, Japan, and wondering if he should emigrate to Brazil or to the United States.

Over the years, I have moved gradually from playing traditional koto, under my first teacher, Seiko Shimaoka, to developing my own approach to technique and vocabulary. The transition was at first tenuous, and I often feared that Shimaoka would attend one of my concerts of music outside the traditional koto sphere. While she never did so, at one lesson she mentioned that any disobedient students could be expelled from the school and have their costly certificates revoked if the teacher so requested. Feeling vaguely guilty, I immediately apologized for any potential problem I might be creating.

- 1969: I'm eleven years old, and the doctor is wrapping plaster on my right arm to make a cast; I have fractured my arm hitting a white boy who called me "Jap."
- Trans-sounding, transcending, transmitting, transducing, trans-ethnological soundings.
- *Sounds, sounds like, sounds true, sounds good, sounds funny, sounds like my mother used to make, sounds like that old commercial for cigarettes (remember when they had commercials for cigarettes?), sounds like chinese pop, sounds sexy, sounds like i might get the gig, sounds like you just made that up, sounds like he might have hit her, sounds like they're*

losing, sounds official, sounds like a good idea, sounds like shit, sound advice, sounds awful, sounds like it's going to be a tough year, sounds like you'll get through it, sounds like my cat is throwing up, sounds like a gun or firecrackers? sounds like you have a leak somewhere, sounds like that girl likes you, sounds like spring, sounds like you're hungry, sounds like she lost interest, sounds like we could have used another rehearsal, sounds better that way, sounds like a ring modulator, sounds too digital, sounds distorted, sounds like that.

• 1884: Capitalist powers in Europe sat around a conference table and carved an entire continent with a multiplicity of peoples, cultures, and languages into colonies (Ngugi wa Thiong'o, *Decolonizing the Mind*).

Sounds. After years of playing the piano, it was a revelation to play a stringed instrument, especially one where the player had direct physical contact with the string, such as the Japanese zither, the koto. On a piano, the piano key is pressed, which moves a hammer which hits the strings, and thus the player's relationship to the actual string is a few steps removed. The inner workings or guts of the piano would be exposed without the protective coverings of the piano lid. Hidden under it, kept from view of the player and the audience, are the internal strings. But with the koto, my hands were touching, grabbing, tugging, bending, pulling, pressing, twisting and scratching. There was a sensuality to this that was open, exposed and vulnerable. Unlike the strings of the piano, one string of the koto could be worked, manipulated to express something very raw, to emote, to sound like a human voice. The production of sounds and timbres became an increasingly effective method for creating music.

Sounds in and of themselves. Can sounds exist in the Cageian ideal? At a brief yet finite moment it is possible for sounds just to be sounds, frequencies undulating in space, devoid of reference, cultural meaning or codes. Kant, although speaking of words, talked about the inability to know a thing in and of itself, apart from the world. Applied to the sonic realm, social context and the external world asserts its relevancy, and continues to frame the context within which sound is produced.

Working with editing software, one begins to learn how many milliseconds worth of an increment of a sound are required for the sound to become a recognizable note, word, or phrase; it's like playing in the game in which one just briefly touches the needle to a vinyl record and then tries to identify the piece from that micro-fragment. Discovering how sounds at the most basic level are organized is one of the challenges of composing. After a few seconds, the accumulation of increments of sound becomes recognizable as belonging to a particular instrument or instruments, and a few seconds more reveals whether or not a particular style or perhaps composer is being interpreted. At this point, a tradition, a particular culture, or perhaps an idiomatic style is referenced and located. The act of music-making, of reaching into a deep place where the muse resides, has a profundity far beyond certain aspects of our individual subjective selves, such as what our backgrounds are, how we grew up, or our ethnicity.

As composers we feel that our work transcends class and culture. Our concern is with creating and mediating sounds, manipulating, re-configuring, developing, re-organizing sounds, ideas, motives, and if accumulated sounds eventually express a culture, we become by extension not only manipulators of sounds, but manipulators of cultures and ideas as well. One thinks of Bela Bartok, adding to his already eccentric habits and, in an expression of nationalist sentiment, wearing his traditional Hungarian garb around the house, perhaps to inspire his reworking and reconfiguring of Hungarian music, interweaving it with a more northern European tradition to create a unique voice in the ethnographical landscape of the early 1900s. Or one thinks of the *Tape Beatles,* appropriating sound bites and thereby creating new audio works, works that consider and value the ideas created by the sounds as well as the sounds themselves. In this post-contemporary world of composing, the borders of sound cultures are blurring, and the interpenetration of a multiplicity of sounds/ cultures necessitates new thinking on ethnicity, nationalism, appropriation, and identification.

• 1650: Father Gregory Gracie felt that he detected Semitic blood in the Indians of the New World because, like the Jews, "they are lazy, they do not believe in the miracles of Jesus Christ, and they are ungrateful to the Spaniards for all the good they have done them" (Eduardo Galeano, *Open Veins of Latin America*).

Having your own sound. In the world of jazz and improvised music, musicians are concerned with attaining their own sound, symbolizing attainment of a personhood, an identity. Traditionally the notion of having one's own sound has been imbued with meaning—it meant you had arrived artistically, having achieved a certain passage to an inner circle. This now was your identifiable sound, and having your sound was like having your voice, allowing for an assertion of spiritual maturity, of personal history and experiences. You were no longer a student or imitator, though maybe people imitated your sound. Charlie Parker, in his famous quote, "If you haven't lived it, it won't come out of your horn," exemplifies the notion of one's life experience as a prerequisite for this kind of making music.

• The notion of shame and perception of outsiders on the the family, and by extension, on other Japanese has been one aspect of Japanese culture that has been successfully transplanted to Japanese communities in America. It is increasingly embarrassing that the most famous Japanese in diaspora is a repressive president of a South American country.

The history of Black music is a history of embattlement in a hostile, racist environment, and the term "jazz" came to signify the struggle for freedom and dignity both phenomenally and metaphorically. The development and success of the Black Liberation Movement inspired other minority groups in the 1960s to become activist, asserting a new sense of political understanding and power, and employing new language to describe new identity; thus the terms Asian-American, Chicano, and Native-Americans are replacing terms with derogatory associations, such as Negro, Mexican-American, Oriental, and Indians. Afrological influence has permeated American musical culture, particularly in those musics involved with improvisation in its many streams in America.

The value placed on individuality there is in direct contrast to what occurs in traditional Japanese music where the teaching methods encourage the students to closely imitate the master teacher in both sound and gestures, a method which insures that the music is passed down and preserved intact. Refinement, not innovation, is the goal.

• 1959: Gagaku (Japanese court music) is presented publicly for the first time outside Japan (though Gagaku had been performed in Buddhist rituals at Temples in the United States since the 1930s, these were not public performances); seven years later, in 1966, Gagaku was taught for the first time in a secular setting outside Japan.
• "The only relationship that Japanese understand is that of father and child. He has become the father of Manzanar. The people are his children." (From an interview in 1944 with Ralph P. Merritt, Director of the Manzanar Project; Manzanar was one of nine internment camps in which Japanese-Americans were held during WWII.)
• 1944: My mother is fourteen years old and lives in a horse stall; the walls are papered with horse excrement; the lines in the mess hall stretch interminably; the food is making everyone ill.

Silence. As a structural device for composition. Whether in phenomenal or in metaphorical descriptions, silence, *Ma,* as space between the notes, is a distinguishing element of Japanese music, and it has its roots in the spiritual and philosophical premises of Buddhism. Consider the large, empty space of a Zen painting on a large scroll and with only a small boat in a tiny corner of the painting. This "one-corner style" originated with Bayan (Ma Yuan, fl. 1175-1225) and is associated with the Japanese painters' "thrifty brush" tradition of using the least possible number of lines or strokes to represent forms on paper or silk, a tradition very much in accord with the spirit of Zen. This minimalism is evident also in Gagaku, where, using the minimum of sound and stroke, restraint on the part of all the players yields the maximum impact on the listener. In Gagaku, the concept of *Ma* is that of the essence of a space or interval or emptiness between objects. The very strong emphasis placed upon this *Ma* (*kanji*) is an important aesthetic principle in all of the Japanese arts.

The unspoken, negative space. The non-event, like *itcho* in *Noh* music. If a Kangen piece, for example, consists of 4 beat measures, the interval or *Ma* between each measure is slightly longer than one beat—exactly how long is determined by the musicians *as they play* (to quote Masao Kodani). Since all the musicians face forward, no visual signals can be given. The only way for them to play at exactly the same time is for the orchestra to breathe as one living body. When this *Ma* is achieved, the effect is remarkable. The melody seems suspended for an eternal moment, like the silent cresting of a wave before it crashes on the shore. It is a free rhythm whose interval or *Ma* is determined by the breath of the group.

- 1979: the Buddhist Ministeries of Oakland, California, decide to replace live Gagaku music with Western organ music.

Reverend Masao Kodani, a Japanese Zen Buddhist minister, sits at his desk at Senshin Temple in Little Tokyo, Los Angeles, and speaks quietly. He says that Gagaku is the music that precedes all other Japanese music and by hundreds of years. The Kamakura period was its heyday, but at the end of that period the influence of Samurai methods of teaching took over the country and imposed a very different form of discipline on the arts. All this and much more was described by Reverend Kodani in our interview.

Interview with Reverend Masao Kodani

Masaoka: Could you talk a little bit about the older Confucian theory that if music is harmonious then there is order and balance in the Universe?

Kodani: The Confucian view was not very mystical at all, it was very practical. The five notes of the scale corresponded to the five virtues or moralities. If a cultivated person learned music, then they were also learning morality and ethics, and through that, society would be ordered. It had nothing to do with the mystical power of music, but everything to do with Confucian principles. Music embodied Confucian principles, and by learning it one incorporated morality into one's being. Confucius would say that music is the most important part of government, and I think that's probably true.

M: What is the role of Gagaku in your worship, and how is Gagaku incorporated into your worship at your temple?

K: Gagaku has always been a part of Buddhist temple music, especially in those schools that have ties to the Imperial family. It's used mainly as orchestral music during part of the ritual; some of it is played with the chanting, but generally it's used with the ritual.

M: Have you ever used organ music in your worship as well?

K: Yes, but I don't particularly care for organ music. Organ music is the perfect Christian music. It has this real vertical kind of feel, whereas Gagaku is the perfect Buddhist music, because of the horizontal feel. Organ music soars, it goes up, up to God. Gagaku music is very earth-bound, it has no sense of soaring, it's there, it doesn't go anywhere. You can walk in at anytime of a Gagaku piece, at the beginning or at the end, and it's basically the same. It's just there.

M: How did you learn to play Gagaku?

K: I learned it in Kyoto Temple as part of my training for ritual.

M: Then you came back to Los Angeles to form a group?

K: Togi Sensei was teaching at UCLA, and I asked him if he would teach me, and he said, "yes." So we formed a group. Togi's attitude represents the view of the Imperial Household, that is the very practical side of Gagaku. Gagaku is the only musical tradition in Japan that does not use Samurai disciplinary means. You don't sit straight and listen to your teacher. You could sprawl out

159

on the floor and learn it if you wanted to. It was taught before the rise of the Samurai, and it is the only music to survive the Heian Period. It's very loose, very relaxed; it's very unmilitary. It was only the rise of the military in Japan where you have this strictness, rigidity, where straight posture is important, etc. Gagaku is very relaxed in that regard, even the attitude of the playing. In Gagaku, they kept the tradition of the East Indians, of sitting Indian style. The Heian courtiers were relaxed, they just crossed their legs and and played.

M: What is the difference between Gagaku performed in Shinto Temples and Gagaku in Buddhist Temples?

K: Kagura is the music of Shinto. (Kagura and Gagaku have an overlapping tradition, and share a number of common songs in the repertoire.) The attitude is a little bit different. In Shinto, Gagaku is the music that communicates to the gods. In that sense there is mysticism associated with the music that doesn't exist for Imperial musicians.

M: Often Japanese musicians speak of *jo ha kyu* (literally this translates as 'prelude,' 'breaking away,' or 'hurried') when talking about theory. How do you interpret *jo ha kyu* in Gagaku?

K: Jo ha kyu is part of a larger piece. Usually when you play Gagaku you are playing part of a larger piece (the rest has been lost over time). Compared to Western music, there is a very subtle change in tempo. The difference between fast and running would be minor in Western music. What is fast in Gagaku is still very slow. In the standard Imperial Gagaku, all the mysticism is absent. There is none; it's like the average Western musician playing orchestral music. There is an artistic quality about it, as in Western music, but they wouldn't talk about the mysticism with respect to it. The Japanese are far more practical and down to earth than the Indian Buddhists.

Christian churches go down the aisle and then go up (to God). Buddhism has always been horizontal, it never tries to leave the ground. It is a union between Reality and the Earth.

M: Could you talk about the theory of the modes and their associations?

K: Certain modes are associated with seasons, and they have a certain seasonal mood to them, so when you transcribe certain modes into other modes, the feeling changes. In the old days, the season dictated what was played. In the early period, Gagaku was played on the first day of the New Year. It was not necessarily played for an audience, it was played to align everyone (in the village and at court) in an harmonious way. The music was symbolic of this harmony.

M: I understand Gagaku was also played at funerals with particular modes for funerals.

K: It was played at court functions, state funerals, and things like that.

M: Could you talk a little bit about the significance of the more free playing at the beginning and end of the pieces.

K: Togi Sensei said that initially the freer playing at the beginning was just when musicians would be warming up in a loose way, and it later became formalized, to introduce the main notes of that piece. But originally it was just them tuning up.

M: I have some books that talk about a member of the Togi family who was the first Imperial musician to announce that Gagaku would now accessible to anybody, both in the teaching and performing, when before there were strict laws that said only Imperial musicians could learn Gagaku.

K: Yeah, that was Togi's grandfather. The Togi family traces its lineage to the first Emperor of China, Chi Huan Ji.

M: So in the Tang Dynasty, early Gagaku was also used for entertainment.

K: What we have today in terms of orchestras, performing, say, as entertainment at the White House, that was what Gagaku was like in the Tang dynasty. There were many drinking songs in the Gagaku repertoire, and they were actually used as background music for drinking fests.

M: And in Japan it was used at Sumo matches and horse racing events.

K: Whatever the court activity was, it was the official background music. It was like Muzak. Like Handel's *Water Music* to accompany the King boating down the Thames. Gagaku was used in a similar way. Parties, receptions or whatever. Gagaku was just like Western classical music, and it represented all of Asia at one time. Only it died out, except in Japan and to a certain extent Korea, whereas Western classical music has survived. When I was in Japan there were only two Gagaku societies outside the Imperial household, and now there are twenty or thirty, so Gagaku is experiencing a minor boom right now.

• Togi Suenobu, my Gagaku master, an Imperial Court musician who traces his family lineage more than 1,200 years, for many years taught the music and dance at the University of Los Angeles. He has since returned to Japan. A number of Gagaku ensembles exist outside Japan, and they all can be traced directly to Togi Suenobu.

- October 11, 1906: the San Francisco Board of Education directs school principals to send "all Chinese, Japanese, and Korean children to the Oriental School" (*Strangers From a Different Shore*).

Conducting the Chi: Masaoka Orchestra

- RECONSTRUCTING CONDUCTIVE IDEAS AND MOVEMENTS FOR SOUND INSTRUCTION AND INSPIRATION
- Clear systems for composing and conducting

Gradually I became inspired to develop a conducting method based on some of the things I had learned over the years, working with a cultural crosscut of conducting traditions from Gagaku and East Indian music, from working with Cecil Taylor, and from observing the methods of Butch Morris and John Zorn.

The impetus for founding the orchestra was based on the desire to have a hybridized, inter-cultural, electronic-friendly, intermedia orchestra that could perform my compositions. Having my own orchestra allows me to develop specific techniques involving the dialectic of composition and improvisation, and it allows me to explore conduction as a means of creating a new orchestral concept in contemporary music.

Gagaku conducting is unseen by the audience but it is essential to the music making of the orchestra, and it is one of the most intriguing aspects of the music. The conductor, or master, sits directly on the floor facing the ensemble. All four limbs are in use, one arm directing the strings, the foot pounding out thuds to the taiko drummer, and another hand bringing in the winds. With the Gagaku orchestra all sitting in cross-legged position, the conductor has full range of sight even seated on the floor.

As Reverend Kodani pointed out, Gagaku, though extremely formalized, is relaxed in comparison to other, later traditional Japanese arts. Before the advent of Bushido, the samurai and militaristic feudalist ideology, the-Heain-styled kimonos were worn loose, without the rigid obi. And the teaching of the tradition was undertaken with informality, not only for Gagaku musicians, but for all players of instruments such as the koto and shamisen as well.

So I'm watching conductors and thinking that their visual presence serves to inspire the musicians to play well and with fresh ideas. What impact could a conductor have on the collective *chi* of an orchestra, approaching the orchestra as a single body, a body whose meridians and yin/yang might be balanced and manipulated. If the original idea of yin and yang is expressed in the shaded and sunlit parts of a landscape and these were the material of agrarian China, what about dynamics and parameters of sound as material for contemporary applications? How is silence and sound reflected in this balance?

—Movements start from the sacral area. The conductor is to keep the sacral area "quiet and firm."
—Movements are to be carried out in a circular direction. Although the arms and legs appear to move "angularly" in their sockets, in actual fact they describe either circles or semicircles as they swivel in their joints.
—Whenever possible, the conductor is to exercise FULL CONCENTRATION and produce GRADUAL INTENSIFICATION, although it is permissible to break this for the sake of unpredictability.

There are numerous ways to incorporate movements into conducting. Already existing hand and arm signals—for example, two hands cupped together forming an O with thumbs together and other fingers touching might be imposed on the circular movement as a signal to play more consonantly, listen to each other, match pitches.

Conducting in a moving semi-circle makes for greater visibility for the musicians, too.

Not all tai'chi movements are smooth; it is a martial art, and it includes sharp, energetic, and angular movements as well fluid ones. These movements may be used to indicate more percussive action by the musicians.

• 1997: My master teacher of Gagaku is working in a major Shinto Shrine in Tokyo, performing Gagaku music for corporate executives who hope it will bless their business deals or to assure that their new cars won't be lemons.

Cecil Taylor's conducting cannot be separated from his notation—letters in space on the paper. He conducts from wherever he happens to be on the stage, sometimes in back of the musicians, sometimes among or off to the side, a roving conductor. It was in the rehearsals rather than in the actual performance that I was better able to understand his compositions. For instance, he would tell the louder saxophones to stop playing so the strings could be heard, producing something like an inverse of conduction, telling people to stop playing, rather that telling people to begin. Taylor was instructing people to go out; he was creating a negative space in the overall sound canvas.

Butch Morris was in Amsterdam during the period I had a residency there, so we got together for lunch at an Italian restaurant on the Rembrant-plein. He was showing me his conduction instructions and various commands to elicit memory, rhythm, looping, sustain, etc. He talked about trying to get funding for the ensembles, how it was difficult to keep it going, how he always had to do everything himself—the writing of the music, the producing, the concerts.

As Butch Morris pointed out, Louis Andriessen had started out with his own band on the street, and many years later he turned to "scored" composer so that he could write for other (or any) ensembles. Both these composers had worked from the ground up (had 'paid their dues') and the thought gave me a grave sense of the amount of work and perseverance that is necessary if one is to have one's work performed by one's own orchestra.

We took a cab to the Icebreaker, and I left Butch there. He said his brother was playing with Arthur Blythe that night at the Bimhuis, and he would get me in if I wanted to go.

• My relatives in Fukuoka, Japan, take me to a temple, and the courtyard is filled with trees. Little rolls of paper wrapped in ribbons are tied daintily to the fragile branches. What's in the rolls of paper? Prayers faxed by students from all over Japan praying for a good grade on their exams.

Improvising with a symphony

Performing with the Rias-Orchestra in Berlin with the Berlin Opera afforded me the opportunity to be conducted by Dr. L. Subramaniam and to observe his hybrid conducting techniques, which combine Indian tabla counting systems with more standard Western conducting.

The Torrance Symphony conductor had a Dr. Jekyll and Mr. Hyde quality, depending on whether there were problems with the orchestra or not. Composer Mark Izu's score allowed me to be a principal performer, and for large sections I was to improvise with the symphony. We stayed in Torrance, California, for a week rehearsing the piece with the conductor, the symphony, and with the narrator, Brenda Wong Aoki. Unamplified, I had room in both quiet sections and raucous, louder sections to really play. After years of improvising in so many contexts, this situation felt very natural, and in many ways it was much easier than improvising for long periods in a duet situation.

India

On the way to the rehearsal at the Bangalore School of Music from my hotel, I saw an ox sleeping on the sidewalk. In the next block an enormous cow was eating from a garbage can. I came across a tent city with hundreds of low canvas tents pitched on sand. The tents were of various colors—pale yellow, beige, ivory—the colors of sandstone. The children were dressed in cotton rags of muslim with bits of cloth wrapping their hair. The women wore long saris of sandstone-hued muslim, and everyone's skin was covered with the dust-like sand, everything drifting in one color.

At the concert hall, a woman in a blue sari gave me a sandalwood necklace. Its scent was dusky and soon after I noticed that every place had its identifying aroma, affecting my moods and thoughts. Science and magic may exist harmoniously side by side; there are gurus who materialize stones from flowers, and physicians wear them around their neck.

Dr. Subramaniam conducted the Indian musicians with a precise delicacy. I detected movement of the fingers, seeming to utilize the techniques of counting the complex tabla rhythms of classical Indian music. This was combined with Western style conducting. For days I watched and played in response to Dr. Subramaniam's conducting, and the delicacy of the movements made a lasting impression on me, long after the final sounds of our playing on the stage had evaporated.

The day after the concert, I went out into street in front of the hotel and hailed one of the motorized rickshaws that run on two pistons, like a glorified lawnmower.

At a nearby temple near Mysore, a snake charmer was playing a double-reeded wind instrument with a gourd as a sound chamber. Fascinated, I watched and listened to the various snake-charmer musicians gracing the foot of the Hindu shrine. While the tradition of snake charming is not Hindu, its roots are nonetheless to be found in Indian mysticism, stemming from the desire to interact and control nature, symbolized by the cobra. There was a little girl with a snake who played when her mother grew tired and took a break. Only one man had a cobra, others had another kind of snake. You could see the fangs had been removed. The music had a quality unlike any other, incense was burning and little children were begging for rupees for the musicians. As I gave a handful to one little girl, three more children came running up, then nine, it could go on and on, in an endless need for rupees.

Being a center in India, Bangalore is famous for its technology, but it is also famous for its spirituality. Famous gurus with enormous powers are pictured every ten feet; their photographs are hung above the drinking fountain in the silk shop, above the cash register in the restaurant, beside the women's restroom in the train station. Their presence is felt everywhere and by everybody, and this omnipresence is even stronger than that of the iconography of the cross, since the image of these faces belonging to real individuals evoked specific and immediate presences.

An evening with LaMonte Young

LaMonte Young's tendril beard accentuated the quick angles of his head movements, turning to the left, then to the right.

It was two in the morning, and LaMonte was playing old cassettes for Lucas Ligeti and myself. We were listening to one of his first recordings, of "All the Things You Are," in which he plays (with considerable chops) soprano saxophone, and Billy Higgins is heard on drums. Then fifties bebop lines were folded into another musical space as he played his "Trio For Strings." I was transfixed and deeply inspired; I could hear those string sounds in my work with bowed koto. The sounds were sparse, and floated in space.

A walk with Rohan de Saram

Someone is rolling a $125,000 son-of-Stradivarius cello down Shattuck Avenue in Berkeley, where muggings are daily occurrences. Rohan de Saram, cellist of the Arditti String Quartet, is in town and has been showing me new bowing techniques involving harmonics, how to work the nodes, the use of various pressures, how to utilize the sides of the bow string, techniques for ideal vibrato, ways of bouncing the bow, etc. We were to perform a concert with Bruce Ackley of ROVA Saxophone Quartet, bassist Stefano Scodanibbio, and Rohan was staying at my house for a few days. During this time, he gave me several lessons on bow technique and demonstrated on koto the most effective bow hand position for the koto. He was very comfortable bowing the koto, and it looked as if he had been doing it his whole life. My koto-monster was given yet another way in which to sing, scream, whine and bellow.

MUSIC SUFFERS

EYVIND KANG

Music isn't dead but held captive. They only allow a peep at music, which is kept prisoner within a parade of falsely glamourized forms. But like a corpse which has been overly made up, the forms are glamourized to the point where music is no longer recognizable.

Why do we perceive the form of music, not its actual flesh? Music is flesh; it is molecules. Forms of music may be depraved or noble, fragile or strong—aren't the passages between them growing unfamiliar? In these ages music suffers like a body whose inner workings have been kept hidden away.

I don't believe in the glamourized forms of music, but persist in attempting to negotiate a microcosmic NADE that could illuminate passages between forms, like veins under skin.

Music & Food

I wanted music to be sweeter, less opaque. But in a dream, my grandmother was urging me to swallow ko chi chung, & it was undeniably delicious. & my other grandmother, my amma, whose face had once appeared (though slightly elongated) in the center of a violin, was teaching me to eat fodselsdagkage, & I was delighting her.

Sometimes I think, "I've had no music to create or perceive." But the surfaces of music keep sliding down my throat. & these are basically memories of something I heard, or premonitions of what I wanted to hear. Hunger provokes the creation of music. & the mind keeps spitting up thoughts to be held buoyant by the hunger for music.

Have you heard of children who play with their own turds? A "composer" of music does something like that. & its a shock to feel molecules of shit on your fingers when you thought you were composing music. "Composers" don't create music, they only redistribute vibrations that would be occurring anyway, regardless of anyone's intentions. There's an old song that says "not a second time." Well, I've always wondered, "why not a 3rd time or a 4th time?" A pattern in the occurrence of events becomes recognizable. One gets the feeling of living through pre-existing forms of sickness & health, sadness & happiness, etc.

In a dream, the suffering of the body had become the locus of a hunger for music. Within the possibility of a NADE, I could remember a body like that, not a body that lived & died, but one that was continually living & dying.

Half-life of a NADE

In certain regions there are spies who sneak under the water, using a straw of bamboo to breathe. For them, that bamboo must have been like an umbilical cord to the embryo. & there are embryos within embryos within embryos.

I believe that within each molecule there must be NADEs—so many of them. & who is lurking there?

the living NADE

the elegance of continuousness of vacuous experience
vacuous by means of its continuousness, the lack of form
& lack of "lack" of form.

the ceaseless repetition of "instances"
which, although different from one another
are never in a fixed form to be perceived.

child singers are saying "pa," "ma"
"dha," "ni" & "sa."
& many children were singing "papa"
& "mama."

one can do little but submit
to the living NADE
embedded in mineral's particles.

The "Composer" is at the Mercy of Music

Like the scientist who named the motion of some molecules after himself, the "composer" will be out of place for bearing information which never belonged to him, never entered his mind. But more than the others, the safe ones, the "composer" is at the mercy of music, lies in the peril of its wake. What is music? It cannot be created by "composing," "improvising," "performing," "recording," or even "listening." I believe that music should be grown on trees, to be plucked like a fruit without the extravagance of a harvest.

These constellations which lie behind the sky, in outer space, are not accessible to my vision by any permutation of events or objects. Nothing should be said about the precise & aquiescent NADE, appearing like the apparition of a human face in the ground, the mineral. & the sky is sure to be "pierced," although it is going to remain present, choking.

THE THREE-FOLD EAR
AND THE ENERGIES OF ENTHUSIASM

(Dedicated to Laverne D. Weisser,
Independence Day 1928–Earth Day 1997)

Z'EV

From the Great Above the Goddess opened her ear to the Great Below.

—Hymn to the Sumerian Inanna[43]

I have eaten from a drum, I have drunk from a cymbal, I am an initiate of Attis.[44]

43. Catherine Keller, "Goddess, Ear & Metaphor: On the Journey of Nelle Morton," *Journal of Feminist Studies in Religion*, vol. 4, no. 2 (Fall 1988).

44. George E. Mylonas, *Eleusis and the Eleusinian Mysteries* (Princeton: Princeton University Press, 1961), p. 291.

The Outer Ear

(**N**ote: idiosyncratically I include the 'ear-drum' as part of the outer ear.)

the ear lobe

1. Absent in all other primates, the ear lobe is an erogenous zone and has at times functioned as a sexual/devotional symbol and offering. Severed ears at some point became a substitute for the castrated phallus sacrificed to the Great Mother in the Cult of Attis.[45]

The Cult of Attis also shared with both the Dionysian and the ancient (first and second Temple) Hebraic cults the prominence of the cymbal rather than the drum as the musical accompaniment for their rites.[46]

"In Egypt devotees offered their ears to the Goddess Isis, and until the early decades of the Christian era, sculpted ears were offered at the shrines of the Great Mother in other parts of the Middle East."[47] Many of

45. "Ear" in Benjamin G. Walker, *Encyclopedia of Esoteric Man* (London: Routledge & Keegan Paul, 1977); and "Attis," in Barbara G. Walker, *Women's Encyclopedia of Myths and Secrets* (San Francisco: Harper & Row, 1983).

46. For the use of cymbals relating to prophecy, see 1 Chronicles 25; for their use relating to praise and meditation, see Psalms 50; for their use as accompaniment to ecstatic dance, see 2 Samuel 6.

47. Walker, *Encyclopedia of Esoteric Man*.

these shrines have been identified as caves, capable of symbolizing not only the uterine but the auditory canal as well.

2. The metaphorical identification of the Ear and the Goddess has been reclaimed and reinterpreted by the feminist *thea*logian Nelle Morton;

"the more divine act," she says, "is *hearing to speech* rather than *speaking to hearing*."[48]

48. Nelle Morton, *The Journey is Home* (Boston: Beacon Press, 1985), p. 54.

"The spontaneity with which we as human speakers [sound makers] articulate ourselves becomes fundamental in the course of cosmic history"; "liberation would occur as we let ourselves be healingly heard, by each other and in those depths where we encounter Wisdom"; "'Hear our prayer,' of course, has always been an important refrain.... But the prayer does not then make sense as a request.... It may be superseded by the varieties of meditation, centering and visualization Morton's story reveals, and by modes of communal attunement to sacred presence and a channeling of collaborative energies."[49]

49. Keller, "Goddess, Ear & Metaphor."

the ear drum

1. The archetypical drum resides within our skulls; the tympanic membrane tensed at the end of the auditory canal, and as such it extends the axiom 'as Above, so Below' to 'as Within, so Without.' This classic esoteric axiom, generally attributed to Hermes-Thrice-Greatest, also has very strong traditions ascribing it to Maria-the-Jewess, identified as Miriam the sister of Moses, who lead her troupe of women drummers in music and song (and most likely dance as well) at the Biblical crossing of the Sea of Reeds.[50]

In Middle Eastern culture the drum was primarily a woman's instrument and terra-cotta figurines of female drummers are among the most prevalent representations at Neolithic and Iron Age sites in the Middle East.[51] This tradition is currently being revived by Layne Redmond in her work with the *Mob of Angels.*

2. The sixteenth hexagram of the *I-Ching, YÜ,* is the only hexagram which is related specifically to both sound and music. The Taoist Liu I-Ming in his Commentary[52] notes the special property of *YÜ* (translated as 'Joy') is 'proper timing in action.' In context this relates to the sounding of the proper rhythm at the proper time, a major

50. Exodus 15: 20, 21; song text, Exodus 1-17.

51. Carol L. Meyers, "Of Drums and Damsels," in *Biblical Archeologist* (March 1991).

52. I-ming Liu, 18th century, *The Taoist I-Ching,* trans. Thomas Cleary (Boston: Shambhala, 1986).

factor contributing to the capacity of sound to cause specific effects. The whole of the tantric musical system of *raga,* for example, incorporates a precise day and time designation for each piece. Except for remnants in the Eastern and Roman Catholic churches, this aspect is unfortunately absent from Western musics and their performance.

YÜ is also sometimes translated as 'Enthusiasm,'[53] whose Greek etymology is *en* ('in')+*theos* (divinity), carrying the root meanings of both 'inspiration' and 'possession by the divine/power(s).' It is fairly universal that sounded rhythms, on whatever implement, are the vehicle whereby trance (inspiration) or identification (possession) are attained, and as such this strengthens the hexagram's relevance.

53. Richard Wilhelm, trans., *The I-Ching,* rendered into English by Cary F. Baynes (New York: Pantheon, 1950).

The image inherent in the hexagram, 'thunder rising from the earth,' was seen as the prototype of music. So we find in the commentaries, "the Earth and Thunder issuing from it with its *crashing noise* form *YÜ*. The ancient Kings, in accordance with this, composed their music..."[54] and "it fell to music to [...] construct a bridge to the world of the unseen."[55] Finds from old Europe show that "the epiphany of the Goddess is inseparable from the noise of howling and clashing," and of her initiates it is said that "they clash the cymbals of the Great Mother."[56] The associations in these examples make clear how both drums and metals have found their preeminent place in sacred/ritual musics, thanks to the complexities and intensities their use can produce. The intentional activation of the drum/rhythm 'without and within' and the identification of the practitioner/participant with an "Other" ('above and below') are focused here at the ear drum, gateway to the middle ear.

54. Z. D. Sung, *The Text of Yi King and its appendices* (New York: Paragon Reprint Corp., 1969).

55. Wilhelm, *The I-Ching.*

56. Marija Gimbutas, *The Goddesses & Gods of Old Europe* (Berkeley: University of California, 1982), p. 183.

The Middle Ear

The middle ear is composed of three small bones, the hammer, anvil, and stirrup, which transmit the energies pulsing the ear drum to the inner ear. Through their action these pulsings are intensified by a factor of something over thirteen times.

The choice of names for these bones and their association with the smithy is mirrored in both the myth of the origin of the Pythagorean theory of music and the use of drums and metals as the shamanic instruments *par excellence.* Pythagorean harmony consists of three concords, the discovery of which is said to have been made by Pythagoras upon hearing hammers striking a stirrup held with tongs against the anvil of a smithy. Attaching the heads of the hammers to cords of equal length and substance, he developed his theory. Many versions of this story, in an attempt to efface the shamanic element, relate it only in terms of the lengths of the cords. (And speaking of stirrups, *riding* and equestrian imagery in general abound in both metallurgic and shamanic lore.)

"For Pythagoras, numbers were the principles and elements of all things and composed the proportions of the whole world."[57] In respect to this, the beats composing rhythm patterns gain their power through the value of their proportions, seen in the quantity of *beats* separated by *rests* in the phrasing comprising a particular rhythm. Proportion literally translates as 'for one's portion,' and inherent to it is a notion of destiny.

57. William Stirling, *The Canon: an exposition of the pagan mystery perpetuated in the Cabala as the rule of all the arts* (London: Garnstene Press, 1974).

58. See Z'EV, *Rhythmajic: Practical Uses of Number, Rhythm, and Sound,* 1992.

When sounding a proportion/rhythm, then, one is invoking *a course of events,* the intention of which varies with the particulars of the 'timing in action.'[58] Individual rhythms are also capable of multiple effects, again depending on one's intention.

The smithy was where the cymbals, gongs, rattles, castanets, and etceteras were created for the rituals of the Goddess. The intentions: "rites calling for…meditation, prayers and acts of worship" executed during the creative processes composed the oral aspect of the craft traditions.[59] In many studies, representations of cymbals are often interpreted as shields, and hence ritual musicians have been repeatedly described as armed warriors.[60] This same school of interpretation also sees the butterfly symbol of the Goddess, especially when rendered in metals, as a double-headed axe. It's the paranoid school, for whom the *joy*ous sound of thunder is the voice of an angry god.

59. Mircea Eliade, *The Forge and the Crucible* (Chicago: University of Chicago Press, 1978).

60. J. E. Harrison, "Kouretes and Korybantes," in *Dictionary of Religion and Ethics* (New York: The Macmillan Co., 1921).

61. Robert Graves, *The Greek Myths* (New York: George Braziller, 1957).

In view of this, consider the myth that relates how Hephaestus, archetypical smith of the West, releases Athene (Wisdom) from Zeus's skull to spring out "fully armed with a mighty shout."[61] In light of the aforementioned 'noise of howling and clashing,' we see here the smith/shaman releasing Wisdom to manifest as/through sound.

In myth, Hephaestus is intimately related to the five male Dactyls born from one handful of the ten fingerprints which the goddess Rhea, in her birththroes bringing forth Zeus, was said to have left on the Earth at Mount Ida, and hence the use of *dactyl* to mean *finger.* These Dactyls knew all the secrets of nature. Inventors of metallurgy, they were *the* smiths and they were

also regarded as masters of both music and the healing arts. They were said to
have been the teachers of Pythagoras.[62] Their five sis-
ters (Rhea's other handful) were equally knowledgeable and they are recorded as having initiated Orpheus
into the Mysteries of the Goddess.

Orpheus is another figure with both shamanic
and musical associations, although his instrument was
primarily the voice.[63] As regards his 'lyre,' while now
applied to one particular instrument, *lyre* was originally a generic term given to music itself. Its strings,
three or seven in number, symbolized either the Goddess in her tripartite
aspect or the seven celestial bodies (Moon, Mercury, Venus, Sun, Mars, Jupiter,
and Saturn).[64]

Meanwhile, back in the smithy, the relation of the blacksmith to the
shaman is prevalent throughout shamanic cultures, and an Ur-Smith is active
in many of the initiation rites in the 'inner' Underworld. This Ur-Smith is generally concerned with that part of the initiation process which includes the dis-
membering of the novice (followed often by immersion in a cauldron) and his
or her reconstitution as a shaman, frequently with some bone(s) having been
replaced by metals. Pythagoras himself was reported to have had a golden
thigh-bone. Related traditions also include the use of stone crystals in this
process, and in many of them crystal is held to be of celestial origin.

A Yakut proverb says, "A shaman's wife is respectable, a smith's wife is
venerable."[65] Charis, the first of the Three Graces, is
in some versions of the myth the wife of Hephaestus.

At their most important sites of worship,
the Graces, as forces of Nature, were personified by
meteorites.[66] In universal traditions, meteorites were
the first, and in some cases the only, iron worked by
cultures/societies. Their explicit celestial origin and mode of a arrival as a flaming stone made them an obvious focus for the mysteries which accumulated
between and around those creating from them. Many of these mysteries,
joined by others from the traditions of glass makers, glazing potters, and dyers,
when interacting with Hellenistic science in that cauldron of syncretism
known as Alexandria (circa 500 BC to 300 AD), produced what is now known
as alchemy. And among the 'founders' of alchemy, our same Maria-the-Jewess
is to be found. She is credited with discovering the first practical use of

62. K.F. Smith, "Magic (Greek and Roman)," in *Dictionary of Religion and Ethics.*

63. George Luck, *Arcana Mundi: Magic and the occult of in the Greek and Roman Worlds: a collection of Ancient Texts* (Baltimore: John Hopkins University, 1985).

64. Fabre d'Olivet, *Music Explained as Science and Art,* trans. Joscelyn Godwin, (New York: Harper & Row, 1987).

65. Mircea Eliade, *Shamanism: Archaic Techniques of Ecstasy,* trans. William R. Trask (Princeton: Princeton University Press, 1972).

66. I.F. Burnes, "Charities," in *Dictionary of Religion and Ethics.*

hydrochloric acid and with the development of the water, sand, and oil baths, vessels which are indispensable in modern chemical laboratories. The most important of her vessels, the double boiler, is still known in French by her name, *le bain-marie.*[67]

67. See "Alchemy," in *Encyclopaedia Judaica* (New York: Encyclopaedia Judaica, 1972).

The Inner Ear

The inner ear is also referred to as the *labyrinth.* In fact, the inner ear is composed of two labyrinths, one inside the other. An outer, 'bony labyrinth' encloses an inner 'membranous labyrinth,' which includes the chattel, or sea shell. This is where the real action is, for it is here that the dynamics which have so far been 'physical' will achieve true transformation. The energies which pulsed the ear drum and were then concentrated by the middle ear are now transmitted through the *oval window* to the fluid in the inner labyrinth. This begins a hydro-electric process. The fluids of the chattel vibrate, which in turn stimulate the neurons along the basilar and tectoral membranes of the cochlea. As neural impulses in the voltage of the central nervous system, the exterior energies have now been transformed back into the realm of electricity, which I feel can be regarded as a 'physical' form of light.[68]

68. See "Ear," in *Encyclopedia Britannica* (Chicago: Encyclopedia Britannica, 1989).

Throughout the world, both the cave and the labyrinth have had primary roles in both initiatory and offertory rituals. The etymology of *labyrinth* is from (*labrys*) double axe (butterfly)+(*inth*) extent/house of. The Labyrinth of Crete, which enclosed the Minotaur, was fashioned by Daedalus, a later name for the same energies personified by Hephaestus, who indeed occasionally appears in the genealogies as an ancestor of Daedalus.

In some of the myths, the Labyrinth was not a walled or subterranean construction but rather took the form of the labyrinths which can still be seen on the floors of European cathedrals, the one at Chartres being an outstanding example. Such labyrinths were the sites of ritual dances of the Goddess, with their 'descents' in their turnings to the left and 'ascents' in their turnings to the right, symbolizing the congruence of the Underworld with the Celestial.

Across the valley from the Cathedral at Chartres is a cemetery which is contemporary with it. In this cemetery, at roughly the same elevation as the Cathedral, stands a very large, very old, tree. One gets the same 'unearthly' earthed feeling standing there as upon arriving at the center of the labyrinth in the Cathedral. This 'polar' dynamic also occurs in the inner ear, where there is also a *round window* on the chattel just below the oval window. This is sometimes referred to as the secondary ear drum and it pulses out as the energies from the oval window are pulsing in.

Such double movements (right-left, in-out, etc.) are often represented in sacred images as a double spiral. The Taoist Yin-Yang symbol is one variation of this form. In Chinese myth, Yu the Great is reported to have achieved the creation of nine sacred cauldrons. Five of them correspond to Yang and four with Yin, thus symbolizing the union of opposites in an image of cosmic totality.[69]

69. Eliade, *The Forge and the Crucible.*

Thus the cauldron/furnace/spiral/labyrinth forms a new matrix, an artful 'uterus' where the ore/participant experiences 'maturation' through refining. Within this complex of associations are the roots of both practical metallurgy/ alchemy/chemistry (and note that there are traditions which say that Paracelsus, an alchemist also claimed by chemists, spent time in the mines of Bohemia) and the mystical/tantric practice of speculative alchemy.

One of the more visible members of the "invisible college of the Rosicrucians" of the early seventeenth century was Michael Maier, physician to the emperor Rudolph II. Maier, who in his published works also engraved his own etchings, considered the whole of alchemy to be encapsulated in the last six words of chapter I, verse 2 of *Genesis*:

$$\text{ורוח אלהים מרחפת על־פני המים}$$

whose common translation is: And the spirit of God hovered over the face of the waters.

A variety of associations related to the preceding comments can be derived from this phrase by applying some traditional forms of Scriptural exegesis. The six Hebrew words are composed of 23 letters. 2+3=5, the symbol of quintessence and the result of the Alchemical Art. 2x3=6, which is the numerical correspondent to both the sun and gold.

In addition to their verbal character, Hebrew letters also have numerical equivalents, and some words in which the numerical values of the letters total 23 are *goldsmith* (10+1+2+5+4), *engraving* (1+9+10+3), *orgasm* (2+6+9+6), *riddle* (1+4+10+8), as well as three words which are formed through permutations of their same four Hebrew letters: *prayer* (10+10+2+1), *force* (1+10+10+2), and *correspondence* (1+2+10+10).[70]

70. All of these, with their spellings/proportions, are capable of functioning as rhythms, with their 'meanings' construed as intentions. See Z'EV, *Rhythmajic.*

As to the words themselves, the first word, denoting *and the spirit,* appears in other locations in the Scriptures, denoting *breath* (*Genesis* 17, verse 5: the *breath of life*), *wind* (*Psalm* 18, verse 11: *the wings of the wind*), and *touch* (*Judges* 16, verse 9: *The touch of the fire*).

The second word, denoting *God* (or Goddess), is a feminine plural of five letters. Its first three letters can form a semantic unit which in its Arabic form denotes *to worship,* while its Hebraic form denotes variously *to howl, an oath,* and *to invoke* or *charm.* (The song/howling of Orpheus can be considered in terms of this.) The last two letters of the second Hebrew word may denote *sea* (*Exodus* 13, verse 18: *the Sea of Reeds*), *west* (*Genesis* 13, verse 14: *westward*), and *reservoir* (I *Kings,* verse 23f: described here is the Artful *Sea* of the Solomonic Temple, a bronze cauldron containing some 10,000 gallons of water).

The third word denoting *hover* consists of five letters with numerical values (400+80+8+200+40) which total 748. A different word (400+300+10+8+30) with the same numerical value of 748 denotes *whisper, to/a spell, to/a charm, secret art,* and *to heal:* "The place where the whispering for charming purposes is done (i.e., the ear)."[71]

71. Marcus Jastrow, *The Dictionary of the Targumim, the Talmud Babli & Yerushlami, and the Midrashic Literature* (New York: Judaica Press, 1989), p. 703.

A variant parsing of (400+80+8+200+40) produces (40+200+8) denoting *to finish, to anoint, to heal.* Its mirror image (8+200+40) denotes *to dedicate for sacred use* and *the fisherman.* The remaining two letters (80+40) denote *two, sustenance,* and *to begin.* (400+80) denotes *the drum, the hollow of the hearth,* and the *furnace/stove.*

The traditional *hover* is drawn when the middle letters (80+8+200) are considered the semantic unit, with the first (40) and the last (400) construed as grammatical additions. (40+400) denotes *death* and (400+40) denotes *perfection.* (80+8+200) denotes *to vibrate, hover, tremble, cherish, fertilize.* (200+8+80) denotes *the potter, the creatrix, the wheel.* A Yakut parable relates that the first smith, shaman, and potter were all of the same blood.[72]

72. Eliade, *The Forge and the Crucible.*

The fourth and fifth words are joined in the written texts (10+50+80+30+70) and together denote *over* or, more properly, *over the face.* The fourth word (30+70) denotes *height, heaven, above, to yoke* or *to bring about* (depending on pronunciation). The fifth word (10+50+80) denotes *face, countenance, movement, to turn, (to) free, (to) empty,* or *twilight* (again depending on pronunciation). The five letters together total 240. Alternate totals of 240 include (10+200+10+20) denoting *Kiri Ram,* "an imitation of a musical sound for beating time to dancers,"[73] and the *Light is Come* (*Isaiah* 60, verse 1).

73. Jastrow, *The Dictionary of the Targumim*, p. 636.

The sixth and last word, *the waters,* is composed of four letters totaling 95 (40+10+40+5). Removing the initial letter (5), which is the particle *the,* leaves the word *waters* (40+10+40), which retains the same meaning when read from the right or from the left. In this actualizing of the right/left spiraling action, the transforming nature of water is represented.

The whole of the next verse of *Genesis,* verse 3, can be translated as "And the charming waters composed, hearing light: and the light returned." This verse brings this consideration of the mythos of the ear full circle to the process of hearing. As with all sense perceptions, the actual processes are admitted by Western science to be a mystery. In light of this, and in closing, it is most telling that the songs sung by the Nine Muses are designated as *mnemosyne*: the *memory* of what is, what was, and what will be. True music? No one writes it or plays it so much as you remember—to—hear it.

CHAPTER
15

MAIM THAT TUNE

GUY KLUCEVSEK

The first piece I heard that made me want to be a composer was Steve Reich's *Come Out,* which I heard in 1969. Reich recorded the spoken phrase "come out to show them" on two channels of a tape recorder, first in unison and then with channel 2 slowly beginning to move ahead. As the phase begins to shift, a gradually increasing reverberation is heard which slowly passes into a sort of canon or round. Eventually the two voices divide into four and then eight. What begins as pure speech ends as pure sound, with the ear focusing on the clash and clang of sibilants.

This music, eventually termed 'minimalism,' that Reich was creating along with his contemporaries Philip Glass, Terry Riley, LaMonte Young and others had a profound impact on me. It introduced me to a micro-world of sound, where what one heard was not just the notated sounds, but the 'psycho-acoustic' phenomena produced by those tones. Although my music has undergone some radical stylistic shifts over the years, I have always tried to emulate the minimalist's economy of material and means, and the search for the unknown inside the familiar.

The basis for most of my own music is melody, but not in the traditional sense of pure song. I'm more interested in exploring how we experience the same melody in different contexts—e.g., by changing the meter which underpins it, shifting its metric feeling, splitting it up between several voices, changing the mode of the melody, putting the tune through the stylistic ringer, or presenting simultaneous, independent versions of a single melody.

Three "Microids" (1991) is a set of solo accordion pieces inspired by Bela Bartok's *Mikrokosmos,* a series of graded studies for piano which explores unusual scales, harmonies, rhythms, and meters, many of them derived from the folk music of eastern-Europe, which Bartok collected. The first "Microid," "My Right Foot, on the Other Hand," is a study in *polymeter*—i.e., the simultaneous use of two or more meters—in which the theme remains basically the same throughout, while the accompaniment adopts a new meter for each variation. Following is a breakdown of what happens in the piece.

Theme: melody alternates measures of 6/8 and 3/4, while the accompaniment does the opposite [Fig. 1];

Figure 1.

Var. 1: melody still 6/8+3/4, but accompaniment is now in 5/4, divided 2+3. This is made possible by the fact that the theme is 30 (quarter note) beats long, which can be equally divided by both 3 and 5 [Fig. 2];

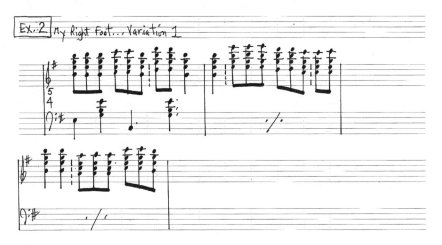

Figure 2.

Var. 2: melody alternates freely between 3/4 and 6/8, accompaniment in 5/4, divided 3+2 [Fig. 3];

Figure 3.

Var. 3: melody 3/4+6/8, accompaniment in 10/8 (double time), divided 3+3+2+2 [Fig. 4];

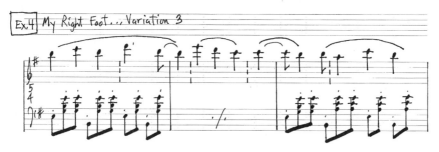

Figure 4.

Var. 4: melody alternates freely between 3/4 and 6/8, accompaniment in 10/8, divided 2+2+3+3 [Fig. 5];

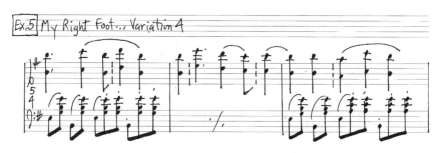

Figure 5.

Var. 5: melody and accompaniment now both 3/4 + 6/8, but accompaniment is one 8th-note ahead of melody, creating a phasing effect [Fig. 6].

Figure 6.

What I was asking in this piece was how do we hear a melody when we change the meter of its accompaniment? Do we now hear the melody in the meter of the new accompaniment, with new accents in the melodic line, or do we hear the melody the same as we did originally? There is no one answer to this, but my guess is that most people hear two simultaneous meters happening, at least in part. As a performer, I find that the meter of the accompaniment seizes the aural foreground, and I definitely articulate the melody accordingly, creating a tension between, e.g., a melodic line which suggests 3/4 and accents which suggest 5/4.

I used a related technique in *Stolen Memories* (1993). By shifting a melody's relationship to an ostinato, I was able, in effect, to generate three new melodies [Fig. 7-10].

Figure 7.

Figure 8.

Figure 9.

Another device I frequently use is *hocket*—i.e., splitting a melody between two or more voices, so that as one sounds, the other is silent. I got interested

Figure 10.

in this through my instrument, the 'free bass' accordion, which has a wide, over-lapping range between the two hands, creating a shift of timbre when tones are passed back-and-forth between them. In my arrangement of Charlie Haden's *Silence* for The Bantam Orchestra, I use this hocket technique in three ways:

a) trading melody notes between right- and left-hand keyboards of the accordion—by doing this very slowly, and overlapping the notes, you get 'beating' caused by amplitude modulation and a slight pitch fluctuation between the two keyboards, as well as a subtle, but distinct, timbre change [Fig. 11];

Figure 11.

b) alternating melody and counter-melody notes between two instruments [Fig. 12];

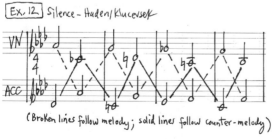

Figure 12.

c) alternating melody and two counter-melody notes among three instruments. (For purposes of the example only, I've used *circles* to represent melody notes, squares for counter-melody #1 notes, and *diamonds* for counter-melody #2 notes, so that you can follow the path of the lines through the voices.) [Fig. 13]

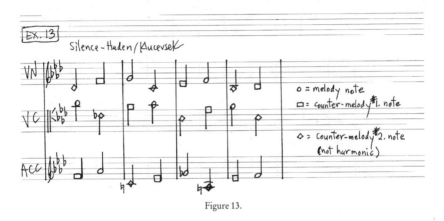

Figure 13.

What I like about using hocket is that you begin to hear a melody not just as a line, but as a succession of tone colors as well, especially when you get into two- and three-part counterpoint.

I also like to change the mode of a scale while maintaining a constant tonal center [Fig. 14], as opposed to the traditional practice of modulating, in

Figure 14.

which the tonal center changes, while the scale remains the same. By changing one or more notes in the interior of a scale, you can drastically alter the nature and mood of the melody which can, in turn, suggest new ways to go with the material. The following passage from *The Singing Sands* (1991) uses four different G-pentatonic scales in the space of eight measures.

As you may have gleaned by now, theme-and-variations is my form of choice. And probably the technique I rely on most heavily within this form is stylistic variation, often suggested by posing questions to myself like: what would this tune sound like if played by a cajun accordionist, a country fiddler, a klezmer clarinetist, a bluegrass banjo picker, or an eastern-European brass band?

A good example of this practice is *Altered Landscapes* (1994), a seventeen minute accordion solo written for a dance by David Dorfman. The theme is in G-Aeolian mode (natural minor) and first appears in hocket between the right and left hands [Fig. 15].

Figure 15.

A number of stylistic variations follows, including a song without words [Fig. 16];

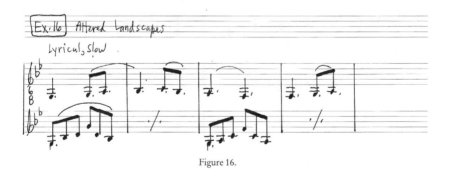

Figure 16.

a waltz in French bal musette style [Fig. 17];

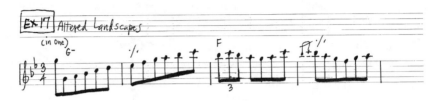

Figure 17.

a Russian (or Zorba the Greek) dance which begins in an exaggeratedly slow tempo and gradually builds to a furioso climax [Fig. 18];

Figure 18.

a hornpipe or sea chanty, in G-mixolydian [Fig. 19];

Figure 19.

a variation on the previous sea chanty, played bagpipe style, with lots of filigree ornamentation [Fig. 20];

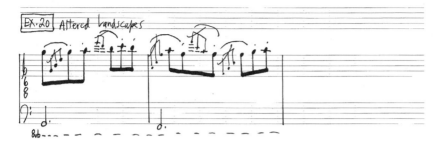

Figure 20.

a highly-improvised melody in the style of Romanian *doina*, using a Bartok-like key signature of B-natural, Eb and Ab [Fig. 21];

Figure 21.

an ending chorale, again in G-mixolydian [Fig. 22].

Figure 22.

In *Tesknota* (1993) I tried a looser, more improvisatory approach to both melody and counterpoint. It is a piece in four voices for four-eight melody instruments or two pianos. The melody consists of note heads only, divided into phrases, with no rhythmic values assigned.

In the version for eight instruments, two players are assigned to each part, which may be played in any octave, so long as both players on a part are in the same octave. The piece begins with a monophonic melody, played in heterophony by two instruments—i.e., both play the same melody independently of one another, with the proviso that they wait for one another at the end of each phrase, so that the piece proceeds one phrase at a time [Fig. 23].

Figure 22.

Tesknota eventually builds up to four melodic lines, played independently by eight instruments, like the delicately balanced units of a mobile [Fig. 24].

Figure 22.

What I like about the structure and conception of this piece is the careful balance between independence and self-expression—playing the melody at your own rate, in your own way—and ensemble interaction—being aware of where all the other players are at any given time; no easy task, especially when the piece splits into four lines/eight players.

The elasticity of this approach to ensemble writing recaptures for me the wonder and excitement of the psycho-acoustic phenomena I first heard in Reich's *Come Out,* while relying less on process and more on personal choice, improvisation and chance. It is a method I hope to explore further in my search for new ways of working with melody.

Works Cited:

Emanuel, Carol. *The Singing Sands* recorded on *Tops of Trees* (Koch International, 1995).

Klucevsek, Guy. *Altered Landscapes* recorded on *Altered Landscapes* (Evva Records, 1998).

Klucevsek, Guy and The Bantam Orchestra. *Stolen Memories* recorded on *Stolen Memories* (Tzadik, 1996).

Klucevsek, Guy and The Bantam Orchestra. *Tesknota* recorded on *Stolen Memories* (Tzadik, 1996).

Klucevsek, Guy. *Three "Microids"* recorded on *Transylvanian Softwear* (John Marks Records, 1994; reissued Starkland, 1999).

(All compositions © and published by Guy Klucevsek Music, BMI, except "Silence," by Charlie Haden, Liberation Music, BMI.)

ELEMENTS OF IMPROVISATION

for Cecil Taylor and Anthony Braxton

MARILYN CRISPELL

Music…has to do with a lot of areas which are magical rather than logical.
The great artists, rather than just getting involved with discipline, get to under-
stand love and allow the love to take shape.[74]

The very joy & freedom of art & life is the hidden presence of insecurity.[75]

Acrobatics performed without a safety net are not
automatically more astonishing than if the net is
there; it's just a messier business if somebody falls
on his face.[76]

It is certainly true that a criterion for true art, as
opposed to its cunning counterfeit, is its ability to
take us where the artist has been, to this other different place where we are free from
the problems of gravity. When we are drawn into the art we are drawn out of ourselves.
We are no longer bound by matter, matter has become what it is: empty space and light.[77]

74. Cecil Taylor, as quoted by Gary Giddins.

75. Stephen Morrissey, "The Insecurity of Art:
Five Statements," in *The Trees of Unknowing.*

76. Steve Lake, FMP/*Improvised Music.*

77. Jeannette Winterson, *Sexing the Cherry.*

Elements of composition:

The use of rhythmic, melodic and harmonic elements and motives (two or more elements joined together to form a logical whole) in the development of an improvisation/composition

(Improvisation as spontaneous composition…)

Adding together motives (as moveable 'blocks,' or permutations) to form compositions

Beginning with an interval (the most primal musical relationship), rhythmic figure, harmonic block (a 'block' of harmony in and of itself, not necessarily related to traditional harmonic function within the major/minor tonality system—harmony used for purity of sound), or any combination of these, and transposing them, adding imitative/continuous elements, or con-trasting elements

Beginning with a melodic line and varying it in any possible manner (transposition, retrograde, inversion, etc.); melodic lines made by clusters; the importance of the shape of a line; modulation from one motif to anther: can be abrupt/contrasting or continuous/evolving

Use of scales created from harmonic blocks to form melodies (i.e., the possibility of seeing harmonic blocks as scale fragments)

The use of phrasing as a very personal matter—like speech; phrasing as an important stylistic element

The use of 'rhythmic approximations' (i.e., *relative* note value feel in rhythmic interpretation, rather than literal interpretation in the traditional way. Thus, a phrase may be written out where the notes in the right hand do not match the total number of beats of the notes in the left hand—rather, it is an approximate feel, more loose, free and spontaneous; even when rhythms are written out in my compositions, they are meant to be played fairly freely); rhythm as an important stylistic element

The use of color and texture

The use of poetic texts/meters as inspiration for improvisations

The development of a motive should be done in a logical, organic way, not haphazardly (improvisation as spontaneous composition)—not, however, in a preconceived way—rather in a way based on intuition enriched with knowledge (from all the study, playing, listening, exposure to various musical styles, etc., that have occurred through a lifetime—including all life experiences); the result is a personal musical vocabulary

True creation "lies in a perception from insecurity…not merely the repetition of the past or remaining within the security of ideas and beliefs, where the mind can move only within the field of the known and the dead" (Stephen Morrissey)

Music for more than one instrument:
- 'pointillistic counterpoint' (simultaneously played, superimposed layers, related to but not dependent upon each other)
- or imitative, supportive, dependent upon each other
- or totally collective with no preconceived, superimposed structures whatsoever

- various instrumental combinations (solo, duo, trio, etc., using any of the above relationship patterns)

The placement of composed sections in an improvisation or interpretation of a traditional piece can be varied (i.e., not only or even at the beginning or end of a piece)

It is possible to play traditional compositions by capturing their feel, using them as springboards for improvisation, rather than being forced to play them in a traditional manner (although knowledge of the traditional interpretations and manners of playing can only enrich the new interpretation); in fact, they can be used as concepts to imitate or contradict

The concept of playing an improvisation against a tape of another improvisation or a written composition (in which elements of improvisation could be included). (These notes were originally written for use in teaching.)

ALL THE RAGE

BOB OSTERTAG

By the early 1980s I was feeling that my music was more and more cut off from the rest of my life, and indeed from the whole world beyond a tiny New York City art scene. I left. For nearly ten years I worked as an organizer and writer in and around El Salvador. When I returned to music at the end of the decade I wanted to make music that would help me to integrate my life instead of fracturing it. I decided to write a trilogy of pieces dealing with, in turn, grief, anger, and joy, because that seemed to be the order I was working through things in my own life.

The first piece of the trilogy is *Sooner or Later*. Completed in 1990, it is created almost entirely from a recording of a young Salvadoran boy speaking at his father's funeral. When the Kronos Quartet approached me about a commission after hearing *Sooner or Later,* the time seemed right to tackle anger.

Then, in October 1991, California Governor Pete Wilson vetoed a gay rights law that had been ten years in the making and which he had specifically promised to sign while campaigning for gay votes only a short time before. Riots broke out within hours, and in San Francisco the California State Office Building was set on fire. I took a portable tape recorder to the riot and recorded everything I could. I came home and decided what the project would be: I would have a string quartet play a queer riot.

Next, I sifted through the recorded material and ferreted out those sections that to my ear suggested music: chanting or screaming which had a sort of musical phrasing, windows smashing, and so forth. Much of the sound was colored by the omnipresence of whistles which many queers carry as a basic self-defense tool against gay bashing[78] and which emerged from people's pockets by the hundreds during the riot.

78. A recent survey by the *San Francisco Examiner* indicates that over one million hate-motivated assaults against queer people take place in the United States each year.

I then set up these isolated audio fragments in a digital sampling keyboard and began to shape them into a composition. I used very little conventional electronic signal processing. Instead, I broke the original sound down into very small blocks, and strung them together in sequences that were close to the way they had originally occurred yet had a more musical structure. As a visual analogy, imagine I had filmed the riot, snipped the film into individual frames, and strung them back together in such a way that movements that suggested dance were developed into a full dance form. By carefully preparing the set-up of the sounds in the sampler, I was actually able to play these creations in "live" improvisations, which I recorded and then edited into final versions.

I chose this way of working for a reason. The point was not to transform the riot into something else but to use music to bring the listener *inside* the riot. Not in the gimmicky sense of creating an audio illusion of actually being in the riot, but to get inside the energy, the passion, and most of all the anger. I found that the moment I started using more conventional sorts of electronic processing (phase shifting, filtering, delay, etc.), the riot quickly became something else. So I limited myself to reproducing the original audio as faithfully as I could, and composing with it using the methods I have described.

While I was satisfied with the results of this work in terms of the music, I worried it would be too easy for listeners to be overwhelmed by the *crowd*—that the very intensity of the crowd would become a emotional barrier for the listener. A spoken text seemed like a good addition—a text that would let the listener in by somehow presenting, in a very personal way, the emotions and passions of one individual in the crowd.

I had attempted to interview people during the riot but it proved impossible. There were undercover cops taking pictures of everything, and it was just too crazy trying to explain to complete strangers in the middle of a riot that I wanted to record their most intimate feelings because I was a composer writing a piece about anger for a string quartet.

I asked writer/artist David Wojnarowicz if he would collaborate on a text, and he agreed. But David was sick with AIDS. For months David and I talked and waited for him to get well enough to work on the project, but he never got well. David died before he could hear the finished piece.

The text was then written on very short notice by poet and journalist Sara Miles. It draws on both her life experiences and my own, and is divided into four parts, dealing with growing up queer, gay bashing, AIDS, and love.

Eric Gupton of PomoAfroHomos (Postmodern African-American Homo-sexuals) read the text for the recording. The composite queerness of the final result was just what I wanted: a real-life mixture of the voices of three queers—a white woman, a black man, and a white man. It was intimate and personal yet bigger than one person/gender/race. With this done I could finally turn to the writing the parts for the quartet.

My idea was to have the quartet actually *play the riot*. So, in one way or another, I developed all the string parts directly from the sounds of the riot. To put it simply, I used the computer to pick out pitches that were present in the sound of the riot, and those would become notes for the quartet to play.

In actual fact the process was much more complex. The riot audio is extremely dense sound, so using pitch analysis technology to extract anything musically useful from the barrage required considerable technological savvy and many many hours of simple trial and error. I used a different strategy with the technology for each section of the piece, depending on what aspect of the riot I wanted the quartet to play. This was directly related to how I had "played" the audio on the digital sampler, which in turn was directly tied to the content of the original riot recording. Thus, though there are many layers of work in the music, in the end it presents a pretty integrated package.

More difficult than getting the pitch sequences, however, was putting them in musical rhythm. At this point, I had a series of pitches I could listen to synchronized to the playback of the riot audio, but they were not in any musical time. So I would listen and ask myself, "If I were playing this part, what tempo would I be feeling?" Since the source audio was a riot and not a written piece of music, I found that the implied tempo would frequently wander. When it wandered too far, I had the choice of writing a tempo change into the score, or editing tiny fractions of seconds of the audio to make the tempo more steady. I used both these methods in different sections of the piece.

Once I had a "map" of implied tempos, I added time signatures (which in some places had to change quite rapidly) and rounded off the durations of the pitches generated by the computer into musically meaningful values.

Asking an ensemble to perform in this manner with an audio tape created unique kinds of problems. Most compositions that combine audio tape with live ensemble performance either use a tape which has audio content with an obvious pulse or a click track the musicians hear via headphones during performance, or they are written in such a way that the live performance does not have to be minutely synchronized with the audio from the tape.

Since my objective was to have the quartet *play* the riot, there was no alternative to the musicians taking the tempo from listening to the riot, despite the fact that the implied tempos changed frequently, wandered, and at times were far from obvious. A good deal of rehearsal time was spent listening to the tape repeatedly while I explained, "Here the tempo changes from such-and-such to so-and-so. Count the time from when the window breaks to when the woman screams. At the new tempo, that's a quarter note."

Some examples will make all this much clearer.

Fairly early on there is a section I created from the sound of a woman screaming. Using the sampler, I looped the section so it repeated again and again. I made two separate copies of the sound, heard from opposite extremes of the stereo field. Each time it repeated, I inflected it. But I set it up so that the same inflection gesture would force the left copy sharp and the right copy flat. The whole section is played twice. The first time the inflections are very slight, so they are perceived more as a phase shift within one scream. The second time they are more drastic, and eventually pull the two copies of the scream out of synchronization with each other altogether, so the listener perceives the result as two screams in a sort of hocket.

I wrote the string parts so that each violin "plays" one of the screams. First I made a working copy of the audio, and filtered out, as close as I could, everything but the screams. Then, after much fiddling with the software, I made an extremely detailed analysis of the pitch movement within each scream. I then took that information, rounded off the durations down to a 32nd note, and spread it across measures counted at the tempo implied by the length of the loop of the scream. The end result was a finely nuanced transcription of each scream, and violin parts that at first glance made no musical sense whatsoever but when considered while listening to the tape were quite comprehensible (though still dauntingly difficult to play) [Fig. 1-2].

Figure 1. Bars 78-81.

Figure 2. Bars 78-81, CONTINUED.

Here the inflections are quite small, and you can see how the two parts are slightly out of sync, with the first violin playing a little earlier and higher [Fig. 2].

Figure 3. Bars 106-109.

This is the second time through. The inflections are much more dramatic, and the parts are farther apart both in time and pitch.

The above example shows a section where the relation of string part and audio is directly perceived by the listener. Here is one where that relation becomes much more opaque. The tape contains sounds I created by piling up sound upon sound of windows breaking in various rhythms, to the point that the composite sound becomes a sort of roar of broken windows. Perplexed at first as to how to create string parts from it, I finally decided that since what was interesting about the sound was all the movement in the upper reaches of the audio spectrum, I would work with that.

I made a working copy of the audio and filtered out everything but the high end. Then I made a very finely detailed analysis of the pitch content, resulting in hundreds and hundreds of very short "notes." Then I simply sifted through them, keeping those I thought most important, throwing out others (in fact the vast majority), moving things a bit here and there, until I had shaped them into what seemed like a musical line. I then spread them across measures at a tempo that was close to arbitrary, as there was little in the original data to imply a tempo. Even at this point the notes flew by quite fast, and I wanted to go for a harsh, dissonant feel in connection with the breaking windows. So I collapsed many notes into double stops at a duration of the original two combined, which then of course required further adjusting to make them playable on the various instruments. Finally, I transposed whole part down five octaves and made it the cello part, and orchestrated the other instruments to enter one at a time, each doubling the part an octave up from the previous instrument to enter [Fig. 4].

Figure 4. Bars 175-184.

For those sections of the piece where the tape contains nothing but text, I transcribed the voice line, word for word and inflection for inflection, and had a soloist "play" the voice. I was in part inspired to do this by the work of René Lussier, whose composition *Le Trésor de la Langue* works in a similar way, though René develops it in another direction entirely. Here again the problem of notation was tricky since the text was spoken in a natural, conversational style and thus had no real tempo. In *Trésor*, René opted for notating accurate pitches but approximate durations, which served the purpose of emphasizing to the musician that in the end the part is not to be synchronized to a tempo but to the spoken voice. I opted for spreading the rhythms very precisely across measures counted at a fixed tempo that was again fairly arbitrary. This way, the musician could still ultimately perform to the actual spoken voice, but could also rehearse any section desired with a metronome and precise rhythmic markings [Fig. 5].

Figure 5. Bars 219-225.

Each member of the quartet was given a part with two staves, the instrument's and a tape staff on which I notated the tape as precisely as I could. What is on the tape staff varies considerably section by section. Here the tape staff actually has two voices: the chanting of the crowd, and the comments of one individual heard on the tape [Fig. 6].

Figure 6. Bars 165-167.

Here is a section where I have indicated only the broadest rhythms of very dense sounds from the riot. Notes with xs for heads indicate windows breaking; standard heads indicated pitches that can be picked out from the din but have no easily identifiable source [Fig. 7].

Figure 7. Bars 303-312.

Here I have notated a simple outline of the sounds on the tape from which the violin parts were made. Note they are provided with two "cue" screams first to provide them nine beats during which to establish the tempo [Fig. 8].

Figure 8. Bars 52-59.

The final section presents issues which make it, I think, the most beautiful and also the most difficult to play. I had an image of someone smashing windows with tears pouring down his cheeks.

I began with a section of the riot where someone yelled "Burn it" three times. When looped appropriately, the shouting became a very musical phrase lasting for four bars of 4/4 time at a clearly implied tempo. I set up the sampler so that, with each repetition of the phrase, I could improvise with looping tiny sections of the sound back on itself. This gave the sensation that with each repetition of the phrase different parts of the sound get stretched, or snag on something before flowing on down the stream. After recording my improvisations, however, I edited the results so that the phrases were spread over 4/4 bars counted at a tempo that held steady. The result was that while each individual phrase would stretch and snag, the following one would arrive on a downbeat that had not snagged at all but came on an absolutely steady pulse.

This gave exactly the effect I wanted: the music seems to stumble and sway under its emotional weight, but at the same time marches resolutely forward.

The string parts here are essentially are extremely detailed transcriptions of the voice shouting "Burn it," and the parts follow every little crack and choke. This was also the effect I wanted: to put the moment under a microscope and magnify every detail, then help others get inside of it by making it into music.

Here again the notation posed a problem: I could notate simple rhythms against a tempo which staggered in complex ways, or I could notate rhythms that would appear much more complex against a steady tempo. While the former approach would have produced a part that would appear much simpler on the page, I chose the latter method since it reflected what I really wanted to happen in the music. Also, this way the part could be rehearsed correctly without the tape.

For the quartet, I think this is the most difficult part of the piece. In order to be effective, the string playing must be exactly synchronized with the tape, otherwise the effect of the detail of the transcription is completely lost. However, hearing the tape strongly skews the musicians' sense of tempo. If the musicians' sense of time wanders with the tape the parts no longer synchronize with the audio, and they always find the downbeat of the next phrase comes sooner than expected since that actual tempo does not "snag."

The piece closes with the viola playing the "Burn it" melody unaccompanied by either the quartet or the tape. In part this decision flows from the entire logic of the piece, of bringing out the essence of the moment through music. And the lyric, almost vocal qualities of the viola make it ideal for the solo passage.

But I had a more personal reasons as well. Hank Dutt is the violist in the Kronos Quartet, and his lover Kevin is living with AIDS. I want *All the Rage* to be a piece that speaks to a general, human anger anyone can feel. But first and foremost I want it to be a piece for queers. I wrote it for *our* anger, for who we are and how we feel with violence coming at us from every side, with the intimate parts of our lives discussed every day in the media by arrogant bigots who have not the slightest clue what they are talking about, with so many of us sick and dying. I wanted *All the Rage* to end with Hank alone playing his viola, playing the most passionate music I could write. It is a sort of present for Hank, and for Kevin.

PROPOSITIONAL MUSIC: ON EMERGENT PROPERTIES IN MORPHOGENESIS AND THE EVOLUTION OF MUSIC

Essays, Propositions, Commentaries,
Imponderable Forms and Compositional Methods

DAVID ROSENBOOM

Abstract

This article describes the author's point of view about creative music making, termed PROPOSITIONAL MUSIC. According to this view, composing involves proposing models for whole musical realities, emphasizing the dynamic emergence of forms through evolution and transformation. The author discusses related areas of music, science and philosophy that influence this view, including morphogenesis; music as a vehicle for exploring human knowledge; the emergence of global properties; the nature of forms; comprehending initially undefined or imponderable forms; some premises with which to approach making propositional music; some fundamental steps to consider in constructing methods for composition and improvisation; the natural emergence of networked interactivity; how substantive phenomena emerge and spread through complex dissipative and resonant processes; implications of the infosphere for art making; the relationship of propositional music to society; and potential sources of new mythology for our culture.

Introduction

How is the universe evolving? What is the natural form of its evolutionary trajectory? What is the place of humanity and intelligent information processing in this evolution? Is the collective mind and body of music an active component in this transformational scenario? How do we perceive music in which the language of composition evolves and emerges in the LISTENING EXPERIENCE and is not known, a priori? The mental state required to search for intelligence outside of ourselves—given that the nature of that intelligence is unknown—is both invigorating for the human spirit and indispensable for the health and survival of our species and that of our evolutionary successors.

The only thing absolutely universal about music, I believe, is that all cultures seem to have something to which they refer with an utterance in their language that we translate into the word MUSIC. Beyond this, music is one of the most wonderfully open and, consequently, abstract forms of activity known to human beings. It admits an enormous variety of definitions, presuppositions, cognitive models, uses and cultural meanings. It is nonsensical to approach music with fixed assumptions about given, innate conceptual models. Often, we may be required to traverse the farthest corners of human thought in constructing truly revealing musical experiences.

Because music making can be one of the most unfettered forms of expression we know and because its evolution is so thoroughly enfolded within the processes shaping the universe, music is an appropriate subject to be united with cosmological, epistemological and scientific investigations of evolution. Musical expressions may result from volitional acts transmitting intended messages, or they may emerge seemingly involuntarily to articulate some of the global characteristics of our social and intellectual order. In my own music, the predominant, unifying metaphors are those of MORPHOGENESIS and EVOLUTION.

It has been deeply inspiring to discover through a life of creative music making that in studying how musical forms and functions grow and change, one can be led through territory as broad and ripe with implications for humanity as any art, philosophy or science. I hope to traverse some of that territory in this article and explore interdependencies among evolving musical languages, human evolution, the emergence of intelligent information-processing and critical levels of interconnectedness among human beings that could lead to new myths powerful enough to aid in healing our society. Though space will not permit fully developing each area, suffice it to say that ideas from every one have spawned experiments in musical forms for my own compositions. The intent is not merely to show how ideas from philosophy or science can be applied in music. Rather, it is to integrate all of these areas in an evolving worldview with music as a starting point, laboratory, and playground. In this regard, I have chosen to identify music made from a particular experimental point of view as *propositional music.* I will introduce some subject areas that may appear quite technical. Remain undaunted. They are meant to provide some conceptual pickaxes that can be useful in mining idea nuggets from the relevant terrain. They will become clearer after further contemplation. The intent is to unfold ideas that connect music—a bottom-up starting point—to a top-down view of its implications for our evolving universe and humanity within it.

Propositional Music

I am interested in musical thinking that includes the view of composition as the proposition of musical realities—complete cognitive models of music—using propositional musical language accompanied by a propositional language of music theory. This may also be related to what is called speculative music and speculative theory. The terms "experimental," "new" and "avant garde," however, have become distorted by historical and stylistic associations and are useless when applied to music at this point.

The term PROPOSITIONAL MUSIC refers to a particular style of musical thinking in which the act of composing includes proposing complete musical realities. It presupposes no extant model of music and no predefinition of a proper critical stance about music. It does, however, assume that it is possible to differentiate between composers throughout history and in our present time period. Such differentiation implies no value judgment or hierarchical categorization according to significance. Rather, it refers to what may be regarded as essentially distinct mind sets that composers have adopted about their activities.

Many composers, being possessed of great skill in the crafts of composition, approach their activities assuming that a definition of music lies implicit in the nature of human behavior. Their task is to understand it and exercise acquired skills with the greatest expressive incisiveness they can muster. This adoption of an assumed definition of music may be consciously explicit or unconsciously hidden. It bears no relevance to questions about quality. It leads to a spectrum of music making that ranges from extensions of preexisting STYLES of concert music to various kinds of musical FUNCTIONALISM, such as are found in COMMERCIAL musical products. In essence, the focus here is on the uses of music, albeit the uses of something predefined.

Composer Anthony Braxton terms this mind set about composing STYLIST COMPOSITION.[79] Here the implication may be that the composer has chosen to master a given style and uses its power in his/her arsenal of expressive tools.

79. Anthony Braxton, *Tri-axium Writings* (Dartmouth, NH: Synthesis Music and Frog Peak Music, 1985).

By carrying the techniques of a style beyond previous practice, a composer may create LANGUAGE-EXTENSION music. By this I mean a kind of music that extends the language or materials of a given style, but that still assumes a definition of music that is given a priori.

Braxton refers to another kind of music that he terms RE-STRUC-TURALIST. By this he means composition that changes or redefines a musical language, often inventing entirely new forms and materials. This may come closer to what I mean by propositional music; however, it may also carry different implications. For example, one may re-structure a given musical form (sonata, theme and variations, gradual process, etc.), but still work within the confines of a pre-existing, assumed definition.

Propositional music, as I use the term here, refers to a different mind set about music. It assumes that prior to engaging in a compositional act, the composer asks and then answers the question, "WHAT IS MUSIC?" Furthermore, propositional music may involve inventing a definition of music and then proceeding to operate within that definition. We may invoke the concept of COGNITIVE MODEL here and say that the composer of propositional music works by first creating a cognitive model of music and then proceeding to make music that is consistent with that model.[80]

INVENTED COGNITIVE MODELS OF MUSIC CAN BE HEARD. This often involves learning. We do not completely understand how much learning through cultural exposure is involved in establishing the many givens of our standard musical models. For example, in Western music it is generally assumed that a chord, such as the dominant seventh, involves a *dissonance* that must *resolve.* However, if one listens to this chord as a continuous drone for a very, very long time, one may find that this *unstable* structure loses all of its urgency for resolution. It may come to produce a perfectly settled feeling, just as the tonic triad does, particularly if it is tuned so that the frequencies of its individual notes are separated from each other by intervals that approximate whole-number ratios (3/2, 4/3, 6/5, etc.). One can easily experience such phenomena by listening to the extended-time music of LaMonte Young.[81] After such an experience, one becomes acutely aware of the particular assumptions we have adopted as the basis for understanding the grammar and syntax of functional Western harmony. One begins to see even the concepts of *consonance*

80. David Rosenboom, "Cognitive Modeling and Musical Composition in the Twentieth Century: A Prolegomenon," *Perspectives of New Music* 25, Nos. 1-2 (1987): 439-46.

81. I am referring particularly to performances by LaMonte Young's ensemble, *The Theatre of Eternal Music,* in which I participated during the late 1960s and early 1970s. These performances often lasted several hours or even days when presented as part of the *Dream House* installations with sound and light compositions by Young and Marian Zazeela. It is very difficult to adequately represent this group through recordings, however one can experience a sampling on Young and. Zazeela, *The Theatre of Eternal Music: Dream House,* LP record (Paris: Shandar Disques, 1974).

82. The score for Erik Satie's *Vexations* consists of 32 bars of music that is to be played 840 times resulting in a performance that is far too long to distribute with conventional recording media. The following are incomplete or excerpt recordings: Satie, *Vexations,* Reinbert de Leeuw, pianist, LP record, includes 35 of the 840 repetitions (Holland: Philips 4104351, 1983); Michel Dalberto, pianist, LP record (Paris: Erato STU 71336, 1981, released on compact disc, 1986); Alan Marks, pianist, compact disc, includes 40 of the 840 repetitions (Berlin: London 4252212, 1990).

and *dissonance* for what they are: profoundly ethnocentric notions that are unique to the common practice of European diatonic music. Erik Satie's *Vexations*[82] offers another such experience, this time with extended-time repetitions of tritone intervals and fourth-chords. After listening to this composition, these sonorities never sound the same again.

Consequently, studies in psychoacoustics or music cognition which assume the dynamism of functional harmony—with its concepts of tonal gravity, resolution, and directed, developmental form—suffer from the limited focus of a fixed frame of reference, not unlike that which prevented physicists from understanding the relativity of the cosmos for so long. We have many examples from twentieth century music in which the musical components that articulate the forms of compositions do not come from the traditional harmonic matrix and, sometimes, do not even involve pitch in the way we normally think of it. Radically differing notions of time and how it progresses also appear in both Western and non-Western music.

Propositional music, then, involves the creation of complete cognitive models of music using propositional musical language, sometimes accompanied by a propositional language of music theory. Composers may adopt different models at different times. They might create new models for practically every piece they compose, or they might adopt extant models and act as propositional composers only to a certain degree. Any mix of these stances is viable. We also assume that when the word *composer* is used, we may be referring to a large variety of actual musical practitioners. By *composer* I often simply mean, the *creative music maker*. This may include creative performers, composers, analysts, historians, philosophers, writers, thinkers, producers, technicians, programmers, designers and listeners—and the listeners are perhaps the most important of these. The term *composer* is just a convenient shorthand. To the extent that music is a shared experience, audiences must understand that this experience can not take place in a meaningful way without their active participation. This requires a view of LISTENING AS COMPOSITION. LISTENERS ARE PART OF THE COMPOSITIONAL PROCESS. They must take an active role in creating musical experiences.

The past 300 years or so has been a time of profound change in ideas about nature and reality. These have been accompanied by fundamental revisions in our thinking about science, philosophy, perception and the arts, and have required us to recast our ideas about who we are and where we fit in the cosmos. Music has reflected practically every such change, as have the other arts—particularly the visual arts. The pace of this recasting has accelerated during the twentieth century. It is to be expected, therefore, that this century's musicians would have an intense involvement with new musical propositions.

I have no doubt that such figures have appeared in other periods of music history; however, our knowledge of them may be scant. It is wise to adopt a degree of suspicion about the light cast on seminal figures by the written historical record. Those about which we hear the most in any given period may or may not be those to whom we can attribute the qualities of true innovation. Very often, the propositional composer may be overshadowed by the stylist practitioner. History does us a disservice when its writers are not cognizant of ideas related to propositional music or musical model building. It is often said by historians and musicologists in academe that their educational goal is to enable students to be informed critics who can distinguish between the *good* and the *lesser* of our musical predecessors and to correctly distinguish *innovators* from *culminators*. Culminators are, clearly, the more highly valued of these two groups. This improper pedagogy impedes the evolutionary progression of music. It fosters in students, who are newly informed listeners, a tendency to approach their own musical time period with a basic attitude of suspicion and mistrust.

Music as an Instrument for Navigating the Idea of Knowledge

Socrates is said to have asserted that true knowledge, untainted by conditioning, is innate in humans at birth and that learning and teaching are processes of retrieving that knowledge so that it may become evident in conscious experience.[83] Can music be used to work towards this goal? Absolutely.

83. Howard Gardner, *The Mind's New Science, A History of the Cognitive Revolution* (New York: Basic Books, Inc., 1985).

The potential of music to combine abstraction with feeling, along with its dependence on the physics of tone (vibration) and time, make it an ideal discipline within which to explore the essential qualities of human knowledge. Music may balance the cerebral and visceral in any conceivable mixture. Music accepts all and is devoid of any assumed mind-body differentiation. It can be used to investigate perception, to represent philosophical systems and embody models of nature. It can be thought of as a model building discipline as well as a medium of expression. As long as we do not succumb to the pressures of conformists to adopt an a priori definition of music, it remains open and unadulterated.

In order to engender a unique style or language—a usual prerequisite for continuity and even a shred of universality—composers build, whether consciously or not, complete cognitive models of music. Often, the music's strength depends on the degree to which the model is complete, consistent, and well ordered, even if, upon first hearing, we cannot perceive what the essential features of the model may be. No composer whose music we remember and value highly today has escaped the task of extending the domain of musical language, at least to some degree.

Achieving a clear understanding of 20th century music can be particularly difficult, partly because the cognitive models associated with it have evolved at an accelerated pace and have split into a plethora of developmental streams. Only occasionally do these merge into what may appear as temporary mainstreams. For the adventurous at heart, however, this is precisely what makes ours one of the most exciting and exhilarating musical epochs in which to live and one which brightly illuminates the collective human intellect, body and spirit.

Music may illustrate virtually any human activity, from socio-physical gestures to complex mental constructs. Consequently, the analogies that can be drawn while attempting to identify universals and reduce music to elaborations of these is seemingly limitless. The musical *universal* may be a Holy Grail and the search for it a never-ending crusade. Additionally, music may not only be illustrative, it may elaborate or extend human activity or become an entirely unique activity, in and of itself. It seems to be true, however, that the existence of music is a human universal. All cultures appear to have something that we choose to *call* music.

Propositional Music and Society

This definition of propositional music provides us with the means to differentiate among creative music makers. Again, it does not imply critical judgment. It does imply a particular orientation to music making regarded as fundamental and unique. This profound difference often goes unrecognized by listeners, observers, critics, historians, musicologists, other composers and, perhaps, even most musicians. It lies at the root of immense misunderstandings revealed when such individuals approach and react to the music of contemporary innovators while operating inside paradigms associated with some extant definition or cognitive model of music that simply doesn't apply.

Such misunderstandings also become apparent when we take the time to probe deeply enough to understand something of the models at work in music outside our own cultures. Non-Western musicians often have fundamentally different ideas about music and its uses that are often overlooked or badly misrepresented. Scientists who study the phenomena of music or music perception consistently make the mistake of approaching the object of their study as if they already know what it is. They act as if all that is necessary is to find the complex patterns of neural organization and information representation in the brain that agree with a presupposed assumption of how music works. Most of the time, their writings reveal a lack of consideration that the domain of music can contain multiple and often strikingly different, cognitive models.

Audiences must also understand their responsibilities in creating musical experiences. Most take the view that music is something done to them—that what they receive for the price of admission is an opportunity to become completely passive, allowing performances to be fired at them as if they were willing targets in a shooting gallery, the quality of performances being judged by the pleasantness of the aesthetic bullets penetrating their eyes and ears. Furthermore, this assessment is usually limited to measuring the conformity with which those bullets fit a presumed definition of music or the skill and dexterity with which such conformity is achieved.

Perhaps a musical relativity admitting multiple points of view, frames of reference and operating models is what we require. We must educate the populace to understand that music making can involve creating entire musical universes, each built on its own unique assumptions and provided for inquiring souls to explore.

Comprehending the Undefined

The universe is a SELF-ORGANIZING SYSTEM in which transformation, evolution and change enable ENTELECHY (actuality). Time is an axis of experience over which features and forms are articulated on other axes. Music is fundamentally involved with sculpting experiences in time. Outside of time, existence is undefined. To participate in the evolving universe, a state of mind must be maintained in which the INTELLIGENT ORDER contained in observations must be sought without prior knowledge regarding the nature of that intelligence.

ORDER may be defined as giving attention to similar differences and to different similarities (to paraphrase David Bohm).[84] The beauty of this

84. David Bohm, *Wholeness and the Implicate Order* (New York: Routledge & Kegan Paul, 1980).

definition lies in the assumption that order is an ACTIVE form of manifesting DISTINCTIONS, not a rigid objectification. In essence, all forms of distinction produce CALLS, (in the sense of G. Spencer-Brown's use of the term),[85] making reference to particular differences around which unique SINGULARITIES in space-time are created. These are particular distinctions with which we associate properties that result from our observing them interact with other such distinctions. In PSYCHOLOGICAL TIME, such calls are always temporary. Emanating from each singularity, within the dimensionality of each call, is a ZONE OF INFLUENCE (a region within which a singularity is able to interact with other singularities), which is characterized, in part, by a notion of STRENGTH, associated with interacting FORCES, that decreases over DISTANCE from the singularity until the zone of influence becomes undefined. (For a musical composition based on these ideas, see my *Zones of Influence*.[86])

We have here a kind of VERBIFICATION of the NOUNS of our language, which, in the arts, evinces a new kind of DEMATERIALIZATION with which we must become comfortable emotionally. We can rest when we realize that the alternative—attachment to stasis—accelerates extinction. Our best chance for survival is to become part of the agency of change and accept our own transmutation into the forms which will eventually inherit our developed characteristics. Such dematerialization may ensue from a natural tendency to unbind what was materially and unnaturally fixed in the first place, returning it to a natural state of dynamism and freedom to evolve.

The development of CYBERSPACE, defined as the broad realm of electronic memory, will accelerate this verbification. Such an INTERACTIVE space encourages focus on the discourse of imaginal dialogues. Objects valued in such networked exchanges will be preserved by circulating in RESONANT NETWORK WELLS, just as perceptions and synthesized memory IDIOLOGS persist in any evolving nervous system.

Though science shoulders the burden of hypothesis, experimental verification and fabricating models with predictive value, science and art share a

85. G. Spencer-Brown, *The Laws of Form* (New York: E.P. Dutton, 1979).

86. D. Rosenboom, *Zones of Influence*, five-part composition for percussion and computer music systems manuscript (Santa Clarita, CA: David Rosenboom Publishing, 1985). A musical composition inspired by ideas of interacting singularities within zones of influence, self-organization, chreods and local orderings. The following is a recording of the first part: "Zones of Influence, Part I, The Winding of a Spring, a) The Stochastic Part, b) The Tripartite Structure," on Rosenboom, *Roundup, A Live Electro-Acoustic Retrospective* (1968-1984), audio cassette with notes ('s-Hertogenbosch, Holland: Slowscan Editions, and Hanover, NH: Frog Peak Music, Vol. 7, 1987). A CD recording of the complete work is currently in progress. Two other compositions by the author that depend entirely on the idea of self-organizing emergent forms are *On Being Invisible* (1976-1977) and *On Being Invisible II (Hypatia Speaks to Jefferson in a Dream)* (1994-1995). In both works, musical forms emerge as computer software uses a partial model of musical perception to make predictions regarding the structural significance of events in its sound output stream. These predictions are then tested by analyzing auditory evoked responses from performers' brains and the results are used to guide further evolution of the music. The first of these works is for a solo performer and the second is an interactive, self-organizing, multi-media chamber opera.

poetic aspect: that of creative communication about newly conceived orders.[87] Poetic perception is largely determined by point of view. Mathematics may be considered a language through which nature speaks. Because of the purity of its logic and calculus, some may assert it to be devoid of the vagaries of poetic imaging. Mathematical impressions, however, can display extraordinary beauty, partly through this natural purity, in the same way that the poignancy of artists' insight can manifest in re-conceiving the boundaries of language. Though art is not required to predict the future behavior of the universe, artists may exhibit intense interest in considering it, and, in common with scientists, be inspired to make CREATIVE PRODUCTS THAT REVEAL NEW ORDERS.

87. Note the derivation of the word *poetic* from the Greek *poiein*, meaning "to make."

A useful task for art may be to provide exercises in COMPREHENDING THE UNDEFINED. How can the mind conceive of EMPTY SPACE, EQUILIBRIUM AS GENESIS, SUBSTANCE AS ASYMMETRY?

On Ponderability

An interesting phenomenon of scientific language bears relevance to the substance of forms, the idea of that which is PONDERABLE. Albert Einstein discusses the idea of the ponderable, particularly when referring to the PROXIMITY OF PONDERABLE MASSES, in his descriptions of the non-homogeneous geometry of relativistic space-time.[88] Distinctions in physics are sometimes drawn around that which is thinkable and that which is UNTHINKABLE. Physics, itself, is sometimes described as a SYSTEM OF THOUGHT, as that which is consistently thinkable.

88. Albert Einstein, *Relativity, The Special and The General Theory*, 15th ed. (New York: Crown, 1952).
89. Howard Gardner, *Frames of Mind, The Theory of Multiple Intelligences* (New York: Basic Books, 1983).

If one subscribes to the theory of MULTIPLE INTELLIGENCES[89] musical forms may be regarded as that which is musically thinkable—not necessarily in the verbal domain, but rather in the MUSICAL INTELLECT. Consideration of ponderability may also involve DEGREES OF PONDERABILITY, analogous to STRENGTHS OF DEFINITION. Elsewhere, I have described a logical model of independent, interacting spaces in which these spaces emanate from singularities (entities of distinction) and are allowed to have degrees or strengths of definition.[90]

90. David Rosenboom, "On the Invocation of Spatial Metaphors," manuscript in progress. Santa Clarita, CA, 1988.

Often, that which is thinkable is determined by a perceived need to maintain a particular world order. For example, the wide-spread objection to

Kepler's formulation of elliptical orbits for the planets was a reflection of a fear that unless orbits were perfectly circular, their paths would not repeat precisely, as would be required for permanence and immortality. Even the law of constant area was not adequate balm for this wound to the canon.[91] Thus, an unfortunate but recurring contra-position is cast between myth and science, a relationship weakened by lack of understanding for either. Circles were required for the denial of death and the denial of the eventual end of all things. Today, a phenomenon with even greater potential to stimulate cognitive dissonance lies in the characterization of planetary systems as CHAOTIC, possessing complex dynamics that are DETERMINISTIC, yet fundamentally UNPREDICTABLE and capable of exhibiting sudden, CATASTROPHIC changes in behavior.

91. The law of constant area is a principle stating that the area covered by a line drawn from a focus of the orbital ellipse to the planet will swing over an equal area during each unit of time as the planet proceeds on its path.

Aristotle distinguished POTENTIALITY from ENTELECHY, (complete actuality). Perhaps, evolution involves the transformation of minds such that what is now potentiality, i.e. currently UNTHINKABLE, becomes entelechy in the future, i.e. ponderable within entirely new cognitive paradigms.

Form and Cause

FORM and CAUSE are inextricably bound in the Western mind. It may be useful to consider the origins of our notions in this regard and our predilection to conceive form as stable substance.

Aristotle's idea of FORMAL CAUSE, perhaps as brought to us through the Medieval Scholastics or, at least, as interpreted in its most banal form, lies at the root, even today, of misapprehensions regarding form in art. This predominantly held idea is infused with a sense of the static. This stasis feeds resonating detectors for mental categories that support particular cognitive models needing reinforcement. One distinguishes sculpture from lumps of preformed raw material with the aid of these models. However, the ORDER SEEKERS evolving inside individual minds may extract ordered perceptions from the UNFORMED lumps, calling into question their unformedness in a profound way. What we refer to as FORMED, by contrast, is usually imbued with the INTELLIGENCE OF THE FORMING AGENT, which we somehow distinguish from the natural order of the unformed lumps.

A view of forms as DYNAMIC MORPHOLOGIES, however, calls into question the distinction of these separate intelligences. Form emerges. Form evolves. Forms emanate from points of singular genesis, defining the space

213

surrounding them, along with sets of dimensions and axes for describing their dynamic processes of change.

During the later Christianization of Aristotle, it became necessary to cast his ideas in a form suitable for the religio-political ruling forces of the time. In interpreting Aristotle's thoughts on teleology—the study of ultimate purpose and over-all design in nature—Aquinas identifies natural or suitable ruling agents as those of strong INTELLECT, their intellection being most evidenced by a thorough comprehension of CAUSES.[92] But the presuppositions underlying a worldview permitting the idea of causes depends on a HIERARCHY OF ORDERING AGENTS. By extension, one is led to the necessity of inquiring as to what ordering agent acts at the top of this hierarchy. Weak intellect, combined with a strong, emotionally driven demand for answers, leads to the invention of gods, born out of the necessity for controlling agents. Because this worldview originates from within a model of intellect, these gods tend to be conceived of as DOUBLES of human forms and though endowed with unimaginably greater power to perpetrate cause, can be appealed to emotionally as agents of ULTIMATE WISDOM and PURE INTELLECTION.

92. Gerald Holton, *Thematic Origins of Scientific Thought, Kepler to Einstein*, rev. ed. (Cambridge, Mass.: Harvard University Press, 1988).

A further problem with this view lies in the distinction it draws between knowledge and information. It posits that knowledge is possessed by self-directed entities, while information is possessed by natural objects. All this leads to the notion that ANIMATE objects must be directed by DIVINE AGENTS and that INANIMATE objects are moved—i.e. made animate—by some agent in the controlling hierarchy. God moves man and man moves rocks. And, because everything seems to move towards an ultimate BEST STATE, we have a fundamentally melioristic worldview. A view based on DYNAMIC MORPHOLOGIES may, in contradistinction, lead one to question the rigid differentiation separating animate from inanimate objects. It may come to seem that all things are animate.

In recent times, some Western minds have begun to assimilate the impermanence of all forms and its ramifications for art making. The evolution of many constructs in Western philosophy has been coerced by the psychological demand for permanence in all structures—the heavens, the molecule, the atom, the fundamental forces and cosmological constants—when all life experience reinforces the presumption of CONTINUOUS PROCESSES, INTERACTIONS AND MORPHODYNAMIC CHANGE. Even the idea of numbers—the most purely permanent construct we have and the foundation of mathematics—is a cognitive pretext born of the continuous interaction of forces in the mind driving the obligation to DIFFERENTIATE, to identify one and then two. Humans must, it seems, attempt to act as ordering agents. To do so they must direct energizing forces through CHREODS,[93] forming channels for information flow and resulting in the SPREAD OF ORDERED PHENOMENA. Following this, they must bear the burden of erecting a CALCULUS OF INDUCTIVE INFERENCE with which to INTEGRATE the results.

93. For a full definition of the chreod, see Reve Thom, *Structural Stability and Morphogenesis* (Reading, Mass.: W. A. Benjamin, 1975).

On global scales, all distinctions result from INTERACTION, not from the hierarchical imposition of ruling agents handing down ordering forces onto lesser agents. Those who act as ordering agents, *as all life forces do,* and who view themselves as RULERS operate under an illusion. They are interacting, ordering agents in consort with all regionally effective forces. It may be that all hierarchical (i.e. global) descriptions are synthetic extractions. It may be viable to view only atomic level events and elements as foundational and all else as emergent, summary phenomena.

In the present age, which now includes the global phenomenon of CYBERSPACE, defined as the realm of collective, electronic memory, INTERACTIVITY through electronic communication NETWORKS naturally emerges as a consequence of self-organization. The only requirement for this is a technological society comprised of a critical mass of individuals. It has been hypothesized that in a universe with the proper values for certain of its fundamental physical characteristics, known as cosmological constants, intelligent information processing will naturally evolve.[94] If this is true, then such electronic interactivity is a clearly foreseeable phenomenon of nature.

94. John D. Barrow and Frank J. Tipler, *The Anthropic Cosmological Principle* (Oxford: Oxford University Press, 1986).

Musical forms have been misapprehended as ruling agents rather than emerging properties of interacting components. Hierarchical descriptions of forms do not, by definition, require such ruling orders. Our interpretation of the word *hierarchy,* though, is unconsciously and profoundly imbued with an interpretative overlay inherited from post-Neolithic DOMINATOR societal structures. Other models for society may have flourished on Earth in the past. Riane Eisler has aptly described the contrast between these dominator and earlier societal models based on PARTNERSHIP. A return to partnership models may be required for us to continue participating in evolution in the future.[95]

95. Riane Eisler, *The Chalice & The Blade, Our History, Our Future* (San Francisco: Harper & Row, 1987).

Development of a good understanding of musical forms depends on the extent to which mental models can be constructed that represent musical information in a manner appropriate for the forms in question. Also, the components of formal analysis must be understood as ACTION TERMS, entities that can stimulate the formation of sometimes unpredictable relationships and provide tools for exploring musical environments. For example, a CHORD should be thought of as a MUSICAL VERB, not a noun. It is a channel of action, a temporary marker for movement, a signpost with arrows on a road leading to somewhere on the continuously stretching rubber sheet of musical space-time. Subtle ideas such as implication, expression by omission, feeling and context will also weigh in with their individual idiosyncrasies.

A worldview emerging now includes these notions: ruling and ordering agents are illusory; all forces act; entities of distinction interact; forces are of different RELATIVE strengths; all agents of order arise from self-organization and are locally effective; information is channeled though chreods, creating local orderings and ZONES OF INFLUENCE.[96] This worldview is expanding rapidly during our time, offering new paradigms for perception, evolution, cosmology, physics and the genesis of ideas.

96. Rosenboom, "On the Invocation of Spatial Metaphors."

Emergent, Global Properties and Wholes

Configurations of a whole often produce perceptions that transcend that suggested by atomistic, bottom-up analyses of component parts. Such entities may emerge as a consequence of organization and size. In fact, consciousness itself may result from super-organization among the electro-chemical-physiological components of the body that could not have been predicted by a deliberate engineering of their combinations. EMERGENT PROPERTIES appearing at certain levels of organization among energy-space-time-information units may reveal a fundamental principle of the universe. Groups of sufficient size and organizational complexity may create the instrumentality for higher-level formal phenomena to materialize.

From the wave structures of elementary singularities in the quantum world emerge the characteristics of ponderable matter and the global properties of materials. We experience these as the sensory qualities of matter—textures, the nature of building materials, the tactility of moldable stuff, such as clay—

and the formal features of sounds we hear. Other global properties appear at various levels of organization in the quantum metaphor.

Particular properties or behaviors often appear in a system as its sheer SIZE and COMPLEXITY are increased. This may be fundamental in the phenomenology of the universe. For example, the emergence of self-reflexive consciousness may be a consequence of the sheer size and complexity achieved by evolving molecular organization. The observations of CATASTROPHE THEORY show that particular levels of organization among processing units may place a system on one or another side of a CUSP, a boundary separating zones in a map of system behaviors. At this point, the fundamental STATE of the system may undergo a radical change. In physics, we speak of the PHASES or states of matter. At super-high heat and density, matter may undergo several such phase changes, as must have happened during the first few microseconds of cooling after the Big Bang, beginning time and space as we know it. The more familiar sudden changes of state—from gas to liquid to solid—that take place as simple physical variables such as heat and pressure are continuously varied also reflect such catastrophic reconfigurations of what we perceive matter to be.

Clearly, some of REDUCTIONISM and some of HOLISM may be operative. However, neither extreme position makes sense. In the brain, we speak of billions of neurons or processing units. No computer has yet been built with billions of processing units.[97] There are, however, billions of human beings on the Earth, ever more closely linked to each other by various communications media, including a self-built, electro-optical nervous system. If evolution continues in such a direction, and barring self-annihilation, a catastrophic cusp may be crossed. When this happens, a fundamental change of state in earthly society may occur and a GLOBAL, ORGANIC CONSCIOUSNESS may emerge. In any case, what the holists observe as integrative behavior and what the reductionists can not seem to explain by means of algorithmic organization of component units may be better understood by considering integrative behaviors as fundamental phases or states of systemic behavior, obtaining under certain constraints of organization, which may shift catastrophically at certain points along the axes of these constraints.

To paraphrase Gardner paraphrasing Wittgenstein, knowing every brain connection involved in concept formation won't help you understand what a concept is.[98] Musical experiments with distributed processing and global

97. Bear in mind that a transistor can not be compared to a neuron, the latter being enormously more complex in its operative behavior.

98. Gardner, *Frames of Mind*.

communication links among geographically distributed performers have been taking place for some time. These may be producing new kinds of organization and conception that could not have been predicted just by knowing the connections.[99]

99. Such experiments have been a major focus of activities at the Center for Experiments in Art, Information and Technology (CEAIT) at the California Institute of Arts in Santa Clarita, California, often in collaboration with the Electronic Café International, Santa Monica, California.

Comprehending Emerging Beauty

One who carefully observes the spread of a phenomenon throughout a population—the constituent parts of any interacting group—can witness how easily a group of sufficient size can become a medium for newly emerging forms, any of which carries the potential for manifesting tangible substance. The spread of ideas throughout a human population is an example. Such emerging forms influence the way in which a population interacts with another population, often with real, material consequences. When viewed from the top down, these consequences may easily qualify as corporeal and palpable.

Detecting and perceiving newly emerging forms requires continuously evolving frames of reference. Because it is by definition impossible to conceive new orders of intellect from within pre-established frames of referential mind, it becomes necessary for nature to evolve an exploratory mind state in which the recognition of new orders—the perception of new messages—carries with it the fundamental transmutation of those inquiring minds that perceive and recognize. New forms in art and music can be agents of this transmutation. Such metamorphic actualization, such entelechy, will occur in the universe. Forces on the obverse will become extinct, as always in the natural order.

Notions of BEAUTY are often phrased in some way involving the creation of striking SIMPLICITY emerging from an underlying COMPLEXITY among uncountable and unknowable component parts. A growing community of musicians, allied artists and scientists are exhibiting a keen interest in attempting to understand notions of complexity, as it is being cast the modern context. This is a natural result of the need to explore transformative processes as we participate in the evolution of a massive, COMPLEX ADAPTIVE SYSTEM: namely, the human family.

Musical Givens

What, then, are the givens of music? These are very difficult to identify. However, it may be reasonable to assume these two:

1. Music usually deals with SOUND.

We may take the Kantian view that the universe exists in ordered fashion outside our own mentality and propose, by implication, that music deals with sound having a physical order: ACOUSTICS.

We may assume that the mechanisms of SONIC PERCEPTION in the ears, brain, skin, organs, bones, etc. result from a degree of predetermination by means of genetics and, therefore, that the perception of sound is guided by certain parsing principles indigenous to the organism: PSYCHOACOUSTICS.

For some, sound may, in truth, provide a convenient metaphor for VIBRATION, LIMIT CYCLES (oscillation in dynamical systems) or WAVES (displacement in space proportional to time). Thus, music may be represented, if only abstractly, in the repetitive phenomena of any or all parts of the universe.[100] Our perception of sonic vibration remains abstract enough—i.e. free enough from parsing into semantically charged or biologically significant categories at relatively high levels of feature extraction in the brain for it to function in this foundational realm of universal symbolism. We can, unquestionably, *hear* sound in waves, whereas we are not as overtly conscious of *seeing* light as waves. Furthermore, the frequencies of sound overlap the frequencies of tactile sensations and rhythmic pulsing. It is easy to imagine a role for sonic perception as the brain/body's way of sensing relatively high-speed events—those which arrive and repeat faster than the usual fare of environmental changes. The perception of light waves remains somewhat problematic in this regard. Optical stimulations are immediately parsed by the primary visual sense mechanisms into categories such as the primary colors and various object, shape and movement classifications. These dissections have evolved to benefit the organism in its environment. However, they seem to be a somewhat arbitrary breakdown of the continuous light wave spectrum. They also overlay hierarchies of meaning on purely abstract physical phenomena at lower levels in the brain's information processing than is the case when we are hearing sounds.

100. It may be significant to point out the importance of sound metaphors in religious descriptions of creation: in the beginning, there was the *word*; according to the Judeo-Christian tradition; sound is also a primary phenomenon in Hinduism.

2. Music making is usually, not always, a SHARED ACTIVITY.

Music tends to involve shared experience among individuals in a social structure, whether human or non-human.

Compositional Method

A composer's license includes the opportunity to construct entire universes. It may be useful to consider some fundamental steps in constructing a compositional method. These may be unique for each individual and may apply to single works or bodies of work. Much music is made without overt consideration of these steps, of course. However, certain basic assumptions will always have been adopted, whether or not through conscious choice. Becoming aware of one's underlying premises through self-examination and retrospective analysis often aids in further developing creative processes.

• CHOOSE YOUR UNIVERSE. What is the UNIVERSAL SET for a work? The universal set will describe a domain of COMPOSITIONAL ATTENTION and the kinds of distinctions that will be made as a result of compositional thought and choice. Thus, the items that will receive attention in composing are delineated. What are the elements of formal concern? This may include naming the parameters that will carry information that articulates forms. Note that these are GENERATIVE parameters, not necessarily ANALYTICAL ones. How will composer(s), performer(s) and listener(s) act as ordering agents in the musical experience? Note that MUSICAL ATTENTION may be directed towards things outside the realm of formal processes, particularly in listening. Compositional attention may also be directed towards things not traditionally considered to be musical.

• HOW WILL THE UNIVERSE BE ORDERED? (Not, "how is it ordered.") List the potential GENERATIVE RELATIONSHIPS among distinctions in the universal set. For example, in the expression, aR_nb, a and b are related to each other by relation, R_n. Can these Rs be listed? One useful composing tool is known as the RELATIONSHIP MATRIX. This is an array that shows whether the elements of a set are considered to be related to each other or not and, if so, how. Note again that these are generative relationships determined in the process of composing and are not necessarily given a priori. Some of James Tenney's writings[101] have provided a good description of the relationship matrix.

101. James Tenney, *Meta + Hodos and META Meta + Hodos* (Hanover, NH: Frog Peak Music, 1986).

• WHAT ARE THE SCALES OF MEASURE FOR PARAMETRIC VALUES TO BE USED? How will parametric values be compared? For example, different types of MEASUREMENT SCALES may be used, i.e. NOMINAL (items are related only by labeling or classification with numbers), ORDINAL (numerical values indicate rank or order), INTERVAL (distances between numbers are equal but with no reference to zero) and RATIO (each value measures a distance from zero) scales. Scales for relating pitches, timbres, sounds in spaces, the physical size of instruments, the spectrum of brainwaves and the geographical separation of performers linked in a communications network could all be examples. MULTI-DIMENSIONAL scaling—the construction of a mapping in which the *closeness* of items located in a contrived space of two or more dimensions is considered analogous to their *similarity*—may be used. The axes of such a space correspond to the parameters describing formal characteristics of items contained in the space. The language and means for making comparisons must be decided —e.g. how it will be determined that *a* is more like *b* than *a* is like *c*, and so on.

• WHAT ARE THE LEVELS OF SIGNIFICANT DIFFERENCE FOR EACH PARAMETER? Establish the criteria by which things are to be considered the same or different.

• DESIGN THE COMPOSITIONAL PRAGMATICS NEEDED TO MAKE ARRANGEMENTS AMONG THE DISTINCTIONS IN THE UNIVERSAL SET. Establish the procedures through which unique musical works will be produced.

Various kinds of compositional pragmatics can be classified according to their philosophical premises. For example, an interesting classification can be created in relation to types of INQUIRING SYSTEMS. In the early 1970s, C. W. Churchman presented a particularly stimulating discussion about designing inquiring systems in which he defined inquiry as "an activity which produces knowledge"[102] Establishing an inquiring system involves articulating presumptions that are implicit in particular methods for exploring and investigating ideas. Often, these designs are guided by imagery used to describe nature. Table 1 is a speculative listing of some inquiring systems that are related to musical systems, with guiding images labeled by figures in Greek philosophy. Comments on each system follow.

102. Charles W. Churchman, *The Design of Inquiring Systems: Basic Concepts of Systems and Organization* (New York: Basic Books, 1971).

Table 1:

	Type	Example	Inquiring System Image
1.	causal-permutative	combinatorics	Democretian
2.	statistical-symbolic	stochastics	Carneadean
3.	acoustical-deterministic	harmony	Pythagorean
4.	gestural-biological	semantics	Platonic
5.	syntactic-teleological	grammar	Aristotelian

Comments:

1. Systems involving arrangements or permutations among sets are established in which the rules of combinatorics cause formal results. The imagery invokes the idea of elegantly simple mechanisms unfolding to subsume most of the phenomena in the universe.

2. The laws of probabilities are employed to symbolize behaviors thought to occur in the natural world. All phenomena are fundamentally uncertain in some measure and some individual manifestations of a phenomenon will attain sufficient strength in some aspect to manifest material interactions with other phenomena.

3. The foundations of acoustics determine forms and language elements. The arrangements of orthogonal building blocks—such as harmonics—thought to be given by fundamental physical principles determine the rules by which the individual components of a system—such as scales, tunings, chords, etc.—are identified.

4. The shapes of gestures and other expressions, perhaps arising from underlying biological processes involved in the essences of communication and social interaction, affect the meanings of forms and the semantic content of language. Such shapes may appear in the changes of parametric values—such as melody, loudness, timbre and position in space—over time, and their contours may communicate semantic qualities.

5. A teleological grammar gives direction to and projects points of arrival in forms by means of generative procedures. Particular uses of elements in a form may be taken to have purposive value in relation to other landmarks in the form.

• FINALLY, EXAMINE HOW ANY PARTICULAR CHOICE OF PRAGMATICS—I.E. A SYSTEM DESIGN—CAN BE EXTENDED BY VIEWING THE RESULT AS PART OF SOMETHING MUCH LARGER THAN ITSELF. If we do this the limits of particular sets of images guiding a system's design may remain apparent and new things may be more likely to emerge from creative processes that may be outside the domain of that particular system.[103]

103. I recall stimulating conversations on this kind of methodology with the late Salvatore Martirano during my student days at the University of Illinois and the point about always considering any idea as part of some larger idea emerged from conversations with Robert Ashley.

Improvisation

In one sense, improvisation is simply composition that is heard immediately rather than subsequently. The act of composing for improvisation may involve constructing a cognitive model of music, creating a good representation of the model to serve as a score and communicating that to musicians. The musicians, then, work from a model instead of a detailed score that is laid out in linear time. Composing that is immediately heard and compositions that are subsequently heard can both result from collective, group effort.

Dissipation, Complexity and Resonance

Equilibrium is genesis; substance is asymmetry. Dissipation is a creative process, a generator of complexity.

In acoustics, the displacement of an elastic medium creates POTENTIAL ENERGY. The DISSIPATION of that energy follows through a sometimes CHAOTIC DYNAMICS, enfolding the effects of instabilities in the medium (vibrating body) and its physical support (boundary conditions) and its ability to break up into many, imbedded, increasingly smaller and SELF-SIMILAR dissipative subsystems, all evolving around a set of ATTRACTORS—points in a PHASE SPACE describing tendencies of behavior in an unpredictable but deterministic dynamical system. Our mechanisms of auditory perception, in their constant search to extract global properties, make generalizations and recognize categories and present this information to consciousness as the spatio-temporal morphology of what we call HARMONICS.

The concept of RESONANCE is crucial in this overall picture. It is the tendency for certain recurrent behaviors to grow, as initially infinitesimal vibrations or patterns become self-reinforced, due of the way in which they *fit* within the spatio-temporal geometry of a bounded system, often aided by some feedback. Such behaviors also decay after the initial excitation energy is removed. Alternatively, if the system is wildly unstable, it may break apart. Resonance also involves the idea of COUPLING among systems in which the excitation of one system, in a particular form known as an EIGENSTATE, is transferred to another. In this way, information is transmitted and, further, may be propagated through a medium (population of systems), producing a kind of spatial diffusion of the EIGENFORM. This geometrical notion of communication may, in fact, be more appropriate than our usual one involving the juxtaposition of linear sequences.[104]

104. Thom, *Structural Stability*.

105. David Rosenboom, "Portable Gold and Philosophers' Stones (Music from Brains in Fours)," composition for a group of brain-wave performers and resonant electronic music circuits, on *Brainwave Music*, LP record (Vancouver & Toronto: Aesthetic Research Center of Canada Publications and Recordings, #ST1002, 1976).

In my *Portable Gold and Philosophers' Stones (Music from Brains in Fours)* (1972), a composition for brainwave performers with resonant electronic systems, a musical form results from how members of a performing group are able to achieve a synchronicity of consciousness—another kind of resonance.[105]

Grand Unity

On one particularly poignant occasion I was seated in the Duomo in Milan, thinking and listening to some monks chanting. Groups of tourists and school children were roaming this majestic and resonant space. The acoustical properties of the cathedral's architecture acted like a high-powered lens focused on the crowds. Each time someone called attention to a particularly inspiring feature of the Duomo, soft exclamations spread in waves through the space, interacting with the monks' chanting in complex, harmonious patterns. This created substantial music of great beauty. The process was exactly like the spread of a chemical reaction through a collection of molecules, giving rise to new, material qualities. Each individual member of such an aggregation is, itself, an organized warping or distortion of space/time. A population of such units comprises a potential medium. When such units are recruited through the process of resonance into patterns of organization quantified as information, new phenomena may emerge that can be perceived as substantive on a global level. Such substance may project itself into our perceptions as new distinctions.

A grand unity in all things follows that seems to require only three kinds of description, these being

(1) SPACE/TIME—frameworks defined when processes extend themselves,
(2) ENERGY—changes and distinctions in space/time, and
(3) INFORMATION—order and pattern underlying emerging entities.

These are all the primitives needed. Everything else follows. For example, ponderable matter and psychological processes both arise from the interactions and consequences of these three. Figure 1 presents a speculative visualization of some large-scale emergent properties in the evolution of the universe.

A POTENTIAL SCHEMA FOR EMERGENT, GLOBAL PROPERTIES IN THE UNIVERSE

MEDIUM	A BEGINNING POINT	INFORMATION
	SPACE (N-DIMENSIONS)	
	———— WARPING ————	
	(PRIMARY PROCESS)	
MATTER/ENERGY		PARTICLES/WAVES TIME
MOLECULES		CHEMICAL FORMS/SUBSTANCES
ORGANISMS		BEHAVIORS SELF-PRESERVATION SELF-REPRODUCTION
NERVOUS SYSTEMS		SELF-CONSCIOUSNESS
CLOSED WAVEFORM ENTITIES		CONSCIOUSNESS OF CONSCIOUSNESS
HIGH SOCIAL ORGANIZATION	✣	MACRO/GLOBAL-ORGANISM CONSCIOUSNESS
SUPER-CLOSED-ANTIENTROPIC ORGANIZATION	✣	UNIVERSE CONSCIOUSNESS

Figure 1. From the beginning point of the universe, the primary processes of spatio-temporal warping produce singularities. Therse are grouped into media organized by information and resulting in broader and broader properties, eventually leading to consciousness.
✣Speculative levels which may or may not have occurred in the ontogeny of the universe.

Transformation and Evolution

Self-observation must be subject to similar constraints as those shown by the UNCERTAINTY PRINCIPLE for the physical universe. The mind can not study itself without affecting itself. Ergo, a composer's mind is changed by the act of studying its own representations for music. Consequently, attempting to derive a mental model of musical representation may, in fact, bring that model into a functional existence.

There exists a universal human fascination with TRANSFORMATION. This may stem from a biologically driven desire evidenced by the creation of mythical or technological DOUBLES of human form, by the invocation of occult powers to transform, by transformation in science fact and fantasy and by transformation as an art process. The ability to recognize and manipulate multiple versions of sensory constructs may be referred to as TRANSFORMATIONAL SKILL. The brain works on, or transforms, images for a variety of purposes, including the following: (1) to test for the identity or similarity of two things, measured over the axes of some perceptual space, (2) to produce novel variations of some image for creative or humorous purposes and (3) to construct expressions relating to common or socially understood ideas.[106] This skill appears to be valuable for survival. It aids in perceptual recognition and facilitates the creation of useful outputs or products. It must function in both top-down and bottom-up hierarchical processing.

Accepting continuous transformation as a fundamental principle of the universe may require a redefinition of ego. This may involve a struggle against the possessiveness that is so fundamental to status and survival in a hierarchical society. The musical forms of transformation, improvisation and loosening fixed notation may all result from an innate and INTUITIVE drive. Intuition—the immediate apprehension or knowing of something without the conscious use of reason—may result from an important biological mechanism that responds to the underlying morphodynamics of the universe. When combined with open-minded REASONING, these two forms of INTELLIGENCE may lead to improved SYSTEMS OF JUDGMENT.[107]

New ideas in the arts and sciences of dynamical systems, evolution, cosmology, dissipative structures are giving glimpses of possible reconceived realities. These are not just reductionist approaches to dissecting the bank of a priori human observations derived within previous paradigms. We are now capable of imagining new paradigms and even testing them through technological or other simulations, especially in the arts. In this way, we can anticipate observations we might make from within potentially new paradigms. The synthesis of new paradigms can be considered an artistic process in which change is a given.

Sources of New Mythology

These ideas may provide a ground against which modern narrative may be developed, providing a basis for a new art with psychological power and cultural strength.

In the last century or two, art making moved from a SYNTHETIC-HIER-ARCHICAL paradigm—that of generalized concepts being constructed within the cognitive framework of higher things operating over lower things—to an ANALYTIC-REDUCTIONIST paradigm of processes being broken down in search

106. These ideas emerged in discussions with Stanford psychologist Roger N. Shepard surrounding the occasion of his talk, "The Structure of Pitch Perception," as part of the Seminar in Formal Methods Series presented at the Mills College Center for Contemporary Music on 14 November 1985. See also his paper, "Toward a Universal Law of Generalization for Psychological Science," *Science* 237 (1987): 1317-23.

107. For a musical work inspired directly by these ideas, see David Rosenboom, *Systems of Judgment,* seven-part composition for computer music systems and auxiliary instruments, *CDCM Computer Music Series,* Vol. 4, compact disc recording (Baton Rouge, LA: Centaur Records, 1989).

of underlying explanations contained in relationships among component parts. Now, art making may be moving to a new paradigm of HOLARCHIC-INTERACTIVE descriptions with EMERGENT PHENOMENA.[108]

Synthetic-hierarchical work was fraught with symbolist content derived from an imposed higher mentality and reflecting blinding, socio-politico-religious orders. These may have originated when the agrarian, ecologically aware, partnership-based societies of the Neolithic were supplanted by the warring, dominator societies that followed.[109] Such dominator societies could only be maintained through subjugation of otherwise freely inquiring human minds. This was accomplished by means of enslavement to vindictive, vengeful and threatening religious icons that has lasted to the present day. The more cool, analytic-reductionist emphasis of inquiring into the nature of human perception, cognition and the conscious and unconscious mind—typifying modern art of the late nineteenth and twentieth centuries—freed art from the baggage of this highly charged, unquestioned symbolic and emotional lexicon that weighed it down.

108. For a description of the synthetic-hierarchical and analytic-reductionist paradigms, see Paul C. Vitz and Arnold G. Glimcher, *Modern Art And Modern Science: The Parallel Analysis of Vision* (New York: Praeger Publishers, 1984).

109. Eisler, *The Chalice & The Blade*.

During the current era, art seems to be moving towards a natural confrontation with the beautiful, holarchical forms of the natural universe. This is happening on many levels of society. The common theme is INTERACTIVITY. This includes heterogeneous socio-cultural interaction and global, technological networking.

During recent centuries, scientific themata have evolved with such power that, when combined with empirical investigation and phenomenic verification, they have succeeded at denuding traditionally powerful myths of their power to guide society. New myths may arise from a critical level of interconnectedness. Such mass phenomena are sure to evince emergent properties. Hopefully they will be accompanied by images of sufficient power to garner forces of healing within our culture once again. Cultural crossings, with imaginal dialogs circulating in communication networks, may become the art objects of focus. This may be accompanied by a new phase of DEMATERIALIZATION in art. Objects may be created as INSTANTIATIONS of experience or EMBODIED REALITIES, growing out of the current notion of VIRTUAL REALITIES. Myths based on continuous transformation and change are needed to help humanity become comfortable with its necessary evolution toward partnership-based societies. Art can help, partly by bridging cosmogony and theogony in modern language.

Anthropic Cosmological Future

An intriguing set of ideas in speculative cosmology arises from what are known as ANTHROPIC COSMOLOGICAL PRINCIPLES. These are stated in various strong and weak forms. All are involved with questions about whether the particular, critical values for physical constants that have, according to theory, allowed the universe to evolve life forms, intelligent information-processing and the potential for self-observation are innate and inevitable. The validity of these lines of reasoning are hotly debated among cosmologists and it is beyond the scope of this text to trace them. However, if one assumes that only a remarkably restricted range for these values is compatible with a universe that eventually forms galaxies and delicate life forms residing on planets, then some of the logical outcomes proffer strong ramifications for the future course of evolution.

In the section on FORM AND CAUSE above, I stated that interactivity through electronic communication networks naturally emerges as a consequence of self-organization. This idea is related to the most speculative theory of an anthropic cosmological future, namely, the *Final Anthropic Principal (FAP)*, which states that *intelligent information-processing must come into existence in the universe, and, once it does, it will never die out.*[110] All activities of intelligent beings involve information-processing. Did the universe evolve the way it did in order to produce such living processors of information and observations? Certainly the universe is only *known* to exist because such processing capability has evolved. Can the forms of human activity reside in a medium other than the body? Can technological society produce other structures to support such activity, such as artificial bodies and intelligent, reproducing machines? Will the current research into artificial life and adaptive knowledge-based systems produce the ultimate inheritors of our essential forms? Who will be the audience in our future universe?

110. Barrow and Tipler, *The Anthropic Cosmological Principle.*

The Infosphere; Who's the Audience?

The emergence of a new dematerialization is a natural byproduct in the evolution of an INFOSPHERE, defined as the realm of the communal, electronic brain—akin to the biosphere. Dematerialization is also related to point of view. From the bottom-up, the circulation of patternings in cyberspace appears without substance. If one could have a view from the top down, however, these emanations may appear quite material.

Visualizing PROPOSITIONAL REALITIES requires cognizance of the degree to which terms of reference—i.e. measuring tools and metrics—are imbedded inside these realities and are subject to their LAWS—i.e. their thinkable terms of description and prediction.[111] Virtual realities manifesting in cyberspace may not carry with them overt descriptions of such thinkable laws. They may require discovery within rather than a priori communication. To be in the condition of searching for intelligence contained in instantiated realities requires transformative skill.

111. Note the importance of prediction to the human species in constructing mental images.

Who is the audience of the infosphere? Increasingly, it will be comprised of participants in networked exchanges. Differences will always exist among individuals who are more or less involved in creativity and innovation. However, the traditional differences separating creator from consumer will be recast, and the roles of creative individuals, formal models and art objects will undergo yet another re-examination. Coming societies will require transformative skill on many levels, akin to that required for intelligent musical improvisation.

Natural selection will insure that a planetary society that is incapable of structuring itself along the lines of cooperative transformation will not survive. Increases in the mobility of populations and global communication are forcing interaction among people with diverse cultural backgrounds. Such admixture of peoples is probably the most powerful energy source currently driving our cultural transformation. The fact that the technological facility to create global, interactive networks, with virtual and embodied electronic realities is being developed at the same time as this growth in cultural juxtapositioning will result in major transformations of society. We can only partially glimpse these at present. We know that emergent, global properties among many interacting components are fundamentally unpredictable. Therefore, we must be able to recognize them and interact in what we determine to be the appropriate manner, using our best judgment and without having full knowledge in advance.

The greatest single threat to human survival presently known is that the population of minimally sentient human beings will increase beyond the capability of the Earth's environment to sustain life and that the collective intelligence will not have advanced far enough to bring controls to bear on preserving our support structure. Furthermore, current societies are becoming bogged down in huge bureaucratic structures arising from organizing principles that are focused primarily on the legalities of individual liability. More of society's time and energy is consumed by managing blame, retribution and protection against responsibility than on creative thinking, education and inventing solutions. Time will tell the story and nature will act to choose appropriate outcomes.

Glossary of Some Important Terms:

ATTRACTOR—A set of points in a multi-dimensional phase space—used to describe the behavior of a dynamical system—toward which points originating in nearby regions of the phase space—known as the basin of attraction—will move as the dynamics process unfolds (usually in time).

CALCULUS OF INDUCTIVE INFERENCE—Mathematical procedures in which broad, large-scale or general characteristics of something are inferred by induction from the results of calculations carried out on smaller-scale constituents.

CALL—The indication and/or naming of a distinction, usually made with reference to one or another kind of content.

CHREOD—A topological construction that describes the projection or spread of an evolving, morphogenic process into a region of space-time, given a defined beginning known as the initiation set of the chreod. This is related to the idea of a morphogenic field, which also attempts to describe the spatial diffusion or region of influence of a morphogenic process. See also, ZONE OF INFLUENCE.

CYBERSPACE—The realm of global electronic memory, comprising the entire electronic communications and information-processing network with all its capacity for storing information and its potential for interactivity among its component parts.

DISTINCTION—The arranging or perceiving of a demarcation separating at least two kinds of content that differ in value.

HOLARCHIC—Having the characteristics of a holarchy, a system or structural entity that results from the simultaneous evolution of processes on both macro- and micro-scales of time, space and cognitive extent. The system or structure is not viewed as the exclusive result of either top-down or bottom-up building processes.

IDIOLOG—The form of processes involved in representing the idea of a quality. Usually used in reference to the encoded form of human percepts or sensory-motor or expressive qualities residing in the electro-chemical activity of the brain's neural networks and memory.

INFOSPHERE—The environment of information enfolding human society, analogous to the atmosphere, biosphere, etc., and usually used in reference to electronically reproducible and transmittable information.

INQUIRING SYSTEM—A set of teleological procedures that have been purposefully designed with the intent of producing knowledge, including methods for measuring the system's performance and the means to make decisions about and to implement changes in the system's components so as to optimize its performance.

MULTIPLE INTELLIGENCES—The idea that human beings possess a number of very distinct and coexistent kinds of intelligence—such as verbal, spatial, mathematical, musical and emotional intelligence—and, further, that no single set of descriptions or measurement assumptions applies with equal validity to all.

RESONANCE—The coupling of two processes, a source and a receptor, in which the excitation of the source results in a similar excitation of the receptor. The excitation of the receptor can also grow or persist when it is re-excited by its own processes, a phenomenon known as *feedback*. When the pattern dynamics of a system are determined by some kind of bounded domain, such as a resonant cavity or fixed vibrating body in acoustics, free-mode behaviors or normal patterns are easily excited, even with minimal coupling strength, when the exciting force patterns match those of the receptor and therefore fit within its system dynamics. Complex resonant behaviors can be observed in electronic networks, societies and ecosystems, as well as mechanical structures such as strings and bells. See also a description of resonance based on geometrical ideas in the section of this article titled "Dissipation, Complexity and Resonance."

RESONANT NETWORK WELLS—Regions within a network of interacting parts—such as an electronic communication network—in which certain processes become contained and reinforced due to their fit within the free-mode or natural operating characteristics of the region, analogous to the quantum theory idea of the potential well, which ensues when the probabilistic wave function for a particle is confined within spatial boundaries of potential energy, resulting in standing wave patterns that are similar to those of vibrating strings or acoustical chambers. See also, RESONANCE.

SINGULARITY—A distinction for which the degree of differentiation among values separated by the distinction is of a high order. A singularity is a point of discontinuity in a continuum—such as space-time or any multi-dimensional representation of a continuum—that is differentiated from its surroundings and is often associated with observable qualities interpreted as being the forms of interaction among the singularity and other distinctions in the continuum. Singularities are also associated with mathematical infinities appearing in solutions to equations used to model continuums, or with critical points on smooth functions that strongly affect the local behavior of systems. The point of origin in the big bang model of the universe and the locus of black holes are often referred to as singularities, because at these points the curvature of space-time becomes infinite. The term is used in the author's work to refer to the locus of warpings in any field—determined by the dynamics of a set of parameters defining a multi-dimensional space—which result in entities of distinction being identified that are capable of interacting with each other.

TONIC TRIAD—A musical chord constructed by simultaneously sounding the first, third, and fifth notes of a standard major or minor scale. The first note of the scale is also known as the tonic, or note which defines the musical key, and this triad is said to be built upon the tonic.

ZONE OF INFLUENCE—A topological idea defining the region of space-time surrounding a chreod, inside which energy and information processes that are channeled through the chreod can affect events. This is similar to the idea of the light cone in relativity, which describes the limits on communication or the propagation of a process through space-time due to the speed of light.

Note:

SMALL CAPS	important terms and vocabulary words
italic	particular, highly specific, unique usage
SANS-SERIF	
SMALL CAPS	emphasis

Publication Note: The first version of this article was written on the invitation of John Zorn in 1993. A considerably revised and reorganized version was published in two installments in the journals, *Leonardo* (30:4, 1997) and *Leonardo Music Journal* (7, 1997), by MIT Press, Cambridge, Mass. The version presented here is a third revised and complete one prepared especially for *Arcana: Musicians on Music.*

EARPLUGS

MARC RIBOT

Hi. My name is Marc. I'm a guitarist who points extremely loud amplifiers directly at his head. Often. Sometimes as often as two hundred fifty nights a year for the past twenty years. Doctors say this could make one's ears howl, create an uncomfortable sensation of density in one's head, and eventually make it impossible to hear human conversation. Yet I persist—why?

It's true most amps sound better at volumes loud enough to fray the edge of notes with the subtle distortion that is to electric guitars what make-up is to a drag queen of a certain age. Not accidentally, as manufacturers in the late fifties and early sixties raced to design equipment with less and less distortion, guitarists turned up louder and louder to subvert their efforts. Nor are guitarists alone in this desire to strain.

We seem to love broken voices in general: vocal chords eroded by whiskey and screaming, the junked out weakness of certain horn players, distortion which signifies surpassing the capabilities of a tube or a speaker—voices that distort, damage, but (at least in performance) don't actually die. The singer pushes through the note, the horn player eventually finds breath, the amplifier struggles on but doesn't explode and become silent.

Was this always true? I don't know. Maybe it means something that representation of the struggle (once shown by the trembling effect called *vibrato*) to maintain the distance necessary to hold an instrument or sing a note in the face of overwhelming emotion is signified in our time by a direct attack on the equipment itself. True vibrato sounds old fashioned to us; think of Django Reinhardt's guitar sound, Caruso's voice, Guy Lombardo's saxophone. Somewhere along the line an inflation occurred in the currency of romantic pain, and the price of our musical fix was more than mere notes could pay.

Another word for distortion is low fidelity. Maybe we distrust our voices and that's why we're unfaithful to them. Beginning in the mid- to late-

sixties, producers of guitar equipment began to recognize our need to be
unfaithful by making equipment designed to produce distortion. Some amps
had little knobs on them saying "distortion," with numbers one to ten.
Although the public at first confused guitarists who fell for this maneuver with
creators of genuine damage such as Jimi Hendrix, the sounds produced soon
became completely predictable.

My chief complaint against many practitioners of heavy metal guitar
in the early seventies through the early eighties is that I can immediately tell
that their distorted sounds are not really placing
their amps at risk. To whatever extent I have a moral
sensibility, this offends it. I prefer the subtler but less
predictable distortions of the forties and fifties (e.g.,
Charlie Christian, Hubert Sumlin, Pee Wee Cray-
ton, Ike Turner, Chuck Berry),[112] a time when amp designers weren't such wise
asses. Still, the total deafness of metal musicians to these considerations lends
them a certain charm all their own.

112. Not that I'm nostalgic—contemporary
inheritors of this tradition of sonic risk
include Robert Quine, James Blood Ulmer,
and legions of others more or less influenced by some or all of the above.

The astute reader may point out that a smaller amplifier would produce the proper ratio of "clean" signal to distortion at a lower volume. True.
Also true: I've often used Marshall stacks—large, loud amps. This was because
I wanted to preserve at all costs the option of playing with a partially distorted
sound—using a larger amp turned up *almost* all the way—rather than be
trapped with the over-distorted sound (produced by having a smaller amp up
all the way) typical of late sixties white blues players.

If subtle distortion is make-up, the heavy, homogenous distortion of
these guitarists (Eric Clapton, in a phrase demeaning to women everywhere,
referred to his sound at the time as "woman tone") amounts to a type of air-
brushing. This is especially true when it is used in conjunction with the type of
grandiose large room reverbs and echoes supplying every amplified squirt in a
garage band with the imaginary ambiance of the Milan Central Train Station. It
is the sonic equivalent of fascist architecture. The effect (and probably the intent)
is to eliminate the little clicks and imperfections that belie the god-stature of
the guitar hero and to give the impression that the guitar is a strong bellowing
voice rather than a frame for frail pieces of metal whose vibrations soon die.

All guitarists fight this death, this logarithmic decline into silence, and
its implied presence in every note may be one of the reasons guitars (more than
bowed or wind instruments, whose notes can be sustained at will) have long
been linked to sadness and despair. The guitar is the essential instrument

of the blues. Picasso chose it to accompany images of death during his "blue" period. The best known piece of the first guitar hero virtuoso, John Dowland (16th century England), is titled "John Dowland Is Always Sad."

Some guitarists fight it by squeezing the last bit out of a note with vibrato. Others use the mandolin technique of picking many notes very fast, hoping no one will notice (the best known example being Francesco Tarrega's *Recuerdos do la Alhambra*). Volume also works. The sound from the amp reinforces the vibrations of the strings, creating increasingly longer sustains up to the point of feedback. Still, to struggle with the decay and death of notes (in music, things decay before they die) is one thing. To try and actually win seems somehow wrong: a Faustian error. Hence the Marshall stack.

I know. All the above is at best a limited explanation for years of nightly volume abuse. Those with a Freudian orientation might by now be tempted to see this preference for large amplifiers and loud sounds as a type of…compensation.

Dear reader, let me assure you—nothing could be farther from the truth. Still, the ghosts of early musical traumas do hover over the volume knobs, urging me to acts of excess as surely as grandma's memories of childhood deprivation kept pulling her back to the refrigerator long after her stomach was full.

The experiences in question are of a type rarely described by music critics, yet so obvious to musicians as to be practically nameless. As soon as I started playing in public, I began to experience the struggle between the "power" of my amp (then a lovely Ampeg B-12) and the social and economic power of band leaders, club owners, paying members of the audience, band members, etc.—the ones Sartre was talking about when he said, "Hell is other people."

Critics tend to write about material conditions of music making as if they were a neutral garden in which little artistic seedlings, fertilized perhaps by the critic's own careful attentions, grow slowly towards the light of aesthetic beauty.

What's missing from this perspective is an understanding of social constraints: sublime moments interrupted by enraged diners who can't talk over their shrimp boats, the harsh criticism of newlyweds who feel your style is spoiling their blessed event, etc.

The relation between amp wattage and social power can be even stickier within bands, those little units which invariably replicate the most dysfunctional elements of their members' families. What guitarist hasn't endured horrible meetings in which electronically deprived members of the band (drummers, sax players, vocalists) attempt to reason with them, appealing to a sense of compassion and egalitarianism usually altogether lacking in their own rock 'n' roll will-to-power personas, or, that failing, resorting to threats or brute force? This banal scenario is a usually doomed attempt to check the famous "dialectic of rock and roll," which can be heard played out on many a stage nightly: you turn up, so I turn up, so you turn up, etc.

Technology being advanced as it is, the only possible end point to this escalation is the limit of human endurance—and here's where distortion/volume as a metaphor meets the medical phenomenon.

When acoustic pain occurs in the theater of rock (and judging by those hilarious clips from decades past, every one of its mutations has been initially felt as brutal or painful, no matter how benign sounding to later ears), the pain of the audience is compensated for by their pleasure at the spectacle of the sacrifice of the musicians, who, since they are standing closer to the amps, are theoretically experiencing even greater and more destructive pain. In fact, mammoth sound systems in the hands of deaf or sadistic sound persons often make the room volume louder than the stage volume, but this only heightens the theatrical effect. In this illusion, the musician is both sacrificial victim and magical protector who filters the dangerous volume levels through his / her body (literally standing between amp and audience) to protect the audience. This ritual is not unlike the shamanistic practice of filtering strong poisons through their bodies so others can enjoy the less toxic residue by drinking their hallucinogenic piss. In a reversal of Star-Kissed Tuna priorities, rock audiences are more than willing to suffer bitter acoustic phenomenon in order to achieve ritual/aesthetic satisfaction. Thanks, Charlie.

I don't know how they do the trick with the poison mushrooms, but the truth about playing loud is this: on a really good night, nothing hurts—not howling volume, not airless rooms at sauna temperatures, not bleeding calluses, not a fever of 103, not a bottle in the head, not a recent divorce. Nothing much. Not 'til later.

So—the unresolved social conflicts of the bad are translated by ever louder sound systems into a theater of pain for the audience, and everyone goes home happy. But the shamans are cheating. They are going deaf or using earplugs, enabling them to avoid indefinitely the consequences of intra-band social failure, and violating the shamanistic pact with the audience—feeding them the poison undiluted. The audience, of course, senses this deception and begins to go deaf or use earplugs themselves, degrading the entire spectacle (and necessitating/giving birth to alternate theatrical forms such as stage diving). The bands in turn sense their lapse in shamanic power and crank it up still louder.

Oh my. Where will it all end? If the birth of symphony orchestras foreshadowed the arrival of parliamentary government, and the Beatles pre-figured the hippie commune, one can only imagine what post-Bosnian nightmarish total failure of language is lurking noisily in our futures, blocked out/symbolized/invited by the earplugs I wore on the gig last night. Don't blame me: doctor's orders. But what's even more depressing…

Thanks to Ann Marlow for feedback of the literary kind.

CHAPTER 20

PAULINE'S QUESTIONS

DAVID MAHLER

Composer Pauline Oliveros posed nine questions for fellow composers on NewMusNet, a conference of the online service Arts Wire. She prefaced her questions by asking, "Regarding survival—would a discussion around the following questions be useful?"

What follow are my responses, edited and fleshed out, but in essence the same as what I wrote online. I have rearranged the order of some of the questions, with the intention of providing more continuity to the issues raised.

Underlying these responses is my belief that musical stylistic prejudices are unimportant now, and certainly subject to continual reassessment. What begs discussion today is not style (with so much of the world at our ears upon demand, arguing over style seems a littlemind activity), but rather how the music gets done. If my responses (and Pauline's questions, too) sometimes seem glib or to range broadly, there is, finally, just one question being asked and responded to here—the question of how the composer gets along in the world today.

Q: As a freelance composer/performer how have you survived?

Through the good graces of friends. That's all there is to it. Everything else I do and have done for survival—playing in various ensembles, conducting a 1920s-style dance orchestra, writing comedy for the radio, teaching music to small children, teaching adult music workshops, practicing public art, playing piano rags in homes, leading singing groups, performing at nursing homes, working as a children's librarian, playing organ in churches, directing choirs, organizing concerts, acting, writing and editing for hire, accompanying singers—all pale in comparison to the basic, comforting knowledge that there is someone(s) accepting my musical offerings and helping sustain me.

I am able to do many different musical activities well and with ease—activities that don't, on the surface, relate directly to my work as a composer (and that don't generate much money, either). But in spite of occasionally grumbling about how I spend my time, I've never had to strictly compartmentalize my life into "work to make money" versus "work to make art." That's just me. Some friends find a clear separation between their money work and their art work to be helpful.

In this regard, I hear composer/life insurance executive Charles Ives saying, "The fabric of existence weaves itself whole. You cannot set an art off in the corner and hope for it to have vitality, reality, and substance. There can be nothing "exclusive" about a substantial art. It comes directly out of the heart of experience of life and thinking about life and living life. My work in music helped my business and my work in business helped my music"— this, in response to criticism that Ives did not participate directly enough in the musical scene of his day; that he chose a safe route by going into business.

I also hear composer Peter Garland pointing out that the tradition of radical music-making in this country is partly a story of composers helping each other. For instance, it's common knowledge that Charles Ives used some of his money to further the causes of a variety of composers, by, among other things, bankrolling concerts and supporting Henry Cowell's publishing ventures. It's also well documented that Lou Harrison turned the tables and gave Ives support by editing, copying parts for, and conducting the first performance of Ives's *Third Symphony*, which piece eventually won for Ives a Pulitzer Prize (though Ives was not impressed with the idea of the prize). It's even fairly well known that a short while later, during a time of critical need for Lou Harrison, Ives sent Harrison half the money from the Pulitzer. What I didn't know until a few years ago, however, was that it was a young John Cage who informed Ives of Harrison's need, and ultimately brought about the monetary gift from Ives to Harrison. Who among us doesn't also have a story of our own regarding personal aid tendered us by another composer? Or by another individual, composer or not?

By assistance, support, or aid, I don't just mean money. There are many needs. Money is only one.

(Incidentally, I like the word sustain in place of survive. Survive has such a desperate tone to it, whereas sustain at least sounds like I'm getting something done in the process of trying to hold my life together!)

Q: What is your current situation?

I live from month to month, if not week to week. I don't feel threatened by that, most of the time. In the boat I'm in are many other passengers. Like most of my companions, I am indebted to friends and credit card companies.

It is important to find ways to live cheaply but well, to be successful at being poor. The government of the United States, and much of society in fact, seems determined to have citizens who are wealthy, but I'm not going to fall for that. Living cheaply but well, that's my preference.

I like to describe myself as independently poor; that is, I have made a choice about what I will and won't do, and one thing I won't do is live my life solely for the purpose of making money. That said, I will also say that I like to have money in my pocket. If I don't know where my next dollar is coming from it affects my work as well as my relationship with other people.

Lately I've been thinking about the fact that many people I know, artists and non, well-off or not, are forced to earn more than they can use. What happens then is that an economy develops around the idea of being money-responsible for the future. For instance, what started out altruistically enough, I would guess, as the life insurance industry, has bloomed into a fixation on "financial security" and all the ramifications thereof. Here I'll bring Charles Ives back to the forum. As I read him, Ives really believed that the value of life insurance was in "equalizing the misfortunes" among citizens. That has a slightly less selfish sound than the reasons offered today for buying insurance.

In a way, music is the perfect expression of a security-less existence— at least music as I hope I practice it. That is to say, music exists in time. As such, it has no security. It sounds and then it is not sounding. It can't be frozen and stockpiled. It's either taking place now or it isn't. In addition, the whole act of making music is involved with danger, from the merely physical and mechanical and human delicacies of instruments, singers, equipment, and performers, to the psychological difficulties of playing and performing. Lou Harrison wrote in his *Music Primer*:

> The miracle is not that so much music exists, nor that so much of it is beautiful— but, rather, that it exists at all. Most music is produced by some fluke of nature— harpsichord jacks just barely pluck & then repass the string, bows just barely pull the strings & then proceed, the plucked string may balk or buzz, even vocal chords grow hoarse & raw. Reeds may or may not vibrate, flutes may wheeze or refuse, lips lapse infirm! Thank heavens that anything works when it does—& the musicians too!

(And to update—patchcords weaken, magnetic tape turns brittle, computer memory fails.)

John Cage wrote, (in 1949!) "Let no one imagine that in owning a recording he has the muse. The very practice of music is a celebration that we own nothing." Composers are subversives in this sense: in a time when people are being exhorted to believe that it's not enough to be alive and active and productive now, that somehow you've got to be all those things to the future, too, composers are, in the absurd act of writing and playing music, sharing a reality of a different sort, namely Cage's grand idea "that we own nothing."

Q: What information or services would help you continue to survive?

Physical space appropriate to music making and "trying things out" is my biggest need right now. It relates to the broader question of how a composer who is not affiliated with an institution finds the space and tools with which to do his/her work. My own needs are simple because I like to work with what I'm given. But there are times when I long for a space that is two-way quiet— where I don't disturb others through my work with sound (and am able to work unselfconsciously), and where I am not disturbed by what is becoming an increasingly aggressive sonic environment. Ideally, I seek a freestanding building, as opposed to one space in a building with many spaces. I suppose a cinder block structure, 600 square feet minimum, would be fine.

Here I'll digress a moment and talk about some of my past relationships with spaces. I have worked at home through most of my composing life. Home has ranged from small apartments to a 2000 square foot loft. I've never had a space where I could regularly work with more than one other musician at a time, with the exception of when I was working at *and/or* (an artists' organization) in the mid- to late-seventies.

For a brief time about four years ago I rented an office space in a building with architects, designers, printers, and various small businesses. It was a little space, probably 200 square feet, but I moved in my upright piano and other music-making tools. It felt good to be among people who worked regularly and, in many cases, independently. I do think that my presence in the building was of great interest to people in some of the other offices. A number of them mentioned to me that they enjoyed hearing the music from the hallway. Some lingered to ask questions and invited me to see what they were up to in their own offices. My tenancy was short lived; a brief letter from the manager informed me that it just didn't work to have a musician in the building, and that there had been a serious complaint. I had no lease, so out I went, mostly disappointed that there was never any direct confrontation with either my accuser or the manager concerning my expulsion.

For a few months after that experience I tried to find alternative studio space, but with no success. Even in an older, concrete building—a large building filled with visual artists, writers, and publishers—I was told that musicians were not welcome. In my explorations of that building I did notice one musician in residence. Surrounded by graphic designers at drafting tables along the circumference of an enormous room, in the middle of a large, nearly vacant space there stood a young man at an electronic keyboard, earnestly working away, listening to his work over headphones that covered his ears. He could have been in his kitchen or he could have been in the middle of the Boeing Aircraft plant in Everett, the largest building in the world. The physical space of his music making was totally inconsequential. While this arrangement may have worked for him, I don't like to cut myself off from the physical, spatial and acoustic surroundings of my music.

What I thought was my best proposal for finding space (and it's an idea that I would still love to have come to fruition) I presented to an employee at a large insurance company. This employee had free reign to administer a rather substantial art program for the company. My proposal was this: hire me as composer-in-residence for a year. Give me an office space in which to work. Let me compose music that might be of use for special occasions that the insurance company would want to celebrate. During lunch hours I would form a company choir that would meet a few days a week. Once a week over the lunch hour I would make a presentation in the elegant company auditorium, sometimes presenting guest musicians or composers, and sometimes just sharing with the employees some of my ideas about music. I would also indoctrinate them in the history of the U.S. musical experimentalists. Still not a bad idea, I think, though the proposal was rejected.

One basic issue concerning space for conscious sound making is that our society has become so unconsciously noisy that the idea of dedicating space to sound making probably seems curious to many people.

Q: Is your music functioning in your community or beyond?

Somehow, yes. The "somehow" is because I only feel that it's functioning when I look back at what has already taken place. It never seems like much is getting done until I look back and see accomplishments.

I try to establish my own community, or define community in a way that suits the work I do. I am always on call—that is, I will tackle almost any type of composing or performing situation requested, as long as I am paid for it and the work isn't degrading to me or to the music.

My favorite way of getting music out is through commissions. A simple, well thought out commission is hard to beat as a meaningful and expeditious way of generating new music. Everyone involved is important and has his/her role. The commissioners provide the impetus, the financial support, and the rationale. The composer provides music for the occasion or for the performers. The performers are entrusted with the pleasures of bringing something new to life. And the audience listens in the spirit of the gifts that have been passed down the line.

By commissions, I mean requests in which money changes hands. The music community still mistakenly refers to a request to write for free as a "commission," but that is not a commission at all. And my interest in commissions is primarily in the area of private commissions, as opposed to commissions that come about through grants. I get most excited when individuals put their money and ideas on the line to help generate a new piece of music. Then a strong bond is created between the money given and the work produced, and everyone—commissioners, composer, performers, and audience—approaches the project with their ears a little more attentive than they might otherwise be.

Similarly, in performing I try to create situations in which there is a commitment from the audience. Small audiences in small spaces, including homes—that's my preference. I think the trick is getting music into people, or reminding people of the music that is within them—planting seeds in individuals, as opposed to broadcasting.

Yes, my own music is functioning in my community, and it is making a difference in people's lives.

Q: What happens when grassroots music spreads to large venues?

Art that is conceived small can't be placed in a larger setting without being substantially changed, and vice versa. I guess the conception of the piece is what seems important—whether the music was *planned* to take place in a large setting. In music, there is an assumption that anything can work in a large setting, as long as we add amplification proportionately—which is one of the reasons why amplification, or overall amplitude, has replaced acoustic spatial considerations in most music.

Q: How do we show the continual rip-off of our research and our music by commercial interests?

I don't think there is a solution to this problem. As long as there are those who use ideas strictly for personal gain, there is little defense against the misappropriation of our ideas. This is part of the bigger question of finding the rightful forum for what we do. I return to John Cage's concern that music is becoming more and more an object. For instance, when well-intentioned programmers at National Public Radio use quarter-minutes of unidentified compositions to segue from one feature to another, we have an example of our music being used as an object, or at least as a device. Who created this authorless music, I want to know? Why is no credit given? Why, indeed, should music devised for listening to over an extended period of time be presented to the listener in dismembered segments? Let the announcers or the station be treated in the same way, without identification, out of context, and see how they like it. I find this no less disturbing, no less a rip-off, by the way, than if someone makes a commercial that clearly steals musical ideas from a composer in order to sell a product.

Q: How do we get them to fund us?

Who is the *them* here? What are we offering in return, or what is the connection between funder and fundee? Why should I want someone's money without also getting their understanding and enthusiasm? A big-picture solution to the survival crisis of composers may be more rooted in identity than in funding, at least funding in the impersonal way that grants are often administered.

Q: How could we strengthen our position in the social fabric of our country?

Let's see...how do we become indispensable?? Wouldn't that be something!

Like any kind of change, change in how composers are perceived best takes place on a one-to-one basis. (At the same time, we seek accurate, regular representation from those who presume to speak on our behalf to mass audiences.)

It seems to me that we need to deal with the whole issue of sound in our lives and sound in the environment if we are to make any inroads into strengthening our position in the social fabric of this country. For instance, I see/hear nothing salutary or social about urban noise levels that virtually rule out the possibility of carrying on a conversation. Whether walking down the street or sitting together in a restaurant, people ought to be able to converse. It's hard to believe that composers will be taken seriously in their communities if sound itself is treated with the casualness and disdain evidenced by life around us. Perhaps if composers become part sound conservationists, we may be appreciated and respected more for the work we do.

On the other hand, it's just a shame that composers doing valuable work in expanding the theoretical base of music can't also be part of the social fabric. I speak here on behalf of difficult work—that demands much from the listener. The issue is education of the public as individuals capable of interest and understanding. A piece of new music heard once remains strange. Heard twice or more it becomes familiar, and audiences bestow an allegiance to the work simply because it is recognizable—it is no longer threatening.

A goal should be to have music—many kinds of music with many uses—be a regular part of our lives. And new work ought to be a natural part of our many musical experiences. In that regard I have long viewed the words "WORLD PREMIERE" with suspicion. If we need to tout a work as a premiere it's a sign that we're not doing enough new work. Our lives ought to be peppered with new work all the time, and in a very natural, "business as usual" way.

Popularity is not the same thing as being an integral part of the social fabric of the country. A populist mentality seems to have a cultural stranglehold on music.

Create a situation—just one situation would do—that involves your audience or community, where and whatever that might be, in a direct experience with your own work. Don't be a capital A artist about it by placing yourself above your community. Don't underestimate your audience. Don't insist that they understand what you do. Let the experience and whatever honest reactions come out of it be the desired end.

Let what you do take place in time. Think of the memory of the event or performance as being part of the piece, a part that will give you a strong tie to many of your audience members, who will never forget what you did, and will be changed by it. Ignore those who aren't satisfied only with what you offered, but want there to be some way that they can *own* what you do, too. In a time when many people think an event is real only if it has been captured on video, leave them with the memory. A good experience can only be enhanced by memory.

Shun categories for all you're worth. Categories are the work of small minds who want to understand everything. When your work is categorized, people assume they understand what you do, and the moment you are understood you will be dismissed.

Accept enigma. Nearly every day I am confronted with Ives' "My God! What has sound got to do with music!" Or I wrestle with Morton Feldman's "Do you know what communication is for me? Communication is when people don't understand each other. That's what communication is. Because then there is a consciousness level that is being brought out of you, where an effort is made."

Grants and other second-hand ways of making connections to people have little lasting value if the only connections made are between composers/musicians and the granting agencies. Money spent to further the cause of composers ought to foster allegiance. Granting agencies are in the *business* of giving money, and allegiance from granting agencies is very different than allegiance from an individual who gives in respect for what you do, rather than as a business. Another way to think about it: granting agencies are dedicated primarily to the idea of funding composers and new music, often based on the concept of "work of the highest quality." On the other hand, an *individual* who gives money to a composer is giving a personal, emotional salute of recognition and approval, often based on that composer's needs rather than on some standard of excellence. This kind of relationship, between a composer and an individual who gives money, is founded on stronger, more vital ties than the relationship between composer and agency. In fact, in my experience the private donor is less interested in the notion of 'work of the highest quality' than in the notion of supporting one particular person, or even supporting the concept of the composer. It is only in the abstract world that the phrase, "...of the highest quality" has use. In real life, (not that there is any such thing!) sophisticated heirarchies based on quality fail to account for the idiosyncratic dreamer, the uncategorizable misfit.

When one leaves behind notions of "work of the highest quality," one also confronts the issue of the possibility of failure, in the conventional sense. As one enlightened individual said to me, after I asked him for money for a commissioning project, "You mean we won't know beforehand what we'll be getting? I love it! We're funding something, and it could turn out to be awful!"

I don't mean these remarks to be disparaging toward foundations and granting agencies. They serve their purpose. Many dedicated, thoughtful, and innovative people staff the various philanthropic organizations that support composers. I treasure strong friendships in those ranks. However, to make a more direct connection to your community, whoever that might be, it makes sense to me to seek support from the people who are part of that community.

Another community-related thought—help those you come in contact with to know something about your musical forbears. If you mislead people into thinking that you are engaged in some mystically generated original act of genius, you may be the last composer to ever have an audience. That is what has happened to Beethoven and Mozart—elevated to sainthood—and for many people those two are, indeed, the last composers to have lived. It's difficult to help people know the exploratory tradition in music, because there is such an enormous gap in the musical consciousness of most people. Almost every other art form has done a better job of connecting itself to its recent past than has music. (If you're not sure about your lineage, a toothy, provocative source for ideas is "The American Experimental Tradition—A Personal Perspective," from Peter Garland's book, *In Search of Sylvester Revueltas*.)

Q: Who do we need to speak to or wake up?

Ourselves, mostly. Our significance to the community around us will increase in proportion to how much we value our own work, and to how thoughtful we are in presenting ourselves.

Beginning in the mid-1970s (my choice of date because that was the flowering of the new-music-presenting alternative space) composers began to ask for and receive fees appropriate to the work we were doing. These fees, paid by presenting organizations loosely referred to as alternative spaces, came from grants, concert admissions, organizational membership programs, and donations, in descending order of financial impact. (For many presenting organizations, grants were nearly the *sole* source of program funding.)

Two oversights may have occurred during the golden days of the composer as circuit rider on the alternative space circuit, oversights whose consequences affect today's composers. First, little connection was made between the composer and the actual source of the money that paid the composer. Given the relatively impersonal nature of grants, often applied for and administered thousands of miles from the sources of the money and the music, composers had little knowledge of where their fees were coming from. In the headiness of actually getting paid for our work, we rarely asked such questions.

Further, we were often negligent in our understanding of the additional support systems that existed in order for us to be well paid. Again, money is only one part of the need of composers. It's a serious part, to be sure. But it is good for us to pay attention to all the means by which our music is made and promoted, including availability of newer technologies and equipment, space for rehearsing, performing, and trying things out, and the mechanisms by which one nurtures attentive and committed audiences.

Of course, this painless arrangement of simply dropping out of the sky, presenting a concert, picking up our check, and heading to our next destination didn't last forever. As granting sources directed their attentions elsewhere or simply went out of existence, and as more and more young composers interjected themselves into the circuit, composers found that fewer presenting organizations could afford the fees previously paid, or could even offer a gig at all, and the golden days were suddenly tarnished. (Incidentally, I don't mean to imply that the seventies and early eighties afforded lots of composers a financially stable existence. However, a relatively large number of heterogeneous composers received credible support for their work, on a fairly regular basis. For a brief period of time, there really existed a viable circuit of performing opportunities that made it economically possible to be a working composer.)

The second oversight connected to the activities of the seventies and very early eighties was that the support system in place worked to the benefit of the solo composer/performer almost exclusively. So, many of us were not only cut off from direct contact with the source of our fees, we were also cut off from other musicians, too. Ensemble-based music, or performer-based music, where the composer was not also the performer, was rarer than the solo composer/performer music. As a consequence, when solo composer/performer opportunities began to dry up, many composers were left isolated from their musical peers, that is, from the community of players and singers who might have helped keep this new music alive and in the consciousness of audiences. One of the real benefits of the ascendency of the new music improvisation scene of the 1980s was its inclusiveness of lots of players. Whereas many of us, as solo composer/performers in the seventies, unwittingly segregated ourselves from the bigger world of music around us through our exclusively solo acts, the next generation of composers cross-cultivated themselves in a big stew of composers and players—indeed, erased the line separating creator and interpreter.

Returning to the question at hand, we do ourselves a service when we consider our composerly relationship to the whole world around us. Some implications of this are: know where your money is coming from. Make it be as direct as possible. If you are able to work locally, enthusiastically seek out local money to support what you do. On the other hand, if what you are about has broader implications, don't expect to use small local sources to fund your activities.

Ask big! Expect to be well paid for what you do, or at the least, expect a respectful response where money is concerned. Cultivate many sources of support. Try to work often and regularly, as though what you do is fundamental to the lives of your constituency.

Keep lines open to other musical explorers, whether they are stylistically like-minded or not. Place yourself in the continuum of composers. Learn from the many creative ways composers sustained themselves and each other in the past. Finally, know that what you do now will affect composers in the future, too.

A PERSONAL PEDAGOGY

MARK DRESSER

The focus of this article is on those extended contrabass techniques and sound resources which I have been developing over the past twenty years.

Finding and developing one's own music is what I have always understood to be a central impulse and basic responsibility of the creative musician. I have always been involved in a rich and varied musical experience. I grew up in a Reform Jewish American home in Los Angeles during the fifties and sixties. My musical sensibility was nurtured by my parents, particularly my mother, a folklorist and amateur musician. We had weekly singing and guitar-playing Hootenannies at our home; this was my first experience playing music with others. Soon after I participated in several community orchestras as well as neighborhood rock and jazz bands. In retrospect the often maligned L.A. scene really had quite a lot to offer with its clubs, free outdoor jazz concerts, and an outstanding community of musicians. Alternative radio, especially Pacifica's station KPFK, had an equally significant influence on me. Besides broadcasting a wide range of avant-garde and folk music, KPFK gave me a venue to perform my first free improvisations live on the air.

I had the good fortune as a teenager to study with jazz giants Red Mitchell and Ray Brown as well as the beloved classical pedagogue Nathaniel Gangursky (and much later with the Italian virtuoso Franco Petracchi). At age seventeen, I met Bertram Turetzky, the contemporary contrabass virtuoso who has been responsible for more solo literature being written for the instrument than any other musician of any century. He became my primary teacher. I heard immediately and at length how improvisation influenced the development of his personal instrumental vocabulary and how his new language informed young composers who made this language their own. More impotantly, I learned fundamental lessons about universal concepts of musicality and musicianship that transcend style, such as how a vocal approach towards the line and a dance-like approach toward rhythm are keys to unlocking musical phrases.

An orientation towards improvisation, codification of new sound resources, and fundamental musicianship has been central to my development as a
player and a composer. My experiences and life long study of the jazz tradition
has interacted and influenced my performing free improvisation, European
classical traditions, pop music, diverse folk music, and various contemporary
concert music. I am reluctant to compartmentalize my understanding of different musical styles. Instead, I prefer to view my music as a sum of my collective
musical experiences, all converging into one world of sound. A tradition is not
a static set of principles in which conformity produces the essence. It is a living
relationship, a personal dialogue in which a not too reverent attitude towards
the past informs the future.

Of the many parameters of music, timbre or tone color, is the component of music most difficult to express in words and notation. Because of the
orientation of our notation system, timbre is generally and unfortunately
reduced to hyper-specific technical descriptions of particular instrumental
performance practices. This way of thinking about timbre is particularly problematic for the improvisor whose personal sound vocabulary may be insepara-
bly linked to rhythmic and pitch considerations as well as issues of physical
continuity, energy dynamics, and total attitude. This inherent complexity has
motivated me to understand the components of sound on the contrabass.

Examining sound resources solely in terms of technique tends to reduce
the musical issues to mere bowings, fingerings, and pressure gradients, giving
an incomplete picture of the total musical context. Nonetheless, it is useful to
isolate the sonic building blocks, so long as we appreciate the extent to which
they can later be musically transformed by improvisation and composition.

Pizzicato Artificial Harmonics

Pizzicato artificial harmonic production, commonly referred to as "harp" harmonics, is not a new technique. It is of value to the modern musician not only
for its unique sound color but also for the information it provides about the
relative location of the harmonic series of changing fundamental pitches. This
information can help significantly with other "extended" techniques including
specific flautando, subharmonics, and multiphonics. "Harp" harmonics are
produced by lightly touching the string at a harmonic node with the right
thumb and then simultaneously plucking the string with an adjacent finger
below the thumb. The location of these harmonic nodes is relative to the
proportion of the string length defined by the left hand finger. For example,

251

the octave node for *E*1, on the open *D* string is at the same location as *E*2. So if *E*1 is depressed with the left hand and the pizzicato artificial harmonic is plucked at *E*2 the *E*2 will sound as a harmonic. This technique yields pizzicato harmonic pitches that are higher in frequency than could be played with ordinary pizzicato technique. It allows for large interval leaps between the fundamental and the harmonic without moving the left hand. This creates a new idiomatic possibility. Bass virtuoso Stefano Scodanibbio, for example, has composed a piece in which he performs "harp" harmonics simultaneously with both hands on the outside strings creating a beautiful contrapuntal and polyrhythmic texture [Fig. 1].

Harmonic Series up to the 7th partial

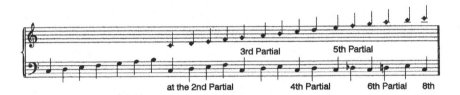

Figure 1. *Pizzicato Artificial Harmonics.*

Harmonic Specific Flautando

According to the *Harvard Dictionary of Music,* flautando bowing is "a flute-like effect produced by bowing very lightly over the fingerboard." If this technique is refined, the individual harmonics of any fundamental can be activated by bowing lightly over the individual nodes.

Harmonic specific flautando technique, or "falsetto bowing," produces a beautiful and expressive sound. It enables an instantaneous transposition of an octave or more without changing the left hand. The technique is essentially an artificial harmonic generated not by the left hand but by a precise bow placement on a harmonic node, using a stroke with a relatively quick attack and no bow pressure. With a relatively fast follow through, the bow travels in the same horizontal plane, thereby maintaining the same harmonic partial. Dynamics are created by bow speed not bow pressure. A spin-off benefit of this technique is that in the process of isolating harmonics individually, the contrabass player can gradate the harmonic spectrum from the extreme tasto region to extreme ponticello. As one learns about the relative location of the harmonic series on any fundamental pitch, one becomes acutely aware of the changing harmonic relationship of the right hand to the left hand. This informs the ears, eyes, and hands. When we return to normal bow weight, an enriched sense of color results.

The first step in the process is to locate the first harmonic, the octave. This may be precisely isolated by employing the artificial pizzicato harmonic technique previously described. For example: Play an *E*b one half step above the open *D* string. Without changing the left hand, use the pizzicato artificial harmonic technique to locate the harmonic two octaves above. Place the bow exactly where the right thumb was and draw a straight stroke with no bow pressure. The resultant "falsetto" note will be an *E*, one octave above. Note that the pizzicato result was two octaves higher. The reason that the arco pitch is one octave lower than the pizzicato pitch on the same node is because the bow itself actually blocks the second octave by acting as both a bridge and harmonic activator at the same time. Try changing the left hand note to *E* natural (one half step above). The right hand must move up proportionally, with the left hand staying in the same harmonic plane, a basic principal of timbre control. The role of the left hand is the same as in traditional technique: to make strong contact with the fingerboard so that all of the harmonics of a pitch can be activated [Fig. 2-3].

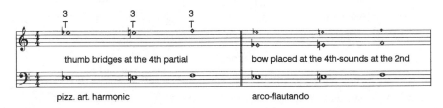

Figure 2. *Harmonic Specific Flautando.*

If the flautando harmonic does not sound, there are three probable reasons: 1) the bow is not placed directly on the node; 2) the bow stroke is not maintaining a consistent horizontal plane at the node; 3) there is too much bow pressure on the string. A fourth, improbable reason may be that the strings are totally dead, or the instrument is set up poorly. I use Thomastik Spirocore strings, an admittedly bright and harmonic rich string, but I have experimented with a variety of strings and have had success with every one I have tried so far.

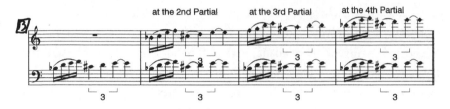

Figure 3. *Harmonic Specific Flautando.*

Scales and arpeggios are efficient tools to abstract the technical issues of clarity of pitch and rhythm as well as articulation. They can be equally successful tools in terms of sensitizing and abstracting the issues of timbre. Apply flautando harmonics to chromatic scales, diatonic scales, and melodies over the full range of the instrument. I recommend playing a phrase that stays in one left hand position at the fundamental and then repeating it at the octave harmonic. With a little practice, a visual sense as well as a "feel" will develop with the bow as to where these nodes lie and the appropriate bow weight and speed. Later try to activate the harmonic at the fifth above the second octave of the fundamental using the same procedure; locate the node with the pizzicato harmonic and then use flautando technique to achieve the result an octave lower. Then move up the overtone series and isolate the higher partials. A next step is to alternate between the fundamental and various flautando harmonics. It is worth mentioning that ascending in the harmonic series has a tendency to produce multiphonic bands. This is because the distance between the partials becomes closer to one another as the overtone series ascend. The musical possibilities compound as one gains more ease in switching quickly between harmonic partials. Once you can accurately locate and isolate the flautando harmonic you can enhance this technique with traditional expressive devices such as vibrato and sliding ornaments.

The World Below the Fundamental

Contrary to traditional bowed string sound production principles are phenomena in which frequencies lower in pitch than the fundamental are excited by implementing a specific kind of bow pressure. This is commonly referred to as "subharmonics," or "subtones" [Fig. 4]. I became aware of subharmonics in 1980 as an accidental result of distorting the vibrations of the strings during

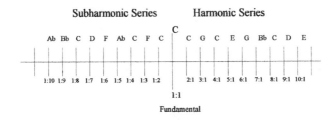

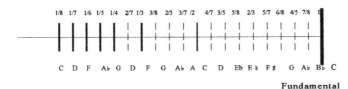

Figure 4. *Subharmonics.*

an improvisation. I continued to investigate these lower sounds on my own. In 1983, I met physicist Robert Keolian, then a graduate student of Professor Isidore Rudnick of the UCLA Physics Department. Mr. Keolian showed me his research on subharmonic phenomena in underwater wave formation. I played the bass for him as he listened and watched the speed of the string vibrate with the aid of a stroboscopic timing light. On one given fundamental we charted eighteen different lower pitches, albeit unstable. My first musical application of this research was "Subtonium," recorded in 1983 at the UCLA physics lab echo chamber and performed on a contrabass violin on loan from the Catgut Foundation.

In theory, a subharmonic series exists in inverse proportion to the harmonic series. For every subharmonic there is a harmonic series built above it—in effect, harmonics of the subharmonic. In addition, there are two different distortion phenomena, one affected by pressure and location, the other by bow speed. For example, using "harp" harmonic technique, locate the second octave above the fundamental and apply a downward pressure with the bow while drawing it horizontally. The fundamental can be flattened to a half step below. If there is too much bow speed, the pitch can be raised. This can be observed by pulling the bow fast on an open string; the pitch will momentarily go sharp. Between subharmonic production and the interrelated effects of pressure distortion and speed distortion, a range of lower pitches can be generated on each fundamental, dependent on the skill of the player. Virtuoso violinist Mari Kimura, for example, has developed an impressive discrete control of this technique and has composed compelling solo music utilizing subharmonics as a core component.

How to generate subharmonics

To produce an octave below the fundamental, on an *Ab* one half step above the open *G* string, use the "harp" harmonic technique to find the node two octaves and a fifth above the fundamental. Draw the bow and apply a simultaneous downward pressure focusing on the point of contact of the hair to the string. On the bass, in contrast to the violin, having a less-than-full left hand pressure aids the subharmonic attack. The sound quality is inherently gritty; however, subharmonics can be controlled and alternated effectively with ordinary arco technique. If first attempts prove unsuccessful, try drawing the bow vertically, pressing up into the string. The friction will produce a lower pitch. Then change the direction from vertical to horizontal to sustain the pitch. With experience, your stroke will get smaller and smaller until a lower pitch can be generated at the level of the smallest attack. Employing subharmonics in a pitch-specific manner depends upon mastering the attack and maintaining a consistent tension on the string. My own experience has shown that bowing at the nodal points are the place of least resistance which aid the production of pitches in the subharmonic series rather than the interrelated distortion effects [Fig. 5-6].

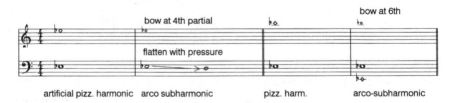

Figure 5. *Subharmonics.*

Figure 6. *Subharmonics.*

Once a lower octave sounds, even for a moment, the technical problem becomes that of sustaining the subharmonic. The next level of control is to be able to oscillate between the fundamental and the subharmonic in one bow. The model of the "accented legato" stroke is good for developing this skill. The next needed skill is to be able to transpose the subharmonic at different fundamentals. First attempts will likely be unsuccessful but with consistent practice, a "feel" for how the bow controls the string will be gained. The entire process is one of *teaching* the string to vibrate in an extraordinary way using a technique that manipulates the string with the hair of the bow in an unorthodox manner.

Improvisationally, the world of subharmonics is a powerful and evocative sonic resource. Subharmonics also have great potential in pitch specific contexts. It is a fair question to ask if subharmonics are a realistic alternative to a fifth string or a machine extension for the bass player in the orchestra? Certainly notes below the low *E* string of the four string contrabass can be generated arco. However, the velocity of pitch change is limited, so functionally the answer is no.

Multiphonics

Multiphonic production is common practice with woodwind and brass instruments but is rarely broached with string playing. It is the result of various conflicting messages being sent to the string via left hand placement, bow pressure, bow speed, and the vertical placement of the bow. As a result, the string registers different frequencies simultaneously, thus creating a complex sound composed of adjacent harmonics, the fundamental, and difference tones. This is analogous to splitting the air column in a wind instrument. Effective multiphonics can be produced by using a combination of techniques developed with natural harmonics, flautando harmonics and subharmonics. They are most easily produced at nodes above the fifth partial where the higher partials are closer together.

How to produce a major chord multiphonic

1) Place the left hand finger touching broadly but lightly at the *D*, an augmented fifth above the open *G* string and play the natural harmonic. This corresponds to the 8th partial, very near to the 19th, 13th, 18th, 11th, 14th, 17th, 3rd, and the 5th partials. 2) Draw an energetic bow stroke placed midway between the fingerboard and the bridge. Similar to subharmonic production technique, a more subtle bow force interrupts the normal vibration of the string. The closer the bow is to the bridge the greater the higher partials content, creating a more complex, but decidedly less "major" sounding cluster [Fig. 7].

Figure 7. *Multiphonics*

Once multiphonics are successfully produced they can be modified by bow speed which will effect dynamics, and by left hand pressure which will effect pitch. A vibrant multiphonic will characteristically be accompanied by a sensation of the whole string vibrating underneath the left hand finger.

Two-Handed Pitch Generating Technique

Left hand hammer-on and pull-off technique has been common practice for at least thirty years of bass playing. If the same technique is performed by the right hand as well, new idiomatic musical options are accessible. Microtonal and large interval combinations are now playable in ornamental, melodic, harmonic, and polyrhythmic contexts [Fig. 8-9].

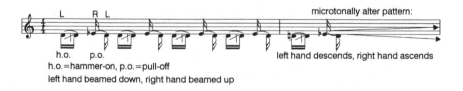

Figure 8. *Two Handed Hammer-on and Pull-offs.*

left hand ascends, right hand descends

h.o.   p.o.   etc.

Figure 9. *Two Handed Hammer-on and Pull-offs.*

The "double glissando" is a two-handed pizzicato looping technique. A left-hand glissando (usually ascending) alternates a "pull-off" at the note of arrival while the right hand catches the glissando at the original point of departure. This glissando can be repeated as an effect or as a melodic and rhythmic device and is loud enough to project at the same volume level as normal pizzicato [Fig. 10].

Pull off from the first note of a slur to the next.

Gliss from the grace note to the eighth
Left hand plays notes beamed down, right hand beamed up.

pull off to the quarter

Gliss-up from quarter

Figure 10. *Pizzicato Double Glissando.*

Bitones are two simultaneous pitches on a single string created by a hammer-on. Both the portion of the string from the nut to the left hand as well as the normal sounding portion between the left hand to the bridge are audible. When this technique is executed with both hands, three to four pitches can be played simultaneously [Fig. 11]. I have employed this technique in the opening of "Trenchant," a collaborative tape piece with Lamont Wolfe, composed solely from sounds of the contrabass. The two handed bitone technique was captured by placing one of two microphones over the fingerboard.

bitone resultant pitches

h.o.

h.o.

all on G string

left hand beamed down, right hand up

= non-sounded depressed pitch

Figure 11. *Bitones and Double Bitones.*

Bitone and double bitone technique is naturally soft and of a limited projection capability. This limitation led me to copy a pick-up design used by guitarist/composer Tom North. An electromagnetic pick-up is suspended over the nut and hovers above the pitches behind the half position [Fig. 12]. It amplifies all the sound information from the vantage point of the nut, including bitones, harmonics, and pitched buzzes. In essence, this device turns the bass into an instrument with two bridges; it's almost like having two instruments. With addition of a volume pedal, one can make an array of subtle sounds audible within an ensemble .

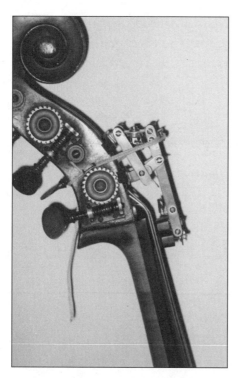

Figure 12. The "Giffus" Pick was designed by
Don Jacobson with electronics by Bill Bartolini.

Conclusion

I hope to have demonstrated that around any pitch there is a whole world of related pitches, timbre, and derivative sound that are accessible on the contrabass. Exploring these phenomena is more than an occasional enhancement of traditional technique. For me, it is a direction for improvisation and composition.

The pragmatic realities of making a living in music have oriented my studies of extended techniques in relationship to performing in metronomic time and tempered pitch. To better understand natural harmonics I have charted the specific harmonics which lie underneath each fingered equal tempered half step. As a result, I encountered the adjacent harmonics between the half steps. I went through a similar procedure of detection and discovery in my desire to understand bitonal harmony. I learned that there are bitonal intervals that are "in tune" with themselves but are out of tune to the open string: tonal yet microtonal. Obviously there are other poignant musical conceptions other than those that are centered around metronomic time and tempered pitch.

I find the overtone series, subharmonic series, and distortion principles rich with suggestive implications. If applied to the world of time, a single rhythm in a specific tempo would become a rhythmic projection in a world of tempos, both slower and faster and variable. Applied to notation, pitch and rhythm might be augmented with poetic imagery, symbols, and explicit improvisational instructions to spark the performers imagination and fantasy in regard to color, mood, and energy. It is not so long ago that "allegro," the Italian for "happy," meant more than a relative tempo marking. Our conceptual vocabulary has changed, and we need a new set of metaphors to reflect those changes. It is not naive to imagine that one day multi-stylistic performance and improvisational skills will be the general level of the modern performer, even in the orchestra.

A BRIEF CARBONic HISTORY

ELLIOTT SHARP

In pursuit of the Ir/RATIONAL

Ir/Rational music is a useful pun to describe what I try to manifest in my compositions.

I was invariably asked, "Well, just what kind of music do you make?" This question might be asked after someone had heard me or before. To me, it was "the music that I do." At the time I moved to New York City in 1979, I began to clarify ways to explain and categorize it—a process not only of focusing my own processes and concerns but of separating them from the surrounding genres and movements.

Certain elements of sound and process were clearly manifest as overriding concerns in my work. I also had a very clear notion of what it wasn't: I felt no resonance with the academics—I used "rock instrumentation" and dynamics and tended to play in clubs and lofts but my own music wasn't considered rock by most who heard it. It definitely wasn't jazz although filled with improvisation. Even with improvisation as a vital and major element, structure and syntax were always prime considerations. Sometimes I used elements of motoric repetition (inspired by funk and rock and non-Western musics) and accretive or phasing processes, but I knew that it was not minimalism (especially given the socio-cultural milieu of the Minimalists—the Soho seventies) nor did it carry the baggage of socialist realism or the appropriation and irony of post-modernism. As I scanned the list of isms, I deleted them.

The solo concerts were always the most concentrated and truest representations of what I did and the essence lay somewhere within them. I decided in December 1980 to release on my zOaR label a cassette of excerpts of solo gigs from the previous year and decided on the title "Ir/Rational Music"—a title that would include this cassette, a series of future solo releases, and a general description of my approach to composition.

ir (an IRresistible pun)—the acoustics of sound in space and in the ear
and its connection to the to perceptual engine:
the overtone series, difference tones, feedback, volume effects, <define
melody>, <define groove>.

the rational: structure and order, algorithms of use and process, formal
systems of organization, social and genre context, cross-reference.

overall—the ir/rational—chaos, intuition, the tangential.

Non-linear improvisation is an essential part of ir/rational music—
improvisation brings the music to life; it transforms the static into the
dynamic; the individual effector in the sonic flux.

A Brief Carbonic History

The band CARBON was first conceived in April 1983 to be an anti-silicon
sound: earthy, jagged, pulsing, and direct. It emerged from work on the fringes
of the early hardcore and improv scenes with my band I/S/M and with The
Hi-Sheriffs of Blue and Mofungo. Powered from the bottom by Jonathan
Kane's monster drums and Rick Brown's hammered bass and steel drum and
fueled mostly by rage and amphetamines, the band made an ugly blur of sound
at our first gig, The Speed Trials Festival, captured in the track YTYKYD on
the Homestead SpeedTrials compilation. Personnel shifted in the ensuing
months and Marie Pilar entered the picture (replacing Rick) to sing, scream,
yammer, and to play the slab, and David Linton (a long-time friend and collab-
orator) eventually replaced Kane on drums plus metal percussion.

Invented instruments: The slab—homemade horizontal bass with four
strings, movable bridge (to yield different tuning ratios), and pickups at
each end with separate outputs (to yield stereo fields). The pantar—a
steel top from a large storage drum fitted with tuning pegs for four
strings plus a domed cymbal serving as a bridge, amplified by contact
mike and with a sound not unlike a tamboura crossed with a dumpster.
The violinoid is a violin neck mounted on a solid wooden body with guitar tuners, a metal bridge, and pickups on either side of the bridge.

In the Fall of 1983 my growing disenchantment with "the Downtown
scene" and my own work and personal life led to a seven-month hiatus from
music. I felt that CARBON had become a "reactionary" band—not in the

notion of anti-progressive but in that that music was too-much filled with anger; too-much in reaction to external events. I was disgusted with the insular, smug and predictable music of the scene. At this same time, I completely lost patience with the sacred totems of post-modernism: appropriation, deconstruction, and irony; and found myself attracted to mathematical studies that had been put aside for some years—especially that of the Fibonacci series and the geometry of the Golden Section.

> The Fibonacci series is a number series generated by summing a number and it's predecessor, beginning with (0,1). Thus, (0, 1, 2, 3, 5, 8, 13, 21, 34, 55, 89, 144 . . .). The average of the ratios of adjacent numbers in the series forms the proportion known historically as the Golden Section, *Phi* (1.61803...). *Phi* has been employed for millennia in architecture and art and reveals itself in nature as the logarithm representing the spiral found in such places as galactic form and construction, the cochlea of the ear, the shape of the DNA molecule, and growth patterns of flower petals, seedcones, ramhorns, and the shell of the chambered nautilus.

One cold night in March, having eaten a supper of psilocybin mushrooms, I set out to explore the ratios of the Fibonacci series. In so doing, I found that certain ratios of adjacent Fibonacci numbers coincided with ratios of just-intoned intervals. I translated these ratios to a tuning on electric guitar with 1/1=C and restricted myself to playing only the open strings and overtones using various picking and tapping techniques. The intervals from low->high were C(1/1) Ab (8/5) C' (2/1) G' (3/2) A' (5/3) and C" (3/1). I was astounded at the results—liquid harmonic melodies pouring off the strings. It was just after midnight when I began playing, sunrise when I stopped. The results were so encouraging that I decided to dig in deeper with a number of strategies for utilization of the Fibonacci series. Besides the primary approach of harmonic tuning, these included mapping the ratios to rhythms and to proportions for structures. In addition, the ratios were applied to various other instruments, including bowed strings (a natural), saxophones (because I played them) and trombones (because I liked that instrument's purity of tone and the relative ease of producing overtones, its ability in the wrong hands to produce an astounding array of onomatopoetic sounds, its relation to the dijeridu and the ragdung, its pedal tones, and its essential simplicity.)

Over the course of the next two months, I composed the cores for six pieces that were fleshed out in rehearsals at the basement of One Morton (aka

Studio Henry) and in one concert at Plugg, Giorgio Gomelsky's loft on 24th Street. I wanted to fuse the old math and the natural overtone series with sounds and techniques from many of the non-European musics that I loved and learned from and the extended techniques and sounds and rhythms of the urban life. The band included Linton, Mark Miller, and Charles Noyes on a variety of drums and percussion instruments, plus Lesli Dalaba on trumpet. I played an old Hohner doubleneck guitar/bass that I had rebuilt and retuned, soprano sax, bass clarinet, sopranino clarinet, trombone, and voice. We soon went to Martin Bisi's studio in Brooklyn to record the pieces that became the album CARBON.

The next phase consisted of building a performing band and a reper-toire. The band clarified into a loose pool of players who knew the vocabulary and syntax of the pieces and my approach to the why of them. CARBON var-ied in size from a duet with Bobby Previte to the nine musicians required to perform MARCO POLO'S ARGALI. In 1985, I became aware of the fractal geometry of Benoit Mandelbrot through an article in *Scientific American* and became increasingly excited by it. I felt a resonance with Mandelbrot's mapping of mathematical functions to forms and phenomena from nature including tur-bulence, chaos, and seeming randomness and felt that my approach to music was also a mapping of these forms and phenomena. Exploring on my comput-er the many regions of an iterated Julia set, I felt that I was looking at a picture of time—not linear at all but jagged, reticulated and looping. With the album FRACTAL (1986), I set out to construct pieces based on various aspects of frac-tal geometry. Each piece had shifting elements of structure and guided improvi-sation, layers of interlocked order and chaos. I looked to the math for catalysis, inspiration, and allusion—I was not interested in generating tables of fractals to construct musical material—too mechanistic, too academic. At this time, I also began using a MIDI converter on the guitar-half of my doubleneck to drive a sampler. By sampling sounds, processes, and phrases produced through the extended techniques that were to form the sonic cores of compositions and from the various homemades, an additional reflexive and recursive element could be layered into the mix as well as greatly extending my timbral range.

LARYNX was the piece that prompted the next manifestation of the band. Commissioned by Brooklyn Academy of Music's NEXT WAVE Festival and performed November 13-14, 1987, LARYNX was composed for a thirteen-member version of CARBON including the Soldier String Quartet, four drum-mers, and four musicians doubling brass instruments and slabs and pantars.

LARYNX is analogy: the orchestra as throat. It follows as corollary to the throat as orchestra: throat-singing as practiced by the Arctic Inuit and the khoomei singing of Siberia and Mongolia, as well as by related jawharp techniques found throughout the world. The natural overtone series is the melodic core of much of these musics and of much of LARYNX. The Fibonacci series was used to generate tunings, rhythms, and melodic/harmonic material as well as shape general structural proportions. I wanted the music to dance on the always-changing boundary between a structural geometry derived from the Fibonacci series and a fractal geometry of turbulence, chaos, and disorder. The explicitly-ordered materials are embedded in a dense flux of multiple processes—layers of micro-melodies and micro-rhythms, dense cross-talk between the players. With each transformation, new landscapes and new processes emerge.

> LARYNX is constructed in six major sections with five interludes. The opening and closing use all four drummers: Bobby Previte, Charles Noyes, Samm Bennett, David Linton; the remaining sections each feature one, with the others playing slabs or samples. Each drummer has developed a unique sound and vocabulary; I enjoy the contrast between them as well as their understanding of my compositional syntax. This applies to all of the musicians in CARBON who are given instructions of varying degrees of specificity in the different sections (ranging from exact rhythms, notes, or playing techniques to more general notions of density and texture.) The same processing algorithms are mapped into each section, cross-referencing them while yielding radically different sonic results. One is transported (via the interludes) into each section—the terrain is different yet the functional identity of process is the same (an analogy from topology applies: a torus is a torus is a torus.) The interludes form a cycle of their own while connecting the cycle of main sections. The first interlude is brass and brass samples, the second—pantars, the third—the string quartet, the fourth—slabs, the fifth—the doubleneck alone.
>
> On instrumentation: All string instruments were tuned to the just ratios of 1/1, 3/2, 8/5, and 5/3 (translating to C, G, Ab, and A.) Throughout the piece, string instruments were predominantly played using only open strings or their overtones while brass instruments used open pedal tones of these notes and their overtones. There are, however, a number of places in LARYNX where the players are called upon to use the variety of their own idiosyncratic extended sound-production techniques, well outside any "system."

After LARYNX, I wanted to return to a small band-format and assembled Samm Bennett on drums, percussion, sampler; Linton on drums and tapes; and electric harpist Zeena Parkins (doubling on slab and keyboard). All players had a huge timbral range—anyone in the group could deal the woofer frequencies or the tweeters, beats, melodies, or pure noise. This group played a few versions of the extended piece JUMPCUT and a number of short pieces, issued as DATACIDE in 1989. The focus was on song-forms, each defined by widely varied parameters.

Personnel went into flux again and the European touring band in 1990-91 included Parkins, bassist Marc Sloan, samplist David Weinstein, and BLIND IDIOT GOD drummer Ted Epstein. For these tours we were joined by Bachir Attar, the leader of the Master Musicians of Jahjouka, on rhaita, guimbri, and flute. The LARYNX sets were filled with three- and four-minute blasts—the sets with Bachir were pulsing psychedelia, a mythical locus half-way between New York and Morocco. Around this same time, I was asked to be part of a "new klezmer" compilation being produced by Edek Bartz and Albert Misek (who perform as Geduldig and Thimann) for an Austrian label. I adapted a 17th century melody for a version of CARBON consisting of Epstein on drums and metal and Mark Feldman on violin and baritone violin. I played bass clarinet, soprano sax, and the doubleneck and came up with STETL METL, the sound of CARBON as a WarsawGhettoBlaster.

For the next record, TOCSIN, Joseph Trump replaced Epstein on drums and the band's groove deepened. TOCSIN was mostly song-structures with very little "formality"—I had decided that CARBON should not hew to any specific agenda but should be the carrier of many mutant strains. Central to the band's sound was the use of extended timbres—sometimes to orchestrate a melodic or harmonic idea, sometime to function as the entire sonic hook. To today's ears, a pungent sound can function just as a catchy melody or lyric refrain once did.

SERRATE (May 1991) and ABSTRACT REPRESSIONISM: 1990-99 (February 1992) extended CARBON again to ORCHESTRA CARBON. SERRATE used pairs of instruments: strings, brass, samplers, guitars, bass and slab and based on processes of fragmentation, decay, and violent change. ABSTRACT REPRESSIONISM was written for eight string players, drums/electronic percussion, and the doubleneck and reprised many of the processes at work in my string pieces but recast for low-budget orchestra.

The personnel of the TOCSIN band continues. The latest realizations are the albums TRUTHTABLE (1992 Homestead), AMUSIA (1994 Atavistic), and the most recent, INTERFERENCE (1995 Atavistic.) The core band (augmented with the Soldier String Quartet plus two bass clarinetists) also appears in the new composition for ORCHESTRA CARBON, RHEO~UMBRA, premiered in April 1996 in New York City at the Knitting Factory.

AWAKE AT THE WHEEL

Observations in overdrive

GERRY HEMINGWAY

Frosty the Snowman knew the sun was hot that day
So he said, let's run and have some fun, before I melt away.[113]

Art is a realm of thought experiments that quicken, sharpen
and sweeten our being in the world.[114]

113. Steve Nelson & Jack Rollins (*Hill & Range Songs,* 1950).

114. Wendy Steiner, *The Scandal of Pleasure: Art in an Age of Fundamentalism* (Chicago: University of Chicago Press, 1995).

Sounds, details, a moment noticed amongst many. To build something, so many parts to chose from, what shape, what's my skyline? It's interesting to me as an artist to ask why we make the choices we make and as an observer and consumer what works and doesn't work. I got into making music because I love to listen to it. Find me some new sounds, by way of a cool record cover. What will come out of those speakers, turn out the lights, turn it up. It was a different time. The late sixties and early seventies were imbued with a music culture that rippled with adventure. I can remember dragging speakers outside, listening to mixes I had made using Subotnik, Ali Akbar Khan, floating on an inner tube and enjoying orange sunshine. Who in the hell has time for that these days! Who stops long enough to remember that the sound around us, also inside of us, can be like a sanctuary? When I can do, I do, and I do so in many different ways. There was one night on a hotel porch in Merano, Italy. There was a river nearby, the wind breezed the leaves, the occasional car passing by drew shapes in the night air. I stopped just long enough to feel that complete space. To some degree I equate these sublime moments with the soul of music making. With all this fired up talk about what is and isn't jazz, or what constitutes serious concert music, I walk back to that porch, or I try to make a music, or hear a music that takes me to that sanctuary. And why not; life as an adult seems dominated by paperwork, stress, and fiscal responsibility, with little time for what once was creative input.

I make something resembling a living as an improvisor and a composer; two interrelated disciplines. After doing this for over twenty years, I have given a lot of thought to the importance of harmony, constructs, language, timing, health, polyphony, juxtaposition, transition, ritual, tension & release, humor, cinema, sequential and lyric forms, density, migratory patterns, groove, rigor, science—to my way of thinking all of these elements play an interdependent role in making music.

Language is a good place to start. I use the word to encompass the unique vocabulary that I along with many of my colleagues have developed over the years in order to expand the expressive possibilities of our instruments. Also referred to as extended techniques, I first got serious about codifying this aspect of music-making when I began collaborating with Earl Howard in 1980. Earl helped me catalog a wide variety of scrapes, rubs, cymbal harmonics, altered envelopes, trills, combined resonances, and any other sound I could produce that might have some musical value. His purpose in doing this was to organize these sounds into a composition, which I later recorded and released on *Solo Works* entitled "C & D." What I elicited from this process was a more rigorous way of looking at my materials for composition. I also approached the further development of my vocabulary in a more systematic, scientific manner, which made me more aware of the ways a particular sound technique could be applied or fitted to a compositional directive.

Around the same time, I was thinking about how to develop harmonic content for my instrument, particularly in the solo context. I focused for some time on developing sound techniques that were of a continuous, sustained nature. I was then able to construct chords by combining and layering these sustained sounds. In addition to offering distinct pitches, or clusters of pitches, these sustained sounds also had what I would term 'sonic character.' I use this term to describe a group of sounds that together form a distinct harmonic identity that might elicit something like our reaction to a diminished or dominant chord. When these sounds are organized in a series, they resemble the way we hear a pitched harmonic progression as an evolution of color; a peregrination from one point to another. When I look at harmony this way I liken it to a rigging that adjusts the sails to catch the wind, propelling the boat on its journey. By establishing a harmonic foundation in a solo work, all of the other horizontal aspects of a composition are given a frame in relation to a vertical progression. In essence, this reconstitutes a well-developed method for making an abstract soundscape more coherent.

As a listener at a concert or in reviewing my own work, I often ask, why these notes, these sounds, this feeling, this just about anything in a piece of music. I grapple with the meaning of a work and also with the desire to create music that connects with something beyond ourselves which we can no longer remain blasé about. I've noticed that if there is a governing harmonic logic then there is a likelihood that the material of a piece of music will rise above itself by virtue of its harmonic coherence. But then, of course, there's content....

One night, in the mid-seventies, we were crowded into a station wagon on our way from New Haven to the new Five Spot on St. Marks to see the Art Ensemble of Chicago. A woman, whose name I can't remember, deep into music school at the time, was quizzing me about composition. How can I write music if I haven't studied theory and harmony? I was not even twenty at the time, a dropout after one semester of college, still naive in many respects and full of oats. I assuredly replied, "I'd rather not be locked into previous theorems about how music should be constructed, what rules harmony should follow. If I just keep writing what I hear I'll get to something else." She politely wished me luck. My older and slightly wiser self finds itself now humbled every day by Bach, Ellington, Schoenberg and the Blue Sky Boys, and as I find time, I chip away at the intellectual process I put aside in favor of experience. However, my intuitive nature has led me to some interesting if not irreverent conclusions. One of the things I have noticed is that composers have certain preferences with harmonic color and intervallic choices and these tend to earmark their work. This could suggest that the colors we gravitate towards reflect some encoded identity.

My awareness of this and of other patterns has served me as a tool for targeting tactics that challenge my comfort zone. It is one of the more interesting aspects of freelancing as a performer, where I am continually being challenged to adapt my language to the precepts of whomever is directing a project. Often this means not being able to rely on that which comes naturally. In the case of harmony, for instance, I recently started to focus on major tonalities as a way of jarring my tendency towards minor scales and harmonies. I feel the process of investigating, evaluating and restructuring our patterns of creativity is significant in aiding the larger cause of moving music forward as an art form.

When I was apprenticing on the South Indian *mrdangam* with Ramnad Rhagavan, I used to spend a lot of time at his house in Middletown, Connecticut, where admittedly I was learning more about cooking then drumming. One day I was listening to Ramnad's nephew, L. Shankar, practicing a *Kriti* on the violin. A *Kriti* is a theme or rag that is repeated four or more times. Each time it occurs it goes by faster, in relation to the *tala* (beat). It does so because at the point of each repetition, the subdivision increases from say 4 to 5 and then on the next repeat from 5 to 6 and then from 6 to 7 and so on. More and more of the theme gets squeezed into each beat. It's quite difficult to do as your relation to the *tal* is continually shifting. Not so daunting for my man L. Shankar. What he was practicing was displacing the downbeat by one subdivision so that the rag never touched home base. Talk about getting out of your comfort zone!

Then there is groove, another word for connectedness or entrainment (synchrony in life forms). It's an aspect of life that everyone has experienced at one time or another. In music it's not a passive experience. You need to get in it for a drive. I am not just talking, ow! take it to the bridge. Musical groove for me extends beyond the auspices of beat and dance. Like harmony, it is a kind of glue that brings together all the elements of a piece of music, the way a line connects the dots to form a picture.

It was to be one of the few times I would get together with Mark Levinson to play, just he and I, bass and drums. The conversation in between music making led to Mark's experience of hanging out with Jimmy Garrison, whom Mark heard with Elvin and the quartet many times. Mark tried, as best as words would allow, to describe what went on between Elvin and Jimmy; the way they heard 4/4 as more of a 12/8, giving Jimmy more places within the beat to shade his emphasis, the way Elvin's touch on the cymbal enveloped the bass notes. "Listen to Elvin's growl and grunts when he plays and between that and what he plays you can begin to discern the way in which he & Jimmy find their sound together." I would describe what they achieve as a kind of rhythmic harmony.

It is a kind of magic that goes on, as slippery and elusive as it is overtly felt. As with some grooves in African music that suggest so many articulated syncopations without actually playing them. Have you ever flipped on the radio and come across a mambo or funk groove and for the first few seconds heard the time completely differently than it was designed? Then something in the music cues your ear and suddenly the clave couldn't be more obvious. This kind of experience was part of what fed my interest in manipulating the elements of a groove so that a listener or other players could have more than one viewpoint to a rhythmic construction, not unlike an Escher drawing.

The way I first approached this interest with my compositions was by using phasing patterns. I shared this interest along with Anthony Davis. Indeed the first document of this direction of my music from the mid-seventies was the work "Kwambe," which was performed by a group that included Anthony. At the core of that work were three vamps, one in 7/2, another in 4/2, and the other in 2/2. Whatever was in 7 would need to be repeated 4 times to return to the original starting point and conversely whatever was in 4 or 2 would need 7 repeats to coincide with the 7/2 material. All the melodic material was crafted to fit this mathematical scheme so that by the end of the theme everything landed on one.

My interest in this way of structuring rhythmic and melodic material got some of its root from my study of Carnatic music. The rhythmic compositions of that tradition continually find elaborate ways to subdivide the meter or *tal*, always adhering to strict rules of symmetry. A solo, in this tradition, compounds long phases into shorter and dicier combinations which then, as if by magic, finish squarely back at beat one of the tal. Taken to its extreme, the masters often delight in giving the listener a hell of time finding the beat let alone the *tal.*

A later work for solo drums, "Trance Tracks" explored this interest in more depth [Fig. 1]. For this piece I took my floor tom off the floor and strapped it around my back so that I could play both heads of the drums; a set up similar to that of the *mrdangam.* I used each of my limbs to demarcate an

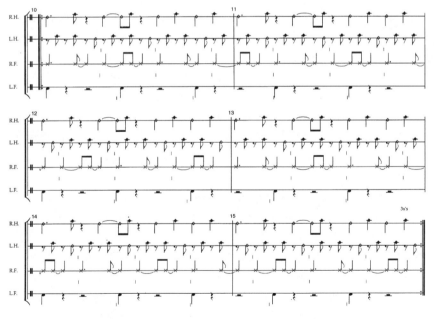

Figure 1. *Trance Tracks.*

individual meter. The right hand begins with 10/4 and one by one combines this phrase with the left hand doing 3/4, the right foot 4/4 and the left foot 2 against 3/4. All of these meters take 60 beats to fully cycle. Here's what that cycle looks like in notation:

I also experimented with repetitious patterns that freely phased around each other keeping only a common quarter or half note as a relationship. "Junctures" on the first quintet record is a good example of this structure. In that piece 7/2, 13/2, 9/2, 12/2 and 3/2 are represented by each instrument in the beginning of the work. Later other lengthed repetitions replace the initial vamps. The music inspired a nice alternate title, "Funk of One" which in some ways does describe the result of all this cross-metering; a reduction of all these clever numbers to the basic pulse. However, I also found that this musical situation had other implications, among them that the players would find their sense of the groove continually shifted as they either played their vamp or improvised. This would mean that each individual's material would sometimes suggest another tempo and/or meter and/or feeling, and that in turn would affect the other elements of the groove; a kind of chain reaction of groove.

This coincided with my developing pieces that simultaneously layered several tempos together. "Outerbridge Crossing," the title track from the same recording as "Junctures," used a dotted quarter note as a link between two tempos. The primary tempo's relationship to the secondary tempo is quarter note equals dotted eighth. I arranged this second layer of tempo so that the dotted quarter of the primary tempo becomes the 2 & 4 (backbeat) of the secondary tempo. The melodic material alternates phrases in 6/4 and 4/4. The underpinning either swings the dotted quarter or articulates a 12/8 feel. After the first exposition of the material a collective improvisation follows that divides the group in two with the bass and trombone playing 4/4 feel in the primary tempo and the cello and baritone sax playing a 4/4 feel in the faster, secondary tempo. On the drums I jump between the two tempos, like the vaudevillian plate-spinning act.

My interest in layering two or more tempos has continued to evolve since "Outerbridge Crossing." The progression of pieces that follow include "Special Detail," "The Checkerboard laughed and eluded everyone," (from *The Marmalade King*) and the more recent "Perfect World" [Fig. 2]. All three of these pieces have the dotted quarter serve as the anchor. "Perfect World" is a piece of many layers. Most of the material is scored in 6/4. The bass line continually shifts between different tempi. Here is an excerpt from that bass line:

Figure 2. *Perfect World.*

In Bar 1 the four dotted quarter notes are grouped as a four note phrase. The shape of this phrase reappears many more times, bar 3, 10, 12 etc. Although it is a six beat phrase in the primary tempo, the feel of the phrase is a slower tempo 4/4. It also implies 12/8. The double groupings of eighth notes imply a double time 4/4 (bar 11, 16). Other groupings of eighth notes support the 12/8 feeling (bar 4, 8). Then there are quarter note triplets again using groupings that suggest a faster tempo inbetween the primary tempo and the double time (bar 2, 13, 14).

The clarinet's and cello's melodic material, phrased in 4/4, dances around on the shifting ground of the bass line. The real twist however is what the trombone is doing. His part is written and phrased in a swinging 4/4 but his quarter note equals everyone else's dotted quarter. The drums play both the dotted quarter (with the feet) and a rhythm (with the hands) that states the quarter note of the primary tempo while also suggesting 3/2. Are you still with me?

Then there is the bridge (beginning in Bar 18) which has the bass and drums take the quarter note triplet (3 over 2) and use that as the basis for a new tempo in 4/4. The clarinet swings right along with the bass and drums with the melodic material. The trombone and cello play repeated diads as accompaniment that shift harmonically with the melody and also gradually accelerate in speed. The acceleration moves from 3 over 4 (quarter notes) to 4 over 4 to 5 over 4 to 6 over 4 to 7 over 4 to 8 over 4 and before everyone runs out of breath, the whole band shifts back to the original 6/4 and continues the exposition of that material.

The way in which I utilized this accelerating accompaniment and also the subdividing of the original 6/4 to create other layers of tempo is in some ways a direct outgrowth of what I learned from the study of South Indian Carnatic Music. I think this is a good example of something exciting that is happening in music these days. Ideas, concepts, and forms are being assimilated into our choices and interests as composers. I also see this as I look at the key moments in the evolution of music and art. It is a process of transformation and evolution which I liken to the Panda's thumb. This thumb developed over time to assist a voracious appetite for bamboo and therefore the possibility for survival.

Assimilation needs to be differentiated from the direct borrowing of previous ideas. I see the latter as a manifesto for post-modernism and a *modus operandi* for most popular music. I don't particularly relate to this concept as a composer but I do relate to and enjoy some of the results, particularly in rap music. De La Sol is one example that comes to mind. Where I get off the train, though, is when I hear talk that puts limits on the evolution of art. I hear this chiefly from the jazz music spokespeople who claim that jazz does not swing (and therefore is unworthy of our listenership) unless it is rooted in (which really means replicates) the previous tradition. Sounds like a value system in bed with our corporate/fundamentalist times. As far as I have observed, my jazz heroes went left when everyone else went right. And had they not checked out what was around that other corner we would all be dancing to big bands in segregated halls. No, I am interested in how all the information available to us can be processed to carry on the 'tradition' of *evolution.*

For instance there is music that doesn't need a discernible beat to swing. The same principles of connectedness apply. I once was listening to an interview on WKCR-FM with a pianist who had been working for some time on the music of Milton Babbitt. He remarked that, after learning the music from the page (no small matter given the notational complexities Babbitt is fond of), he would then begin to hear and play the music through a process of physical memorization. This would eventually lead him to being able to express the music as an internalized series of gestures. A very rigorous process in this case leading to a very open and in my view swinging conclusion. When I listened to his performance it felt like his music; it danced in his own way.

The backwards end of the envelope, where many of these musical principles would die of affixation, has its *raison d'être* as well. I could think of no better example than the Shaggs's earliest recordings. Here is a music that is so oblivious to the rules, so out of the loop, that no one's quite sure where it landed from; it's so wrong it's right. A lot of people find this recording to be a sort of a party favor, as it really is so whack. But I think what makes it happen is that there is a radical collision between us as listeners and a musical situation so unique, naive, and stubborn that we dazedly find familiarity with its soul. My reaction when I first heard the recording was similar to the first time I heard "Ghosts" by Albert Ayler—a joyful disbelief.

My point with these examples is to demonstrate that there is no one handy way to reduce the element of swing in music to the confines of a style or an idiom. I look out at the stars at night and am reminded that there is no one way to look at our existence, let alone what swings. If anything, I receive more understanding by remaining flexible about what I perceive. When I think about how a musical experience achieves its groove, for instance, I find that many roads lead to the same destination and each trip is different.

The musicians whom I have had the good fortune to have been out on the road with all share a unique ability that could best be characterized as a survival technique. It's a kind of humor that starts with reducing our shared experiences down to a short lexicon of words and phrases. Those phrases then get applied to other situations, always to comic effect, and, before we know it, no one but us can find any sense of humor in our conversation. Of course you have to be properly exhausted to appreciate this form of repartee. More than anything else what makes these moments of comic relief come together is timing. And it's the same in music-making. In the realm of interpreting or improvising there are so many approaches to the placement of a musical idea, the turning of a phrase.

Looking at humor is in many ways a good (not to mention fun) way to appreciate timing. Working the crowd or the room is really the comic's way of defining a relationship between the material he or she generates and the way in which it is received. It is always different, not unlike the musician's awareness of acoustic and concentration in the room. Great comics achieve much of their effect through the spaces they leave between words. One need only picture Jack Benny's wry smile, which gives him an extra second or two to drop the punch line for maximum effect. Or Derek & Clive (Peter Cook and Dudley Moore) who make pure music out of drunken repartee. Their content, which is either absurd or insulting and almost always way over the top, becomes secondary to a liquid rhythm in the banter they mostly improvise together. It is chemistry, where the elements that are present, commingle naturally. It is in these moments that we, as audience, have a chance to be lured into a freedom in which our regulated lives are suspended, but where we retain our capacity for reflection and judgment, and from which we return with a more heightened awareness of how our choices and tastes both define and confine us in our everyday world.

There was a period, shortly after I moved to New York in 1979, when I had next to no work as a musician. I hooked up with some friends in a similar situation and together we spent the majority of the next two years ripping apart and rebuilding a brownstone in Brooklyn. The commute, which averaged over an hour each way, allowed my interest in literature a major feeding. I must have read at least eight books of Faulkner, amongst others, and with his work in particular I became more aware and excited by the layering of meaning, the shifting of perspective, and how structure, content, form, varying textures, and contradictory styles can find cohesion by keeping a relation to a single foundation. In many of Faulkner's work that foundation was the *Bible,* set on the stage of Yoknapatawpha County, Mississippi. Take for instance the use of the triad (father, son, holy ghost), which shows up in many guises even at the level of language itself, as in triads of adjectives or nouns appearing in groups of three (e.g., "a dim hot airless room," "the dead old dried paint," "a dry vivid dusty sound," "Miss Coldfield in the eternal black which she had worn… whether for sister, father, or nothusband none knew," "he would abrupt [man-horse-demon] upon a scene," etc., just to point out a few on the first two pages of *Absalom, Absalom!*). From the grandest themes to the smallest of details, Faulkner continually crafted relationships, so that every aspect of a work found resonance and meaning.

There is so much to talk about on this subject alone, I will have to address it in detail some other time. But I wanted to bring it up in the context of this article to address once again my fascination and excitement with the ways materials we work with as composers and improvisors can ascend to another level of meaning when we craft the content of our ideas in relation to a discernible form or framework. A skyline if you will.

The sun was already orange as dusk moved quickly through its deep winter tempo. By the time we had reached our exit on the highway, the orange that had reflected on the icy snow had given way to the cool dark gray blue of twilight. "Back way," commanded Jordan from his car seat; a ritual now popular in our ride home from school. This night, however, more colors awaited our journey through the rural landscape of farms, tractors, and cornfields that Jordan so enjoys. White fire engines, spinning red lights, and fire belching from a collapsing farm roof ricochetted off the icy trees and frozen stream. We pulled off the road to watch this rare display. Like many farms near where we live, this one has been steadily decaying; with no more money to keep its past glory alive. Jordan is riveted, fascinated by the work of the fireman, the glow of the blaze, the eerie excitement of this destructive event. I wonder, as we complete our journey home, how this moment, so potent to the senses, will find its place in memory.

279

HOW WE EAT OUR YOUNG

MIKE PATTON

If music is dying, musicians are killing it. Composers are the ones decomposing it. We are as responsible as anyone—although we'd love not to admit it. We lash out at 'The Industry,' blaming things like corporate structure for our shitty music—but we are the ones making it. We open the box they've given us and jump in, wrap ourselves up, and even lick the stamp. Why? Insecurity—the need for acceptance—maybe even money. We're not thinking about our music, just about how it looks. One would rather have the warm tongue of a critic tickling his asshole than the tongue of his spouse. It gives him a sense of validity and power. He seems to defy gravity. Maybe it is simply because he doesn't know what the hell else to do. He sees it coming—but freezes with panic like a deer in the headlights. Don't laugh—I've done it and you probably have too. And it has undoubtedly affected our music. (But have we learned anything from it?) We know that we are mostly a lot of slobbering babies who need constant stroking. We realize also that in the moral order of society, we occupy positions similar to the thief, pimp, or peeping tom. We know that even if one has the pride of a bull, it is hard enough just to remain *focused* in this world. It gives us millions upon millions of images—distractions—all saying the same thing at the same time: DO NOT THINK. If your fantasy and desire give you migraines, how easy it is to forget them when there is so damn much to *look* at. Our creations die quickly when abandoned like this. Do we realize that we are eating our young? It seems the passion that moves us is accompanied by an incredible urge to squash it. It is as quick as a fucking reflex—a conditioned response. Is it a sexual problem? A puritanical one? The most intense and convincing music achieves a sexual level of expression, but what we normally feel is frigidity and limpness. It is just too easy for an artist to 'socialize' his desires when life tells him that cardboard is OK. You should be ashamed of yourself! What is your fucking problem? If you don't come out, sooner or later you'll die in there. Use chunks of yourself. Bodily fluids. Look left and right. Sift through others' belongings. Borrow. Steal. And try to achieve some sort of pleasure while doing it. This excitement should increase and intensify when you visualize it being shared by a number of people. Think about it. If it comes from inside you, it is automatically valid—it just may or may not be good. Because if it is not communicating in some way, its pleasure is as short-lived as a quick fuck in the back room. It doesn't mean *shit*. The labor of many composers is to construct elaborate walls of sound—but we often forget to leave a window or door to crawl out of. How can we survive in these clever little rooms? We must eat our creations or we'll starve. At this point, we've heard what we've wanted to hear—our ears have shut down. We've resigned as slaves to our own gluttony. But if we have boarded up our learning environment, our only way out is to teach what we know. Will they listen? Why should they? Because they need you as much as you need them. You can save them from being swallowed up by the world—they can save you from being swallowed up by yourself. Young and old players should be constantly seeking each other out and *using* each other. They should develop a healthy exchange of smut—and learn to wear each other's masks. In this kind of environment, incredible things can happen. Music can emerge that is athletic and personal. Music that is riddled with contradictions—impossibilities. And *that* is the shit that defies gravity.

PLAYING WITH FIRE:
DRINKING—AND BURNING—
IN THE DREAMTIME

PETER GARLAND

An Aboriginal bar bush fire dreaming journal: drinking in the Dreamtime. For Jim Pomeroy, of whose death at forty-seven, of a blood clot in the brain, I learn a half hour before catching the train to Alice Springs, Northern Territory—the central desert of Australia. We are already used to the sadness of our friends dying young of AIDS or in car accidents—to hear of someone dear dying of 'natural causes' at forty-seven is unexpected and tragic.

The train trip up is twenty-two hours on the "Ghan" from Adelaide to Alice Springs, over 1500 kilometers. Sunset is luminous, like an aurora borealis; the last blues of ending twilight shimmering in a red sandstone sky. Dawn is equally dramatic—a spreading richness of red, diffusing as the globe of the sun peeks up from as flat a horizon as I've ever seen in the open. A landscape of kangaroo and emu. Old cattle and sheep stations—a reminder of two claims for the land's ownership. I read Leslie Silko's *Ceremony* nearly cover to cover on the train—in between long contemplation of the landscape and the passing of time in the context of one's own life and friend's death.

Port Augusta is a stop five hours out of Adelaide. Our Aboriginal singing teacher at the University of Adelaide's Center for Studies in Aboriginal Music, Billy Mungie, is a Pitjantjatjara from the northern part of South Australia. He sang for us two Port Augusta songs (Amiwara is his name for the place—but, he explains, the dreamtime spirit there is dead, destroyed by the changes). The songs have a very wide pitch range, at least one and a half octaves, and are extremely expressive—contrasting with the narrower pitch range of the *Inma Nyi Nyi* cycle (Zebra Finch Songs) from up north that we'd been studying. I think of those songs and his words about Port Augusta as I browse in the terminal after a Bundie (Queensland rum) on the rocks. Knickknacks, baseball hats, a rack of porno mags, dirty postcards, and a bar.

At night I watch a parade of people back and forth to the bar (in the car behind us). A half dozen Anglos, a big fat young Aboriginal man (a beer gut if there ever was one), and two Aboriginal girls who had knocked down whiskey and cokes behind me in the bar in Port Augusta. The girls get louder and more aggressive, punchy drunk, as the night wears on. They are amusing actually, more so than the uptight young punk with his girlfriend and his heavy metal earphones (to a cassette player) cranked up to volumes I could hear until past midnight.

Sunrise is rapturous, as I've said, and at 9:30 a.m. we pull into Alice Springs. I get a room at a backpacker hostel type place. It's by itself, and in fact is a one-person house trailer. I couldn't feel more 'at home' out in the desert. It's a 'Texas touch' Jim would have appreciated.

My first night in Alice Springs, I check out the town, looking for the bar where the Aborigines drink. I find it next to the regular pub at the Old Alice Inn. Appropriately enough, I suppose, it's called "The Other Place," and it's packed on a Friday night. Almost all Aborigines exclusively, plus a few "outback" types—what we'd call in the States white trash (I do not mean to be derogatory —this bar is far more interesting than the one next door full of young outback yuppies). A chance to listen to native languages being spoken, and to study faces and people. The white guys who work the bar are big and muscular—they have to do double duty as bouncers also, though by the gentle way they get several overly-drunk Aborigines to leave, they seem to know their business (or perhaps I should attribute the gentleness to the Aborigines? They seem to leave the white people alone, very carefully so—though Australia is a free country, there is no doubt in Alice Springs who the first- and second-class citizens are). The bar scene reminds me of Gallup, New Mexico, and of native people there who have drunk too much and have experienced too much anger and cultural displacement: their anger, released through alcohol, is vented at themselves. There is a clamor of voices, people talking loudly. Near me a woman is arguing vehemently with a man—the language, at least, is beautiful to listen to. Some old white guys are making passes at drunk Aboriginal women. None of this drunkenness seems happy. The bar faces the Todd River, which runs through the center of town. Most of the year it's a dry sandy wash—many of the local Aborigines sleep there.

The next night after an exploratory hike out in the hills north of Alice Springs, I go back to the bar. A young man in a black tank top T-shirt sits down next to me to order beers for himself and his buddy. On each arm, from the shoulder down to the elbow, are an amazing set of ritual scars in parallel rows, the thickest row protruding a good quarter-inch above the skin. I smile and say to him, "That's an impressive set of scars you've got!" "Tribal law," he replies.

Sunday is devoted to a long hike, thirteen kilometers each way, along the trail I'd checked out the day before. The Larapinta Trail, it starts at the Old Alice Springs Telegraph Station about three kilometers out of town, as one follows the banks of the Todd River. The desert is hot, bright, luminous—the Australian sun is so intense I keep my arms and neck covered, but my lips dry up and get chapped after two days exposure. The plants seem familiar—or, rather, the general desert vegetation or patterns of it—and yet they are completely different: acacias, corkwoods (a tree with thick, corky bark and silvery blue needle leaves that almost gleam in the midday brightness). Mallees, shrub-like trees whose multiple trunks or stems all emerge from the ground. Witchetty bushes, at the bases of which witchetty grubs are found, a thick white wood-boring worm, which is considered a delicacy and eaten either raw or lightly fried (I had one in Adelaide, and the taste, under a white cream and black pepper sauce, was nutty and flavorful). Also spinifex bushes, round needle-cushion mounds of stiff grass. Lots of saltbush, light grayish green like the ones I know in New Mexico —but again different. Also different is the complete lack of cacti in such a terrain.

The mountains are ancient, hundreds of millions of years old, upthrusts of rock which have been polished down into mesa tops over the years—cliff edges that loom above talus slopes of boulders and plant life. On the hike out I run into a female kangaroo and her baby—or joey, as they're called in Australia. They are not overly frightful, and we stare at length at each other with seemingly equal curiosity (I'll eventually see so many kangaroos and euros that I lose count). I disturb a flock of birds in trees across a dry creek bed— though I cannot see them clearly enough to do more than guess at their identification by their calls. At certain points in the trail, one arrives at hill tops with 360 degree views. As I go higher, more distant mountains begin to appear to the southwest, and one gets a view of the big valley between opposite ridge systems that climaxes, looking south, with the greenness and trees around Alice Springs. In rocks in a dry creek bed in a deep canyon I encounter a small waterhole with water that's clear and not algae-green. Various small animal tracks are in the sand, in a part where the water has evaporated and receded— kangaroo or wallaby most likely (also telling by several fresh feces at the pool's edge). It's good for cold face-rinsing after three hours in the burning sun.

I head north up the valley and can see where another wedge of ridge comes down the middle between the two main ones, and effectively ends the big valley—the ridges glow almost pink in the midday heat. Other nearby hills seem like big piles of reddish-orange boulders, rising up out of a landscape full of stones. I walk through this terrain thinking of its history and mythic life in the Aboriginal story traditions: that so much of this landscape is named and has a story from the Dreamtime associated with it. There are few ruins in Australia, unlike New Mexico, but the very morphology of the countryside shapes its place in legend and is a reminder to me of a human history embedded in this landscape. Later I read that the long ridge opposite me, and a particular high point on it, is a Dreaming place of the Dingo Ancestor, and that my day's hike ends just short of Euro Ridge, named after the Dreamtime doings of a euro (kangaroo-like animal) Ancestor. On my way back I am stopped mid-trail by the cry and presence of a bell bird in a nearby tree top, and an eagle does a swoop over a small valley and comes to a watchful rest at the top of a far tree.

Two days later it's out to some of the more dramatic gorges, canyons, gaps between ridge systems, waterholes. Sheer geology dominates here: red cliffs, boulder strewn slopes, cave mouths scattered here and there. I climb up to one cave by Ellery Gorge waterhole—the back of the roof of the cave has been blackened by fire smoke. The creek beds are marked by river red gums like cottonwoods denote water in New Mexico. White ghost gums (gums are various eucalyptus), called so because of how they stand out in moonlight, are scattered around too, a couple growing in seemingly impossible rocky cliffsides. Ormiston Gorge is the most dramatic, an open area surrounded by hills where cattle were grazed and watered by the (now dry) stream bed running through it, called for that reason "the Pound," leading into a deep canyon that yields around a bend to a luscious cold, deep waterhole that I swim in. Again there is no doubt that such a generous place in the midst of harsh desert has a long and rich human history and occupation. In the distance is Mt. Sonder, a dominant presence across the horizon like one of the sacred mountains of the Navaho.

> "They took almost everything, didn't they?"
> The old man looked up from the fire. He shook his head slowly.... "We always come back to that, don't we? It was planned that way. For all the anger and the frustration. And for the guilt too. Indians wake up every morning of their lives to see the land which was stolen, still there, within reach, its theft being flaunted.

115. Leslie Silko, *Ceremony* (New York: Penguin Books, 1989), pp. 127-28.

And the desire is strong to make things right, to take back what was stolen and to stop them from destroying what they have taken...."

"Look," Betonie said, pointing east to Mount Taylor towering dark blue with the last twilight. "They only fool themselves when they think it is theirs. the deeds and papers don't mean anything. It is the people who belong to the mountain."[115]

A few days later I'm in Tennant Creek, six hours north of Alice Springs. The town has only 3200 people but does have a gourmet restaurant where in one night I have delicious osso buco and the next roast quail. Would I ever run into this in the middle of the California desert?

The night I arrive I'm walking down the main street checking out the town. A young fat Aboriginal girl in a dirty light blue dress staggers out of a bar I was looking into, asks me for a cigarette. She doesn't quite seem to believe it when I say I have none, as I pat my empty shirt pockets in proof. She goes, "Come on, give me a smoke." Her eyes are bleary and non-seeing. Suddenly she drapes her arms around my neck and says, "Where are you staying? I'm sleeping outdoors. It's cold. Let me stay with you." I laugh and say no, the hotel management wouldn't be too happy with that (and besides, I'm staying in a dormitory). At that moment a couple who appear to be her parents walk out of the bar. They seem less concerned with the girl than with trying to convince me to buy them a four liter container of Coolabah, the white wine that's the scourge of the Aborigines. The older woman asks, "Can I trust you?" I say sure—then they ask me to buy them the wine, because the bar won't sell them any more as they're too drunk. The woman goes, "You're a white man. They'll sell it to you." I say, "Sure! At 10 p.m. a white guy comes in and wants four liters of Coolabah? They'll know what I'm up to. Besides I don't know you. Maybe buying you wine would be a bad thing. Maybe you've had enough. I just arrived here; I don't know what the situation is."

Meanwhile the girl still has her arms draped around me; she seems too drunk to do much else and seems to be hanging on for sheer stability. She says, "Buy us the wine." Her father nods, and adds, "Buy us the wine, and you can have her," looking at the girl. At this I protest that I'm not after ass—but it's certainly the first time I've been made such a good offer.

The hike the next day is out to a dam. On the way there, I pass an elderly gray-bearded Aboriginal man with a thick walking stick accompanied by his wife, and we exchange friendly smiles and greetings. Four large hawks circle overhead, three cormorants call to each other across the artificial lake, and a lone pelican floats regally about. The water is revivifying in this heat—I float on my back and watch the hawks circle over me. On the way back I crack open a rock with large quartz crystals inside. That night, in the bar, after too many beers, I almost get into a fight with a young Aborigine. He starts to get angry at hearing my talking about "black people." When I realize he's yelling at me, I confront him, and as women rush up to separate us, I just tell him that I'd been saying it was nice to be in a bar where black people and white people are drinking and playing pool—together. The situation is defused and I sit down and buy myself, and him, another round of beers. This bar is a contrast to the scene I encountered in Alice Springs (though later I hear a white guy chuckle and say how he'd just seen an Aborigine "pull off a perfect one"—have his friends distract the owner, while he ran off with a box of wine from the liquor store. By his tone, one infers that this is, to him, 'typical' behavior).

Katherine, Northern Territory. This hike today out to the gorges is hot, grueling. The heat here has a humid edge, even now in the 'dry' season, that saps energy. Even two swims in the gorge do little but alleviate the heat exhaustion for fifteen minutes each time. The terrain is dry savannah. Palm trees, dry gold-brown spear grasses that after a season of rains are almost waist-high. The countryside is flat, scorching, with rock outcroppings, part of the larger canyon system, that form low hills and vales. In the not-so-far distance a long gray column of smoke is rising from a brush fire. I wonder that I don't see spotter planes flying overhead as I certainly would in the U.S. As I hike I keep an eye on it, to gauge its movement and direction. I am naturally nervous, from all my years in the dry western United States, of the sudden, ravaging effects of fire in the wilderness. Although as the afternoon progresses the fire seems to be moving no closer, I surprise two kangaroos at a waterhole who bound off without the semi-tame curiosity I've encountered before. At the end of the day, I run into my reward for the day's exhaustion: I surprise a flock of red-collared lorikeets feeding in wild fig trees—green parrots with bright blue and red coloring around their necks and heads who look just like the more well-known rainbow lorikeets. They do not fly far away, and look at me with that impish parrot curiosity I've known in my own pet Mexican parrots. In another tree, as close as I've ever seen one, is a blue wing kookaburra, with its long, thick pointy bill. With that beak, he looks like he's grinning at me.

That night I hit the quieter of Katherine's two Aboriginal bars—watch some good pool players, listen to the language spoken in these parts. A young man comes up and starts talking; his name is Andy. He starts to explain the aboriginal system of clan and family relationships, according to which he seems to be related to almost everybody in the bar! He asks if the blacks in America have this kind of relationship system, and he seems pleased when I say no. And as someone comes by and grabs Andy's cigarette, and later another person his beer, he again laughs and explains that these people have free right to everything that's his, and vice versa, because they are all family. Another Aboriginal man named Trevor, who's a good pool player and for whom I've been rooting, comes up between games and asks me about the Los Angeles riots that are currently going on. He tells me, as he sips on his nephew Andy's beer, that he saw the news on his TV, and he adds, "It made me cry when I saw that." I tell him how the people are angry, how the politicians have robbed the country for twelve years. And that if poor people are stealing shoes and food now, how does that compare with rich white bankers, developers, and politicians looting millions? And leaving our cities and systems of social welfare cynically depleted, and with a whole generation of poor people ravaged by drugs and killing each other? It makes me think of the songs of Bob Marley: "How many rivers do we have to cross, before we can talk to the boss?" (*Burning and Looting*) and "Slave driver, the tables are turning. Catch a fire, or you're gonna get burned" (*Slave Driver*). The legacy of the Reagan-Bush era is coming to roost in the burning streets of Los Angeles. And this black man in Katherine, Northern Territory, cries at seeing this violence, and he says to me, "It can't happen here, I hope?"

A bit later, a stocky, drunk Aborigine comes into the bar and in a loud voice starts singing about "Waylon and Willie"; that makes me think of Jim Pomeroy and Texas (as did the country and western music I heard blaring from one of the trailers in Ngalpa Ngalpa, the Aboriginal community on the outskirts of Tennant Creek). I drink enough beer to revitalize myself, eat in the food stalls at the once-a-month (first Saturday) Katherine "Tick Market" (like our "flea markets")—Cambodian chili beef and beef satay sticks. I realize that attempting a hike like I did today was a mistake in this kind of climate.

Darwin. Last night I went out to smoke a joint and watch the famous Darwin sunset over the Gulf of Arafura. It was a clear twilight, and the sky gradually turned a pink salmon color. In the distance I began to hear, from what was obviously a very loud sound system, music that, despite my incredulity, appeared to be African. I made my way down the beach esplanade to check out the source of the music. Darwin was having a May Day concert, sponsored by the Northern Territory trade union council (for some reason both the Northern Territory and Queensland were celebrating the holiday on Monday, the 4th). And indeed it was African music playing over the loudspeakers. An older union man was the MC for the night; and coming from the anti-union, anti-labor USA, I found it sweet to hear the radical talk this man gave out between sets—about labor solidarity, support for the freedom struggle in East Timor. The theme of this outdoor concert festival is "Many Voices, One Cry: Peace, Freedom, Justice. May Day 1992." I buy a T-shirt with that logo to give to a friend and actually (for the first time in my life) get a 33% discount for being unemployed (I laughingly explain that being a 'self-employed composer' is exactly the same thing). A bunch of folk music acts one always sees at these events play, as the sky turns a rich tapestry of blues and reds with the sunset's finale. I eat one of the freshest and tastiest garlic squids I've ever had from a Chinese food stall as I watch the sky show. Walking back towards the music area, my attention is drawn to a long flat truck bed with an array of percussion instruments covering the length of it. There are four trap-sets, two sets of steel drums at either end, a synthesizer and banks of speakers, plus numerous other sets of drums and cymbals. Young Aboriginal boys are sitting around in base-ball caps, drinking Cokes and trying to look cool—though they are obviously a bunch of nervous and excited teenagers. They are due to play in another twenty minutes; so, ignoring the folk singers who are still on the main stage, I hang around waiting to see what this band is about. An Aboriginal man comes up and stands next to me—together we wait (there's a beer stand about ten yards away). The folkies finish and the labor announcer says, "And now we present a favorite since 1988, the May Day Percussion Band!" (I'm surprised— I thought, despite the arsenal of drums, that there would be guitars.) It was obvious that these youngsters were going to be into levels of musical energy far beyond that of the folkies, but I am blown away by what I hear. Eleven people come onto the truck bed, an even mix of whites and Aborigines. The synthesizer starts up a bass marimba type melody line, and the band is off and kicking! There are a couple of older white guys—one, in a black cut-off T-shirt looks like a leader; he's playing African double iron bells with a cigarette dangling from his mouth, trying to look tough the whole time. If he is a teacher, this ensemble is certainly an inspired product! My attention turns to the Aboriginal teenagers in their baseball caps, wailing on the trap sets like cool professionals. It's a long truck bed, and the music is very loud and dancey—apparently the young drummers at the far end can't hear the rest of the ensemble, as they gradually go out of sync in each tune—that way creating fabulous, and probably unintended, polyrhythms (with totally 'cool,' detached, self-confidence). The crowd loves it, and this eleven-piece percussion ensemble just cooks, from beginning to end. the bass melody line in the synthesizer is simple but satisfactory—it's the polyrhythms set up along the length of the flatbed that keep the textures totally unexpected and interesting. And damn!—watching young people get totally into some really good music is an inspiration to this older, somewhat jaded musician (having just spent six weeks in the dry atmosphere of a university music department). These kids' set totally renews my belief in music.

A group of Aborigines moves up in front of me; a drunken Aboriginal woman starts dancing with a pair of white hippie lesbians. She totally wipes them out in terms of dancing sensuality. It's fascinating, watching rock and roll dance movements that are clearly Aboriginal in origin. Whoa! Hot!

The MC comes back on the main stage and introduces the "May Day Chorus," and a group of teenage girls (mostly) and boys come dancing on-stage singing an African liberation song! They are being conducted by another teenager—he's just basically keeping the beat and dancing around himself. These teenagers are wonderful—they move and sway to the rhythm of their songs with a natural, uninhibited enthusiasm that brings me back to the concert area (I had been about to leave, after the percussion group). This is what music is all about, the sensual joy and movement, in a supportive community context. They sing a Peter Tosh song (actually, his version of a Motown hit), that sounds as alive and fresh as the original (can you imagine a youth choir sounding like that?). It makes one aware of how far and wide classic reggae's 'liberation' message has reached.

They are followed by the "May Day Band," featuring a dark Islander bass player and a young white female singer, who rock the crowd to an appropriate evening's finale. Their guitar player spins out African type licks, giving the music a definite tropical feeling, in keeping with the ocean only 100 yards away. The drunken Aboriginal woman whose dancing I'd admired earlier comes uninvited on-stage and joins the band. Australians are a bit sedate about dancing, but I'm moving my hips as I sip on a final beer and watch all this, the most wonderful, real, workers' May Day I have ever experienced. Once again, as at Christmas time in Jalapa, Veracruz, young people—teenagers—have re-energized me and my faith that music is a magical, life-affirming force—something so special that devoting one's life to it is no doubt worthwhile. "Keep on walkin' and don't look back."

Two days in Kakadu National Park. Flat tropical forest wetlands. River systems and swamps and marshlands, leading back to a rocky wooded plain that is cut off by the rising escarpment that signals the beginning of Arnhem Land.

The night before, watching the sunset over Darwin Harbor had been strange. On the far shore I'd noticed columns of smoke from two bush fires. As the sun disappeared and the sky darkened, I began to notice another source of light on the horizon, a red flaming color, but more concentrated, not letting out the rays of the setting sun. Then I realized it was the larger of the two fires—and that those were flames I was seeing against the far horizon and dark sky. How many thousands of acres must have been burning to see that large a mass of flames over such a distance? It appeared like an hallucination.

On the drive out to Kakadu I learn that this is the time of year for the 'burnings'—the beginning of the dry season. That the area is so wet naturally that the dry grasses are burned, as had been the Aboriginal tradition for thousands of years. These deliberate burnings have a number of beneficial results: 1) the dry bushlands are burned early in the season while there is still plenty of water and hence the burning prevents later, worse, more destructive fires; 2) many seeds of trees and grasses are released due to the burning, which in that sense actually replenishes the vegetation; 3) though I'm not sure of this, it may also be a good form of insect control in these swampy areas (though these Aboriginal burning methods were also practiced in the desert regions). Many of the grasses aren't killed, but merely burned down, and a live root system and low mound remain; and likewise the trees survive this periodic burning—the Australian trees' answer to this is to have highly inflammable barks and leaves that burn quickly, leaving the inner plant alive and continuing. All through this trip into the Kakadu, I see these brush fires, dozens literally.

The next morning we're in a boat floating down the Mary River before sunrise. I remark that the sky seems so big because of the simple fact that the horizon is so indefinite, receding into the sky. There are water channels between gardens of pink and blue flowering water lilies on both banks; actually the idea of 'shore' recedes as we go further into this system of interconnecting waterways. One of the first sights that greets us is a huge white-chested sea eagle, perched on the gray trunk of a dead tree. It's a flat horizonless landscape of water lilies, palms, and green bush—standing above it are the dead gray trunks of the many trees that have grown, then drowned, in this water-flooded environment. The sun rises over a terrain of bird cries: storks, jabirus (stork-like birds with black heads), magpie geese, brolgas (another stork-like bird, larger than the jabiru, and with more of a crooked neck), dozens of hawks and ospreys, wedge-tail eagles, and white cockatoos. The scene seems prehistoric, nature in a time before humans walked the planet; timelessness in an avian, tropical swamp. The birds don't seem to be afraid of us; not so much because they're tame but because this is their environment, and we humans matter little, in the immensity of it.

That afternoon, hiking to a waterfall that hurtles off the escarpment and fills a waterhole below, I stop at a rapids in a stream. Turning, I encounter a small rainbow pitta—it's a bird with almost no tail, but with a flash of red beneath, and iridescent blue-green patches on its wings. Alone in the woods like this, it seems like a messenger bird from the natural world, that other folks, hurrying through a landscape, eager to take photos (the same ones everyone takes) of 'pretty' spots, don't slow down, listen and look, long enough to find. The next day, it's a lone wedge-tail eagle flying over me on the rocks as I look over a valley to Nourlangie Rock, the shape of its figure (and wedge of its tail) outlined perfectly against the blue sky.

The sky over the flat ocean is definitely more symphonic in scope, if I may use such a term, than those in the desert or plains. The lack of a horizon gives a deep three-dimensional depth to the sky, and the sky itself assumes the function of a changing landscape. Though I'm here in the dry season, a slide show I see at park headquarters in Kakadu gives me a sense of the famous lightning storms and rains here. I am struck immediately by the way the Aboriginal mythology of the region springs from these natural phenomena: the importance of the Lightning Spirit, who has hammers on his knees and elbows with which he pounds out the lightning: the fierce, wrathful nature of his portrayal as it's mirrored in the intensity of these dark storm clouds and spectacular lightning displays, the significance of the Rainbow Serpent in a country where one can see great distances and where rain storms pass over in a downpour and move on. It was when I witnessed this same thing in the American southwest that I understood the significance of rainbows and lightning in Navajo cosmology, and it's exactly the same here: a religion that is a kind of deification or personification of the imagery and drama of nature.

On the bus heading south, beyond Katherine, as darkness takes over from twilight, the bus drives through a zone of brush fires, burning on both sides of the road all around us right up to the edge of the highway. The bright orange flames, the crackling sound, the smoke smell of burning dry vegetation, and the blackness of already burned-out areas gives the scene, once again as on the cliffs at Darwin, a hallucinatory quality—as if we are driving through the end of the world, and everywhere, to the edge of sightlines in the oncoming darkness, the land is burning.

Back in Alice Springs, it almost feels like being back home. There was an unusual downpour, with a violent electrical storm, two days before I arrive, and there is now water in the previously dry Todd River that runs through the middle of town. All the vegetation is still giving off a rich desert smell of wetness—it's as if the water looses a flood of sweet vegetal odors in this dry, harsh land, as sudden and dramatic as the flash flooding which sweeps over the riverbed and washes up to the train tracks several meters above.

I buy a painting in the morning at the gallery run by the Papunya Tula Artists' Association. The young pony-tailed white guy I buy it from turns out to have been a music student in Adelaide and Melbourne, and we have mutual friends. As I finish the purchase, one of the most famous painters from the Western Desert art movement and head of Papunya Tula, Clifford Possum Tjapaltjarri, walks in. Later I see him in the street, and we give each other a look. Shortly after that I run into Josie, a short, round Pitjantjatjara lady with a frowning face whom I'd met at the pub on my last stay in Alice Creek, and she asks me, in her brusque but endearing way, "Are you headed for the waterhole?" I misunderstand her at first, but then catch on, and say I'll probably see her there later on.

About five I head over to "The Other Place" and as I walk in I notice Clifford Possum sitting at the middle of the bar. I don't have enough nerve to walk up to him and express my admiration for his painting or for that of his deceased (in his late forties) brother, Tim Leurah Tjapaltjarri, whose work I intensely admire. I don't know how he would take such an approach by a white person, whether his reaction would be one of friendliness or coldness. My friend Josie turns up and is drinking with another crowd ('mob,' as they call it in Australia). I'm content to drink alone and watch the goings on. There's a big white girl there, from Sydney, who is visiting her brother who's married to an Aboriginal woman. She's drunk already and loud, and various Aboriginal men are making passes at her, which I watch with amusement (she's wearing a fishnet type woolen blouse with not much on underneath). Things get loud in the bar, and the pub owner himself comes out (the first time I've seen him there) and tells people to quiet down or he'll shut the bar. I myself lean over and tell the man doing all the yelling (punctuated with lots of 'fucks') that he's being too loud, but he's too drunk and oblivious. A half hour later I leave (shortly after Clifford Possum does—I look for him in the street, but he's gone) and have dinner over in the white section of the pub (not out of racism—I hope!—but so that I can eat quietly rather than in front of a whole bunch of people who aren't eating). After dinner, about 7:15, I go back over to the Aboriginal bar, only to find that the owner has prematurely closed it down due to the rowdiness. Josie and the drunk white girl Debbie (I'd expected her to have been picked up by an Aboriginal guy by now) are outside, so we decide to go to another bar—in fact, the one next door, the Old Alice Inn, which seems to be almost entirely white. The owner of the pub had seen Debbie's earlier shenanigans and is in the doorway when she tries to get in; he refuses her entry (she, in her sexy outfit, doesn't quite pass Australian 'dress codes' either). Debbie starts swearing and gesturing at him, yet he stands his ground, and before we know it a police truck pulls up (Josie tells me later that the police had been across the street and seen the whole incident). Josie and I are standing there (we should have dragged our friend off) and Debbie continues cussing out the cops—and suddenly she is pulled into the police wagon and driven off. Josie and I look at each other in helpless frustration; another mixed Aboriginal man watching this stomps off in a rage. We go off for another beer—I say to Josie, "She was getting out of hand, but it was no reason for the cops to take her away. That was pure macho cop-ism." Josie agrees, and then I add: "Also, it was a case of a white girl playing fast with black guys; and it's one thing if white fellows do that to black women, but not the other way around." We go to another bar, apparently the only other one downtown that serves Aborigines. There's only one other Aborigine sitting there drinking by himself. Josie goes: "I've seen him here once before, drinking alone. He must not be from around here." After a round, we move up to the bar counter, and Josie starts a conversation, only to find that he's from Western Australia, as many of her husband's family are, and they have plenty of acquaintances in common. So the conversation turns from the frustration of the recent arrest to the marvel of close clan and marital relationships among Aboriginal people who've actually never met each other before.

There seems to be a law in Australia that men can't piss in public places. I am doing just so, off in a dark corner to one side of a bank, when a police wagon drives by two minutes later—in fact, I notice, it's the same one that pulled Debbie off to jail. That they are patrolling for types like me is obvious from the fact that there's no road here, they are driving through the plaza of a mall. This is not the first time my guardian angel has saved me from the Australian police when peeing (or smoking) in a public place. Long live 'free' societies!

The next two days I take a quick trip to Uluru and Kata Tjuta—also known as Ayers Rock and The Olgas. The European names—Alice Springs likewise—seem entirely out of place in a land that has known European presence for only some 150 to 200 years, compared to 40,000 years of Aboriginal occupation. The Aboriginal people now have reclaimed ownership of this area, and with that has come the return of its indigenous name, which seems entirely appropriate. It points to the fact that these European names in themselves—The Olgas, Mt. Connor, the Musgrave Ranges, Katherine—represent an act of appropriation and cultural theft. As does the strange word 'Aborigine'—they should be called 'Australians' and some appropriate word thought up for the European foreigners and new arrivals.

Uluru is a nightmare of organized tourism—the most visited tourist destination in Australia. There are literally twenty tour buses going to each site at the same time—with the apparent attitude of giving people their twenty-minutes glimpse of a place, time enough just to take their silly snapshots. People nowadays confuse traveling with merely going somewhere—checking off a list of places, countries. "I did Bali." "I was at Ayers Rock." The 'proof' or certificate of that is the photograph. These people are capable of taking pictures of a place without even seeing it. Many, after clicking the shutters of their cameras, turn their backs on this magnificent rock formation they've traveled thousands of miles to see, and engage in idle chatter with other tourists—exactly as if they were in a shopping mall. We do the 'sunset viewing,' then all go back to the campground and hotels for our various dinners, catered or otherwise. That night not a single person leaves their group of fellow tourists to walk alone in the desert, to study the night-time visage of the land and Uluru. I walk out to a lookout spot and soak up the silence and stillness of the landscape lit up by a three quarter moon. In the early morning, awake in my sleeping bag, I hear the distant cry of a dingo, lonely and mournful like that of his cousin the coyote. That call seems to encapsulate my feelings about this violated landscape.

We're awakened at 5:30 to climb Uluru. Already there is a column of people making their way up the steep bare slope. The incline is about 30% and the going is assisted in places by a chain to hold onto. I feel hesitant about going up, having read that the Aborigines do not climb it for cultural reasons, and although they have given permission, they would prefer us not to climb it.

But hundreds of people are going to ignore this, today and almost every other day, so I join the desecration and go up too. The wind blows fiercely as if in reproach. At the top I watch the sun rise over the flat expanse of the landscape. A British tourist says something that tickles my sense of humor and yet summarizes the trivialization of this sacred spot: "I drank a whole lot of beer last night, and this morning I wake up on top of this bloody rock!"

Back down at the bottom, with the morning sun fully bright now I still see a line of people descending and ascending, looking from the distance like nothing so much as a column of ants. And we think of ourselves as an 'advanced' civilization! Uluṟu stands as a magnificent reproach, and despite all this, inviolable.

In Uluṟu National Park I came across more information on Aboriginal fire management practices:

> When the Aṉangu (traditional people) used fire for managing the country, they would start fires which were generally small and close together, creating a mosaic pattern of burned and unburned terrain. The effect of this burning strategy was to create a diverse habitat which provided excellent conditions for wildlife.
>
> Many of the animals in the arid zone find spinifex an unpalatable food. For several years after spinifex has been burned, it is replaced by soft palatable grasses and small shrubs. This regrowth encourages small mammals, birds, reptiles, and, in particular, the red kangaroo, rufous hare wallaby and bilby/rabbit-eared bandicoot to move onto these areas to feed. Because the burnt areas were small, the smaller less mobile animals could shelter in the remaining patches of spinifex. Many animals and plants became dependent on the fire regime maintained by Aṉangu, and in turn Aṉangu were dependent on those plants and animals....
>
> The traditional burning practices were largely stopped when Aṉangu were driven from the region, particularly during the 1930s. This was followed by good rainfall in the 1940s. This created a large build-up of fuel, with no burnt patches to prevent the spread of wildfires. Consequently, approximately a third of the Park was burnt in 1950. A similar set of circumstances led to approximately three quarters of the park being burnt by two wildfires in 1976.
>
> The pattern established by these fires was one of large areas of burnt country with occasional unburned patches. This created a uniform vegetation pattern which was in direct contrast to the mosaic pattern that had existed. Consequently a number of animals suffered from this dramatic change.
>
> About one third of medium-sized animals found on the Park eighty years ago are now locally extinct.[116]

116. "Fire Management," *Park Notes,* (Uluṟu National Park).

That night after my return from Uluṟu and Kata Tjuta, I stop by The Other Place for a beer after dinner. Josie is there, playing on the electronic poker machine. She waves me over and I greet her, then take a seat at the bar. Later Josie comes over; with her is an attractive well-dressed young woman with a frizzy Afro hairdo. I learn that she's studying to become a school teacher, and we talk about how important it is for Aborigines to get into teaching—to give the young people a start in dealing with the modern white world while affirming traditional Aboriginal values. An older woman comes over and laughingly squeezes me, saying we met the afternoon when the white girl Debbie had been there. She keeps telling me I need a woman, implying that she's the one—if I'll just buy her another rum and coke. Periodically she comes back, tickles me—at one point slyly smiling, she asks me if I "want it front or back?" I ignore her attempts to get me to buy her a drink and tell her I've sworn off women. On the other side of me at the bar is an older man with straight slicked-back hair who introduces himself to me. His name is Peter, which calls for another round of beers, and I find out he's a painter. I ask if he paints in the western Desert style known as dot painting—a semi-abstract style like aerial maps of the landscape telling stories of the Dreamtime. He says no, that he's a landscape painter, which is not as fashionable currently. I say, "Oh, like Albert Namatjira?" (the famous originator of what's called the Hermannsburg School, after the Hermannsburg mission west of Alice Springs, which is no longer a mission and has been reclaimed by the Aborigines). Namatjira is much like Georgia O'Keefe in New Mexico, in that prints of his are sold everywhere in tourist shops—but he's a less radical artist than O'Keefe. "He's my uncle," Peter replies, but I'm getting used to everyone's being related up here. Clifford Possum Tjapaltjarri comes into the bar at this point and starts talking to Peter. He's looking disheveled and drunk, wearing a bright purple flower print shirt, and I notice that his left eye is almost completely shut, giving him an even wilder appearance. Peter tells me who he is, and he seems slightly nonplused when I say I know of him, that he's a famous painter (the landscapists being the poor cousins now, money-wise and in public acclaim). Peter introduces us, and Clifford glares at me with his one good eye and says, "I am Possum." I reply that I admire his painting, but either the remark doesn't register or he ignores it, and eventually he drifts off to the other side of the bar. An elder with a beautiful face wreathed in a gray beard comes over, greets Josie and my teacher friend, and is introduced to me. The teacher tells me that he's on the council of elders that supervises the school, and the old man says yes, that's so, and that he's not always in here "with the grog" (booze). Some young men come over and start talking to him. Aborigines seem to have a wonderful, directly emotional way of conversing—they quickly become animated and expressive, and it's not just because of the alcohol. At one point the old man exclaims, "I am *Tjapaltjarri!*" (the same family name as Clifford Possum). He turns back to me and says, "You must be a nice bloke—to be in here talking to us, trying to know Aboriginal people." He strokes my face with his hand and exclaims in surprise, "You do not have to shave!" I quickly explain that I had just shaved two hours earlier and that I'm not normally this smooth. A youngish to middle-age woman comes up and starts talking to the old man. He smiles at me and explains, "That's my mother," even though she's obviously much younger than he, a good fifteen years at least. I laugh and shake my head—I've given up trying to figure out Aboriginal relations! When Tjapaltjarri leaves the bar, he gives me a little peck of a kiss on the cheek, his beard rubbing against my skin. I am exhausted by the past two days' trip to Uluru and think about leaving myself. I turn back to the teacher and Josie. One of the first questions the former had asked me was whether or not I was married, so now I ask her, pointing at the rings on her fingers. She says no, and when I explain what those rings imply to me, she slips one onto another finger. I ask her age, and she says twenty-seven. Josie is forty-two or forty-four, but she looks old enough almost to be my mother—her physical size and hard living and permanent frown (I don't think in all our hours of conversation I ever really saw her smile) make her appear so. She has the toughness, self-control, and wisdom of a long-time drinker. I really begin to respect and be fond of her for this quality of wisdom obviously born of experience, and I'm developing a comradely affection for her. I can hardly keep my eyes open from fatigue, so I get up to go. The teacher gives a sign that she wants a hug or something; instead, we kiss, on the lips. Hers are moist and inviting—I am surprised and shy. I am not about to get into heavy kissing in front of all the males in this bar, so I give her a friendly but polite kiss. Josie then motions for me to kiss her, which I do, on the cheek, with a brotherly squeeze of the shoulder. And I'm out the door.

Eating breakfast in Alice Springs one morning, I notice an old faded poster describing local sights. One is simply a big stone. This large rock, chained off in the Railway Yard, tells the story of an Aboriginal legend. Beneath it I read the following:

Gnoilya (Wild Dog) Tmerga. Known as Wild Dog Rock. This stone is associated with a great, white Dog man who came from Latrika away to the

West and wanted to kill the Dog Men at Choritja (Alice Springs). When they saw him the local Gnoilya men sang out, "See, this is your camp, sit down." So he sat down quietly and remained there, this stone arising to mark the spot. If the stone is rubbed by the old men, all the camp dogs begin to growl and grow fierce. The last one to rub it was one of the old Inkatas (head men) who did so soon after the white men came to try and make the dogs bite them.

My last day in Alice Springs I'm up at 6:30 and off by 7 to hike out finally to Euro Ridge on the Larapinta Trail. The sun is not up yet, but the day is cloudy and overcast—a blessing actually because in the full heat the walk I'm taking, fourteen and a half kilometers each way, would be difficult. There's a trail that goes off the main track just outside of Alice Springs. Instead of following straight along the Todd River, it winds among the low hills and fallen boulders. In the early morning, kangaroos abound—some I encounter straight on along the trail; several I see outlined against the sky, perched on rocks on hilltops. Coming around a corner I surprise a small black rock wallaby, a smaller and shyer creature than the kangaroo. Crows, magpies, and galahs (gray cockatoos with pink-red chests) are flying in the treetops. I sign the register at the beginning of the Larapinta Trail, which commences three kilometers outside of Alice Springs near the Old Telegraph Station and notice that since my last trek out there some eighteen days earlier, only fourteen people have signed in. It's amazing that this trail, so close to Alice Springs, seems so little used; indeed, I encounter no one else this day.

I've determined to make it out to Euro Ridge for personal reasons, to ask the land and its animal beings for power, spiritual strength. As with the Indian custom in northern California, those on a vision quest walk out into the lonely places, the mountains where only wild beings dwell. I'm a child of the late twentieth century and the modern USA, but I have come out here for the same reasons. Therefore I am determined to make it to the top of Euro Ridge, resting place of the Euro Ancestor.

I make it quickly out to the Charles River, where there is more water after the recent rains, and I rinse my face in the same small waterhole as I had previously. As I ascend to the hilltops where I begin to get the expansive views, I notice that the cliffs on the opposite side of the valley are a gray-green color, different from the pink-red of the bright hot days several weeks before. At the foot of Euro Ridge, on a slope above a stream bed, I hear, then see, a kangaroo-like creature disappearing in the mulga and witchetty bush shrubbery. The path ascends steeply up the ridge which consists of two humps with the south edge dropping in a vertical rocky knife edge to the valley floor. The closer, lower, eastern hump is supposed to represent the head of the Euro Ancestor; the higher western one its back. I stop at the latter for food followed by a smoke. Getting up and walking to the rock ledge, I surprise another wallaby which scurries away, down the nearly vertical cliff face. It is enough for me; between this creature and the other I'd seen below, I have seen the 'signs,' been allowed audience with these shy animal spirits, however fleeting. I stand on the cliff edge and gaze out on a landscape whose magnificence words are too impoverished to describe. Today I feel as if I've taken another step in shedding my European ancestry, in my search for the Euro Ancestor. In the cliff face at the very peak is a little sheltered enclosure created by a slab of rock that has tumbled over. It is actually accessible by a precarious series of footholds. By the presence of droppings, it appears to be a rock wallaby shelter. I can also imagine it in the tens of thousands of years of Aboriginal presence on the land, as a secret hiding place for sacred totemic stones and boards. So many times in these hikes out to powerful sites, I have encountered such places! On my way back, I come round a corner in the trail and there in the top branch of a dead gray tree is a large white-chested bird with a long pointed thin beak, which cranes its neck out and, calling across the hillside to a hidden partner, gives its song to me. In the riverbed of the Charles small black birds with a flash of white on their wings and a yellow edge to their tails are busy nest building, carrying twigs from the river up to the treetops, and big deep nests. Nature is alive, and it is full of message: we 'modern' humans have simply lost that language; other cultures less advanced but perhaps more wise still retain some of that knowledge.

I get back to town in time for the last hour of "Happy Hour" (*sic*) at The Other Place. I see Josie playing the poker machines and wave hello at her, then sit down alone at the bar. I need two quick beers just to relieve my thirst and exhaustion. Clifford Possum comes in, sees, but does not greet me. After another round I go back to my room, drop off my bag, change into more comfortable shoes, and go eat. After dinner I go back to the bar and seat myself on a bar stool. I drink alone most of the evening, talking occasionally to someone. An old man with a gray beard sits down next to me with a bushman's hat on, smiling peacefully and babbling incoherently in his own language. He says something to the barmaid, who doesn't understand. I nod to her to give the old gent another beer—he seems totally blissful and non-threatening to anybody. He smiles broadly when the beer arrives and says something to me, still in his own language. I smile back. Later a slim man with gray curly hair and a trim beard and intelligent eyes comes over to order a drink. He asks me if I haven't been up in Katherine recently, that he thinks he'd seen me there. We establish that he probably had, and I notice the difference in his facial features. By now I've come to appreciate the different look of the northerners from the Western Desert Aborigines. I like this man, especially for his smile and gentle demeanor, in this bar brimming over with latent emotional violence.

I get up and as I walk across the bar, I notice Clifford Possum holding up an empty bottle, about to throw it across the room at an empty garbage can. He looks totally bombed, so calmly, smiling, I walk by and take the bottle from his hand and myself throw it away. I sit down next to him, but he's obliterated and hostile. A woman he'd been talking to earlier comes over, so I get up, offer her my chair, and get another one and sit down next to them. At this point, Clifford goes into a rage and starts yelling at me: "Get the *fuck* out of here! Get the *fuck* away from my sister!" There's a wild, violent look in his face, accentuated by his beard, bushy hair, and one good eye. It's a nasty, incoherent scene, so I get up and move immediately, with a quiet word and hand on the shoulder. Depressed by this incident, I decide not to hang around much longer. I've had enough of alcohol and its destructiveness.

I walk outside behind a group of four young guys and notice that it's drizzling rain. A big young white bouncer is standing guard at the entrance, and we start talking about drinking and Aborigines. He says: "I guess that's the way they are. I've seen them down at Port Adelaide and they're just the same." I start to defend them, saying, well, there are other factors at play, when a police wagon pulls up and two cops step out and begin to hassle the four young men, still standing under the verandah. I watch this and can see a situation of growing tension develop, even though these young guys hadn't been doing anything. I interrupt my conversation with the bouncer and move toward the policemen and say, "Look. These guys haven't been causing any trouble. They're like me. It's raining and we're just waiting here to go somewhere." The policemen turn and give me surprised hostile looks, and one asks, "Well, who are you?" I immediately get meek (I know cops respond well to that) and quietly respond: "Just a tourist." He arrogantly replies, "Well, thank you," and they turn back to the black guys. But right away they get back in their van and drive off. I grin at the young men and say, "Now, don't talk too loud!" and walk away myself. I've had enough of this; sad, angry, and depressed I lie in bed and think about the Aboriginal people and the curse of the white man's alcohol. Outside and on the roof of my trailer, the rain pours down all night.

Well they gossip in the town and they run the boys down
'Cause they live on wine and beer;
But if they'd stop and think, if the boys didn't drink
There'd be no fun around here.[117]

He lay there and hated them. Not for what they wanted to do with him, but for what they did to the earth with their machines, and to the animals with their packs of dogs and their guns. It happened again and again, and the people had to watch, unable to save or to protect any of the things that were so important to them.... He wanted to kick the soft white bodies into the Atlantic Ocean; he wanted to scream to all of them that they were trespassers and thieves. He wanted to scream at Indians like Harley ... that the white things they admired and desired so much—the bright city lights and loud music, the soft sweet food and the cars—all these things had been stolen, torn out of Indian land.... The people had been taught to despise themselves because they were left with barren land and dry rivers. But they were wrong. It was the white people who had nothing; it was the white people who were suffering as thieves do, never able to forget that their pride was wrapped in something stolen, something that had never been, and could never be, theirs. The destroyers had tricked the white people as completely as they had fooled the Indians, and now only a few people understood how the filthy deception worked; only a few people knew that the lie was destroying the whites faster than it was destroying Indian people. But the effects were hidden, evident only in the sterility of their art, which continued to feed off the vitality of other cultures, and in the dissolution of their consciousness into dead objects: the plastic and neon, the concrete and steel. Hollow and lifeless as a witchery clay figure. And what little remained to white people was shriveled like a seed hoarded too long, shrunken past its time, and split open now, to expose a fragile, pale leaf stem, perfectly formed and dead.[118]

117. "Cut a Rug," ballad by Dougie Young, Aboriginal singer from Wilcannia, NSW, born in Queensland; quoted in Marcus Breen, ed., *Our Place Our Music* (Canberra: Aboriginal Studies Press, 1989), p. 39.
118. Silko, *Ceremony*, pp. 203-04

On the train down to Adelaide, a pre-recorded tape explains the white 'development' of the land we are passing through. How the water to our right in Port Augusta is a man-made lake, with the coolant run-off from the power plant we can see in the distance, and that it is always a pink color (!) due to particular algae in it. And that another port, Port Pirie, is the lead and zinc smelting capital of Australia. The voice tells us that the whites found 'treasures' like copper, zinc, silver. All of this exemplifies the attitude that the land is to be exploited for the markets of capitalism and industrial development. The voice talks about the early settlers crossing the Pichi Richi Pass, and then it condescendingly says that the name is not some kiddy thing but rather the way the whites pronounced the Aboriginal name of the mountain pass. The voice continues to explain how the whites arrived in that region in an unusual time of moisture, farmed the land, depleted the soil, and were then 'defeated' by the normal aridity of the region, abandoning it, leaving the soils ravaged, washed away by rains, dust bowls blown about by the winds. The whites were defeated by this land, but the Aborigines had lived here for tens of thousands of years! Who is the more 'advanced'?

May 18, 1992 *The Advertiser* (Adelaide's daily newspaper) reports:

"Sacred Site Ban Stops $20M Dam"

In a landmark move, the Federal Government has stopped the Northern Territory building a $20 million dollar dam near Alice Springs by using its special powers to protect Aboriginal sacred sites.

The unprecedented declaration delighted the local Aboriginal community but outraged the Northern Territory Government....

The historic decision was greeted with tears of joy, singing and dancing by women of the Arrernte people, traditional custodians of the sacred "dreaming" sites just outside Alice Springs.

Mr. Wootten [author of the report on which the decision was based] found the dam had become "a symbol of identity" for many Aborigines and a test of the respect white people were prepared to give to Aboriginal spiritual beliefs....

Mr. Wootten's report said the area included two dreaming tracks involving the story of Two Women, which was important for Aboriginal women, and the story of the journey of a group of uncircumcised boys, which was of great significance for men. Interference with the sites would have left Aborigines "rejected and diminished, angry and resentful."

I read this as an example of the positive effects of a liberal federal government—in direct contrast to the attitudes of the U.S. government in the last decade, bulldozing logging roads through sacred wilderness in northern California, destroying entire species of wildlife in Oregon to satisfy short-term timber interests, ripping open the sacred Black Hills of the Sioux for mineral extraction to fill the bank vaults of capitalist earth-devouring greed. When will we in the United States learn? Our Indian population may not have the same mythic mapping of the land as the Australian Aborigines, but a time must come when the big patriarchal state religions (Christianity, Judaism, Islam, etc.) will respect the beliefs and rights of other spiritual attitudes towards the land!

The 1992 trip to the Northern Territory seems in a strange way like the fulfillment of a particularly potent, revelatory, and message-laden LSD trip I had in the spring of 1973. It's as if some of the visions that came to me then had actually done so with a resonance that can only be linked with concepts like 'prophecy': fulfillment of what I saw that day was, eventually, inevitable. In that way I link it to a kind of dreaming: to 'become dreaming.' On this trip in 1992, I had become what had earlier been my dreaming.

A group of friends and I had been subscribing to bill-me-later book clubs that spring and had been receiving a steady stream of 'free' books. As I sat in my house on the hill in Val Verde in the desert of southern California, peaking on LSD, I saw the postman leave a parcel off by my mailbox down on the road below. I hastened to get it and found two photo books, *Animals of Africa* and *Australia.* The image of a deep orange-red Uluru is burned into my memory from that day, which ended like so many others with a hike into the desert. Now I was hiking again in the desert, but there before me was—Uluru—as I had dreamed it on a spring day nineteen years earlier.

It is obvious that I have no particular insights nor anything new to offer regarding the Aboriginal people. What I have written here is merely a highly personal and subjectively viewed travel journal. In a sense I may be doing Aborigines a disservice by focusing on what's a traditional racist image— that of the drunken native. There is a larger, deeper, more important and fundamental Aboriginal identity that has nothing to do with the grog and the bars; it belongs to them, and not to some foreigner just passing through. On a more immediate level, it was a quick way, and one of the few, for a traveler to interact, however superficially, with local and Aboriginal people in the kind of neutral (*sic!*) public places that bars are. Also, once I opened my mouth, people realized by my accent that I wasn't Australian, and hence I was myself in a somewhat more politically neutral position, despite my skin color. In the white bars few people talked to me. After ten minutes in an Aboriginal bar, I was usually engaged in an interesting conversation with a local person.

I approached this theme because of familiarity with a similar situation among Native American peoples in my previous home state, New Mexico. I saw my own country and experience reflected in what I viewed in central Australia. It also seemed strangely fortuitous and 'prophetic' that I should read Leslie Silko's powerful novel, *Ceremony*, on the way up north, since in it she writes passionately about what I was subsequently to witness in Alice Springs. 'Ceremony' is also a fundamental Pitjantjatjara concept. *Inma.* Ceremony— and song. This journal attempts to be like a song-line, of my journey from Adelaide to Alice Springs to Darwin—from south to north through the central heart of Australia—and back.

Australia, like the United States, is a political entity of transplanted Europeans living on a land stolen from its original inhabitants, who had lived on it with judiciousness and wisdom for thousands of years. If either country is to forge its own identity rather than perpetuate a secondhand copy of a European original, and if it is to do so without destroying its very character— its beauty and its resources—through capitalist 'development,' it will have to come to grips with its indigenous identity. Not merely that: it will have to embrace that identity and history. The original, indigenous world views may be one of our last hopes of turning the course of things around, or at least of being able to survive the changes and ravages of modern times and restore the land and its inhabitants ecologically and spiritually.

In my last class with him at the Center for Aboriginal Studies in Music, Pitjantjatjara elder Billy Mungie poignantly said to us: "We Aboriginal people have a Dreaming, but we are very poor; we have no money, our clothes are very bad, we have nothing in terms of material things. The white people have everything. They have lots of money, nice clothes, everything they want—but they have no Dreaming."

With thanks to: Stephen and Jin Whittington, Guy and Deetje Tunstill, The Center for Aboriginal Studies in Music at the University of Adelaide, Mrs. Betty Freeman, and John Cage.

CHAPTER
26

STUDYING GAGAKU

LOIS V VIERK

Most Americans wouldn't call me ethnic. I'm a blue-eyed, blond Midwesterner by birth. But my ethnic identity is very strong. I think that this helped make it very natural for me to become immersed in another strong culture.

Most of my ancestors came to this country in the 1860s, around the time of our Civil War. My mother's father, the most recent immigrant, arrived at the beginning of the twentieth century. My ancestors were all German and they settled in German communities in the Chicago area. They went to Lutheran church and sang Bach. They went to Lutheran school where for generations they studied geography, history, math, and religion in German. Even my father, born in the 1920s, spoke German as his first language. For the first fifteen years of my life I lived in this community, eating German food, singing German songs, going to parochial school with other German-Americans.

My family moved to the east coast when I was in high school. I began to meet people from many other cultural backgrounds. Their customs, celebrations, food, folk dances, and languages delighted and fascinated me, and they resonated with the ways I experienced my own ethnicity. After a time I went on to college, studying piano, but soon I felt that something was missing. I needed to find out about other cultures, too. I had to experience and learn to play non-Western music.

So I traveled to the west coast and enrolled at UCLA, which had a real "hands-on" ethnomusicology department. I would be able to work with master musicians and dancers from all over the world. At first I tried to take courses in everything. I loved the exquisite, virtuoso, ensemble music of China with its graceful ribbon- and fan-dances. A musician to one of the royal families of Ghana taught classes in talking drums, with intricate poly-rhythms. Once a week the colorful, dynamic Balinese *anklung* gamelan orchestra rehearsed. And there were folk dances from the many cultures of the former Yugoslavia.

306

So many concerts to attend, too—music from Australia, Korea, Okinawa, India, Mexico, Russia—a musical feast.

But one afternoon as I walked through the halls of the dance department I heard music that made me stop in my tracks. The sound was massive. It cleared out all the thoughts from my head and just made me listen. Extremely loud double reed instruments were playing. It wasn't hard for me to find them. I walked into the room. The double reeds were playing a three-part canon, one instrument to a part. The line was unmeasured and highly ornamented, with sensuous sliding tones. The canon was in free rhythm, with each part keeping just a few seconds behind the previous part. Another canon, this time played by bamboo flutes followed the double reed piece. In these groupings of like instruments, every nuance of melody, timbre, and dynamics in each individual instrument could be heard with intense clarity. The two introductory pieces led into the main piece, begun very slowly by the "orchestra" members, who were sitting cross-legged on the floor. The music quite gradually began to accumulate speed, all the while the dancers moving in what impressed me as an odd and yet graceful way. To my untrained eye it was vaguely reminiscent of tai chi. The rehearsal which I had stumbled upon was incredible to me. Here was an art from that was powerful, strong, loud, and also so very refined and beautiful. It was very satisfying. I knew that I needed to study it.

I soon met the master musician who taught this music (*Gagaku*, Japanese Court Music) and dance (*Bugaku*). His name was Mr. Suenobu Togi. He turned out to be one of the most musical performers I've ever encountered. Mr. Togi was Associate Professor at UCLA for twenty-eight years, and he only recently retired to his home city of Tokyo. Togi-sensei (sensei is the title for teacher) traces his ancestry through generations of Gagaku Court Musicians in Japan back to the eighth century, Japan's Nara Period. This was the time of a mass importation of scholars and artists from China and Korea and they brought important elements of their cultures with them. For about a thousand years Togi-sensei's forefathers have played Gagaku in the emperor's household, as it moved from Nara to Kyoto to Tokyo.

My first class with Togi-sensei was in Bugaku dance. As I think about this, about twenty-five years later, I still immediately want to say "But I'm not a dancer." Although this may be a knee-jerk reaction for a Westerner, the mindset in Gagaku is completely different. Music and dance are part of the same art form. You learn the art form, so you learn everything. My fellow students and

I watched Togi-sensei move and tried to move as he did. We saw the flow of his motion, which I finally realized had a lot to do with the flow of his breathing. As one not used to memorizing with my whole body (though memorizing music at the piano, for example, was always easy) the twenty-minute dances were quite a challenge. Eventually my partner and I performed *Nasori*, a dance for two dragons. We put on the dragon masks, with tiny eye holes, and I didn't think I could even keep my balance. I felt like I was in long, dark tunnel, looking out into blinding lights, and then I had to remember all the steps and move gracefully, besides. I had to practice so long and hard that at least once I'm afraid I drove my fellow dragon to tears. The performance went well, though.

It was clear watching Togi-sensei move and trying to do as he did, that a very different sense of time and phrasing existed here. I loved studying Bugaku though I'm sorry to say I did it for only a couple years.

After beginning Bugaku class I quickly made plans to take up one of the Gagaku instruments, as well. I learned that the ensemble consisted of *hichiriki* (double reeds), *ryuteki* (flutes), *sho* (mouth organs), *biwa* (lutes), *koto* (zithers), and the percussion instruments (*taiko*), which is a suspended "big drum" (*shoko*), suspended cymbal, and the double-headed drum (*kakko*), played by the leader of the group. I began to study *ryuteki*, which literally means "dragon flute." This instrument is made of bamboo, lacquered inside with a substance made from a plant similar to poison ivy, I'm told, and wrapped with cherry bark on the outside. It is open-holed, with seven finger holes. Traditionally a student will study Gagaku by singing a version of all the instrumental melodies, memorizing hundreds of tunes by listening to the teacher, and then repeating. Only after a few years of singing and memorizing will the student be allowed to pick up an instrument. Given the constraints of the university system, Togi-sensei was forced to allow us to use notation to learn the melodies. The notation is a kind of tablature, using simple Japanese characters, and the notation is different for each instrument.

The Gagaku class was led by Togi-sensei, and my private lessons on *ryuteki* were with Mr. Mitsuru Yuge, Togi-sensei's colleague at UCLA. We played many pieces. Many Gagaku melodies unfold quite slowly. The opening tempo may be very slow, with (in Western terms) a pulse of quarter note being less than thirty per minute, the tune being largely in half notes. The beginning of a piece may stay on the "tonic" for a minute or longer, ornamenting it gracefully and unhurriedly. Pieces generally speed up as they proceed and some of them get quite lively. They may last anywhere from a few minutes to over twenty.

Every nuance of melody as played by the flutes and double reeds, every glissando slide, every accent and dynamic shape has a meaning in the musical phrase. Each of the six modes has its own characteristic turns of melody and kinds of ornamentation, and also its own tuning. The pitch *F* for example, in the *ryuteki* part, is sometimes high like an *F*-sharp, sometimes low like an *F*-natural, sometimes rising, sometimes stable, depending on the mode and upon the function of the pitch in the phrase. These factors all contribute to the special sound that each mode has.

Our Gagaku class was made up mostly of Americans. Being Americans it was natural for us to talk a lot and ask a lot of questions: "Sensei, how do you play this note?" "Should I play long tones to practice?" "How do you finger this phrase?" Etc., etc., etc. I think sometimes our talking made Togi-sensei feel we weren't very deeply involved in the matter at hand. How could we learn if we would not listen? But he had patience. He wouldn't answer us in words. He would pick up his *hichiriki* and play for us, then quietly command, "Just do it." There was no choice but to try.

After I had studied with Togi-sensei for ten years, continuing long after I'd graduated from UCLA, he arranged for me to study with his colleague in Tokyo, Mr. Sukeyasu Shiba. Shiba-sensei was the lead *ryuteki* player at the Emperor's Court in Tokyo, the *Kunaicho Gakubu*. Shiba-sensei is an extraordinary performer, as well as a renowned composer, music historian, professor, and flute maker. I attended one of his classes and also received semi-private lessons from him with another American. Unlike me when I first arrived, my fellow student spoke Japanese. But even if I had not understood Shiba-sensei's words at all I think it wouldn't have mattered too much. By then I think I already understood how important it was to "just do it."

In Japan I studied in a more traditional way than I had before, and I memorized many melodies by ear. Shiba-sensei recorded the vocal tune called *shoga* for me of much of the Gagaku repertoire. I sat with my cassette player and sang the melodies back phrase by phrase until I had memorized them. I memorized with my ear, not my eye. I think the music sinks in very deeply this way.

In my two years in Tokyo I didn't learn to play Gagaku without an American "accent" to my sound, I think. Gagaku is the oldest continuous musical tradition in the world. The style of performance is very defined, and over the centuries the emphasis has been on preserving the ancient beauty. Innovation is not a sought-after quality. Change does come, but to suggest any sort of new ideas about performance and have them taken seriously, it takes someone of the stature of Shiba-sensei, who has diligently studied since he was a boy, whose ancestors have been playing this music for many generations, who like his father before him has researched the history, the ancient documents with old notation, and who has published well-respected articles and analyses. And some of Shiba-sensei's ideas are, I believe, in part meant to restore to modern performance what he has discovered in the old manuscripts. To my ears his "newer" style of playing is more dynamic, with clearer phrasing, more exciting and more sensitive to the musical line and to the form of the piece as a whole.

Shiba-sensei is one of the very few composers I know of whose compositions show deep understanding for the traditional and yet are stated with a musical voice clearly from our time. His work deserves to be performed much more than it is. He is from a formal culture, where to be known mainly as a *ryuteki* performer precludes being taken seriously in some quarters as a composer. Yet he writes beautifully and idiomatically for both Japanese and Western instruments. And he is an accomplished Western flutist, since all of the Court Musicians are required to play Western music, as well. I asked Shiba-sensei once what he thought of Western-style composers using traditional Japanese instruments. He replied that he thought it possible to do so with understanding and sensitivity only after many years of study.

Gagaku will be a lifelong journey for me. The intangibles that from the first pulled me in—the power, the timeless beauty, the elegance—are still there. A lifelong reward.

TAPPED TEETH—
TRY DIFFERENT SPEEDS
Notebook Extracts, 1978-96

FRED FRITH

A-A-A-AD-AD-AD-ADV-ADV-ADVA-ADVA-ADVAN-ADVAN-
ADVANC-ADVANC-ADVANC-ADVANCE-ADVANCE-ADVANCE!-
ADVANCE!-E ADVANCE-E ADVANCE- WE ADVANCE!-WE
ADVANCE!- WE ADVANCE!-WE ADVANCE!- CAN WE ADVANCE?-
CAN WE ADVANCE?- CAN WE ADVANCE?- CAN WE ADVANCE?-
CAN WE AD-CAN WE AD- CAN WEIRD- CAN WE?-CAN WE?-CAN
WE?-CAN WE-C WEAK-WEAK-WEAK[119]

NO APAGUEN EL FUEGO DEL ESPIRITU[120]

1977-78

1. Timbre of amplified pizzicato violin with flute.
2. Metal bowl on strings, bowed (use compressor).
3. Voice chord loops with leader inserts as "breath."
4. Dance as ritual/dance as symbol/dance as demand/dance as response.

"our secret longing from the very beginning—the victory over gravity, over all that weighs down and oppresses, the change of body into spirit, the elevation of creature into creator, the merging with the infinite, the divine."[121]

5. Improvised structures—the perception that they mostly consist of "boring" bits that lead to "exciting" bits; but if you attempt to cut out the boring bits by making very short "exciting" pieces, the result is the creation of stereotypes, self-conscious attempts to excite, predictable ways of manipulating the audience…easy to fall into traps, but better to resist simplistic definitions in the first place. Learning to empty yourself before playing. Reminds me of Tai Ch'i seminar with Patrick Watson.

Young man, smiling knowingly: "This is all very well, but what use is it going to be when some guy pulls a knife on me in the street?"

Patrick: "If you understand Tai Ch'i principles, you won't be there!"

119. Text for *The Entire Works of Henry Cow,* created by editing one line of an Art Bears song, contributed to the *Miniatures* compilation LP.

120. Found painted on the wall when I moved into my 13th Street apartment.

121. Curt Sachs, *World History of the Dance* (New York: Bonanza Books, 1937).

6. Edited version still needs editing.

7. Tight, well-played, unconvincing.

8. Isolated rhythmic events/don't worry about repeating something through-out/a few strokes here and there/a drone for two bars/a mosaic of single moments taken from hundreds of disparate elements.

9. Use extreme background and foreground (like screams and fairground music in Hitchcock).

10. Tense serenity—leaves reflected on a brick wall, wind blowing—

    simple (silhouettes) complex (wind patterns)

    not moving (wall) moving (trees)

    kids playing, security guards with night sticks, radio static.

11. Colouring of our actions by what we feel is expected of us. How to resist such impulses. How to remain true to an integrated idea both of self and of purpose.

1979/80

Aigrette garzette   Milan Noir

Héron poupré   Faucon Crécerelle

Flamant rose   Avocette

Buse variable   Rossignol philomèle

Busard St. Martin

Cochevis Huppé

"Now he discovered familiar patterns everywhere, only weirdly mingled and combined, and in this way often the strangest objects fell into order in his mind. Soon he looked for analogies in all things, conjunctures, correspondences; till he could no longer see anything in isolation."[122]

122. Novalis, from *The Disciples of Saïs*.

1981/82

12. Idea of interference—events breaking into/out of the superstructures, sur-faces of pieces.

13. Accidents—accept, embrace, ignore, incorporate, develop, avoid.

"As one conditions oneself by time and by working to what happens, one becomes more alive to what the accident has proposed for one. And, in my case, I feel that anything I've ever liked at all has been the result of an accident on which I've been able to work."[123]

123. Francis Bacon.

14. Hairdryer blown between mike and speaker to offset recording technicians' obsession with cleanness.

1983/84

15. Trigger sound more transparent? (treatment?).
16. To get a better bass sound—hop x-y through light chorus, all top filtered out of chorus channel to make low frequencies move a little...
17. People have started to leave things on my table to see what I'll do with them.
18. Taps/tears/water boiling in a pan/washing machine emptying and spinning 6-string bass/mini-guitar v. abrasive/cardboard box, biscuit tin, double-bass bow.
19. Tokyo subway/ crows in Meiji Shrine/ tapped teeth (or cheeks?)/ try different speeds (slowed down?).

"Half of my painting work is disrupting what I can do with ease."[124]   124. Francis Bacon.

20. Metal rods through strings (open tuning), hit with *soft* beaters/ metronome balanced on strings as pulse.

21. Interlocks, especially using chordal possibilities, creating "melodies" out of interchanges of chordal, timbral and single note patterns.
22. Rapid variations of attacks using volume and other pedals.
23. Melodic material divided through the three voices and made into interlocks, sometimes with three different but related pulses counted simultaneously (not ONLY hocketed).
24. Don't worry about making songs—let it happen at its own pace. Words can be available and 'improvised' as appropriate to the context (not ONLY shouting!).

Later, from the train window
water, wires
smell of diesel fumes
Southern serves the South
dead sky
red light on a scaffold pole
tropical tropical tropical

1984/85

welcome to dreamland

25. Remove bass under end of sax solo for more clear re-entry.
26. Remember to trigger Zorn (but not all the time!)
27. Raindrops wouldn't hurt, introduced half-way through.
28. Careful with extra note!
29. Cut voices from 1' 14" onwards/ remove bass altogether/ introduce Wayne one-third of the way through/more Arto?
30. One static, two mobile, extreme use of physical space, imitation, quite sexy.
31. Construct melodies out of recordings of long notes on different instruments/timbres cut up—record even lengths and edit precisely into loops. (Mellotron principle)

I'm still here and I know what time it is.

32. Limit Tenko's voice (graphic?)
33. What can be taken away?
34. Drum sounds—room? gate? artificial vs. natural/tuning? drum skin rings? oil?
35. Good but not dangerous.
36. Needs de-hissing—lacking middle bite—some fading problems.
37. Gating one instrument with another to tighten up sound.
38. "Dismantle" kit/ different treatments of voices.

"Lovely penguins are popular with us. Their humming makes us feel dancing like a conjuring trick."[125]

125. Seen on a T-shirt in Japan.

39. Utsonomiya-san's analogue techniques:
    - hand-turned Leslie speakers
    - sandpaper the oxide off back of tape
    - noise reduction by putting snare drum near sound source when recording, then cutting relevant frequency in mix
    - change mikes and mike positions for each word or line of a voice track to change character of sound in subtle ways
    - chorus—flap paper over the cone of a magazine attached like a horn to a tiny loudspeaker
    - constantly changing reverb. chamber surfaces and sizes (shiny? dull? open? closed?)

"There is no convenient time to break your leg
   there is no convenient time to submit to force
   there is no convenient time to find your soul
   there is no convenient time to have a child
   there is no convenient time to starve
   there is no convenient time to lose your will
   there is no convenient time to have a flat tire"[126]

126. Rebby Sharp, from "You May Find a Bed."

40. Linn Drum—acceleration/deceleration/ very slow elastic tempi/ use of extreme speeds to create precise melodies/ harmonies (tom triads?)/ triggering (both ways)/metronome calculations to match tempi/ rapid co-ordination without over-density (beyond human capacity, say)/ Use of drum patterns to cue unison elements in unpredictable places (can be left out in the mix, e.g.)/ relative tempi.

41. Linn Drum II—additive/ start from basis of full open relationship between two pulses, then prune—write instrumental lines around the pruned drum parts/ contradictory pulses/ how to improvise…?

1986

42. Energy field

switch switch faint heart

43. Record several (many) sections of different lengths (from two to twenty measures) united by common elements (time signature, tempo, harmonic basis) which can be mixed down in different guises and edited and re-edited into a variety of structural forms.

44. Cut up the mixed 1/2 track tape into random lengths à la Cage, shuffle, re-edit at random without regard to tape direction. Listen. Re-edit until satisfied with structural shape. Notate the resulting music precisely. Create parts, record the edited version back on to the multi-track tape, learn and play the parts along with the edited version on whatever instruments seem appropriate, re-edit as necessary.

45. Two mixes should emphasise opposing elements.

46. Perhaps melody needs to be more broken up—insert trombone playing only parts of it…

47. Shouts, clicks, hisses, gasps, panting.

48. Invent a series of connecting factors that emphasise opposite functions—to exaggerate continuity, or to emphasise fragmentation.

49. City system of grids…geometry underpins emotional reality…city as a series of solid structures full of fluid attempts to create living/moving ones. Try to "paint" music into the walls of the city…

50. Remains at the same level for a very long time.

This should see me out
As if on a steep hill looking down
past the houses at all that ice

51. A bunch of beginnings that never come to fruition. Some kind of under-lying connection but I can't find it. If fragmentation is the important thing, make more of it. Keep shortening fragments and then release into a long flow of movement…Too predictable!

"…apart from the moment of decision as to when to throw, and apart from the consistency and choice of colour, and apart from the choice of the part of the painting at which it is to be thrown, there is also the angle and force at which it is to be thrown, which obviously depends very much on practice and knowing the kinds of things that happen when the paint is thrown at a certain velocity and at a certain angle."[127]

127. David Sylvester, *Interviews with Francis Bacon* (London: Thames and Hudson, 1987).

52. Sudden very short interruptions.

53. Spirals—each loop progressively changing—pitch, length of leader tape, introduction of external elements.

54. Duration? how to keep energy up? what to add? melodic/timbral content? overlaps?

55. Distorting mirror…foreground = rapid pulses fading. Feeling of lack of control…

56. Tension between formal musical representation and the "real" (found sound, sampling).

57. Not only blocks of different speeds, but acceleration within blocks.

58. Recognition patterns of speed-ups and slow-downs—*same thing* must be heard in each unit. Use Linn Drum to calibrate speed changes.

59. Continuous *mix* variations in blocks—adding and subtracting tracks. Multitrack loops.

60. Record different lengths of reverb and insert into master tape instead of leader.

61. War going on in the distance.

Red table
silver light
a grapefruit on the table
a cut out of it which
does not reveal the flesh
in the newspaper
Le Pen's teeth
head thrown back
an article on
genetic engineering
the radio's droning
but I can't hear who it is
shuffling feet and pages turning
outside it's still snow
never stop till Spring

62. Each repetition must incorporate a change.
63. Rattles—water? shimmering, articulate…treat tune *heavily*, background/ foreground.
64. Music box, slow pulse, accordion, Tom singing, *Birds* starts in bits.

"…the great function of art is communication, since mutual understanding is a force to unite people, and the spirit of communion is one of the most important aspects of artistic creativity…Art is a meta-language, with the help of which people try to communicate with one another; to impart information about themselves and assimilate the experience of others…Self-expression is meaningless unless it meets with a response."[128]

"IF YOU ARE MUSICIANS, PLAY!"[129]

128. Andrey Tarkovsky, *Sculpting in Time* (London: Bodley Head, 1985).
129. Border guard to Skeleton Crew, Czech-Hungarian frontier, November 1986, 1:00 a.m.

1987

65. High intensity solo right from the start.
66. Tension between unison and breaking out of it/ surfaces overlapping.
67. Roof below under three feet of water gradually turning orange. Bath of starlings. Trees make a difference.

68. Orchestration of environmental sounds progressing/digressing towards music.

69. Dissassembly.

70. Continuous very quiet melody merging with sounds in the action, e.g. gear-shift, cornering, factory sounds, train, etc.

71. Insects slowly transformed into radio static.

1988/89

"I don't think you can separate childhood from adulthood. I think you are the same person all through your life. So all the sensibilities that energise you as a child sort of flow through. And being an artist means that you can use them."[130]

72. Frailty/quality of decay like bad lungs.

130. Richard Long.

73. Use fast forward defeat sound, v. far away with violin 'stacks.'

74. Use of very slow rhythmic macro-structure containing faster rhythmic micro-structures (Messiaen, Korean music).

75. In multiple counterpoint sections relative levels should be constantly changing.

MEN OF ALL AGES PLAYING CARDS FOR MONEY ON THE TRUNKS OF PARKED CARS[131]

131. In Rio de Janeiro.

76. Structure based on a series of episodes which may or may not be thematically linked (in normal musical sense) but which accumulate a certain power of inexorability. Narratives. Journeys. Metaphorically a lot more relevant than expositions and developments? *Memories of Fire and The Book of Embraces* (Eduardo Galeano). Or Béatrice's collections of tiny images…

1990

77. *Helter Skelter:* React
Don't take any notice
Be influenced
Keep your own direction
Play/don't play with the others
Play/don't play in spite of the others
Play in parallel with the others

• Find a personal language that's coherent, simple, efficient, especially in the context of the ensemble. Don't try to do too much.

• STREETWISE—super-consciousness of the movements and intentions of others. Be aware of everything that's going on—when not playing you should be as aware and as focused as when you are.

• Use the narrative and dramatic aspects of the work to concentrate your energies and give you an emotional context.

• Limitations.

• No music without tension:	sound/silence
	development/stasis
	passion/self-control
	the past/the present
	optimism/pessimism
	what happened?
	what's happening?
	what's going to happen?
• No music without movement:	starting with the fact that all sound
	consists of the movement of air

78. Someone or something is trying to prevent you from playing.

79. Music heard across a wall—sometimes a door opens, but immediately it's closed again.

80. Monumental but fragile.   132. François-Michel Pesenti.

81. Violence hidden behind form.

"Between the violence of a memory and the fact that it isn't theirs."[132]

82. Effect of trying to talk through loud music.

83. Keep repeating senseless actions.

84. Gradually losing the thread of the written parts and starting to invent.

85. The actors are tired of acting but they can never escape from it.

  no sleep coming, nor any prospect of even one bad dream

86. Change frequency picture radically from traditional verticality.

87. Constantly breaking through, but never clearly identifiable.

HOLDING UP A SKULL FOR A SEEING EYE DOG
CERTIFIED LIKENESS OF A BUTCHER'S HOOK
DOCTOR I'M IN TROUBLE WON'T YOU TAKE A LOOK?

88. Sample Didier's lungs/ tight, no gaps/ chains and bells not needed musically/ keep pulses quiet.
89. Make *Dark* more of a shadow of *Mirror.*
90. Wolves much shorter/ let voices penetrate by keeping ending quieter.

1991/92

91. *Portraits d'Inconnus*/ basic principles:
- simultaneity—use of different acoustic spaces and reverbs (especially using analogue methods)
- abuse of recording media (physical manipulation and destruction/ reconstruction of tape, for example)
- varying densities—from one tooth of a music box to several sources at once.
- random volume—each playback will be at one of several randomly determined levels.
- random selection—each sensor will be able to trigger several different sources, selected at random to avoid identifiable sensor—sound relationships.
- lengths should also differ widely to ensure that permutations of combinations are as varied as possible.

92. Enigmatic mechanical repetitions, laughter, incomprehensible voices recorded through bad microphones and replayed at wrong speed, anxiety, suddenness of events.

"photography is a way of shouting, of freeing oneself"[133]   133. Henri Cartier-Bresson.

93. As each recognisable melodic element returns it
should be more and more mutilated, distorted as if by memory.
94. Don't be afraid not to use things, however important they may have seemed.
95. Keep voices primary and tense.
96. Lose seconds here and there if it helps keep things in motion.
97. Highly amplified small and mundane sounds used as rhythm elements.
98. Grid—consists of timed moments at which a limited number of elements are heard in varying relation to each other.
99. Snatches of pre-recorded music synchronised with grid, but distant.

100. Soloists or small groups playing in fixed but unmatched time relations (use phantom click tracks).
101. Grid elements—rice in metal bowl or on guitar strings
>   whirled sounds
>   eating/laughing/bricolage intime
>   train
>   footsteps in snow
>   drummed bass
>   drone elements

102. Losing control is a discipline like any other.
103. First eat, then cook with love.

Finely tuned tremor earthquakes aftershocks
intuition the wind stealing through leaves
ghost in the machine being fearless uncertain
this isn't meant to be 'new'
oblique oppositions and attempts to reconcile them
fragile armour tender stone splintered sure
perpetual motion marching loitering lurching
reaching out falling over leaping sleepy inevitable
you're always faced with choices power
but there's no time strident who decides?

ignore what just happened patience
catch it
pick it apart or break abrasive away
this isn't meant to be 'shocking'
but it's passion excite second nature
silence sudden winter night
illusions as when a tiny sound very close under stars
to your ear chatty lyrical
seems like a huge one heard from a distance

Attack decay repeat delay advance

birds call discreet interference to lake waves lapping
the continuous dialogue between what the musicians know
quiet conviction their technical resources their pasts
and dropping a packing case out the back of a truck

sighing signing off sweet danger
discovered every time they play
sly erotic irreverent
   try again
animal cries it
     swings[134]

134. Contributed as notes to Jim Staley's Don Giovanni CD.

1993/94

104. Eat, clap, hiss, newspaper, sandpaper, shh, tap cheek, sing very quietly, hum quietly close to mike (intimate versions of vocal melodies).
105. Make timing grid more subtle, less systematic.
106. "Il faut nous arrêter au lieu de marcher, marcher…"
107. Mechanical encounters/ mechanical responses.
108. No repetition.

"specialised products will be accurately served by our trained personnel"[135]

135. Announcement heard on Italian Railways.

   From notes to *"Nous sommes les Vaincus"*:
109. Buckets filled with gravel sent by wire, tipped onto metal sheets.
brushes on metal clothing.
breath, mud, grinding percussion.
110. String instrument: two metres long, metal neck, timpani as sound resonator, moveable frets, to be played with beaters, sticks, fingers, bow, mounted on bicycle wheels for mobility…

   Giant bagpipe: vertical pipes, air provided by foot-pump, operated by two people.

   Wind instrument: based on Swanee Whistle, but very large, constructed from PVC piping, use sax mouthpiece.

1995

111. From pre-edit questions to choreographer Paul Selwyn Norton:
     Do we need silence? If so, how much?
     Do you hear anything that's not there?
     How flexible do you want the material to be?
     Is it useful to edit it into a fixed order?
     Do you have any feeling about beginnings or endings?

Do you have any idea what it's about?

Are substantial alterations necessary; if so, in what direction should they go?

112.   Turn whole building into a performance space, like a labyrinth from Art of Memory. Audience has to keep moving. Events timed with stopwatches. Fifty pianos! Live sampling forms basis of final event in the auditorium. Key factor is mix of choral and non-trained voices, texts on theme of refugee. Abrasive interventions from the Rock Department. Oud? Dance element? Duration at least three hours…

"I suppose the whole of art lies in this mysterious conjunction of being able to let go and yet being able to remain sufficiently apart to see where one has to stop."[136]

136. David Sylvester.

Recordings and other composed work to which the above notebook extracts are relevant:

1.   "The Entire Works of Henry Cow" from *Miniatures,* a compilation of one-minute pieces produced by Morgan Fisher in 1979.

2.   *Gravity,* an exploration of world dance music recorded in 1979/80.

3.   *Speechless,* 1981.

4.   *Cheap at Half the Price,* home recordings from 1983.

5.   *Who Needs Enemies,* a collaboration with Henry Kaiser in 1983 that made extensive use of the then new and exotic Linn Drum

6.   *Dense Band,* a David Moss recording with John Zorn, Arto Lindsay, Wayne Horvitz and others, produced and co-composed by FF in 1984.

7.   *After Dinner,* very radically produced by Yasushi Utsunomiya between 1981-83.

8   *Welcome to Dreamland,* a compilation of Japanese music produced by FF in 1984.

9.   *The Country of Blinds,* Skeleton Crew's second LP, mostly written in 1985.

10.   *The Technology of Tears,* dance music for choreographer Rosalind Newman, composed and recorded in 1986.

11.   *Jigsaw,* as above.

12.   *Long on Logic,* commissioned by Rova Sax Quartet in 1987.

13.   Soundtrack for Peter Mettler's *The Top of His Head,* 1989.

14.   *Allies,* music for choreographer Bebe Miller, recorded in 1989.

15.   *Dropéra,* collaboration with Ferdinand Richard, 1989.

16.   *Helter Skelter,* a project to create opera music through working with "young, unemployed rock musicians from the 'quartiers défavorisés' of Marseille," 1990.

17.   Jim Staley's *Don Giovanni,* produced by FF in 1991.

18. *Portraits d'Inconnus,* a gallery installation in Paris with painter Béatrice Turquand d'Auzay, created between 1991/93.

19. *The Previous Evening,* music for choreographer Amanda Miller (and a tribute to John Cage), composed in 1992.

20. *Nous Sommes les Vaincus,* music for invented instruments designed and built by Claudine Brahem Drouet, for the dance production by François Verret, Paris 1993.

21. *Second Nature,* a grid composition for 13 guitars, contributed to the Sub Rosa 'Subsonic" series, recorded in 1994.

22. *Rogue Tool,* for choreographer Paul Selwyn Norton, composed in 1995, premiered in Tel Aviv in 1996.

23. *Impur,* for 130 musicians, large building and mobile audience, performed at L'École Nationale de Musique, Villeurbanne, France, in May 1996.

DEVICES AND STRATEGIES FOR STRUCTURED IMPROVISATION

LARRY OCHS

Since my first encounters in the late sixties/early seventies with the musics of Anthony Braxton and The Art Ensemble of Chicago—and following subsequent encounters with that of Iannis Xenakis and other so-called 'new music' composers—all my composed music has been concerned with the integration of composition and improvisation using non-traditional forms and/or alternative devices, inventing or reforming structures and systems that combine specific expectations (goals) with intuitive processes. These composers' music made it clear that fresh (if not wholly 'original') forms—or structural devices—would work in compositions including improvisation. The improvisational ideas Steve Lacy developed in the seventies, and the structural devices invented by Braxton, Leo Smith, Cecil Taylor, and Roscoe Mitchell, all pointed many of us in a particular direction. And their musics suggested that one could create improvisations employing the *instrumental* language developed through the history of jazz in combination with compositional devices developed by western musicians for so-called 'new music'; what results are hybrid art forms not usually associated with jazz.

The choice of a particular system or set of structures for a piece should be determined by three things: the goal of the composition, the particular kind of interaction the composer is looking for in any portion of the composition, and the contour of the composition. Of course, modifications to one system or another would be dependent upon the makeup of the group one is composing for.

Since 1977, I have been composing music for Rova, the saxophone quartet. There are only so many ways to divide up a quartet; the most obvious is to have one player solo over a repeated rhythmic or melodic line, usually called a *vamp*. Although all the composer-performers in Rova have employed that device at one time or another, we generally try to avoid the obvious. The important thing to remember while reading further along in this essay on devices I have employed is that, in all cases, these formal devices/structures are employed to *get at* the musical requirements of a given piece. It is always the primary goal in any piece to be musically coherent; to tell a story *and/or* to create a mood, feeling, or environment. The devices used in any given piece are employed with the sole intent of realizing the intentions of that composition. And the decision to use (structured) improvisation as a means of furthering those intentions is made in order to create the possibility of realizing even more—more than the composer imagined possible when composing the piece (or section of the piece). Or, at the very least, to allow for the possibility of different—or fresh—realizations of that intention with each performance.

One particular setup that I have employed in pieces (for Rova and for other groups) is the *simultaneous solo* usually for a maximum of three players. The initial concept is simple: each player uses written material from the piece to start with and then expands on this material in soloistic fashion, finding ways to make his or her solo fit with the other players' simultaneous solo statements. The best early example of this was the trio in *Paint Another Take of the Shootpop* (1981). In *torque* (1988) and other pieces composed after it, I added the following rule for each of three players during these triple solos: start from an initial written motif ('idea A'); improvise on idea A until it sets up against the other players' version of idea A; then phase in a new idea ('idea B'), which can be any musical motif that fits the mood of the current overall sound area; phase out the original idea A; play idea B alone with variation until it is clearly set up against the other players' music (that is: play idea B until the relationship between your idea B and the group music can be heard by the other players [and the listening audience]); phase in an 'idea C'; phase out 'idea B.' Etcetera. The pace of the phasing is completely up to the individual player and virtually independent of the other two players involved. Ideas B, C and beyond are created freely by the players, but the choice of new material must be influenced by what the given player hears happening in the group-music. The concept is simple, but a successful realization is most likely to be made by experienced practitioners only.

Another obvious division of a quartet is into two pairs. The *double duo* has been used in many different compositions of mine (and others) in Rova and elsewhere. The following are some examples.

In *New Sheets* (1978) the written introduction sets up two duos: one involving the higher range instruments and one involving the lower range instruments. The low duo (baritone and tenor saxes) plays simpler, slower lines, initially with silences between phrases. The higher duo (soprano, sopranino) is given a written line that is rhythmically insistent. They play on the phrase, alternate parts of the phrase, and improvise around it, building constantly. The low pair builds and relaxes tension throughout, acting like the lead singer of a ballad. Eventually the two pairs link up for the final moments of the piece.

In one section of *Escape from Zero Village* (1980), two alto saxes work together, playing slurred lines in an off-kilter tandem, slowly moving up the range of the instrument while creating serious tension by glissing up and down in a small range of pitches that changes incrementally (getting higher) over the total time of the section. Meanwhile, the tenor and the soprano play soloistically over, around, and under the alto duo. Both tenor and soprano use staccato, declarative lines, with tenor playing as a sub-soloist to soprano. That is, the tenor, while remaining independent from the soprano, nevertheless pays a little more attention to soprano comments than if he was a co-soloist. Both tenor and soprano make declarative statements that punctuate the continuous push-pull of the alto duo.

In *The Shopper* (1986), following an initial series of written heads that include four very short solos over vamp lines, the main improvisational section begins with the soprano soloing over the trio's four-bar-vamp. After the baritone joins the soprano for simultaneous solos over six more bars of this vamp, the alto and tenor, who have been playing the vamp, drop the vamp and hit a brief sound event called a *pivot cue*.* At the sound of each pivot cue, the bari and soprano change simulta-neously to a new, improvised pitch/ sound pattern,

*Term introduced to me by John Zorn in his game pieces

and make the new patterns work together. After four to eight of these in rapid succession, the tenor—who signals all pivot cues—starts a new (improvised) cue that is actually a repeated rhythmic pattern; the alto joins the riff, repeating it exactly in terms of the rhythm, but with choice of pitch selection open to the altoist. This riff will sound very different from the composed pivot cues, and thus this riff cues the baritone to join the soprano in whatever he is doing; thus the baritone and soprano become a duo.

After the two duos set up against each other, any of the four players may, at any time, exercise one of several options. (1) He may visually signal his partner to cut off the current repeating figure, immediately starting a new repetitive figure that the partner must join in on. (Not every riff need be repeated with literal rhythmic accuracy by the cued partner; the player follow-ing the lead of the cuer may choose to imitate the leader's repetitive riff slightly irregularly or slightly out of time, but the relationship thus set should repeat for the length of the pattern's life.) (2) He may cue one of the players in the other duo pair to join him and thus form a new pair with a new riff. When this occurs, the two players remaining from the original pairings may continue existing riffs until one or the other of them signals to the other to join him in a new repeating riff. At that point we again have a double duo, but now in new combination. (3) He may cue the other three players that he will take a solo over the existing repeating patterns. In this case, his partner must hold the pattern until the soloist ends solo (and usually then cues in a new riff). The other pairing should—more often than not—also freeze on existing riff/sounds until the brief solo is over, but this other pair can change if doing so makes sense musically. However, this change is a difficult one to make and tends in our experience to subvert the solo in an uninteresting way. These solos are brief.

All repetitive riffs do not have to be concerned with exact rhythms. Some will be sound blocks and/or repeat for a specific duration with microtonal pitch changes; others could be intervalistic declarations. Anything is possible so long as it hooks up musically with what the other pair is playing at the time of changing.

Both *Planetary* (1995) and *torque* (1988) contain introductory sections in which one duo plays a repeating vamp while the other duo plays a duet (initiated by written material) over (louder than) the vamp line. This is, at its most basic, a simple variation on that idea of solo over vamp mentioned early in this article. In *torque*, however, the duet consists of two simultaneous solos (à la Dixieland music). *torque* has the baritone and tenor repeating a 'typical' bouncy, rhythmic unison-line over which the simultaneous solos play traditionally. In *Planetary*, I change up on this cliche a bit by having the tenor and soprano play a dreamy high line in unison while the duo-ing baritone and alto briefly trade declarative riffs (thinking rap), then gradually begin to overlap and play simultaneously around, over, and under the vamp-line.

In the first structured improvisation in *When the Nation Was Sound* (1993), a twenty-five minute piece with many sections and subsections, a more traditional form is also employed (or at least it can be considered traditional within European-based 'new music' of the 20th century). Following a brief, introductory theme, all four players improvise using notated lines only. Two duos —duo 1: two *E*b altos; duo 2: two *B*b tenors—are instructed to play these notated lines as written, but not necessarily in unison. In fact only the altos' first notated line is definitely played in unison, and that only briefly. However, many of the lines are played by the pair at the same time, but out of phase. Some of these ten notated lines are in both duos' parts. All lines but one are highly energized and played *rubato*, with feeling. There is one melancholy melodic motif that, by the time of the recording, was being played only by the altos. The tenors have a rolling rhythmic figure that they constantly refer back to while moving consecutively through the other lines, in their own time. Several of these lines reappear in variation throughout the piece. See notated examples [Fig. 1-2]:

Figure 1. *When the Nation Was Sound.* Part for two tenors (*B*b)—Section 2.

The device of providing written lines—to be played when the musician chooses but without the addition of freely chosen material—is perhaps the most common form of structured improvisation employed by 'contemporary classical' composers. It is also a potentially deadly, boring device because 1) musicians have a real problem making the material sound spontaneous and

Figure 2. *When the Nation Was Sound.* Part for two altos (in Eb)—Section 2.

2) the lines themselves are the problem: overworked, too complicated, no feeling.

The device works in *When the Nation Was Sound* for a couple of reasons, the most important of which is that the three other players in Rova are improvising artists. They know how to breathe life into the lines and make them their own. And they understand what it means to hear the other players' music and to blend their own contributions into it. The resulting orchestral sound is the paramount goal. And though the art of the improvisor seems like a lesser discipline to some, that notion is consistently disproven by classically trained musicians who, when given a chore similar to that required in *Sound,* simply obstruct realization of the group sound and the composer's ideas.

The device also works in *Sound* because all the lines 'relate' or 'fit over' the first lines given to each duo to initiate the improvisation. Then, the free-jazz feel of the section allows the players the freedom to flow organically from line to line, and the overall flow of the group-sound prevents sudden changes in material by any one player from disturbing the overall flow of the section. It's like well-kneaded bread: composed of independent materials, it all melds together into one coherent unit while still allowing for an unusual inclusion to 'make sense' within the context of the whole.

In *Triceratops* (1993), written for the saxophone octet called Figure 8 (Rova plus Tim Berne, Glenn Spearman, Dave Barrett and Vinny Golia), I had eight players to work with instead of the usual four. The group performed in a semi-circle:

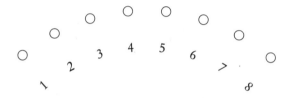

In one five to eight minute section, towards the end of this twenty-five minute piece, notated motifs set up a structured improvisation consisting of three simultaneous duos. The duos take place at positions 2, 5 and 8 with the three pairings being players 1-2, 4-5, and 7-8. In other words, player 1 will move towards position 2, player 4 to position 5, etc. The players already at position 2, 5 and 8 are the 'leaders' of their respective duos. It is up to each partner to make sure that he is playing in a complementary *and* similar style to that of the 'leader.' Each of the three pairs are given musical materials that contrast with what has been given to the other pairs. Thus at the outset of this structured improvisation one hears a trio of duets.

As you will have noticed, players 3 and 6 are not involved initially in the three duos. They wait until the players in the duos have developed the given thematic materials, and then player 3 or 6 may walk over to any of the three 'positions' and enter it, signalling 'out' one or the other of the two members of the pair, and beginning to play new (improvised) material. At that point player 3 or 6 will have become the new 'leader' of the duo, and it is incumbent upon the other player to mutate what he has previously been doing so that it can work with the new leader's idea. The new leader's job when entering is to introduce improvised musical material that relates to the overall orchestral sound being created by the trio of duets at the time of his entry. He can choose from any of five musical areas suggested by the composer or go for something else that he hears the music demanding.

In other words, while players 1-2, 4-5, and 7-8 have been playing, players 3 and 6 have been listening to the overall group-music. When player 3 or 6 hears something—when he hears an interesting way to influence the existing group-music—he chooses one of the duos whose sound he wants to alter, walks to the duo position, and interjects his new musical idea into the group-music as described above.

The player he replaces then becomes one of the two listeners to the group-music. And he continues as a listener until he is inspired to rejoin the group music with a new musical idea. (The two listeners can also do a limited amount of conducting; they can indicate to an existing duo to raise or lower their dynamic level, for example.)

In the recorded version of this piece, the general thrust of this structured improvisation is highly energetic and generally dense, but any musical outcome is possible here. And there is no requirement as the section unfolds that all three duos must always be in contrast to each other. It is possible that the group-music would progressively thin out and quiet down, for example. The leaders of the duos have the option of leading their duos into territory that complements or is similar to one of the other pre-existing duos.

In *The Secret Magritte* (1993), a piece written for an extended ensemble involving Rova plus two pianists, two bassists, and a percussionist, there is a double duo of sorts at the beginning of Section 4. A drone (eventually elaborated on) is kept up by the two pianists. Over the drone a bass-sopranino pairing and a bass-soprano pairing take turns relating a 'fierce story.' *The Secret Magritte* is a fifty minute work that slowly moves through a landscape of varying terrain. In this double duo, the only direction given the double duo is to make up this 'fierce story' over the dynamically loud piano drone. The process for realizing this 'story' is as follows: duo 1 or 2 is always cued in by the saxophonist in the pairing. If the saxophonist points to the bassist, then the bassist knows that on the next cue by the saxophonist, the bassist will continue the story by himself (solo). If the saxophonist points to himself, then the saxophonist solos on the next cue. If no finger-pointing occurs before the cue (which is most often the case) then the duo members enter virtually simultaneously with the saxophonist as 'leader' and the bassist as 'accompanist'; the bassist must in a split second come up with music that continues the story and works with what the saxophonist is introducing. (In reality, both players will have to adjust to each others' starting points.) A pair continues to play until the *other* pair cues itself in, at which point the first pair must stop immediately.

And thus a continuous story—or series of statements—is made by the two pairs. With each pair change, the forward motion of the music can be slowed or sped up, made more or less staccato or legato, loud or soft, spare or intense, etc. But again (as with all these devices), the main concern is that the group-music *happen.* This is not about a competition between the two duos; this is about realizing a section of a composition using a method that optimizes the skills of the improvising artists and inspires them to play the music in ways not even imagined by the composer.

If we compare the last few sentences of my discussion of *Triceratops* with the last few sentences above we will come to the points I want to make in the final part of this article. All the discussion thus far has been about the formal structures within which the improvisation takes place. Just like chord changes in traditional jazz, these formal structures can be used for any group and with any composition. Some adaptation to the kind of instruments employed will have to be made, and some changes in the rules could be necessary—if (for example) one, the number of players involved were different or two, certain players were not mobile due to the instrument they play. But these formal questions aside, it's important to recognize that the musical or thematic mater- ial that sets up the structured improvisation is the key to how the group music will sound in most cases. In other words, three factors differentiate one piece from another, not the formal structure of the improvisation itself, and those factors are: what the player is given as starting material, what the player is given as finishing material, and the limits of expression put on the improvisa- tion by the composer. Thus, the structures, just like chord changes in jazz and blues, or modes and rhythms in Indian music, or the sonata form in traditional European music, are neutral; they themselves do not dictate the musical out- come of a given composition.

For example, the double duo set up in *The Shopper* is a derivative of a double duo form created by Jon Raskin for his piece, *The Pond,* composed one year earlier. In *The Pond* the individual player could choose pure sound or melody or rhythm or a combination of these and other musical parameters when initiating an event. In *The Shopper,* the composed material played prior to the improvisational section sets up an aggressive, forward-moving improvisation, and my verbal instructions limit the variables that each player can choose from to make repeated riffs; all the limits being constructed so as to sustain the mood of the piece.

torque and *Planetary* also show how compositional material affect an improvisation. I wrote *Planetary* in 1995 with the sole intention of creating a new context for the structured improvisation created originally for *torque*. Rova enjoyed playing *torque* for many years because the structured improvisation that makes up most of the piece remained wide open to possibility. After a long while however, we did start spinning our wheels, repeating ourselves in the macro (group sound) if not necessarily in the micro (individual solo phasing process). It wasn't the structure for the improvisation that became stale but rather the written music. So in *Planetary*, the written music sets up a very different mood out of which to improvise; slight alterations to some of the rules of the improvisation also freshen up the process and inspire us to discover new playing areas.

I can offer yet another example of how composer intent rather than structure determines musical outcome: both my piece *The Shopper* and Steve Adams' *The Farallons* (1995) are primarily double-duo structured-improvisations. But whereas in *The Shopper* the duos are aggressive, forward-moving, and focused on rhythmic repeating riffs, the double duos in *The Farallons* consist of held-pitches; two-pitch chords set one against another, with duos changing on signals from either partner in any order at any time. Thus *The Farallons* has a dreamy quality throughout; the solos over the held pitches are slow or plaintive—what the composer wants here—rather than the high-energy solos blasted out in *The Shopper*.

So it is then that a composer working in structured improvisations that are not formulaic must balance his/her desire for control with his/her desire to provide a vehicle for the players. If the closed system that is a composition is so loose that anything that happens is admissible, then one might as well jettison the writing and play freely. On the other hand, a piece can be judged to be successful by the degree to which the composition acts as a springboard for musical invention by the players, directing their energy and creativity to realize the composers intent while still leaving room for the individual players to expand on the original concept and make a creative statement.

Works Cited:

Figure 8. "Triceratops," on *Pipe Dreams.* Black Saint, 1994.

Ochs, Larry. "The Secret Magritte," on *The Secret Magritte.* Black Saint, 1994.

Rova Saxophone Quartet. "Escape from Zero Village," on *Saxophone Diplomacy.* Hat Hut CD, 1992; LP 1983.

____."The Farallons," on *Ptow!* Victo, 1996.

____."New Sheets," on *Cinema Rovaté.* Metalanguage, 1978.

____."Paint Another Take of the Shootpop," on *Saxophone Diplomacy.* Hat Hut, 1992; and on *As Was.* Metalanguage, 1981.

____."The Shopper," on *The Aggregate.* Sound Aspects, 1988; and *Long on Logic.* Sound Aspects, 1990.

____."torque," on *This Time We Are Both.* New Albion, 1991; and on *Long on Logic.* Sound Aspects, 1990.

____."When the Nation Was Sound," on *Vol. 1: The Works.* Black Saint, 1996.

The Pond and *Planetary* are not documented on CD as of this writing.

AGAINST RADICAL CONTINGENCY

STEPHEN DRURY

ONE

Although presented on occasion as a startlingly new advance in the philosophy of art, the idea that a culture uses the trappings and value systems of the art-works it produces to re-affirm its participants' membership in that culture has been floating around at the level of common sense for a long time. The specter of the 'opera lover' dedicated to showing off her new fur while oblivious to the music or of the scene maker more concerned with making the guest list than understanding the band's lyrics serves to confirm, at least to outsiders, the fundamental hollowness of the art; it seems no more than a context in which attitude can be put on display. Even the 'true' opera fanatic discussing Pavarotti's high Cs *ad nauseum* provokes the suspicion that he is really celebrating his own refined taste and thus displaying his cultural capital, his rank in the hierarchy of culture vultures, rather than participating in an experience which makes him feel more profoundly human. The catch-phrase, "value is radically contingent," codifies these suspicions and provides the perpetrators of academic, liberal, multi-syllabic discourse a way to avoid the demands of art; instead they load the cannons of multi-culturalism so they can fire away at classical European culture's canon of 'accepted masterpieces,' a knowledge of which, in simpler times, was deemed fundamental to an educated life.

The idea behind radical contingency is that the values of any particular art or genre—Western concert music, Noh theater, the detective novel, etc.— are dictated by the culture's dominant ideology, are dependent on that culture's socio-politics, and are used primarily to create dividing and defining lines between groups rather than to express any basic transcendental human meaning, any intrinsic connection to human experience, perception, or psychology. This contention is bolstered by pages and pages of studies and surveys showing that wealthy well-educated Westerners, especially those born into wealth, tend to listen to opera, attend performances of Shakespeare's plays, and look at Abstract Expressionist painting more than do those at the so-called lower end of the economic/educational scale. The mechanics of affirming class-membership through cultural choices are clearly visible through the entire spectrum of available music (symphonic, punk, "classic hits," rock, New Age, etc.). The recent trend among classical radio stations to play predominantly Baroque instrumental music ("All Vivaldi Radio! All Vivaldi, All the Time!") which serves as high-class aural wallpaper and status diplomas for yuppies who don't want to be disturbed by the sound of a human voice, a cymbal crash, or a dissonance is but one example. Pierre Bourdieu clarifies the many and subtle ways that economic standing, "educational capital," and other social forces contribute to an individual's willingness to declare one work of art 'better' than another.[137]

137. Pierre Bourdieu, *Distinction: A Social Critique of the Judgment of Taste* (Cambridge, Mass.: Harvard University Press, 1984).

But a crucial mistake is made here: confusing value or quality with taste. Marcel Duchamp pointed out that "taste is the enemy of art, A-R-T." Duchamp and Bourdieu actually reinforce each other's positions; when taste and value are confused, the result is not an art-making which defines and enriches the human experience but rather the production and polishing of badges of class and clique. It is here that we see those who dote on Pavarotti's high Cs, the critics who complain about gaudy CD jacket covers, the club-hoppers who sneer at country-western lyrics, and the teeny-boppers who giggle at string quartets. The actual experience of art lies in the private aesthetic realm of the one-on-one encounter with the artwork. All else is taste, class distinction, and socio-economics.

TWO

One of the things that radical contingency seeks to establish is the impossibility of determining relative quality—the impossibility of determining whether one thing is better than another. The arts are not the sciences, and proof of quality is not to be had. But we all feel degrees of relative quality, and the purpose of critical theory is to develop, support and make explicit those intuitions. Forced to defend John Zorn's *Leng Tch'e* to a symphony musician who doesn't like loud guitars and drums, I can use the tools of radical contingency to break down (or at least hold up to light) his class prejudices. But then I need tools of real analysis if I am successfully to invite him to listen to the thing or if I am to explain why I find it more worthy of attention than the Rachmaninoff Second

Piano Concerto (which it is, but that alone doesn't say much). In the process, hopefully, I will reveal and enrich my own understanding of and sympathy for the piece and derive greater and more fulfilling pleasure from the listening experience. The function of criticism is not to decide or declare what good art is, but to explain "why I like it," that is, why it is good art. At the same time, any criticism which is afraid to say "this is good; this is quality" is ultimately a worthless, cowardly cop-out. And at the root of all this talk is the necessarily 'credulous' mind of the creative artist, which must be more open to inspiration and intuition than that of the scholar. I am reminded here of Joseph Horowitz's comment about Claudio Arrau: "Versus the skeptical modern mind, Arrau's is a credulous intelligence, actually susceptible to exaltation or diablerie."[138]

138. Joseph Horowitz, *Conversations with Arrau* (New York: Alfred A. Knopf, 1982).

The theory of radical contingency is a useful toothbrush. Exploring how deeply dependent most artistic forms are on received, unquestioned values helps one see the work freshly and cleanly. The more we are aware of the socio-economic detritus cluttering our view of an artwork, the more intimate our relationship with the art becomes, and the more we become open to new genres and forms. Unfortunately, in its sweeping refusal to recognize the possibility of quality not dependent on socio-economic stakes, radical contingency throws the baby out with the bath water. Rather than opening up criticism to new definitions of quality and the canon to new works of quality, works not based on forms which are the exclusive domain of (for example) white male moneyed culture, radical contingency discards the very *idea*—the very possibility—of a canon. And the concept of a canon is not exclusively a property of high culture. Collections of 'greatest hits,' Nick at Nite, and oldies radio stations, while smothered by a distorting commercial envelope, spring from the same impulse to select and preserve, while in the process discovering and defining the nature of quality in any given genre or medium. The problem with a canon is inherent in its definition—exclusiveness. As a culture's critical thinking about itself evolves, certain works will be nominated to represent 'the best.' What is needed is not the destruction of the canon but a constant challenging and evolution of the canon, bringing in new works of quality which will repay intense scrutiny with deeper knowledge of, and greater sympathy for, more forms of human experience.

Bourdieu seems astonished to discover that a decent education "inculcates" aesthetic sophistication and analytical skills in fields other than those prescribed in the curriculum and beyond its reading lists. He thus betrays ignorance of (what should be) the fundamental purpose of education—the development of an aesthetic sensibility supported by the ability to think clearly, analytically, and, above all, independently. That a student of classical music in the European concert tradition shows a lively, advanced appreciation of bebop, death metal, beat poetry, or film noir is no mystery of an 'entitlement' granted along with membership in high culture but rather one sign of a successful educational process (whether that education came courtesy of academic institutions or through less legitimized channels). The canon as an educational tool is analogous to the piano études of Chopin or Ligeti. By studying a small number of works in depth and with great rigor the aesthetic (or finger) muscles necessary for tackling the larger world of culture (or piano repertoire) are developed and strengthened.

Attributing all possible definitions of quality to socio-economic forces is a dead end. After clearing away useless unthinking assumptions, it tells us nothing about what remains, which is our true, personal, aesthetic response to art. Approaching art from a strictly sociological viewpoint creates a blind spot—the fundamental nature of art is discovered in the private moment at which the contact between the individual listener, viewer, or reader and the song, picture, or poem creates the spark that acknowledges and gives name to our deepest sensations and affirms the fact that we are human. True, socioeconomic forces act strongly on the listener, and thus they greatly influence his or her reception of the song. Initial choices of genres to explore are based almost wholly on circumstances presented by the environment. But here again, taste and value are confused. Any genre, when not operating purely from commercial considerations, attempts to transcend individual circumstances and speak to something more fundamental, more ultimate—from the most sentimental poetry of a high school girl to the most abstract pitch class manipulations of an unrepentant serialist. To speak to that something, art relies on certain paradigms of human perception. Two measures of quality in art are how deeply the piece works with and is responsive to these paradigms and the degree to which it successfully challenges and expands them. Robert Rauschenberg has pointed out that if, after seeing a painting for the first time, you don't somehow change your mind about something, either the painting is not very good "or you're a damn fool." Advanced art tackles the twin responsibilities of comforting and confronting the observer.

According to Jung, the mind is responsive to a shared set of archetypes, symbols, or myths. Whether these are instilled socially, come as part of the collective unconscious, are a natural product of the physiological structure of the brain, or reflect some deeper, undiscovered set of circumstances is not a question I propose to try to answer here. By "paradigms of human perception," I mean more than simply the habits of taste to which radical contingency calls our attention. I mean something to do with the very structure of the perception apparatus as a whole. The way in which the ear hears, its ability to turn vibrations into pitches or rhythms depending on their frequency (as Stockhausen pointed out), makes things like counterpoint possible. Given a decision to work primarily with pitches and secondarily with rhythms, as in Western art music, counterpoint as a value becomes nearly inevitable at a certain stage of music's evolution. In circumstances not conducive to the creation of instruments of fixed and stable pitch (for example, in sub-Saharan Africa), rhythm assumes a much more dominant role, turning the mind's tendency to fuse two elements into one away from the pitch-oriented counterpoint of Bach and toward the repetitive rhythmic cycles of tribal drumming. Both work with the structure of the mind and of the ear. Western art music, over the long haul, is one culture which (due perhaps to technological development) places particular emphasis on its own change and growth (the challenging of the paradigms of perception, which evolve in a community over time in a way paralleling that suggested by Julian Jaynes).[139] Our culture develops, nurtures, and strengthens these paradigms and causes them to evolve, change, and even to reverse their original meaning. Fast, loud music in a major key means one thing in Beethoven's *Seventh Symphony* and quite another in The Clash's "I'm So Bored with the USA." The idea of counterpoint turns into John Cage's concept of the "musicircus," where completely independent musics are presented simultaneously, with the listener trying to hear them all equally, no piece influencing another in the ear. (For a good example of this, check out Cage's "Apartment House 1776.")

Any set of values, when isolated from the whole process of human perception, can appear equal to any other set, which is why the big picture must be kept constantly in mind in theoretical and critical thinking. For example, consider the comparative value systems of striptease bars. Possible values here include seediness (or lack thereof—and here already we encounter a question as to what constitutes a 'positive' value), number of strippers, attractiveness of strippers, degree of nudity, provocativeness, intimacy, variety, and so forth. A

139. Julian Jaynes, *The Origin of Consciousness in the Breakdown of the Bicameral Mind* (Boston: Houghton Mifflin, 1976).

seedy, second floor San Diego bar near the waterfront several years ago (it has since been torn down) offered a small number of very attractive strippers performing in close proximity to the customers, with the option of a private, nude (both stripper and customer) photo session. Currently San Diego boasts a Pure Platinum franchise limited to topless stage dancing and clothed table dances in a shiny, clean room. (One wonders if these people have ever seen a real striptease club.) Portland, Oregon sports nearly a dozen tiny clubs most of which feature only two or three strippers in perpetual rotation. They run from reasonably attractive to less so. The Pure Platinum franchise in Ft. Lauderdale is filled with nearly two dozen extremely attractive strippers, many surgically augmented, who offer total nudity both on stage and for table-side dances (but no alcohol), while its sister club in New York City shares its squeaky-clean decor but demands suit and tie (on the customer). Lap dances are available at the slightly dingy House of Babes in Orlando (clothed) and the Mons Venus in Tampa (unclothed). The infamous Mitchell Brothers complex in San Francisco goes so far as to offer table-top Lesbian shows as well as private one-on-one sessions, stage dancing, movies, and peep booths. The invariably attractive performers frequently sport body piercings along with other idiosyncrasies of personal grooming. Clubs in State Line, Idaho and Tijuana, Mexico, are known to have permitted on-stage audience participation and are definitely at the seedy (even dangerous) end of the scale.

My purpose here is to show how the methods underlying radical contingency become a self-fulfilling prophecy which defines considerations of value out of existence. Nothing of the above addresses the fundamental aspects of striptease establishments—political (anti-feminist), moral (misogynist), religious (not), or erotic (debatable). Most current analysis of art operates at about the same level. This is merely description and tells us nothing about why we are here.

THREE

Quality is measured according to many standards, all of which participate in the sum. These standards seem almost limitless in number and interact in so many ways that one is reminded of chaos theory, in which a closed system (say, global weather patterns or the movement of individual molecules as a pot of water comes to a boil) with even a small number of variables quickly becomes unpredictable due to the complexity of their interactions. Given the primitive state of psychology as a science (roughly on a level with alchemy) and the immense plurality of values and aesthetics necessary to deal with more than a single piece at a time (let alone a single culture), it's no wonder that some critical writers throw up their hands, refuse to attempt value judgments, and take refuge in mere description. It is difficult—perhaps even impossible—to show why any particular artistic value should be regarded as good or positive. Every proposal gives rise to a counter-example. If you suggest 'harmonic interest,' where does that leave Varèse's *Ionisation* for (largely unpitched) percussion, for example, or African tribal drumming? 'Melodic development' leaves out Stockhausen's *Stimmung,* 'rhythmic drive' misses the first movement of the *Moonlight* Sonata and 'counterpoint' is non-existent in Credence Clearwater Revival's "Lookin' Out My Back Door." Even such hopelessly over-generalized categories as 'complexity' (Satie's *Socratie*) or 'simplicity' (Bach's *Passion of St. Matthew*) are insufficient, not to mention the virtually uncategorizable achievements of John Cage, LaMonte Young, Public Enemy, or the Velvet Underground. And many labels are likely to backfire. The melodic simplicity which serves as a defining characteristic of the slow movement of Beethoven's *Appassionata* Sonata or Bob Dylan's "Subterranean Homesick Blues" becomes the liability which wrecks Bruce Springsteen's "Born in the USA" and America's "Horse With No Name," which share the same sing-song three-note melodic gamut (two more notes than "Subterranean Homesick Blues" or Elvis Costello's "Pump It Up," for all the good those two notes did).

Any given set of values does an incomplete and possibly misleading job of signifying artistic achievement. Radical contingency fails, however, when it attempts to deny the existence of quality, however slippery the labels attached to it may grow. In attributing the power of Schubert's *Der Leiermann* or Hank Williams's "Ramblin' Man" to purely sociological forces, radical contingency not only runs away from uncovering why these songs *truly* affect the listener as they do, it also misses the deep-rooted similarity of two songs held dear by listeners at opposite ends of the socio-economic spectrum. Both speak of feelings of rootlessness and alienation, forces which drag the singer (against his will) constantly away from stability or a sense of home or belonging. Both are so simple and so emotionally naked as to invite the question, "Is this Art?" Both are starkly constructed—two chords each, extremely stripped-down melodies, bare but evocative accompaniment. Both discover a simultaneously fearful and comforting conclusion. Schubert's rejected fugitive, deceived by an unfaithful lover, travels through a winter landscape of desolation and madness seeking death. The open fifth in the left hand of the piano proves to be the drone of a hurdy-gurdy played by a lonely, frost-bitten old man surrounded by snapping dogs. With a combination of horror and resignation, the fugitive discovers his doppelganger in the old man. He releases his soul to the old man whose hurdy-gurdy provides music for the fugitive's songs. Two melodic fragments alternate obsessively, changing only at the moment of recognition at the very end. In "Ramblin' Man," the four-note melodic formula rises once and then plummets an octave and a half. Each eight-bar phrase repeats this formula with a text that begins each time with a ray of hope and immediately dashes it as the melody falls:

> I can settle down
> and be doin' just fine
> 'til I hear an old freight
> rollin' down the line.
>
> Then I hurry straight
> home and pack,
> and if I didn't go
> I b'lieve I'd blow my stack.
>
> I love you baby
> but you gotta understand
> when the Lord made me
> He made a ramblin' man.

Throughout the song variations are wrought on this wedding of text and music, offering a rainbow of takes on elements of the scene, filling it with complex mixtures of hope and despair. The extraordinary final verse is a reconciliation with and longing for death as powerful as anything in Schubert. The descending phrase, until now weighted with despair and defeat, becomes a gentle release downward into the place of rest denied the ramblin' man for so long:

> And when I'm gone
> and at my grave you stand,
> just say God's called home
> your ramblin' man.

FOUR

These are some of the things I expect from critical theory: a vigorous belief in art, the courage to take a stand, an attempt to share the substance of the aesthetic experience, a clarification to me of my own aesthetic experience. It must bring intuition and impression to a conscious level. It must determine what characteristics the separate values of two or more observers, groups, or cultures have in common, and what this says about the most basic human perceptions and needs for artmaking. It must tell me why I do indeed feel something that could be described as transcendence or exaltation when experiencing Beethoven's *Hammerklavier* Sonata, Ives's *Fourth* Symphony, or Talking Heads' "Cool Water." And above all, it must demonstrate humility—art came before theory and continually escapes the grasp of the scholar.

Special thanks to Scott Michaelsen of Michigan State University, an imaginative, thoughtful, and provocative scholar, who first introduced me to these concepts and disagrees with nearly the entirety of this paper. Thanks also to Warren Nichols of New York City and Philadelphia, and to Crystal of the House of Babes in Orlando, Florida.

"WE ARE REVEALING A HAND
THAT WILL LATER REVEAL US"

Notes on Form and Harmony in Coltrane's Work

JOHN SCHOTT

Each man his own academy—Cecil Taylor

Following his death in 1967, the ideas that informed John Coltrane's music, or rather his music up to 1964, became a standard for improvising virtuosity. Techniques derived from his work were reduced to easily graspable pedagogical principles and set forth in numerous publications[140]; mastering his compositions *Moment's Notice* and *Giant Steps* became the rite of passage for jazz musicians it has been for thirty years. The obsession Coltrane demonstrated for practicing, purification, and rigorous treatment of musical material, an obsession virtually without precedent in jazz, became a posthumous boon to the burgeoning jazz education industry, which conferred on Coltrane the sainthood previously reserved only for Charlie Parker. After all, Coltrane, who had resoundingly kicked his drug habit in 1957, was a better role model than the morally ambivalent Parker, who died a junkie.

140. See, for instance, the "Pro Session" columns in *Down Beat,* 1970-1990; the many, many books published by Jamey Aebersold; Ricker and Weiskopf's *Coltrane: A Player's Guide To His Harmony* (Hal Leonard Publications), and David Leibman's *A Chromatic Approach To Improvisation* (Rottenberg, Germany: Advanced Music, 1991).

The demands of pedagogy inevitably simplify complex phenomena, and Coltrane (who it now seems dropped quite a bit of acid in his last years[141]) is only one of many jazz musicians whose legacy is encumbered by this necessity. This isn't such a bad thing: the simplistic improv formulas I swallowed as a student—play this scale over this chord, swing those eighth notes—did finally lead me to a more subtle understanding of jazz styles, by which point I no longer needed them.

141. On Coltrane's alleged LSD use, see Eric Nisenson, *Ascension: John Coltrane And His Quest* (New York: St. Martin's Press, 1993), pp. 166-647.

142. No author given (Wisconsin: Hal Leonard Publications, 1991). Edited, incredibly, by Alice Coltrane!

But the benign distortions of my education are in a separate category from the irresponsible publication *The Music of John Coltrane.*[142] Errors abound in this attempted "fakebook" of 107 Coltrane compositions, but "error" does not begin to describe the travesty that is made of Coltrane's less-easily notated, post-1965 music here. Making no attempt to distinguish composition from improvisation in these pieces, the editors simply transcribe from the recordings one page's worth of what Coltrane played at the beginning of each piece. The heraldic fanfare which marks the true beginning of *Evolution* is therefore omitted, coming as it does several minutes after an opening bass solo. More than half of *Expression* is similarly missing…and so on. No attempt is made to differentiate a freely improvised tenor and drum duet from *Interstellar Space* from a 32-measure tune from *Blue Train*. Throughout the later compositions, barlines are imposed where none are heard, chords are given that contradict the recordings, and the roles of the supporting musicians present are routinely ignored, integral though they may be to the composition's conception. With friends like Hal Leonard, Coltrane doesn't need enemies.

This dumbing-down of Coltrane's work offends me. As a musician who in some part traces his lineage through Coltrane, I feel like someone has been telling lies about my family. The sins in this instance are of omission, of giving simplistic answers to complex questions. The present essay is offered as a corrective.

It has been forty years since jazz musicians began to improvise without prearranged chord changes or forms. The body of work that has resulted is, at its best, the strongest challenge to the musical status quo since the Second World War. What is made of this legacy, by critics, musicologists, or publishers, ultimately becomes our legacy. Exegesis of this music, not for want of intellectual prestige or academic recognition, but according to what we as contemporary musicians find valuable and relevant to our own work, therefore becomes an imperative. There is little hope of our work being understood if we do not also try to elucidate what is meaningful in the work of our predecessors.

My early fascination with Coltrane's work centered on his ability to create long melodic lines that balanced an intricate array of internal tensions and resolutions over chord changes. Essentially, I wanted to know what notes he played over which chords, in hopes of abstracting from this knowledge a modicum of applicable theory, and thereby becoming a better improvisor. Later, a growing interest in the special properties of the total chromatic brought about an estrangement from conventional chord changes in my work, and this begot a fresh perspective on the classic jazz I had grown up with.

Coltrane's development parallels the "emancipation of the dissonance"—in Schoenberg's classic formulation—that took place at the beginning of this century. Both of these great musicians were able to justify previously forbidden dissonances through an expansion of harmonic interpretation.

Mutatis mutandis, we might say that their harmonic conceptions enlarged to the point where they could not play a wrong note; everything became consonant, and at that moment tonality gave way to something new. Although both men expressed a desire to occasionally return to older styles, once they broke with the past, there was no going back.

Reading aspects of Coltrane's work in the light of recent atonal theory brings with it certain risks. Jazz does not lend itself to the "account-for-every-note" approach of classical music analysis; the stuff of an improvised solo, or even a jazz composition, is not the stuff of Brahms. To name only the most obvious difference, jazz lacks a text. The analytical consequences of that difference are devastating.[143] Transcribed jazz solos are conjectures, and inevitably become a demonstration of the inadequacies of our notational system. Furthermore, there is almost no analytical vocabulary for discussing performative qualities like rhythmic inflection or timbral modulations, though these elements contribute as much to a solo's meaning as pitch selection.

143. The notion that classical music has a definitive "urtext" that one can legitimately refer to has recently come under attack. See Roman Ingarden, *The Work of Music and the Problem of Its Identity* (Berkeley: University of California Press, 1986), and Richard Taruskin, *Text and Act* (New York: Oxford University Press, 1995).

It's also true that criteria derived from classical music have been used to "legitimize" jazz. The thinking goes: Beethoven/Europe=thematic development=cultural prestige; therefore: Charlie Parker/America=thematic development=cultural prestige. *Jazz: America's Classical Music,* as the title of one book has it. Such patronizing, if well-intentioned, efforts only reinforce the notion that all musical values stem from Europe.

It's a mistake, I think, to exclude those criteria completely, if indeed that is even possible. Coltrane does not exist in a sealed-off vacuum of African-American creativity. His work is informed by and participates in a dialogue with European (and African, Asian, Latin American...) musical traditions, while not being constrained by them.[144] But more to the point, this essay reflects *my* varied backgrounds, and though I seek to underline a theme running through Coltrane's work, it is in some sense a Coltrane of my invention, a projection of my own work.

144. This was brought home to me when I asked jazz guitarist Jim Hall, who majored in composition at the Cleveland Institute of Music, if he was familiar with Heinrich Schenker, the turn-of-the-century Viennese theorist. He replied that he wasn't, but that he believed Sonny Rollins was studying Schenker in the early sixties. Further research, someone?

My motivation for this discussion is to bring my own disparate influences—creative and theoretical—under one conceptual roof. The following

347

observations are not intended to offer complete accounts of the music under examination. Sometimes I have looked at the frame without mentioning the painting it encloses. I have selectively picked my way through Coltrane's work in hopes of illuminating what is currently stimulating to me in it.

To begin with we must distinguish between two approaches to chromaticism in Coltrane's early work: that which is consonant with the underlying harmony, but, following that harmony, modulates to remote regions or fails to establish any key center; and that which extends, alters or superimposes upon the underlying, tonic-oriented harmony, and thus is dissonant to it. The former is associated with Coltrane's playing on his own, harmonically challenging compositions; the latter with blues and standards. These techniques were not Coltrane's inventions; their beginnings may be seen variously in the music of Coleman Hawkins, Thelonious Monk, Gil Evans, and others. But it was Coltrane who most rigorously mined these techniques for alternative methods of harmonic organization.

145. John Coltrane, *Blue Train* (Blue Note 53428). All citations of recordings in this essay give their most recent issue.

Moment's Notice [Fig. 1], recorded in 1957, inaugurates Coltrane's chromatic journey. It begins with II-V-I progressions in Eb and Db, and expands them to include their lower neighbors.[145]

Figure 1.

The half-step relationship between the two tonalities achieves a higher degree of chromatic saturation than a more conventional progression, such as III-VI-II-V, which also fits the melody, would have guaranteed. At the end of the A section, right before the beginning is repeated, a sudden modulation to the remote region of bIII occurs, derailing what would have been a standard III-VI-II-V progression with a construction parallel to the opening bars. The effect is to destabilize the tonic, and to drive the soloist into a rapid and far-reaching chromaticism [Fig. 2].

Figure 2.

348

Until the eight cadential measures in Eb that round out the form, no key center is definitively established. The prolonged cadence, over a pedal point on V, belatedly confirms the tonic and provides the soloist with a contrasting modal section to improvise on, resolving the tension of the migrating harmony.

Coltrane's ornate, dense improvisations on the chord changes of blues and standards are a logical extension of the practice of Charlie Parker and Dizzy Gillespie. The chromaticism of *Moment's Notice,* and later *Giant Steps* and *Satellite,* is fundamentally different than that which had preceded it. Widely roving harmonies had been used by Monk, Ellington and others, but not at breakneck bebop tempos. The appearance of any key center is so fleeting in these pieces that the bebop soloist's arsenal of upper-structure extensions, passing tones, and substitutions is useless. The solos thus become more consonant with the underlying harmony, comprised primarily of chord tones, 9ths and 6ths, and yet paradoxically more chromatic, lacking as they do the long-range resolutions of the more conventionally tonal song forms.

The technique in *Moment's Notice* of juxtaposing underlying harmonies to produce chromatic saturation receives a different treatment in Miles Davis' composition *So What.* First recorded in 1958,[146] Coltrane continued playing it through 1965 (in his sped-up paraphrase, re-titled *Impressions*), making it the longest running piece in his repertoire. Restricted to D Dorian for the A sections and Eb Dorian for the B section, the piece thus "saves" the notes Eb, Gb, Ab, Bb, and Db for the bridge [Fig. 3].

146. Miles Davis, *Kind of Blue* (Sony 64935).

Figure 3.

The idea of introducing "fresh" notes was a common compositional conceit in European music of the teens and twenties.[147] Here, in a cyclical form, it has the effect of establishing for the soloist two alternating harmonic regions, with—as far as possible given the constraints of the diatonic tonal system—maximal pitch exclusivity.

The consequences of this idea resonate throughout Coltrane's work, most explicitly in his 1965 composition *One Down, One Up.*[148] The 32-bar

147. See Milton Babbitt, *Words About Music* (Madison: University of Wisconsin Press, 1987), pp. 154-155, and Anton Webern, *The Path to the New Music,* English translation (Pennsylvania: Theodore Presser Co. 1963), pp. 50- 51. Webern's example appears to be in error, but his observation is pertinent.

148. There are two recordings, currently available on *Dear Old Stockholm* (Impulse! GRD-120) and *New Thing At Newport* (Impulse! GRD-105). The examples here are from *Dear Old Stockholm.* Like *Giant Steps* (see below), the inspiration for this piece may have been Slonimsky's *Thesaurus.* The identical hexachords are featured in patterns 186, 188, 190, 192, and 231.

AABA form of *So What* is maintained, but the diatonic juxtaposition is replaced with a strictly hexachordal one, making the division of the aggregate into two parts absolute. The hexachords are symmetrical, comprised of two augmented triads a half-step apart [Fig. 4].

Figure 4.

Even several minutes into the solo, the hexachords are kept distinct, yielding only a little to passing tones and 'dissonant' (that is, outside the hexachord) notes [Fig. 5].

Figure 5.

In an essay for *Down Beat,* Coltrane stated that during his second tenure with Miles Davis (1958-60): "I could stack up chords-say, on a *C7,* I sometimes superimposed an *Eb7,* up to an *F#7,* down to an *F.* That way I could play three chords on one."[149] The concept is clear—the superimposed dominant chords introduce the higher, chromatically altered extensions of *C7*: the flat and sharp ninths, and the flat sharp eleventh. Generations of jazz musicians, myself included, have been taught some version of this formula as a Coltrane signature. The device may well have been a practice room etude, but on recordings Coltrane is rarely this formulaic. Indeed, I have been unable to find a single unequivocal example of the above-mentioned device in his solos from the period. The problem is compounded by the elusive identity of

149. John Coltrane and Don DeMichael, "Coltrane On Coltrane," *Down Beat* (Sept. 29, 1960). This quote has often been used as a key to Coltrane's middle-period style, but explication of it usually becomes bogged down in confusion and error. Simpkins insufficiently writes the chords out in chorale style, as if the concept were self-explanatory, and uses the triangle symbol to indicate both dominant and major seventh chords. Cole's example, like many in his book, is a kind of virtuostic, contrapuntal display of errors. The example is in a different key from its description in the text; it is notated incorrectly, with misspelled notes and misplaced barlines; and it bears only a passing resemblance to the passage it purports to transcribe, the end of Coltrane's second chorus on *Straight No Chaser.* See Cuthbert Ormond Simpkins, *Coltrane: A Biography* (New York: Herndon House, 1975), pp. 69-70, 74-75, and Bill Cole, *John Coltrane* (New York: Schirmer Books, 1976), pp. 80-83.

the C7 in Coltrane's example: it exists as a *model,* or mental backdrop that the players spontaneously, and liberally, interpret. When the choices available to them include altering, extending, superimposing upon, or even ignoring the model, then the relationship between the model and its specific realization (or non-realization, as the case may be) becomes highly problematic. The C7 is an abstraction. It exists for Coltrane in the form of a repertoire of possibilities, but for *us,* the listeners, it exists only so far as we can construe its presence in the actual music. As Barry Kernfeld has written, "this music lacks not only a definitive written score, but also a fixed point of reference (the model, the accompaniment, or the solo?) from which to judge whether a tone is harmonic or non-harmonic."[150] The problem with Coltrane's description of his own method then, is that C7 *itself* is superimposed on C7.

150. Barry Kernfeld, "Two Coltranes," *Annual Review of Jazz Studies* II (1983): 13. This article is the essential treatment of Coltrane's style during this period, and offers some tentative solutions to the issues obstructing a theoretical understanding of it.

The death of a style is often the beginning of a theoretical understanding of it. Satisfactory accounts of sonata form did not arise until the mid-19th century, by which time it had become an exhausted, if prestigious, antique. The most interesting and relevant improvised music of our time has little to do with chord changes, and this has been true since at least the death of Bill Evans. The function of chord changes—or rather "functions," since their role in the music of Louis Armstrong, Thelonious Monk, and Duke Ellington is so different—is the least understood element of classic jazz. The preoccupation with scales and chord changes in soloing over song-forms is a relatively recent and pedagogically necessitated phenomenon; linear concerns and voice leading were the primary determinants of note selection in the solos of the masters.

Let us turn to two examples from Coltrane's so-called "chord on chord" period. The first is choruses five and six from a nine-chorus solo on "Sid's Ahead," a blues in *F,* taken from a 1958 broadcast recording by the Miles Davis Sextet.[151]

This is exceedingly complex music [Fig. 6] that does not give up its secrets easily. Remembering the statement by Coltrane quoted above, we note the presence of many triads and seventh chords foreign to the harmony here; some of these are easier to interpret as substitutions than others. The *Gb9* (lacking a b7th) in the tenth measure of the second chorus, for instance, is a common enough tritone substitution, ensuring a strong resolution to the tonic. The *Abmin7* in measure nine of the first chorus varies this procedure by shifting the superimposed bII

151. Miles Davis, *All Stars Live in 1958-59* (Jazz Band EBCD2101-2). The date of the performance is November 1, 1958, not February 1959 as listed on the CD.

Figure 6.

chord from the V (in this instance *D7*) to the I (*Gmin 7*), and then resolving it on beats three and four. The superimposition idea is less helpful in explicating other vagrant chords, e.g. the *E6* in chorus one, measure 4 (an anticipation of *Bb7* by its tritone?).

The passage maintains only the briefest of allegiances to the underlying blues harmony. It does so at strategic places within the form, however, bracketing the chromatic excursions within. Both choruses are made up of two six-measure phrases, which neatly bisect the 12-bar form. In both choruses the first phrase begins by outlining the tonic triad, moves away from it, then ends outlining the subdominant in measure six. The second phrase stays outside the underlying harmonies until measures 11-12, where it confirms the tonic triad. The form is thus defined as two spans,

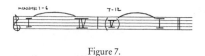

Figure 7.

and in between the triadic landmarks the lines chromatically fill in the registral space. Thus the perfect fifth *F-C* that begins chorus five is filled in over the four measures that make up the I7 region, completed by the *G* natural on the downbeat of measure five. The *G* is the 'fresh' note that marks the change in harmony to the IV region. The first phrase of the second chorus begins with a descending motion from *Ab* to *Bb*; it ends with the same gesture backwards, ascending *Bb* to *Ab*, in measure six. In between these gestures, all the half steps from the *C* of the phrase's second measure to the *B* that is the phrase's highest note are filled in *except* for the *Ab* that begins and ends the phrase.

Coltrane's mastery at sustaining long lines is rivaled in Jazz only by Charlie Parker and Lennie Tristano. The second phrase of the example (beginning measure 7) weaves together several strands of voice leading. A motion from Eb to D is prolonged in the lowest notes, while a descending minor sixth is spanned in the upper register. The middle register fills out the perfect fourth F-Bb. Observe also the intervals that are formed by the notes that mark a change of direction, or are otherwise structurally exposed. In measures 3-6 of the fifth chorus there is a chain of major 7ths; in the sixth chorus a tritone that ends the first phrase provides the impetus for the second phrase.

In the excerpt from *Impressions* below [Fig. 8], the long lines of *Sid's Ahead* are broken up into choked three-to-five note fragments, most often placed in cross-meter to the ensemble. As in the earlier example the solo refers to the underlying harmony only at structural points in the form, in this case at the end of eight-measure phrases.[152]

152. John Coltrane, *Impressions* (MCA 5887).

Figure 8.

A lot of things are happening here, but *D* minor is not one of them! In *So What*, recorded four years earlier, the soloist's adherence to the modal scheme had partitioned the twelve tones. That scheme is still a point of departure in *Impressions,* but within two minutes has become only the merest of outlines. This is free jazz, the underlying form notwithstanding. The many triads in Coltrane's solo are not substitutions, as there is no pretext of functional harmony. The soloist's line is responsible only to itself. All twelve tones are

353

accessible at all times, and it is their more or less equal circulation that keeps them stable, neutral of consonance or dissonance. The passage is harmonically static, and this has the effect of foregrounding the role played by rhythm. The long line is sustained here entirely through rhythmic means: the use of hemiola —Coltrane playing in 3/4 against the ensemble's 4/4—and clipped three and four-note groups, sounding like a phrase trying to start itself over and over again. The agitated fragments struggling to define themselves against a motionless, chromatic background builds a hypnotic tension that was fundamentally new to jazz.

Coltrane's extensive study during this period of Slonimsky's *Thesaurus Of Scales And Melodic Patterns*[153] is well known, but we must put to rest the myth that he cut and pasted patterns from it into his solos. There is in fact very little literal pattern playing in Coltrane of the kind that one finds in Eddie Harris or Yusef Lateef, or in the scores of would-be Coltrane imitators one hears today. The *Thesaurus* was an etude book for the terminally curious Coltrane. Its exhaustive treatment of octave divisions and symmetrical interval patterns was also a goad in his quest for a tonal system that would supplant traditional tonality.

Coltrane's passion for symmetrical harmonic organization reached its peak with *Giant Steps*, recorded in 1959.[154] David Demsey has shown the composition's likely origins in an example of tonal harmonization of twelve-tone melody from the *Thesaurus*.[155] He further analyses the relationship of melody to bass movement in the 16-measure composition, showing them both to be limited to a nine tone, symmetric set that excludes the pitches C, E, and G#, a trichord which is a transposition of the underlying harmonic scheme. The affinities with serial thinking, however, do not end there.

A fusion and culmination of modal juxtaposition and chord-on-chord structures, *Giant Steps* expands *So What's* two tonal centers to three: Eb, B and G. Like *So What*, the keys are chosen for maximum pitch exclusivity. But in *Giant Steps* the changes come very fast indeed, as in the "chord-on-chord" approach, and a more or less constant rotation of the total chromatic results. In Coltrane's solo all twelve pitch-classes are sounded on average every three measures, or roughly every twenty notes. As in *Moment's Notice*, these notes are almost invariably consonant with their underlying harmony, not chromatic passing tones, and thus are structurally reinforced. The first seven

153. Nicolas Slonimsky, *Thesaurus of Scales and Melodic Patterns* (New York: Charles Scribner's Sons, 1947).

154. John Coltrane, *Giant Steps* (Atlantic 8133).

155. David Demsey, "Chromatic Third Relations in the Music of John Coltrane," *Annual Review of Jazz Studies* 5 (1991): 156-57, 169-73.

measures of Coltrane's solo, beginning with the pickup to the top of the form, are one note shy of three complete statements of all twelve tones [Fig. 9].

Figure 9.

Giant Steps is too tightly constructed to allow for a contrasting bridge to dilute its argument. The pedal-tone section of *Moment's Notice* is similarly irrelevant, for here there are no remote regions creating tension in need of resolution. The symmetry of the key centers makes them equally stable, balanced as if in orbit around each other. For this reason solos on *Giant Steps* don't end so much as stop—seamlessly circular, the composition permits no closure.

In a sense, Coltrane destroyed tonality by using it against itself. Employing the most basic feature of the American popular song, the II-V-I chord progression, he sped up the rate as well as the degree of modulation to an unprecedented extent, creating a context for improvisation that allowed for coherent complete chromatic circulation. That Coltrane 'signified' on popular songs like *My Favorite Things* has been commented upon; less well-known is how his harmonic research signifies on the elemental assumptions of Western music theory.[156]

Contemporary with *Giant Steps* is a diagram [Fig. 10] drawn by Coltrane in 1960, and given to Yusef Lateef.[157] The diagram juxtaposes the two whole-tone collections five times around the perimeter of a circle. Lines are drawn connecting each tone to its tritone across the circle, bisecting the circle thirty times. Every fifth tone is enclosed in a box to show the circle of fifths. Each member of the circle of fifths is also enclosed with its upper and lower neighbors in two ovals. The five appearances of the note C are linked through

156. On Signifying see Henry Louis Gates, Jr., *The Signifying Monkey: A Theory of Afro-American Literary Criticism* (New York: Oxford University Press, 1988). For an interesting study of the signifying element in Coltrane's version of "My Favorite Things" see Ingrid Monson, "Doubleness and Jazz Improvisation: Irony, Parody, and Ethnomusicology," *Critical Inquiry* 2 (Winter 1994): 292-99.

157. The diagram is reproduced in Yusef Lateef, *Repository of Scales and Melodic Patterns* (Amherst, Mass.: Fana Press, n.d.). It is also printed on the inset CD tray card of Prima Materia, *Meditations* (Knitting Factory Works 180). Mention might also be made of a statement by Lateef included in the notes for *John Coltrane: The Complete Atlantic Recordings* (Rhino/Atlantic 71984): "One night in the late fifties [Coltrane] asked me several questions, which are as follows: Which two keys have 12 different tones? Which two keys have 11 different tones? Which two keys have 10 different tones? [etc.]." The questions as asked are nonsensical; perhaps Lateef means, "Which two keys contain all twelve notes (i.e. five different tones)?" Even so, the conversation again indicates Coltrane's systematic approach to tonality in regard to aggregate relationships.

355

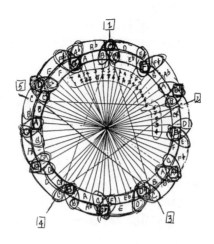

Figure 10.

a five pointed star. At the top, underscoring the inversion-based symmetry of the diagram, Coltrane has assigned *C* the number 1, and then counted outwards in both directions to *F#*. This procedure is repeated for *F#*.

Though the origins of this diagram and its significance for Coltrane are obscure, we may nevertheless make some observations about it. What impresses is the multitude of interconnected paths that are traced through the aggregate. The diagram is a blueprint for a musical journey, linking together whole-tone, chromatic, and circle of fifth formations. His plotting of musical relationships here could well have been used as the basis for a composition or improvisation, analogous to the 12x12 arrays that initiate 12-tone composition. Finally, the appearance of the pentagram opens the discourse beyond the strictly musical, and this is of course entirely characteristic of Coltrane's predilection for metaphysical arcana.[158]

158. The pentagram is one of the world's oldest symbols, thought to derive from astronomical research in the Euphrates-Tigris region 6000 years ago. See Carl G. Liungman, *Dictionary Of Symbols*, English translation (New York: Norton 1991), pp. 43-45, 298-300.

159. Such a study might contextualize Coltrane's intellectual development in the blossoming Afrocentric movement of the 1950-60s, show the bebop musicians—Coltrane's artistic mentors—to be on the cutting edge of that movement, and explore the interdependent use of science (sometimes decidedly idiosyncratic science) and mysticism in Afrocentric thought.

Though beyond the boundaries of this paper, the relationship between Coltrane's musical-theoretical research and his voracious reading in religion, history, and the occult is in need of comprehensive study.[159]

Giant Steps is an extreme point in Coltrane's development. He doesn't seem to have played the piece live, and he soon moved on to looser harmonic structures. But the idea of interlocking diatonic or pentatonic figures to achieve chromatic circulation remained a hallmark of his late style, even as he abandoned the chord changes that had generated them. These ideas inform much of his late music, and in his solos they often appear in the midst of wild, virtually non-pitched, overblown textures, where they have the effect of a fervent testimony summoned up by sheer force of will to dispel the surrounding chaos.

Not all of Coltrane's explorations of organized chromaticism yield large-scale structures. *Miles' Mode,* from 1962, is the sole example of an ordered 12-tone collection in Coltrane's work. The first half of the phrase uses the row forward and backward, then quickly rounds off the melody with a rather clichéd hard-bop cadence in *B* minor, followed by 16 measures of modal improvising [Fig. 11].

Figure 11.

This suggests a pattern of alternating chromaticism and modality, and Coltrane to some extent follows this plan in his solo, although this pattern was not unusual for him at this time.[160]

In *Acknowledgement,* from *A Love Supreme,* [Fig. 12] Coltrane transposes the bass ostinato to each of the twelve keys at the end of his solo, before locking in with the bass and beginning the vocal chant. During these measures McCoy Tyner shadows Coltrane's modulations in a remarkable way; it is difficult to tell whether this is a result of Tyner's prodigious comping intuition, or if perhaps this modulatory foray was charted out by Coltrane beforehand. Though there is no exact pattern to the transpositions, the appearance of all twelve (with the last, *F#,* appearing in the third-to-last repetition) seems unlikely to be pure accident.[161]

These last two examples, one a minor work and the other a passage from a masterpiece, indicate that Coltrane drew upon twelve-tone organization not just for global compositional organization, as in *Giant Steps* and *One Up, One Down,* but for local effect as well. In *Acknowledgement* it prepares the return of the chant; in *Miles' Mode* it sets up two contrasting areas for the soloist to develop. What is remarkable in these examples and throughout Coltrane's career is the shunning of any conspicuous display of these effects. Our attention is rarely called to matters of compositional (or instrumental)

160. John Coltrane, *Coltrane* (Impulse! IMPD-215). Coltrane also maintains the alternating structure in a live recording of the composition from the same year; see John Coltrane, *Abstract Blue* (Telstar Records TRCD 1007).

161. John Coltrane, *A Love Supreme* (Impulse! GRD-155). My example is adapted from an excellent, in-depth study by Lewis Porter, "John Coltrane's *A Love Supreme*: Jazz Improvisation as Composition," *Journal of the American Musicological Society* XXXVIII, no. 3 (Fall 1985).

"A Love Su-preme, A"

Figure 12.

technique, as it was in many of his contemporaries; Coltrane's self-imposed doctrine of purification and humility all but precluded the cool dissertations of the mid-sixties Miles Davis Quintet, or the elaborate counterpoint and labyrinthian forms of Charles Mingus. His art increasingly became one of renunciation and self-censorship, the discipline of the music reflecting Coltrane's search for an order that could encompass the disorder of his times.

The recording of *A Love Supreme* in December of 1964 inaugurated a year in which the suite or extended composition was Coltrane's preferred vehicle. Eight such pieces were recorded, although the designation "extended piece" becomes somewhat arbitrary in this era of long solos.[162] Each piece offers a different solution to the problems of formal coherence and unity in a multi-movement work. Not all of these solutions were equally successful, and only half of these works were approved for release by Coltrane. While the playing is uniformly compelling, one senses with Coltrane the unfinished quality that makes *Suite: Prayer and Meditation, Om, Selflessness,* and *First Meditations* comparatively unsatisfying.[163]

Leaving aside the special case of *Kulu Se Mama,* which was not Coltrane's composition, and which is governed by its chanted poetry and exotic instrumentation more than its music, we are left with three major works: *A Love Supreme, Ascension,* and *Meditations.* The tonal relationships that govern these pieces are no longer characterized by symmetric harmonic plans or methodical chromatic circulation. Those procedures depended on a

162. There is some evidence that *Crescent, After The Crescent,* and *Transition* were originally intended to make up a suite. See David Wild, liner notes to *Dear Old Stockholm* (Impulse! GRD-120).

163. The posthumously released suite *Interstellar Space* is a different matter. The focus here is less on the material than on the challenge posed by its reduced instrumentation, tenor sax and drums. But note also the statement by Alice Coltrane accompanying her recording of *Leo:* "The chart John designed was a musical one with 12 tones correlating to the 12 zodiacal [sic] signs." Liner notes to Alice Coltrane, *Transfiguration* (Warner Bros. #3218, 1978).

rhythmic and formal clarity that had steadily eroded. The dialectics that had previously delineated the music's form—composition/improvisation, consonance/dissonance, pulse/syncopation—collapse into themselves during 1965, as if overwhelmed by Coltrane's obsessive desire to transcend the (musical) material world.

As a result it is often unclear where the writing ends and the improvising begins, or if there is any writing at all. This ambiguity is itself one of the most distinctive features of the music. Instead of the sharp contrasts that characterize his earlier harmonic plans, or the monotonalities from 1960-64, the harmonic organization from 1965 on stresses commonality and continuity. The distinctions between motif, chord, and mode are blurred; it may be more useful to speak of harmonic *fields.* One chord may bleed into the next, as in parts of *Ascension.* A scale or mode may be improvised upon as a non-hierarchic set of notes, without any tonic note asserting itself until the end, as in *Love,* from the *First Meditations* suite. Finally, Coltrane's part may follow a definite harmonic plan that is only vaguely acknowledged by the piano and bass, as in much of *Meditations.*

164. On *Ascension* see John C. Thomas, *Chasin' The Trane* (New York: Doubleday, 1975), p. 195; Ekkerhard Jost, *Free Jazz* (Graz: Universal Edition, 1974) pp. 84-98; Cole, pp. 165-67; and Simpkins, pp. 187-189.

The number of conflicting accounts of *Ascension* attest to the difficulty in discerning its compositional structure.[164] No two descriptions of its musical material agree, and there are no satisfactory explanations by the participants. My reading of the piece [Fig. 13], which makes no claims to be definitive, identifies four harmonic regions:

Figure 13.

The regions progress in order of shared tones, or harmonic overlap: *B* shares two notes with *A, C* shares three notes with *B, D* shares four notes with *C.* They are variously presented as themes (the first and last statements of *A*), motifs (*C*), or scales (*B* and the other statements of *A*). Region *D* is highly ambiguous: uniquely, it always follows its antecedent *C,* and it is often difficult to tell where *C* ends and *D* begins. It seems to be associated with an augmented triad on *F,* sometimes expanded to include the cue note *C.* At other times it is difficult to discern its presence at all, as in ensemble 3, edition two. Each region

359

is announced by a "cue" note, indicated by a whole note in the example, which Coltrane uses to signal the musicians. The regions are always presented in sequence, although it may be a gapped sequence, and are apparently cued ad lib, as a comparison between the two takes shows:

	Edition 1	Edition 2
Ensemble 1	A B C D	A B C D
solo	Coltrane	Coltrane
Ens. 2	A B C D	A B C D
solo	Johnson	Johnson
Ens. 3	C D	A B C ?
solo	Sanders	Sanders
Ens. 4	A C	C D
solo	Hubbard	Hubbard
Ens. 5	B C	A C D
solo	Shepp	Brown
Ens. 6	A B C D	B C D A
solo	Tchicai	Shepp
Ens. 7	A B C	A (or combo of all?)
solo	Brown	Tchicai
Ens. 8	C (D—Coltrane solo)	A B C D
solo	Tyner, Garrison/Davis, Jones	Tyner, Garrison/Davis
Ens. 9	A B C D A	A B C D A

Perhaps the system of cued modes was adapted from *Flamenco Sketches,* the Miles Davis recording that had featured Coltrane seven years earlier. The advance in *Ascension* concerns the freedom of the leader to reconfigure the harmonic sequence throughout the work, thus showing the basic elements in continually different relationships. Despite the considerable liberties of Coltrane's later work, this, to my knowledge, is the only example of formal harmonic components being spontaneously deployed on the ensemble level.

A comparison of the two versions of *Meditations* sheds light on Coltrane's compositional development during this period. The first version, recorded in September, 1965 by the original quartet,[165] is a sequence of five virtually themeless modal improvisations:

165. John Coltrane, *First Meditations (for quartet)* (Impulse! GRD-118).

1. Love   *B*b min.(dorian)
2. Compassion   *F* min. (no 6th)
3. Joy   *B*b Maj.(ionian) also *F*7sus4
4. Consequences *D* min. (phrygian? second tenor solo dorian?)
5. Serenity   *F*# min. (Maj 7)

The progression of tonal centers here is surprisingly awkward. The first four movements are in keys closely related to Bb Maj. or min.; too related, in fact, to convey any large-scale tonal progression. The final movement breaks this pattern, but the remoteness of this key is unprepared by what has preceded it. Nor are the movements strongly differentiated by thematic ideas or orchestration, as *A Love Supreme* had been. The motifs that begin the movements don't stick in the mind—indeed, it is only in hearing the later *Meditations*, where their treatment is vastly expanded, that we retrospectively realize their earlier incarnation. What little form there is is provided by Coltrane's treatment of the modes: in the odd-numbered movements his playing is relatively stable, rarely venturing outside the given scale, where in the second and fourth movements his solos are highly chromatic.

"Once you become aware of this force for unity in life you can't ever forget it."[166] When he returned to *Meditations* two and a half months later, Coltrane drastically overhauled it. Four titles and three motives were retained, but the substance of the earlier version is undermined on several levels. By adding young turks Pharoah Sanders and Rashied Ali to the ensemble, Coltrane all but ensured the desecration of the music's modal and metric boundaries. Compensating for the loss of stability those modes provided, Coltrane now dwells at length on the motifs, grounding each movement before the excoriating solos. What provides unity in the later version is not so much the *what*—tonal relationships between movements or motific associations (though there is that)—as the *how*, a process that the melodic cells of the work are subjected to.

166. Coltrane, quoted in the liner notes to John Coltrane, *Meditations* (Impulse! IMPD-199).

The typical Coltrane motif is pentatonic [Fig. 14], three to five notes, rhythmically square, and unpromising in its potential for development. It often comes perilously close to banality. In part this is due to his search for what he called "a universal expression"; the themes are meant to sound like found objects more than artistic creations. *Welcome* suggests a first draft for *Happy Birthday, Seraphic Light* a ponderous religious invocation. *The Father And The Son And The Holy Ghost*, which replaced *Joy* in the revised *Meditations*, sounds like *Pop Goes The Weasel*:

(phrase repetitions omitted)

Figure 14.

The last note of the motif becomes the first note of its next statement, transposing it by a minor third or perfect fourth, depending on whether the motif is carried out four or five tones. Coltrane repeats it twenty-two times, not pursuing a specific goal or exhausting all transpositional possibilities ($E\flat$ and $G\flat$ are missing), but always adhering to this rule of transposition. At the movement's close he repeats the motif eleven more times, breaking the pattern just once, in the penultimate statement, by transposing the motif down a major second.

Movements three and five are shaped by similar procedures. The motif of *Love* is related to that of the first movement, and is likewise transposed, via a common tone, by minor thirds [Fig 15].

Figure 15.

The motive returns to its original transposition every five repetitions, and with this cyclical plan we are back in the world of *Giant Steps*. This connection is made even more explicit in movement five, *Serenity*, where the motif is transposed by major thirds, as it was in *Giant Steps* [Fig. 16]:

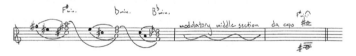

Figure 16.

As with *Giant Steps*, there is a suggestion of eternity in these cyclical modulations; one feels that a process is going on that began before the music started, and doesn't end so much as drift off, or dissolve into something else.

Movements two and four [Fig. 17-18] are more diffuse in their compositional strategies. *Compassion* features a chain of minor thirds, most often linked by half steps. At the close Coltrane reinterprets this material as he recapitulates it, placing the half steps as upper or lower neighbors within the minor thirds. The ending sounds at once different and familiar, foregrounding trichords that had been peripheral in the beginning. (I have simplified the melody for clarity in the example.)

Figure 17.

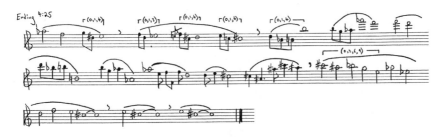

Figure 18.

After *Meditations,* Coltrane abandoned the suite format in favor of terse, self-contained pieces (at least in the studio). Many of these pieces attempt a kind of summation, gathering together several strands that had preoccupied Coltrane at different times. The rhythm remains sprung, and the solos are free, but there is a renewed interest in the intense lyricism that had been the hallmark of his early sixties style. His treatment of form evolves also: continuing a process begun in *Ascension* and *Meditations,* several late pieces tightly interweave composition and improvisation. Most remarkable, and unprecedented in the work of his contemporaries, is the (re)introduction of standard tonal chord changes. Coltrane had begun writing long, quasi-tonal melodies again, as distinct from the fragmented motifs and modal chants that comprised his output in 1965-66. Chord changes were needed to give those melodies specific shadings and underpinnings. Their easy coexistence with the surrounding anarchic harmony is Coltrane's last great achievement.

Offering [Fig. 19] is a series of lyrical fanfares on widely roving chord changes, interspersed with increasingly lengthy digressions that are freely improvised. This is only one of several innovative formal conceptions in Coltrane's late work that were orphaned by his untimely death. The opening slowly fills out the complete chromatic through overlapping statements of the trichord (0,2,7) and its inversion (0,5,7).[167]

167. John Coltrane, *Expression* (Impulse! GRD-131). The trichord (0,2,7) is *the* late Coltrane signature, prominently exposed in *A Love Supreme, Expression, Mars,* and many others.

The note that completes the chromatic, C#, is structurally exposed as the highest note of the melody up to that point.

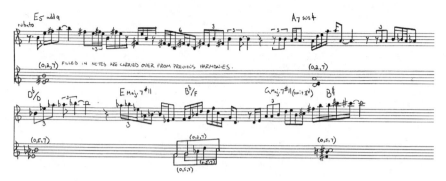

Figure 19.

The notion of a slowly unfolding pitch field is treated in a different but no less remarkable way in *Number One,* from Coltrane's last extant recording session [Fig. 20]. The piece is apparently freely improvised, a rare practice for this period. The musical discourse, however, is completely assured, and every bit as unified as the intricate compositions *Expression* and *Offering.* The basic units here, as in all of Coltrane's work, are pentatonic and whole-tone scales, used complete or in part, and chromatically interwoven. Melodic intervals are almost all 2nds and 3rds. He rocks back and forth on these three and four-note groups, until one element dislodges and gives way to a new group. This new group, as a rule, fills in half steps the previous group had skipped. Coltrane's handling of the long line here is masterful, beginning from the middle register of the instrument and slowly moving outwards in both directions. Note, for example, the chromatic ascent from the *A#* in the fifth phrase through the *G* towards the end of line five in the example. This ascent is animated by a motive of *Bb C C Db* (middle of line three). This expands to *Bb D D Eb* (middle of line four), then *Bb Eb Eb*—arpeggio interruption—*E* at the end of the same phrase. Coltrane's regard for linear voice-leading, which he had honed in the 'chord-on-chord' studies of the late fifties, is here remade, carefully filling out not just the complete chromatic, but almost every note on the instrument. Eventually this deliberative exposition cedes to rapid bursts that take in larger intervals (line six on).

Figure 20.

From 1958, the year of his musical maturity, to his last recordings in 1967, Coltrane's work was marked by extremes: distant harmonic relationships, marathon solos, the sheer volume of Elvin Jones's drumming, the reaching into impossible registers of the saxophone. The fierce concentration and superhuman effort summoned by the musicians to control a musical language on the brink of dissolution becomes in some measure the subject of the music itself. In this respect Coltrane's position is akin to Beethoven more than to any of his own contemporaries. Both were terminal figures of their eras, masters of a language that had become outdated in their lifetimes; indeed, their very mastery had made that obsolescence inevitable. The drama inherent in that position invests their music with a power that is at once heroic and isolated. In their most radical experiments they found consolation and structure in the resources of the past: buried deep inside the chaotic orgy of *Ascension* is a form suggested by *Flamenco Sketches,* just as the *Grosse Fuge* controls its titanic dissonances through Baroque architecture. And of Coltrane's late essays in strict modality, such as *Peace On Earth,* or *Dearly Beloved,* we might transpose what Charles Rosen said of the *Arietta* from Op. 111, the development section of Op. 130, and the introduction to the *Ninth* Symphony:

[They] build an intensity more terrifying and moving than any less inward motion could induce. With all their tension, these effects are essentially meditative in character, and they make one aware to what an extent the exploration of the tonal universe was an act of introspection.[168]

Coltrane rode tonality to the end of the line, exhausting it, exploding it, piling meaning

168. Charles Rosen, *The Classical Style* (New York: Norton, 1971), p. 448.

upon meaning, to the point where the very proliferation of meanings undermined its ability to mean anything, in the conventional (that is, tonal) sense. The tonality of his late music is "tonality"; a memory, a quotation, of an irrecoverable past. Hearing the work of his colleagues Ornette Coleman, Cecil Taylor, and Albert Ayler, we may imagine ourselves to be variously at a down-home gathering, art museum, political gathering, or gospel revival; whatever the scenario, even the solemn pieces cannot mask a bright enthusiasm for the wide open terrain the new music offered. With Coltrane we are always at a funeral, and he is saying a final, private goodbye to the figure in the coffin. (The likely knowledge, by late 1966, of his own impending death makes this metaphor all too literal.) The depth of his feeling of loss gave a special intensity to Coltrane's work that was

I am indebted to Louie Belogenis, Ben Goldberg, Naomi Seidman, and Peter Gordon for discussions that contributed to this essay.

unavailable to the younger musicians, and fueled his search for *unity*—in all its musical, social, and metaphysical dimensions—amid the ruins of tradition.

ABOUT THE MUSICIANS

CHRIS BROWN (b. 1953), San Francisco-based composer, pianist, and electronic musician, creates music for acoustic instruments with interactive electronics, for computer networks, and for improvising ensembles. He is a member of the computer network band The Hub, plays free-jazz with the Glenn Spearman Double Trio, and has performed and recorded his own works with Room. He has also received commissions from the Berkeley Symphony, the Rova Saxophone Quartet, and the Gerbode Foundation. He teaches Composition and Electronic Music at Mills College in Oakland, where he is Head of the Music Department and Co-Director of the Center for Contemporary Music (CCM). His compositions are known for unusual sonorities derived from electroacoustic instruments he has invented (*Alternating Currents*, 1983); the use of live, interactive electronics to extend the sonorities of traditional acoustic instruments (*Iceberg*, 1985; *Hall of Mirrors*, 1987; and *Lava*, 1992); the contrast between mechanized automated electronic sound environments and the spontaneity of free improvisation (*Snakecharmer*, 1986 and *Duo*, 1992); and applications of new technology in performance that change the roles of musicians to each other and to their audience (*Chain Reaction*, 1990; *Wheelies*, 1992; and *Talking Drum*, 1995-96).

Chris Brown

Anthony Coleman

Marilyn Crispell

ANTHONY COLEMAN was born in New York City in 1955. He is a composer and performer (piano, organ, sampler, trombone, voice, etc.) and currently leader of two groups: Selfhaters and Sephardic Tinge.

MARILYN CRISPELL is a graduate of the New England Conservatory of Music where she studied classical piano and composition. She discovered jazz primarily through the music of John Coltrane, Cecil Taylor, and Paul Bley. Crispell combines improvisation with composition, not only in her work in contemporary jazz, but also when playing pieces by composers such as Robert Cogan, Pozzi Escot, and Pauline Oliveros. She is probably best known for her ten years as a member of the Anthony Braxton Quartet, as well as with the Reggie Workman Ensemble, and various solo and ensemble projects with many of the great players in the American and European modern jazz scene, such as Oliver Lake, Roscoe Mitchell, Joseph Jarman, Leo Smith, Anthony Davis, Gerry Hemingway, Tim Berne, Paul Motian, Steve Lacy, Barry Guy, and Evan Parker.

Mark Dresser has been composing and performing solo contrabass and ensemble music professionally since 1972 throughout North America, Europe, and the Far East. His own projects include Mark Dresser's Force Green and the Mark Dresser Trio, performing his music for the French Surrealist film masterpiece of Luis Buñuel and Salvador Dalí, *Un Chien Andalou* as well as the German expressionist silent film classic, *The Cabinet of Dr. Caligari.* Additional original solo bass music was composed for the New York Shakespeare Festival Production of *Henry VI.* Collaborative projects include The Double Trio comprised of the Arcado String Trio and the Trio du Clarinettes. He was commissioned by the Banlieu Bleues Festival in Paris to premier his composition "Bosnia." A founding member of the Arcado String Trio, he also received a commission from WDR Radio of Cologne, Germany, in 1991 to compose "For Not the Law," an extended work for string trio and orchestra. In 1992, Dresser composed and performed *Armadillo* for Arcado and the WDR Big Band. In 1995, *The Banquet,* a double concert for various flutes and contrabass with string quartet was commissioned by Swiss flute virtuoso Matthias Ziegler. Dresser has received grants from the New York Foundation for the Arts and Meet the Composer. He holds both B.A. and M.A. degrees in Music from U.C. San Diego, where he studied contrabass with the seminal

Mark Dresser

Steven Drury

Bill Frisell

virtuoso of 20th century performance practice, Maestro Bertram Turetzky. He was awarded a 1983 Fulbright Fellowship for advanced contrabass study with Maestro Franco Petracchi. As a virtuoso contrabassist himself, Dresser has performed and recorded with many of the luminaries of 'new' jazz composition and improvisation. For ten years he performed with the Anthony Braxton Quartet, as well as diverse groups led by Ray Anderson, Tim Berne, Anthony Davis, Gerry Hemingway, John Zorn, and others. He has made over sixty recordings.

Well-known as a champion of 20th century music, pianist Steven Drury's repertoire extends from Bach to Zorn. He has performed throughout the United States, Latin America, Europe, and Asia, taking the sound of dissonance into remote corners of Pakistan, Greenland, and Montana. His recordings are available on Mode, Tzadik, New Albion, MusicMasters, Neuma, and Catalyst. He teaches at the New England Conservatory in Boston.

Born in Baltimore, Bill Frisell played clarinet throughout his childhood in Denver, Colorado. His interest in guitar began with exposure to pop music, and soon thereafter the Chicago Blues became a passion through the work of Otis Rush, B.B.King, Paul Butterfield, and Buddy Guy. In high school, he played in bands covering pop and soul classics, James Brown, and other dance material. Later, Bill studied music at the University of Northern Colorado before attending Berklee College of Music in Boston, where he studied with John Damian, Herb Pomeroy, and Michael Gibbs. From 1979 to 1989, he lived in New York; he now lives in Seattle. Most recently, he has been performing in a new Quartet with Ron Miles (trumpet), Eyvind Kang (violin), and Curtis Fowlkes (trombone). Other recent collaborations include a tour with Marty Ehrlich and the Creative Jazz Orchestra performing the music of Julius Hemphill. Frisell and

Joey Baron performed Stephen Mackey's *Deal*, a concerto for guitar and drums, with the Los Angeles Philharmonic New Music Group, New York's American Composer's Orchestra, and the San Francisco Contemporary Music Players.

FRED FRITH, composer improvisor, and multi-instrumentalist, has been a fixture for more than twenty-five years in the area where rock music and new music meet. Co-founder of the British underground band Henry Cow (1968-78), he moved to New York in the late seventies and came into contact with many of the musicians with whom he's since been associated, including John Zorn, Ikue Mori, Tom Cora, Zeena Parkins, and Alvin Lussier, among many others. In the eighties he began to write extensively for dance, film, and theater, and this in turn has led to his composing for Rova Saxophone Quartet, Ensemble Moderne, The Asko Ensemble, and a number of other groups, including his own Guitar Quartet. He is also active as an improvising guitarist, performing regularly in a variety of contexts worldwide. Frith is the subject of Nicolas Humbert and Werner Penzels' award-winning documentary film, *Step Across the Border*. He lives in Germany with photographer Heike Liss and their children, Finn and Lucia.

Fred Frith

Peter Garland

Gerry Hemingway

PETER GARLAND: Born 1952, Portland, Maine. Principal teachers: James Tenney (piano/composition), Harold Budd (composition), Wolfgang Stoerchle (video/performance), Clayton Eshleman (American Literature). Editor-publisher of SOUNDINGS Press, 1971-1991. Long friendships/associations with Lou Harrison, Conlon Nancarrow, Paul Bowles, Dane Rudhyar. Two years living in Mexican Indian villages in the 1970s. In the 1980s resident in Santa Fe, New Mexico. 1991-95, a forty-three month trip around the world. In 1997 moved to Mexico. Author of three books: *Americas: Essays on American Music and Culture 1973-80; In Search of Silvestre Revueltas: Essays 1978-1990; Gone Walkabout: Essays 1991-1995*. Fourth book of essays in progress. Special areas of investigation: 20th century American composers, Mexican traditional musics.

GERRY HEMINGWAY has been composing and performing solo and ensemble music since 1974. In addition to receiving fellowships from both the National Endowment for the Arts and the New York Foundation on the Arts, he has also received four commissions from the Parabola Arts Foundation with funding from N.Y.S.C.A. In 1993 he premiered a commission from the Kansas City Symphony with funding from Meet the Composer for a concerto for percussionist and orchestra entitled *Terrains*. Mr. Hemingway's working quintet, his most prominent vehicle for much of his composed work, has toured extensively in both the U.S. and Europe. Mr. Hemingway also performs regularly as a duo with live electronics and saxophone virtuoso Earl Howard. His work as a composer and percussionist includes recordings and performances with Derek Bailey, Leo Smith, Oliver Lake, Ray Anderson, Conrad Bauer, John Cale, and Hank Roberts, among others. For twelve years, staring in 1983, he was a member of the Anthony Braxton Quartet, and more recently he has been performing as a member of the Reggie Workman Ensemble. Mr. Hemingway also participates in a number of collaborative projects, including a trio with German pianist Georg Graewe and cellist Ernst Reijseger.

Composer SCOTT JOHNSON is widely recognized as a pioneering voice in today's movement to redefine and restore the dialogue between contemporary art music and the popular culture which surrounds it. He has played an influential role in the trend towards incorporating rock-derived instrumentation into traditional score-based composition, and in the use of taped, sampled and MIDI-controlled electronic elements within instrumental ensembles. His music has been heard in performances by the St. Paul Chamber Orchestra and the Kronos Quartet, in concerts of his own ensembles, in dance works performed by the Boston Ballet, the London Contemporary Dance Theater, and the Ballets de Monte Carlo; in Paul Schrader's film *Patty Hearst,* and in recordings on the Nonesuch, CRI, and Point labels. Trained in both music and visual arts at the University of Wisconsin, his earliest work in New York included visual/sound installations and performance art. Beginning in 1982, he has performed throughout Europe and North America; first with self-performed compositions for solo electric guitar, tape, and electronics, and later with an octet modeled on the American big band and rock traditions. His most recent ensemble is an electric quartet of violin, cello, electric guitar, and piano/synthesizer, performing both alone as a chamber group, and together with computer-controlled sequences of sampled sound. Concert venues for Mr. Johnson's ensembles have included Lincoln Center's Alice Tully Hall, Merkin Hall, the Knitting Factory, and The Kitchen in New York City, as well as festivals and concert halls throughout the United States and Canada, and in France, Germany, Austria, Switzerland, Italy, and Holland.

Scott Johnson

Eyvind Kang

Guy Klucevsek

George E. Lewis

EYVIND KANG is a violinist and composer who has worked with artists ranging from Bill Frisell to the Sun City Girls. As a composer, he has written for film, theatre, and dance, as well as making his highly personal NADEs.

GUY KLUCEVSEK has composed over fifty pieces for dance companies, chamber ensembles, music theater, solo accordion, and his own groups, including The Bantam Orchestra. His collaborators have included choreographers David Dorfman, Bebe Miller, Susan Braham, Victoria Marks, Karen Bamonte, Angela Caponigro, Mark Taylor, and Anita Feldman; writer/director/visual artist Ping Chong; and the new music ensembles Relâche, Present Music, and Double Edge (2 pianos). Klucevsek received a 1995 New York Dance and Performance Award (Bessie) for his solo accordion score *Altered Landscapes,* written for David Dorfman's dance piece, *Hey.*

GEORGE E. LEWIS (b. Chicago, 1952), Professor of Music in the Critical Studies/ Experimental Practices program at the University of California, San Diego, is an improvisor-trombonist, composer, performer, and computer/installation artist. Lewis is a twenty-five year member of the Association for the Advancement of Creative Musicians, and has presented his interdisciplinary compositions, including works incorporating intermedia and computer technology, across Eastern and Western Europe, North America, and Japan. Lewis's work is documented on over ninety recordings on which he is featured as composer, improvisor, or interpreter. A fairly extensive discography of the work of George Lewis can be found on the website of the

Department of Music at the University of California, San Diego: http://orpheus. ucsd.edu/dept. music/music dept/lewis.html. Other websites with significant information on Lewis's recent musical research initiatives include those of the Center for Research in Computing and the Arts (CRCA): http://www-crca.ucsd.edu/ 95_96/ FACULTY/george.html, and the Association for the Advancement of Creative Musicians (AACM): http://csmaclabwww.cs.uchicago. edu/AACM/.

DAVID MAHLER's scores, writings, and recordings are published by Frog Peak Music (A Composers' Collective). A longtime resident of the Pacific Northwest, Mahler spent his youth at play on the baseball fields of the Midwest (at times alleging to have grown up in Michigan). In southern California under the influence of the early 1970s, he began his musical florescence.

MIYA MASAOKA is a composer/kotoist performing acoustically and with the Laser Koto. In her solo performances, she uses her background in Japanese court music, new music and improvisation to create a span from 9th-century **David Mahler** Japan to sensor and digital technology. With an array of extended techniques that include strumming, bowing, scratching, and thumps, she **Miya Masaoka** uses fragments of koto-created sounds to weave an organic synthesis of the acoustic and electronic. Sometimes more acoustic, sometimes more electronic, she develops timbre-based motives, textures and loops. Using various triggering devices in tandem with live samples, ultra sound, light sensors and digital signal processing, Masaoka captures gestures of movement and sound that cross the lines of world music, jazz, new music, and electronics. She has collaborated with some of the most noted artists of the 20th-century, including Ornette Coleman, Toshiko Akiyoshi, Pharoah Sanders, Reggie Workman, Andrew Cyrille, Steve Coleman, George Lewis, Cecil Taylor and Rova Saxophone Quartet. Her music compositions have led her to varied forms of media and performance. In *"Ritual,"* giant cockroaches crawl freely on her naked body breaking laser beams that trigger samples of their own hissing. Strong imagery, use of the body, technology and a socially engaged impetus are common threads in her work. A site-specific multi-media piece, "What is the Difference Between Stripping and Playing the Violin?" was performed with two erotic dancers and orchestra on Market St. in San Francisco, with Masaoka composing and conducting. Masaoka has also collaborated with librettist Thulani Davis to create the multi-media piece with string quartet, video and Japanese American internees in "Dark Passages" which premiered at the Asian Art Museum in San Francisco. Ms. Masaoka holds a Bachelor of Arts in Music from San Francisco State University, and a Masters in Music Composition from Mills College. She has studied with Suenobu Togi, gagaku master who traces his unbroken line in the Imperial music family for more than 1000 years. She was Director of the San Francisco Gagaku Society for eight years. As a composer, she has received commissions from Bang On A Can, Rova Saxophone Quartet, Meet The Composer and National Endowment for the Arts and others. The midi-koto interface was developed over a period of years and multiple residencies at the institute STEIM in Amsterdam. The Laser Koto was developed by Donald Swearingen, hardware by Oliver D'iCicco.

MYRA MELFORD has won critical acclaim as both pianist and composer on the jazz and new music scenes in the United States, Europe, and Japan. Melford has performed with a distinguished array of musicians, including Butch Morris, Leroy Jenkins, Henry Threadgill, Joseph Jarman, Han Bennink, Fred Frith, François Houle, Marion Brandis, and Anne LeBaron, as well as the Soldier String Quartet and the Splatter Trio. She was recently featured as a guest artist on Butch Morris's *Testament* (New World Records), Henry Threadgill's *Makin' a Move* (Sony), and Leroy Jenkins's *Themes and Improvisations on the Blues* (CRI). Commissions have included a dance-theater score, *My House Was Collapsing To One Side,* premiered at Dance Theater Workshop, New York City, in 1996, Melford is the recipient of a 1994 Arts International Grant to perform at foreign festivals, a 1992 Composition Fellowship from the New York Foundation for the Arts, as well as commissioning grants from Meet The Composer.

IKUE MORI: 1977: moved to New York from Tokyo. Started playing drums, and formed the seminal New York NO WAVE band, DNA, with Arto Lindsay, Tim Wright. 1983: began improvising, collaborating regularly with John Zorn, Tom Cora, Wayne Horvitz, and Fred Frith, among others. 1985: started playing drum machines. Using standard technology, she created her own highly sensitive signature style. Currently she uses three self-programmed machines simultaneously. 1987: with Luli Shioi (on bass and vocal), created the band TOHBAN DJAN, subverting images of orientalism, femininity, and obsessions, combining world music influences and surreal zones within songs. 1990: received an NEA Grant to collaborate with filmmaker Abigail Child. 1993: gave workshops at the International Percussion Festival in Berlin, performed at New York Symphony Space, Jazz Across the Border in Germany, and Derek Bailey's Company Week in London. 1994: awarded Artists-in-Residency at Studio Pass and recorded soundtrack music for *Geek Love.* 1995: composed music for Abigail Child's film *Rubble.*

Myra Melford

Ikue Mori

Larry Ochs

Bob Ostertag

LARRY OCHS is a founding member of Rova Saxophone Quartet, with whom he has performed since 1977. He has also been active composing, performing, and producing CDs for a number of other music ensembles: Room (the new music trio with William Winant and Chris Brown), Glenn Spearman Double Trio, Figure 8 (a saxophone octet), and What We Live (an improvising trio with Donald Robinson and Lisle Ellis). Ochs has been awarded commissions by *Reader's Digest*/Meet the Composer (1989, 1995) and Antwerpen '93 Festival. In addition, he has written original soundtrack music for film and video and composed/performed the music for Leslie Scalapino's play *Goya's L.A.* (1994). He founded Metalanguage Records in 1978.

BOB OSTERTAG's instruments range from cutting edge digital devices to old tape recorders linked with helium balloons. His compositions include solo works for live electronics, computer-generated tape pieces, the repertoire of his touring ensemble, Say No More, and works for other ensembles such as the Kronos Quartet. His work with digital sampling has established him as an influential pioneer in this media. He has released twelve CDs and records of his compositions. The work he discusses in this volume, *All the Rage,* was commissioned by the Kronos Quartet and was premiered by them at Lincoln Center in April 1992.

JOHN OSWALD is Director of Research at Mystery Laboratory in Canada, and Musical Director of the North American Experience. Norm Igma is the Mystery Lab inquisitor. In 1990, Oswald's most notorious recording, *plunderphonic,* was destroyed by prudes in the Recording Industry representing Michael Jackson. He has since released recordings on Elektra, Avant, ReR Megacorp, Blast First, and Swell, featuring transformations of the music and performances of Stravinsky, Metallica, James Brown, Györgi Ligeti, Dolly Parton, and many others. Oswald has most recently completed the writing, directing, and production of a radio play in four interwoven languages (Portugese, Dutch, English, and German), the score for a stage version of the silent movie classic *Metropolis,* and the soundtrack album to the film *Hustler White,* as well as appearing as himself in John Greyson's feature film *Un©ut.* Other recent activities include a sonic motorcade in Brasilia, two wind quintets, an orchestral score, and a dance composition for twenty-two choreographers (including Bill T. Jones, Margie Gillis, James Kudelka, and Holly Small). He has received recent commissions from the Lyon Opera Ballet, Dutch National Radio, Change of Heart, SMCQ, and Radio Canada, and his works are in the active repertoire of the Kronos Quartet, the Culberg Ballet Sweden, the Monaco Ballet, the Deutsche Opera Ballet Berlin, The Modern Quartet, and the Penderecki Quartet.

MIKE PATTON has never written a fucking essay. He has little experience writing bios. He has never scored a film. He has recorded numerous albums with 'rock' groups Faith No More and Mr. Bungle, as well as several albums of his own compositions on the Tzadik Composer Series. He never listens to those albums. He improvises regularly with John Zorn, Ikue Mori, Han Bennink, Otomo Yoshihide, and others. He has toured the world off and on for the last ten years. He hopes to stay home and write music for the next ten years.

John Oswald

Mike Patton

Marc Ribot

David Rosenboom

MARC RIBOT is a guitarist/composer living and working in downtown NYC. He has been a member of the Lounge Lizards (*Big Heart, Live in Tokyo, No Pain for Cakes, and Voice of Chunk*), Evan Lurie's Tango band (*Selling Water by the Side of the River*), The Jazz Passengers (*Broken Night, Red Light, Deranged* and *Decomposed,* and others), Tom Waits's band (*Raindogs, Frank's Wild Years,* and *Big-Time*), Elvis Costello's Rude Five (*Spike, Mighty Like a Rose,* and *Kojack Variety*) and many other bands. In addition, he has performed and recorded with John Zorn (*Kristallnacht, Bar Kokhba, Cobra, Film Works II* through *V,* and the premier recording of Zorn's piece for solo guitar, *Book of Heads*), T-Bone Burnett, Sam Phillips, Arto Lindsay, Syd Straw, The Klezmatics, Solomon Burke, BarkMarket, Cibo Matto, Alain Bashung, Jim Thurwell, and many others.

DAVID ROSENBOOM (b. 1947), composer, performer, conductor, interdisciplinary artist, author and educator, has explored ideas in his work about the spontaneous evolution of forms, languages for improvisation, new techniques and notation for ensembles, cross-cultural collaborations, performance art, computer music systems, interactive multi-media, compositional algorithms, and extended musical interface with the human nervous system since the 1960s. His work is widely distributed and presented and he is known as a pioneer in American experimental music. Rosenboom has been Dean of the School of Music, Co-Director of the Center for Experiments in Art, Information and Technology, and Conductor of the New Century Players at the California Institute of the Arts since 1990. He taught at Mills College from 1979 to 1990, was Professor of Music, Head of the Music Department, Director of the Center for Contemporary Music, and held the Darius Milhaud Chair from 1987 to 1990. He studied at the University of Illinois with Salvatore Martirano, Kenneth Gaburo, Lejaren Hiller, Soulima Stravinsky, Paul Roland, and Gordon Binkerd, among others, and has worked and taught in innovative institutions, such as the Center for Creative and Performing Arts at SUNY in Buffalo, New York's Electric Circus, York University in Toronto where he was Professor of Music and Interdisciplinary Studies, the University of Illinois where he was recently awarded the George A. Miller Professorship, New York University, the Banff Center for the Arts, Simon Fraser University, the Aesthetic Research Centre of Canada, the San Francisco Art Institute, and the California College of Arts and Crafts. The following is the URL for a World Wide Web site with information about the author's work: http://music.calarts.edu/~david.

JOHN SCHOTT: Like the generation of American composers who are now so derided, I too want to make music "as much as it can be." In my case that means absolute abandon, communion and general craziness, *and* maximal structural rigor. For the past several years I have been evolving an improvisational language that takes into account some of the structural assumptions of American post-tonal music, particularly Milton Babbitt and Elliott Carter. I have begun tentatively exploring this in ensemble compositions, notably *Diglossia* and *Jealous Lover,* and in solo guitar performances. Worth mentioning also is my ongoing collaboration with Naomi Seidman, most recently on the birth of our son Ezra.

John Schott

Elliott Sharp

David Shea

ELLIOTT SHARP leads the groups Carbon and Orchestra Carbon, Tectonics, Bootstrappers, and Terraplane. *Racing Hearts,* for thirty-five musicians, was premiered in January 1995 by the Bang on a Can Spit Orchestra at The Kitchen in NYC and *Cochlea,* for thirty musicians, premiered in March 1995 at the Inner Ear festival in Linz. *Lumen* was premiered in May 1996 by the Meridian String Quartet at Carnegie Hall. *X-topia,* for Soldier String Quartet and live electronics premiered at the 1994 Ars Electronica Linz. Other activities have included a featured performance on the NBC-TV show "Night Music"; a live broadcast performance with Qawwali singer Nusrat Fateh Ali Khan at CKUT-FM Montreal; collaborations with blues legend Hubert Sumlin and Bachir Attar, a multi-instrumentalist and leader of the Master Muscians Of Jahjouka from Morocco. He formed zOaR Records in 1978 to produce his own and other extreme musics and produced the compilations *State of the Union* and *Peripheral Vision.*

DAVID SHEA studied composition and theory at the School of Performing Arts in Indianapolis, Indiana, from 1982-84 and the Oberlin Conservatory from 1984-85. Since

1985 he has been active in New York as a composer and sampler player. Known mainly for his six ensemble records, scores for the Karole Armitage ballet and his work in John Zorn's various ensembles, he has also performed extensively in Europe and New York with his own ensembles and tours of solo concerts.

FRANCES-MARIE UITTI transformed the cello in 1975 into a truly polyphonic instrument capable of sustained chordal (two, three, and four part) and intricate multivoiced writing. Using two bows in one hand, this invention permits contemporaneous cross accents, multiple timbres, contrasting four-voiced dynamics, simultaneous legato-articulated playing, that her previous work with a curved bow couldn't attain. She has composed extensively over the last twenty years for two-bowed cello to public and critical acclaim. Györgi Kurtág, Luigi Nono, Giacinto Scelsi, Louis Andriessen, Jonathan Harvey, Richard Barrett, Benedict Mason, Vinko Globokar, J.A. Yim, and Clarence Barlow, among others, have written works for her using this technique. She completed studies with Leslie Parnas and George Neikrug in the U.S. and with Andre Navarra in Europe. After her solo debut with orchestra at age thirteen, she was awarded many prizes, including a Ford Foundation Award, Casals' Master Classes, Diploma d'Onore Accademia Chigiana 1970-72, and she is a recipient of a National Endowment for the Arts Solo Recitalist Grant. Ms. Uitti specializes in works for solo cello with a repertoire extending from pre-Bach to contemporary music. Ms. Uitti has toured extensively in Europe, the United States, and Canada as well as Korea and Japan, and she participates regularly in such festivals as the Biennale di Venezia, the Strassbourg Festival, Halland Festival, Zagreb Festival, Gulbenkian Festival, Arts Musica Festival, New Music America, etc., and for radio and television in Europe, Japan, and the United States. As composer-performer she composed the music and played the lead role in Eric van Zuylen's feature film *Over Orpheus*.

Frances-Marie Uitti

Lois V Vierk

LOIS V VIERK was commissioned by Lincoln Center to compose *Silversword* for Gagaku orchestra, and it was premiered by the Reigakusha ensemble of Tokyo at Lincoln Center Festival 1996. Her chamber orchestra work *Event Horizon* was recently premiered by Ensemble Modern at the Donaueschingen Musiktage festival in Germany. Ms. Vierk is known for directional, developmental music, often building to high energy climaxes. She has been commissioned by some of today's most exciting new music performers and ensembles, including the Kronos Quartet, Ursula Oppens and Frederic Rzewski (pianos), Ensemble Modern, Guy Klucevsek (accordion), Margaret Leng Tan (piano), Music From Japan, Relache Ensemble of Philadelphia, and Bang On A Can Festival. Recent performances include Carnegie Hall, Darmstadt, the Barbican Center of London, the Huddersfield Festival, the Schleswig-Holstein Festival, Suntory Summer Festival '97 in Tokyo, and the Adelaide Festival of Australia. Her co-creations with tap choreographer Anita Feldman are performed regularly in both music and dance venues. Ms. Vierk studied composition at California Institute of the Arts with Mel Powell, Leonard Stein, and Morton Subotnick. For twelve years she studied Gagaku, first with Mr. Suenobu Togi in Los Angeles and then with Mr. Sukeyasu Shiba in Toyko.

JOHN ZORN: *Christabel* (1972), *Conquest of Mexico* (1973), *String Quartet* (1973), *Mikhail Zoetrope* (1974), *Lacrosse* (1977), *Hockey* (1978), *Fencing* (1978), *The Book of Heads* (1978), *Pool* (1979), *Archery* (1979), *Track & Field* (1980), *Croquet* (1981), *Locus Solus* (1982), *Sebastopol* (1983), *Rugby* (1983), *Cobra* (1984), *Xu Feng* (1985), *Godard* (1985), *Spillane* (1986), *Hu Die* (1986), *Road Runner* (1986), *Ruan Lingyu* (1987), *Hwang Chin-ee* (1988), *Cat O' Nine Tails* (1988), *For Your Eyes Only* (1989), *Bézique* (1989), *Torture Garden* (1990), *Qûê Trân* (1990), *Grand Guignol* (1990), *Dead Man* (1990), *Elegy* (1991), *Leng Tch'e* (1991), *Carny* (1992), *Memento Mori* (1992), *Kristallnacht* (1992), *Absinthe* (1992), *Angelus Novus* (1993), *Masada* (1993-97), *The Sand's Share* (1994), *Aporias* (1994), *Dark River* (1995), *Redbird* (1995), *Kol Nidre* (1996), *Music for Children* (1996), *Duras* (1996), *Etant Donnés* (1997) *Shibboleth* (1997), *Orchestra Variations* (1998), *Rituals* (1998), *Amour Fou* (1999), *Contes des Fées* (1999), *Le Mômo* (1999), *Untitled (for Joseph Cornell)* (1999).

Z'EV: If one can be known by the company one keeps then here follows a list of teachers and friends and etc. who have contributed to where I may be at. They are listed in no significant order. In San Francisco and environs: Rav Jerry Winston, the Hogun Rico Joves, David Jeffers, Aeryn Richmond and her Society for the Preservation of Occult Consciousness, Pearl Sofer, Carl Stone, Naut Humon, Barry Schwartz, Mark Pauline, Monte Cazaza, Steve Tupper. In Los Angeles and environs: Bruce Gary, Barry Markowitz, Johanna Wendt, Mark Wheaton, Toby Dell, David Javalosa. In Boston: Michelle Duran. In New York and environs: Roberta Friedman, Louis D'Agostino, Barbara Barg, Barbara Ess, Rudolf Grey, Glenn Branca, Joan Jonas, Simone Forti, Maryanne Amacher, Danielle Steir, Maryann Luvchick, Nik Williams, Steve Speer, Pamela Calvert, Charles Ball, Genesis P-Orridge. In London and environs: Barbara Steveni, Richard Wilson, Anna Bean, Lloyd Trott, Words and Jackie, Jon Wozencroft. In Amsterdam and environs: Dorothea Franck, Babeth van Loo, Van Lagestein, Remko Scha, DJ Dano, Bram Angstrom, Ria Higler, Laurien Wijers, the staff at the Bibliothecas Rosenthalia and Philosophica Hermetica. In Vienna: Konrad Becker, Eugene Rochas. Full biographical and etcetera informations are available online at http://www. touch. demon.co.uk. From this home page two clicks take you to their bullctin board. At this point replace the end tag /bull.htm in the address line to /zev2.html. Then hit enter and the next thing you'll see will be the table of contents to the forty-three pages of textual materials from *One Foot in the Grave*, the retrospective of my work from 1968-1990 which was released by Touch in 1992, and that you can now scroll through to your heart's content, or not.

John Zorn

Z'EV

RECOMMENDED LISTENING

Chris Brown
Duets Artifact
Snakecharmer Artifact
Lava Tzadik
Wreckin' Ball Artifact
Hall of Mirrors Music & Arts

Anthony Coleman
Disco By Night Avant
Selfhaters Tzadik
Sephardic Tinge Tzadik
The Coming Great Millennium
Knitting Factory Works
Lobster and Friend
Knitting Factory Works

Marilyn Crispell
Gaia Leo Records
Circles Les Disques Victo
Santuerio Leo Records
Band on the Wall
Matchless Recordings
Cascades Music and Arts
Altered Spaces Leo Records

Mark Dresser
Green Dolphy Street ENJA
Arcado JMT
Behind the Myth JMT
Three Strings and Orchestra JMT
Live in Europe Avant
Invocation Knitting Factory
Banquet Tzadik

Steven Drury
John Cage: Piano Works, Vol. 1
Mode Records
John Cage: Orchestral Works, Vol. 1
Mode Records
John Cage: The Piano Concertos
Mode Records
Frederik Rzewski: "The People United
Will Never Be Defeated" New Albion
Music of Colin McPhee Music Masters

Bill Frisell
In Line ECM
Rambler ECM
Lookout for Hope ECM
Music for the Films of Buster Keaton:
"Go West" Elektra/Nonesuch
This Land Elektra/Nonesuch
Have a Little Faith Elektra/Nonesuch
Quartet Elektra/Nonesuch
Before We Were Born
Elektra/Nonesuch

Fred Frith
Quartets RecRec Music
Eye to Ear Tzadik
The Top of His Head Crammed Discs
Step Across the Border RecRec
Gravity Ralph Records
Speechless Ralph Records
Cheap at Half the Price Ralph Records
Pacifica Tzadik

Peter Garland
Nana and Victorio   Avant
Walk in Beauty   New Albion
Across the Border   Nonsequitur

Gerry Hemingway
Electro-Acoustic Solo Works (84-95)
   Random Acoustics
Acoustic Solo Works (83-94)
   Random Acoustics
Special Detail   Hat Art
Down to the Wire   Hat Art
Demon Chaser   Hat Art
Perfect World   Random Acoustics
Slamadam   Random Acoustics
The Marmalade King   Hat Art
Chamber Waves   Tzadik

Scott Johnson
Patty Hearst   out of print; available
   2000 from Tzadik
Rock/Paper/Scissors   Point
John Somebody   Elektra/Nonesuch

Eyvind Kang
7 Nades   Tzadik
theatre of mineral NADEs   Tzadik
Dying Ground   Avant
Sweetness of Sickness   RGI

Guy Klucevsek
Altered Landscapes   Evva
Stolen Memories   Tzadik
Transylvanian Softwear   John Marks
Citrus, My Love   RecRec/Swiss
Polka Dots & Laser Beams   Evva
Manhattan Cascade   CRI
Flying Vegetables of the Apocalypse   XI
Scenes From A Mirage   Review

George E. Lewis
Changing With The Times
   New World Records
Voyager   Avant

Shadowgraph   Black Saint
Donaueschingen (Duo)   Hat Hut
Slideride   Hat Hut
Triangulation   Nine Winds

David Mahler
The Voice of the Poet
   Artifact Recordings

Miya Masaoka
Compositions/Improvisations
   Asian Improv Arts
Seance   VEX Records
The Usual Turmoil and other Duets with
   George Lewis   Music & Arts
Monk's Japanese Folksong   (The Miya
   Masaoka Trio)   Dizim Records

Myra Melford
Even the Sounds Shine   Hat Art
Alive in the House of Saints   Hat Art
Now and Now   Enemy
Jump   Enemy
The Same River, Twice
   Gramavision/Rykodisc

Ikue Mori
DNA   Avant
Vibraslaps   RecRec
Painted Desert   Avant
Death Praxis   What Next
Hex Kitchen   Tzadik
Garden   Tzadik
Death Ambient   Tzadik
Synaesthesia   Tzadik

Larry Ochs
The Secret Magritte   Black Saint
Figure 8—Pipe Dreams   Black Saint
This Time We Are Both   New Albion
The Fields   Black Saint
The Works: Vol. 1   Black Saint

Bob Ostertag
All the Rage   Nonesuch
Say No More   RecDec Music
Fear No Love   Avant
Attention Span   RecDec
Burns Like Fire   RecDec

John Oswald
plunderphonic   Mystery Lab
Discosphere   ReR Megacorp
Plexure   Avant
G.R.A.Y.F.O.L.D.E.D.   Swell/Artifact
Elektrax   Elektra/Nonesuch

Mike Patton
Adult Themes for Voice   Tzadik
Pranzo Oltranzista   Tzadik

Marc Ribot
Requiem for What's-His-Name   Crepescule
Rootless Cosmopolitans   Island/Antilles
Shrek   Avant
Shoe String Symphonettes   Tzadik
Don't Blame Me   DIW
Los Cubanos Postizos   Atlantic

David Rosenboom
Two Lines   Lovely Music
Systems of Judgment   Centaur

John Schott
In These Great Times   Tzadik
What Comes Before   Tzadik

Elliott Sharp
Figure Ground   Tzadik
Revenge of the Stuttering Child   Tzadik
Xenocodex   Tzadik
Interference   Atavistic
Cryptid Fragments   Extreme
Field & Stream   Atonal

David Shea
Shock Corridor   Avant
Prisoner   Sub Rosa
Hsi-Yu Chi   Tzadik
I   Sub Rosa
The Tower of Mirrors   Sub Rosa
Satyricon   Sub Rosa

Frances Marie Uitti
2 Bows   BVHaast
Imaginings   chillout
Uitti.Sharp   Lowlands
The Second Bow   Intrapresa/Cramps

Lois V Vierk
Simoom   XI
Outcome Inevitable   O.O.Discs
Manhattan Cascade   CRI
River Beneath the River   Tzadik

Z'EV
Heads & Tails   Avant
One Foot in the Grave 1968-1990   Touch

John Zorn
Kristallnacht   Tzadik
Absinthe   Avant
Bar Kokhba   Tzadik
Naked City: Black Box   Tzadik
Elegy   Tzadik
The Parachute Years   Tzadik
Duras: Duchamp   Tzadik
Aporias: Requia for Piano and Orchestra   Tzadik
Godard/Spillane   Tzadik
Angelus Novus   Tzadik
The String Quartets   Tzadik